Yuping Wang

Distance Language Learning and Desktop Videoconferencing

Yuping Wang

Distance Language Learning and Desktop Videoconferencing

A Chinese Language Case Study

VDM Verlag Dr. Müller

Imprint

Bibliographic information by the German National Library: The German National Library lists this publication at the German National Bibliography; detailed bibliographic information is available on the Internet at http://dnb.d-nb.de.

Cover image: www.purestockx.com

Publisher:
VDM Verlag Dr. Müller Aktiengesellschaft & Co. KG , Dudweiler Landstr. 125 a, 66123 Saarbrücken, Germany,
Phone +49 681 9100-698, Fax +49 681 9100-988,
Email: info@vdm-verlag.de

Zugl.: Brisbane, Griffith University, 2005

Produced in USA and UK by:
Lightning Source Inc., La Vergne, Tennessee, USA
Lightning Source UK Ltd., Milton Keynes, UK
BookSurge LLC, 5341 Dorchester Road, Suite 16, North Charleston, SC 29418, USA

ISBN: 978-3-639-04286-3

Table of contents

Chapter Seven:

List of figures

List of tables

List of acronyms

CALL – Computer Assisted Language Learning

CMC – Computer Mediated Communication

DE – Distance Education

DLE – Distance Language Education

HCI – Human-Computer Interaction

IRC – Internet Relay Chat

ISP – Internet Service Provider

L1 – First language

L2 – Second language

LAN – Local Area Network

NS – Native Speaker

OU – Open University

PC – Personal Computer

SLA – Second Language Acquisition

Acknowledgements

I acknowledge the invaluable support of Professor Mary Farquhar, Professor Nick Knight, Professor Mike Levy and Professor Chengzheng Sun.

My gratitude goes first to Professor Mary Farquhar, who guided me to the research of CALL 10 years ago. Since then I have been fascinated by this area, and completed a masters and a PhD degree in this area, both under her supervision. Her guidance, critique and support throughout this research development have been incredibly valuable to me.

To Professor Nick Knight, I owe special thanks for his prompt and insightful feedback, constructive criticism and friendship. He spent countless hours discussing research methodologies with me, reading every draft of this research and patiently correcting my English. His encouragement helped keep my research and my life in perspective.

I am greatly indebted to Professor Mike Levy, whose advice and expertise were a constant source of inspiration. His profound knowledge and understanding of CALL-related theories and practices have helped shape this research in many ways.

The research into videoconferencing tools was initially inspired by Professor Chengzheng Sun. I am extremely grateful to him for his assistance in funding the technological dimension of this project and in providing technical support. Without his insightful advice, understanding and constant encouragement, this research would not have been possible.

I also wish to acknowledge the help of Associate Professor Junwei Lu, who provided many valuable technical suggestions and much support.

My appreciation also goes to Ms Rosemary Murray and Ms Robyn White, who helped with the editing and formatting of the book.

Thanks are also due to those students who took part in the trial of NetMeeting. They courageously participated in the online sessions, and generously took the time to complete several surveys and to be interviewed. Their participation was invaluable to this research.

I would also like to thank the university for providing me with research funding, especially the academic and equity leaves. These leaves provided me with teaching relief and uninterrupted time for research and publications.

I have been fortunate to have the technical support from the technicians in the School of Languages and Linguistics at Griffith University. Thanks to Michael Colenso, Paul Bosworth, Peter

Smith and Ron Magarry, who answered many of my queries and helped with setting up the computer lab for the experiment and burning the CD.

My thanks also go to Celia Bein, the Acquisition Editor of VDM Verlag Dr Müller Aktiengesellschaft & Co. KG, who answered many of my questions.

Finally, I would like to thank my husband Nanhua Chen, my mother Shouying Wang and my son Leo for their tolerance, unfailing support and love during the course of this research. I dedicate this book to them.

I would like to acknowledge the following journals in which my articles drawing on the raw data and discussions from the earlier version of this book have been published:

Wang, Y. & Sun, C. (2001). Internet-based real time language education: towards a fourth generation distance education. *CALICO Journal, 18*(3), 539-561.

Wang, Y. (2004a). Distance Language Learning: Interactivity and Fourth Generation Internet-based Videoconferencing. *CALICO Journal, 21*(2), 373-395.

Wang, Y. (2004b). Internet-based desktop videoconferencing in supporting synchronous distance language learning. *Language Learning and Technology, 8*(3), 90-121.

Wang, Y. (2006). Negotiation of meaning in desktop videoconferencing-supported distance language learning. *ReCALL, 18*(1), 122-146.

Wang, Y. (2007). Task design in videoconferencing supported distance language learning. *CALICO Journal, 24*(3), 591-630.

Chapter One

Introduction

1.1 Introduction

As a distance language teacher, I have confronted many issues in practice and in theory. For me, the most urgent and significant issues are how distance learners can effectively acquire listening and speaking skills when there is a physical distance between the learner and the education provider, and how cutting edge technology can be utilized to maximize optimal conditions for developing these skills. These questions have challenged me intellectually and led to the theoretical and empirical investigation in this research, an inquiry into oral-visual interaction via Internet-based desktop videoconferencing for language acquisition at a distance.

This introductory chapter provides a framework for the book. It commences with a brief statement of the research focus which delineates the central and subsidiary research questions to allow an overview of this study. It then sets the scene for the rest of the book by briefly introducing the Open Learning Chinese Program taught at Griffith University, Australia, as this program will be used as a case study throughout the research (for details of this program, see Section 1.3). The chapter further examines the course delivery structures of this program in comparison with those of the Open University in the UK in order to identify the needs of learners in the present generation DLE. These case studies highlight the need for oral-visual interaction in DLE. I then outline a possible solution to the provision of such interaction and discuss the significance of the research. The chapter ends with a synopsis of the contents for each chapter that follows.

1.2 Research focus

1.2.1 Statement of research questions

While the concept of distance education has been applauded for such features as flexibility in delivery and minimal teacher contact, the cost for students learning languages in distance mode has been the weakness in the acquisition of speaking and listening skills. The physical distance between the learner and the language program provider has prevented the creation of an effective and interactive language learning environment (Wang & Sun, 2001). My research indicates that Synchronous Computer Mediated Communication (SCMC) supporting oral-visual interaction has not yet been effectively employed in practice to minimize the impact of distance in DLE. At both the theoretical and practical levels, research in the use of this category of CMC in language learning at a distance has occupied only a marginal status, in terms of both quantity and quality, in the entirety of DLE research. This book attempts to fill some of the gaps in this interdisciplinary area.

The argument in this study is that Internet-based videoconferencing tools may, for the first time in history, support real-time oral-visual interaction between second language learners and teachers in distance education mode. The central research question, therefore, is as follows.

In what ways is oral-visual interaction via videoconferencing able to facilitate L2 acquisition at a distance?

In the course of answering the central research question, the following subsidiary questions are closely investigated:

♦ *What are the needs of distance learners in terms of L2 acquisition?*

♦ *What are the benefits and limitations of oral-visual interaction via videoconferencing for L2 acquisition at a distance?*

♦ *What are the implications and potential of such interaction for L2 acquisition in distance mode?*

What are the needs of distance learners in terms of L2 acquisition? To answer this first subsidiary question, this research project sets out to establish that distance language learners do need improved platforms for acquisition of speaking skills. This conclusion was reached by using the Open Learning Language Chinese program at Griffith University as a case study, and by employing contextual materials on distance education. I have argued elsewhere (Wang & Sun, 2001) that the physical distance between the learner and the language program provider has prevented the creation of an effective interactive language learning environment. This problem is particularly acute in the acquisition of listening and speaking skills where spoken interaction is essential, but has been nevertheless missing (for discussion of listening and speaking problems in DLE, see Wang & Sun, 2000; Wong & Fauverge, 1999; Goodfellow et al., 1999; Kötter, 2001; Hampel & Hauck, 2004, Wang, 2004b). The importance of interaction, especially spoken interaction, to second language (L2) acquisition has long been recognized in the literature (see Hall, 1995; Lantolf, 1994; Ohta, 1995; Swain & Lapkin, 1995; Mitchell & Myles, 1998; Kitade, 2000; Gass, 2003; Long, 1996). However, there has until now been no effective way of incorporating this dimension of L2 acquisition into distance language learning. My attempt to find a technology to support an improved platform for the provision of spoken interaction in distance language learning indicates that real-time SCMC, especially videoconferencing tools supporting oral-visual interaction, may be effectively employed to minimize the impact of distance in DLE.

Then, *what are the benefits and limitations of videoconferencing-supported oral and visual interaction in the process of L2 acquisition?* This second subsidiary research question follows on the first. To answer this question, a two-stage evaluation of a L2 learning environment via videoconferencing was designed and conducted with the participation of both on-campus and distance Chinese language learners. In this environment, participants used NetMeeting, a videoconferencing tool, to complete a variety of meaning-focused speaking tasks involving real-time oral-visual interaction with their teacher. Two aspects of the benefits and limitations of this learning environment were evaluated: its technological capabilities and its pedagogical values for L2 acquisition in distance mode. The technological capabilities were evaluated using criteria developed through this research. The pedagogical values were assessed against criteria also developed for this study following research in L2 acquisition, and communicative and task-based language learning theories, especially Chapelle's (2001) criteria for CALL task evaluation. Central to this evaluation is the investigation of the language learning potential of a videoconferencing task, in terms of its provision of focus on form in negotiating of meaning.

What are the implications and potential of oral-visual interaction via videoconferencing for L2 acquisition in distance mode? The data gathered from the two-stage evaluation posed this final subsidiary research question. Recommendations for future research were made based on the empirical findings of the evaluation, and in reference to L2 acquisition theories, especially in terms of the use of videoconferencing, videoconferencing-based task design and performance through oral and visual interaction.

In this study, distance language learning is the field of research, Internet-based desktop videoconferencing is the chosen technology, and the provision of oral and visual interaction for L2 acquisition by distance learners constitutes the core research problem. Thus, this study can be summarized as an investigation of the ways in which videoconferencing-enabled oral-visual interaction facilitates L2 acquisition in distance mode.

1.2.2 Defining videoconferencing for this study

It has to be stressed at the outset that the focus of this study is on *Internet-based desktop videoconferencing,* not other types of videoconferencing. Broadly speaking, from a technical perspective, videoconferencing can be categorized into desktop and studio-based conferencing. Studio-based videoconferencing can be supported by either the Internet or a LAN (Local Area Network) and often involves more complicated set-ups and technology, such as a codec, a multipoint control unit, a studio, and a visualizer. In a campus-based educational setting, such videoconferencing is often designed to conduct lectures across campuses or institutions. The initial investment and ongoing maintenance costs are huge. The studio-based videoconferencing is also place dependent, i.e. all learners have to be at a certain place for a videoconferencing session. These features make the studio-based videoconferencing unsuitable for distance learners, who mostly require an individual, inexpensive and user-friendly platform. In contrast, desktop videoconferencing is a more economical option in terms of initial investment and ongoing maintenance for distance learners. It is also more user-friendly and less place- and time-dependent as the learner can use it on his or her PC (Personal Computer) at home or work. No complicated set-ups are needed. Again, desktop videoconferencing can be Internet or LAN based. This book, with its focus on the provision of oral-visual interaction to distance language learners, will concentrate on the effectiveness and efficiency of *Internet-based desktop* videoconferencing for L2 acquisition in distance mode because this type of videoconferencing suits the distance learning environment better than studio-based videoconferencing.

1.3 Language learning at a distance: The Open Learning Chinese Language Program at Griffith University

In contrast to other disciplines in distance education, systematic and comprehensive distance programs for language learning emerged relatively recently. Most of the distance modern language programs were not developed until the 1980s. For example, the Open University founded in 1969 in the UK did not start its language teaching until 1994, after 25 years of experience in the provision of distance education in many other academic areas (Stevens, 1995, p. 12). Since then, it has been regarded as the "largest modern foreign language learning provider" in the UK (Kötter et al., 1999, p. 55). The international enthusiasm for DLE of the 1980s emerged from the advances in educational technology which promised support for the mastery of language skills such as listening and speaking skills, although drill and practice of grammar were still the main activities at this time.

It was amid this widespread enthusiasm for distance language learning that the Open Learning Chinese program at Griffith University was launched. It was developed in 1991 by the Key Centre for Asian Languages and Studies at Griffith University in collaboration with the School of Modern Languages at Macquarie University. Students enrolling in this program have been quite geographically dispersed, with the majority from different states in Australia and some even from other countries. Involvement with this program as a teacher and course developer has provided me with first hand knowledge about the joy and frustration of these distance language learners. They are delighted to have the opportunity of learning a language wherever and whenever they want, without having to attend classes at scheduled times. Qualifying the positive feelings is the frustration they often feel when they are learning to communicate but without a communication partner in the target language. It would not be an exaggeration to conclude that physical distance prevents effective language learning and teaching from happening. Similarly, without adequate technological support, there are severe deficiencies in distance modes of delivery, particularly in the case of communicative language learning and teaching.

As described in the Study Guide of the Open Learning program, this program is a "relatively 'low-tech' package, only requiring access to a television, video player and a cassette player" (1992, p. 5). Printed matter, cassette-taped texts and videotapes thus constitute the major forms of subject matter delivery. This form of delivery structure has been retained since 1991. Data from two major surveys completed in the 1980s also indicates the employment of the same delivery structure throughout the world. The first was conducted among 89 institutions, of which the majority were in the United States (Stringer et al., 1982) and the second surveyed all the Australian higher education institutions offering modern languages in distance mode in 1985 (Williams and Sharma, 1988). Results from both surveys revealed that "a typical distance-taught language course package consisted of a textbook or textbooks and at least one workbook". If there were other materials, "the audio-cassette was the most common" (Williams and Sharma, 1988, p. 135). Kötter (2001, p. 328) also confirms the provision of a similar course delivery format even at the start of the 21st century by stating that distance language learners, in comparison with writing in the target language for an audience, normally have even fewer chances to test and to improve their speaking skills in authentic communication. When discussing Lyceum, an Internet-based audio conferencing tool developed by the Open University, Hampel & Hauck (2004, p. 66) point out that until 2002, "Open University language students depended primarily on traditional distance-learning methods of delivery such as print material, video tapes, audio cassettes, and occasional face-to-face tutorials…". Judging from the available publications on distance language learning, it may not be imprudent to suggest that a similar delivery mode remains the mainstream media of instruction, despite the recent involvement of computer technology. This is certainly true of the Griffith University Open Learning Chinese Program. Obviously such asynchronous delivery mode is not adequate to facilitate interactive language learning, and cannot satisfy the needs of learners of the 21st century.

In the present structure of course delivery of the Open Learning Chinese program at Griffith University, the acquisition of speaking skills in the target language has been largely left to the students themselves with little academic support and no spontaneous feedback at all (Wang & Sun, 2000). Therefore, none of the three communicative strands (cooperative learning, collaborative learning and interaction) in normal language classroom is available in this distance language program. The students are required to submit three assignments in each study period. Each assignment comprises four parts: speaking, writing, reading comprehension and translation. No serious problems have surfaced in students' handling of the sections on writing, reading comprehension and translation. It is in the section on speaking that teachers and students have experienced the greatest difficulty, as shown in survey results discussed in Section 3.2.1.

1.4   Lack of exposure to oral-visual interaction in distance language learning

It is generally accepted that interaction is an integral part of communicative language learning (Hall, 1995; Lantolf, 1994; Ohta, 1995; Swain & Lapkin, 1995; Long, 1996; McKay, 1996; Kitade, 2000). However, spontaneous oral-visual interaction is missing in the Open Learning Chinese program at Griffith University. The speaking section of the language assignments usually requires students to record a few sentences or passages onto a tape, as the only measure to check students' progress in speaking (Wang & Sun, 2000). The tape is then submitted to the teacher together with written assignments. After listening to the tape, the teacher is only able to point out to the students which sound was pronounced incorrectly, and why it was wrong. For example, the teacher may write comments to warn a student that the *ma* sound requiring the first tone was incorrectly pronounced as a fourth tone. However, this cannot ensure that the student will know how to pronounce the *ma* sound in the first tone after reading the teacher's notes. During my years of teaching with the Open Learning program, I often found myself recording the same passage for some students after listening to their recordings and asking the students to listen to my recording, with the hope that the students would notice the difference between the correct pronunciation and theirs. This is an enormous task for the teacher if there are a considerable number of students. Even so, there is no way to guarantee that the students listen to my recording, let alone ascertain that they can decipher the difference between the correct and incorrect pronunciations. Furthermore, when discussing this type of tape-recorded speaking practice, Goodfellow et al. (1999, p. 268) point out that students "cannot get immediate feedback on their performance". Similar comments or complaints from the students were also heard in our program (see Section 3.2.1). This is because their previous assignments may be returned after they have sent off their next one in which the same mistake might have been made. Even if they receive the previous assignment before they send off the next one, the comments may not be able to register strongly since student memory of the problems may no longer be fresh.

This problem is particularly acute in the case of learning Chinese language, largely because Chinese is a tonal language. Of the many difficulties encountered by beginners of Chinese language, mastery of the tones in Chinese is always a daunting task. There are four tones, or five including the neutral one, which are variations in pitch. McGinnis (1997, p. 228) argues, "[t]he critical importance of tonal accuracy in the development of spoken competence in Chinese cannot be underestimated". This is because a slight variation in the tone can represent a totally different character with a different meaning. For example, *ma* with the first tone can mean "mother" (妈) while *ma* with the third tone can mean "horse" (马). McGinnis (1997, p. 228) further contends that "[t]here is nothing secondary about tone in Chinese, yet to most learners of Chinese as a second language, the suprasegmental feature of lexical tone is so far removed from their native language experience as to render the mastery of tones problematic, neglected, or both". Learners need to hear and watch the pronunciation of the sound in context to be able to ascertain the subtle differences between the tones. Orton (2001, p. 140) also stresses the importance of acquiring tones when learning Chinese by stating that "there needed to be concentrated assistance for English speakers learning Chinese with the major tasks of acquiring tone and characters".

Assuming that the Open Learning students could attain perfect pronunciation and tones, and could remember all the useful phrases and sentences after studying assiduously with books and tapes, spontaneous interaction in the target language is still not available in such a low-tech learning environment. Compared with distance language programs with no inclusion of an oral component (see Stringer et al., 1982, 54 out of 222 sampled), the Open Learning Chinese Program at Griffith University is much better off in the provision of oral skill training. However, there is a serious deficiency in this provision: that is, it does not offer the opportunity for language output in a natural environment where two way oral-visual interaction and communication in the target language can be generated spontaneously as they would in the real world. Despite the limited language input, that is, the provision of audio-tapes and a TV program called *Dragon's Tongue*, communicative and interactional skills do not readily emerge from just listening to and watching the language being spoken. Consequently, students still find themselves lacking a simple spontaneous answer to a very basic sentence that they have practised many times. This is because, apart from being daunted by the speaker's unfamiliar accent and intonation, the Open Learning students are not used to and have not acquired the skills for communicating in the target language. Due to the existence of distance, and the lack of capable technologies, there has been seriously inadequate, if any, training in interactional skills, such as turn taking, clarification requests, filled pauses, and other elements deemed essential for successful language acquisition by scholars in Second Language (L2) acquisition (see sections 2.2 and 2.3). Having never been exposed to real-life use of the target language in face-to-face interaction where visual cues such as eye contact and other body language are presented, they are not prepared for the "unpredictability of social talk" (McCarthy, 1991, p. 137). Furthermore, without these basic communication skills, deep learning and advanced communication skills such as the interpretation of implicatures are unachievable. The low level of communicative competency of distance learners became clearly evident in the later empirical studies of this research and drew my attention to the gravity of the problem of the lack of oral-visual interaction. Informed by the literature on distance language learning, I argue that this is a problem common to most distance language learning programs (similar findings can be found in the Open University program, according to Shield & Hewer, 1999), which needs the urgent attention of language professionals.

The present Open Learning program recognizes the students' needs for immediate feedback on their written and oral assignments and assessments, and attempts to meet the needs by providing a weekly telephone consultation service. A toll free number is put in place for students to contact the teacher when they have questions regarding their assignments and assessments. It is not used for the delivery of teaching materials. However, experience shows that it is sometimes difficult to explain certain concepts and characters without visual support. For example, it is almost impossible to demonstrate on the phone how a Chinese character should be written. This service therefore has its limitations and is ineffective in solving the problem of lack of interactive speaking practice.

1.5   Finding a solution to the problem of lack of oral-visual interaction

Clearly, a highly interactive and synchronous learning environment is conducive to effective communicative language learning at a distance, particularly for the acquisition of speaking skills. Unfortunately this is precisely where most distance language programs fall short. The few earlier videoconferencing projects such as The HIPERNET, LEVERAGE and ReLaTe in the 1990s may have represented the beginning of efforts to find a way of offering oral-visual interaction in distance language learning, but these projects often involve huge up-front expenses and ongoing maintenance costs (for reports and reviews of these projects, see McAndrew et al., 1996; Wong & Fauverge, 1999; Buckett & Stringer, 1997; Wang, 2004). A review of these projects is also conducted in Section 2.3.2. While more and more research on the use of CMC to improve students' writing and reading comprehension is being published, there is a paucity of systematic findings on the effectiveness of CMC in improving students' speaking ability. This book attempts to bridge gaps in this area by investigating a technological and economically viable videoconferencing-based option that allows the learner to orally and visually interact with each other or the teacher at home through the use of their personal computer. The constant improvement in Internet products and bandwidth promises a potential solution to the provision of synchronous oral and visual interaction in DLE.

My investigation into the capabilities of videoconferencing started with a preliminary examination of the available videoconferencing tools. At the start of this research in 1999, NetMeeting, now integrated into MSN, emerged strongly for its potential to support synchronous oral and visual interaction. This preliminary study was then followed by a more in-depth two-stage evaluation of NetMeeting. Stage One evaluated NetMeeting with the involvement of three on-campus students from Griffith University in an intranet environment. Stage Two launched the evaluation in an Internet environment with the participation of five students from the Griffith University Open Learning Chinese program. In contrast to most studies in CMC literature, this research did not stop at the technological level of the investigation. As a focal area of investigation, the pedagogical values of oral-visual interaction via videoconferencing were examined through the performance and completion of the pedagogical tasks especially designed for evaluating videoconferencing. A considerable amount of useful data was collected from this two-stage investigation, from which important conclusions and implications have been derived.

1.6 Significance of the research problem

When discussing distance education in general, Peters (1991) drew attention to the gravity of the problem of lack of interaction:

> Zaochny is the Russian word for 'distance' in distance education. It is remarkable as it means – etymologically speaking – 'without eye contact'. This implies that the decisive criterion according to which distance education can be distinguished from conventional teaching and learning is the lack of eye contact. Distance education does not take place 'eyeball to eyeball' as Wedemeyer once called it. As the eye is the organ of man's innermost feelings, this aspect of apartness is surely significant. We become aware that a whole dimension of the interaction of the teacher and learner is lacking in distance education. The new form of teaching and learning is defined and characterized by pointing to a severe deficiency. (p. 52)

If the lack of eye contact is a severe deficiency of distance education in a general sense, such deficiency can be even more detrimental to the development of the learner's communicative competency in L2 learning, because oral and visual interaction is the core component in communicative language learning. The significance of this study is therefore as follows:

♦ This research identifies distance language learners' need for oral-visual interaction as an important issue that requires urgent attention from distance language professionals.

- ♦ This research evaluates findings and resulting recommendations regarding the ways in which oral-visual interaction enabled by videoconferencing facilitates L2 acquisition.

- ♦ The research directs our attention to the potential of Internet-based desktop videoconferencing in the provision of synchronous oral and visual interaction for L2 acquisition in DLE.

- ♦ The findings from this research may be usefully replicated by other distance language learning programs.

1.7 Organization of book

The main body of the book consists of 7 chapters. Following this introductory chapter, Chapter 2 establishes the significance of the research question by means of a critical review of the relevant literature. This review scrutinizes such theories as interaction, task design and evaluation principles and CMC-based interactions. It also evaluates the provision of interaction in the developmental stages of distance language education. In so doing, this chapter proposes a new taxonomy of CMC-based interaction and the emergence of a fourth generation DLE.

Chapter 3 consists of three parts. Part one reports the findings from two preliminary case studies, laying a foundation for the main empirical study of this research. Part two contains a detailed account of the methodologies employed in this research. It first provides a synopsis of the two-stage evaluation of NetMeeting, including the objectives, procedures, participants and network environments of each stage of the evaluation. This part further points out the formative and qualitative nature and the task-based approach of this study. Finally, it specifies data collected and data collection and analysis methods. Two sets of criteria are then proposed in part three of this chapter for evaluating the technological capabilities and the pedagogical values of oral-visual interaction via videoconferencing respectively.

Chapter 4 presents (with a preliminary analysis) the data collected from the two stages of the evaluation of NetMeeting with both on-campus and distance participants. This chapter focuses on the **technological** capabilities of videoconferencing in the support of oral-visual interaction in DLE.

Chapter 5 provides a detailed account of the data collected from the two-stage evaluation of NetMeeting in relation to the **pedagogical** values of videoconferencing-supported oral-visual interaction in DLE. In this evaluation, tasks were designed and trialled with both on-campus and distance participants, and significant findings emerged.

Chapter 6 further develops the analysis of the findings contained in chapters 4 and 5. In this analysis, recommendations are suggested regarding the effective use of videoconferencing in future applications and videoconferencing task design and performance.

Chapter 7 concludes the book by summarizing the contributions and findings of this research, and discussing the implications of the findings for future research. It also points out that a re-conceptualization of distance language education is necessary and possible as a result of the developments and employment of technology.

Chapter Two

Literature Review: Interactive language learning, CMC, and the provision of interaction in DLE

2.1 Introduction

As discussed in Section 1.2, this research investigates **the ways in which videoconferencing-enabled real-time oral and visual interaction facilitates L2 acquisition by distance learners**. This chapter, consequently, examines the role and importance of interaction in language learning and in the development of DLE.

To pursue this discussion, the chapter proceeds through three cumulative steps. Part One provides a definitional context for this research through a comprehensive review of the literature on the definitions of interaction in general and spoken interaction in particular. This section then moves on to examine the importance of interaction in the context of communicative language learning. Important theories concerning communicative language learning such as negotiation of meaning and focus on form are critically reviewed. In view of its importance to the empirical study of this research, the task-based approach is also discussed in detail in terms of task design and evaluation principles.

Part Two of this chapter focuses on Computer Mediated Communication (CMC)-based interactions, with updated reviews on their recent developments in both theory and practice. In this critical review, a new taxonomy is proposed (Wang, 2004a, p. 376). CMC is a key issue in this research because the central argument in this book is that videoconferencing, a major form of CMC, provides a solution to the problem identified in Chapter 1: the lack of oral and visual interaction in distance language education.

Part Three of this chapter highlights the quality of interaction in the four developmental stages of DLE, from a historical perspective. It is proposed in this section that a fourth generation DLE is emerging with real-time oral-visual interaction as its defining feature (Wang & Sun, 2001, p. 551). The discussion in Part Two and Part Three leads to an answer to the first subsidiary research question: what are the needs of distance learners in terms of L2 acquisition? The chapter's three parts are interdependent and interconnected. Each part is crucial to the investigation of distance language learners' needs as a prerequisite for this research on improved L2 acquisition.

2.2 Part One – Interaction and interactive language learning

2.2.1 Definitions of interaction

As interaction provides a central theme of investigation in this research, we need to understand it conceptually in order to establish a framework and foundation for later discussions on the capacities of videoconferencing to support the kind of interaction needed for language learning at a distance. At the outset, the difference between interactivity and interaction must be clarified, even though they are sometimes used interchangeably in the literature. In this book, the distinction between the two terms drawn by McLoughlin and Oliver (1995, p. 51) is adopted:

> In order to bring some conceptual clarity to these terms, it is proposed that a distinction is drawn between the system interactivity afforded by the technology and instructional interactions which arise through deliberate planning and intervention.

Thus, interactivity is used to describe the capacity of a particular technology whereas interaction refers to human activity. Thus, in this study, interactivity is only used to describe the capabilities of NetMeeting, while interaction constitutes the focal point in the inquiry. This is why the following discussion concentrates on interaction. The concept of interaction will be discussed in relation to recent developments in the field.

Probing the nature of interaction, one cannot help but notice its complexity and hence the problem of defining it. Such complexity lies not only in the inclusiveness of this concept, but also in its evolving roles in a time of technological innovation. In the last 20 years, there is much more research focus on the concept of interaction. As a result it is much richer in content, scope and depth than it did 20 years ago. A review of the literature on interaction reveals two major generic traits of interaction – its social and individual nature. Bates (1997) summarizes the present achievements in the research of interaction by placing interaction in the following two contexts:

> the first is an **individual**, isolated activity, and that is the interaction of a learner **with** the learning material, be it text, television or computer program; the second is a **social** activity, and that is the interaction between two or more people **about** the learning material. **Both** kinds of interactions are important in learning. (p. 100; emphasis in original)

Furthermore, both kinds of interaction can be face-to-face and technology-mediated.

Interaction as a social activity

There is little controversy over the social nature of interaction. In fact the word 'interaction' itself denotes such a characteristic. In other words, interaction is a socially reciprocal action involving two or more people, and it can be face-to-face or technology-mediated.

Twenty years ago, the definition of interaction was largely in the realm of face-to-face mode. Wells (1981, p. 46) used it interchangeably with the word "communication". He suggests firstly that "linguistic interaction is a collaborative activity", and then moves on to say that "linguistic communication involves the establishment of a triangular relationship between the sender, the receiver and the context of situation". Rivers (1987, p. 4) renders Wells' understanding of interaction into a verbal version: "listening to others, talking with others, negotiating meaning in a shared context". Along with more interest and research in interaction, scholars (e.g. Neu, 1990; Oxford, 1995) began to identify the non-verbal aspect of face-to-face interaction (e.g. body languages) and its importance in communicative language acquisition. Oxford (1997, p. 444) defines interaction as "the situation in which people act upon each other" and in educational settings, "interaction involves teachers, learners and others acting upon each other and consciously or unconsciously interpreting (i.e. giving meaning to) those actions".

The above definitions point out that, in a social context, face-to-face interaction involves more than one party, and involves the possibility of reciprocal actions. In other words, face-to-face interaction involves action between at least two parties, be it verbal or non-verbal interaction, and the purpose of interaction is for negotiating meaning.

The rapid development of technology has vastly enriched the content and scope of interaction. In fact, a new term has appeared to denote the influence of technology in interaction – technologized interaction (see Hutchby, 2001). Again, this type of interaction can be individual or social. Telephone and computer-mediated human-human interaction are two of the most important forms of technologized social interaction, offering various types of interaction that have never existed before. In such interaction, the technology is seen as a tool to be used by the human to achieve communication goals, in this case, interaction in language learning. These goals are often achieved through the manipulation of keyboard, mouse, computer screen, video, voice etc. All these naturally affect the nature and scope of interaction which occurs now in a variety of forms.

In comparison with telephone conversation, computer-mediated human-human interaction is the most high-profile phenomenon of the late 20th and early 21st century. It can occur in a context of oral, visual and written forms or a combination of the three, between the learner and instructor, among the learners and/or even between native speakers in the target language speaking countries and learners in their own countries. For example, recent research has focused on interactive writing through the use of Web technologies (e.g. Barnes, 2000; Lamy & Goodfellow, 1999; Negretti, 1999; Pennington, 1999; Appel & Gilabert, 2002; Kötter, 2003; Lee, 2004). It can be asynchronous interaction through e-mails or synchronous interaction through computer conferencing such as Internet Relay Chat (IRC). Oral and visual interaction generated by Internet-based audio and videoconferencing tools has also begun to attract research interest (e.g. (Hauck & Haezewindt, 1999; Shield et al., 2001; Hewer et al., 1999; Kötter, 2001; Hampel & Baber, 2003; Hampel & Hauck, 2004; Wong & Fauverge, 1999; Zähner et al., 2000; Levy & Kennedy, 2004; Wang, 2004a; Wang, 2004b, 2006, 2007). Such interaction offers interactivity similar to that of face-to-face interaction but with, at least, one added value – the interaction between the learner and native speaker when they are miles apart. (for detailed discussion on CMC-based interaction, see Section 2.3)

Interaction as an individual activity

The word "interaction" seems to be in opposition to the word "reflection". In some definitions, interaction is only recognized to occur between two or more people, whereas reflection is an activity of an individual. However, in this book, following Bates, I will talk about 'individual interaction' also. Bates (1997, p. 100) stresses that in individual interaction, the learner interacts with the learning materials, and such learning materials can be computer, text and television. In other words, the other party or parties in the individual interaction is not a human being. Similar to social interaction, individual interaction can also be categorized as face-to-face or technology-mediated.

The "face-to-face" interaction between the learner and text is not a new concept. Such texts usually refer to traditional texts (that is, textbook texts or any paper-based reading materials). In fact, the notion of interaction between the learner and the texts has been developed and promoted by a multitude of research studies on reading comprehension skills (e.g. Goodman, 1976; Smith, 1982; Carrell, 1983; Papalia, 1987; Anderson & Pearson, 1988; Grabe, 1988, 1991; Devitt, 1997; Ganderton, 1999). Central to this type of interaction is the view that reading is a form of dialogue between the reader and the text.

The technology-mediated interaction of an individual nature mainly refers to the interaction between the learner and computer-supported learning materials. This type of interaction appealed particularly to language professionals in CALL in the 1990s. Phrases such as "interactive Web-based reading" and "interactive multimedia" frequently appear in the literature (see Godwin-Jones, 1998; Devitt, 1997; Barty, 1998). When discussing in L2 Web-based reading, Ganderton (1999, p. 50) argues that such reading "can be interactive in the fuller sense of the word, when considered as interaction not just between the learner and the computer, but also between the learner and the text, and indeed among the various mental processes occurring within the learner themselves".

Human-Computer Interaction (HCI) is a recent addition to the repertoire of individual interaction and was especially popular in the 1990s. Unlike computer-mediated human-human interaction, HCI is still in the realm of individual activity, and the computer is seen as a tutor as opposed to the computer as a tool. Interaction between the learner and the computer emerged with the development of computer technology. It is employed when discussing the user friendliness of multimedia packages, which often offer texts, links, audio and/or video capacities. HCI emphasizes "understanding users, their needs and the nature of the tasks they have to complete with the computer". (Levy, 1997, p. 70)

2.2.2   Towards a synthesis of interaction

On the basis of the definitions discussed above, and in view of the capabilities of the present day educational technologies, interaction entails at least the following characteristics:

1. It involves at least two or more parties (e.g. sender-receiver [Wells, 1981]; learner-instructor, learner-learner, learner-computer [Moore, 1989] and learner-native speaker, etc.)
2. It is a reciprocal action – acting upon each other. (Oxford, 1997)
3. It is a collaborative activity. (Wells, 1981)
4. It is a process of conveying and negotiating meanings. (Rivers, 1987)
5. It can involve both social and individual communication. (Bates, 1997)
6. It can be synchronous or asynchronous.
7. It can involve written, oral or visual discourse or a combination of these three.
8. It can be either face-to-face or technology mediated.

Research in computer-mediated human-to-human interaction has begun to gain importance recently, especially in terms of synchronous oral and visual interaction. Such research often investigates the role of the computer as a tool rather than a tutor. This research investigates the role of computer technology as a tool in human-to-human interaction.

2.2.3   Spoken interaction

The concepts and theories discussed above define interaction in a general sense. These definitions provide the necessary background to the investigation into the central issue concerning the current research: facilitating spoken interaction in distance language learning. Thus, interaction is defined for this research as a social activity referring to the type of human-to-human communication that occurs in second language learning. The facilitating effect of interaction to L2 acquisition has long been established and will be further discussed in Section 2.2.4.

As this research focuses on videoconferencing-enabled interaction, the interaction under investigation here is of a spoken nature. Then, what is spoken interaction and what are the characteristics of spoken interaction? According to Stenström (1994, p. xi), spoken interaction "belongs to the area of discourse, which can be defined as 'any unit of language beyond the sentence', such as a dialogue in speech and a paragraph in writing". She further defines spoken interaction as "a joint, here-and-now social activity which is governed by two main principles" – speakers take turns and speakers cooperate (Stenström, 1994, p. 1). With this understanding, spoken interaction can be further analyzed in terms of five hierarchical levels. (see Table 2.1)

Table 2.1   The discourse hierarchy of spoken interaction

The TRANSACTION	consists of one or more exchanges dealing with one single topic: one or more transactions make up a conversation
The EXCHANGE	is the smallest interactive unit consisting, minimally, of two turns produced by two different speakers
The TURN	is everything the current speaker says before the next speaker takes over; it consists of one or more moves
The MOVE	is what the speaker does in a turn in order to start, carry on and finish an exchange, i.e., the way s/he interacts; it consists of one or more acts
The ACT	signals what the speaker intends, what s/he wants to communicate; it is the smallest interactive unit

Source: Adapted from Stenström (1994, p. 30)

It can be seen from the above table that each level consists of one or more units from the level below it, with the TRANSACTION being the largest interactive unit and the ACT the smallest. The analysis of spoken interaction is generally approached from a discourse perspective. The TURN and the MOVE in the above table are often the focus of analysis when discussing acquisition in second language learning, especially, in negotiation of meaning. Turn taking and move types such as repairs and responses are operationalized in the discussion of interactional modification, which is generally deemed beneficial to L2 acquisition (see Varonis & Gass, 1985: Pellettieri, 2000; Fernández-García & Martínez-Arbelaiz, 2002; discussions in Section 2.2.8 and 3.3.9). In the current research, spoken interaction that occurred in the evaluation of the videoconferencing-supported learning environment is a focal point of analysis (see Section 5.2.2). The importance and complexity of spoken interaction are revisited in Section 2.3 in the context of CMC-based interaction. The theories and model for analysing spoken interaction are contained in Section 3.3.9.

2.2.4   The importance of interaction in L2 language learning

The above discussion on interaction points to the importance of interaction in generating "deep-level learning" and "critical thinking" (see Bullen, 1998; Duffy et al., 1998). Other benefits include increased motivation and interest in learning (see Wells, 1981; Rivers, 1987; Moore, 1989; Mason, 1994 and Burke et al., 1997). If interaction adds value to learning in a general sense, it is indispensable to language learning for the simple reason that language itself is a means of communication and interaction. In the area of second language (L2) learning, it is an understanding among L2 professionals that interaction is an integral part of a communicative language learning process (Vygotsky, 1978; Hall, 1995; Lantolf, 1994; Ohta, 1995; Swain & Lapkin, 1995; Long, 1996; Mitchell & Myles, 1998; Kitade, 2000; Gass, 2003; Hampel, 2003). This section specifically identifies the role of interaction in L2 acquisition.

To further understand the importance of interaction to language learning, it is necessary to probe the nature of language and language learning. Recent research seems to have reached a consensus about the basic constituents of language: forms and meaning. Forms refer to the structural properties of the language, more tangible than meaning. They cover a familiar field: pronunciation, grammar, vocabulary, kinesics, prosodics. Meaning is the way in which words and types of sentence construction or rules of grammar are used in a social context (Robins, 1972, p. 18). The definition contained in *Longman Dictionary of Applied Linguistics* by Richards et al. (1985, p. 48) conveys this sense of language: "the system of human communication by means of a structured arrangement of sounds (or their written representation) to form larger units, e.g. morphemes, words, sentences". It would be clearer and more precise to replace "by means of" with "consisting of", hence changing the above definition into: *language is the system of human communication consisting of a structured arrangement of sounds (or their written representation) to form larger units, e.g. morphemes, words, sentences.* Such understanding of the nature of language provides a basis for the communicative language learning approach with an emphasis on the importance of communication and interaction in L2 learning, a theoretical framework adopted in this research.

2.2.5   Communicative language learning

The communicative language learning approach was born when grammar-translation and audiolingual approaches failed to produce learners who could communicate using the target language. Language professionals (e.g. Littlewood, 1981; Wilkinson, 1982; Krashen, 1988) began to direct their attention to those aspects of language learning beyond linguistic properties. Central to the communicative approach is the notion that language is a tool for social communication and interaction. It emphasizes teaching "the language needed to express and understand different kinds of functions, such as requesting, describing, expressing likes and dislikes" and so on. In particular, it "emphasizes the processes of communication, such as using language appropriately in different types of situations; using language to perform different kinds of tasks, e.g. to solve puzzles, to get information". In other words, "using language for social interaction with other people". (Richards et al., 1985, p. 48)

Thus, teaching and learning how to use the target language for social communication is central to the communicative approach. There are two most important features of this approach: the stress on the communicative context where realistic and authentic language use occurs and on language learning as a communicative process. Extended from these two features, some of the characteristics of this approach can be summarized as follows:

1. an emphasis on organizing language learning around its functions such as using language appropriately in different situations, using language to perform different kinds of tasks, e.g. to solve puzzles, to get practical information, and using language for social interaction with other people (Richards et al., 1985, p. 48; McMeniman, 1992, p. 5);

2. an emphasis on learning to communicate through interaction in the target language (Nunan, 1991, p. 279);

3. the introduction of authentic texts into the learning situation (Nunan, 1991, p. 279; Balet, 1985, p. 178-179);

4. a focus, not only on language, but also on the language learning process itself (Nunan, 1991, p. 279);

5. an emphasis on learning a second language as the mother tongue has been learnt, that is, by using it in 'real-life' situations. (Balet, 1985, p. 178-179)

However, ever since the day that the communicative approach appeared, misconceptions about it have thrived, due to "an absence of a well-defined theoretical framework" (McKay, 1994, p. 15). When translated into practice, this approach went to extremes during its early phase. (Thompson, 1996)

Thompson (1996) summarizes four main misconceptions about this approach: Communicative Language Teaching (CLT) means not teaching grammar; CLT means teaching only speaking; CLT means role-play; and CLT means expecting too much from the teacher. Teaching grammar was regarded as old fashioned and thus discarded; language laboratories were rejected because they hindered the communication among learners and between the learner and the teacher. There are in reality various interpretations of this approach. While it enjoys a wide recognition in the field of L2 acquisition, this approach has also been criticized. One of the fiercest criticisms comes from Swan (1985a & 1985b). According to Swan (1985a), despite its many virtues,

> the Communicative Approach unfortunately has most of the typical vices of an intellectual revolution: it over-generalizes valid but limited insights until they become virtually meaningless; it makes exaggerated claims for the power and novelty of its doctrines; it misrepresents the currents of thought it has replaced; it is often characterized by serious intellectual confusion; it is choked with jargon. (p. 2)

However, after his attack on some deficiencies of this approach, Swan (1985b) does admit that this approach can take credit for some achievements in the field of L2 acquisition:

> [t]he Communicative Approach has directed our attention to the importance of other aspects of language besides prepositional meaning, and helped us to analyze and teach the language of interaction. At the same time, it has encouraged a methodology which relies less on mechanical teacher-centered practice and more on the simulation of real-life exchanges. All this is very valuable, and even if (as with religions) there is a good deal of confusion on the theoretical side, it is difficult not to feel that we are teaching better than we used to. By and large, we have probably gained more than we have lost from the Communicative Approach. (p. 87)

To McMeniman (1992, p. 4), the communicative approach has generated a "qualitative difference in the competencies of L2 learners".

Contrary to Swan (1985b, p. 87), I argue that, whatever its vices, the communicative approach is much more than "an interesting ripple on the surface of 20th-century language teaching". It has enriched language learning in terms of both theory and practice. The emergence of the communicative language learning approach should be regarded as part of the ongoing effort by L2 professionals to improve their teaching. Furthermore, this approach has given rise to many theoretical and practical methodologies in L2 acquisition.

2.2.6   Recent developments in the communicative approach and focus on form

Recent development of the communicative approach sees constant debates on whether, how and when to teach grammar in L2 acquisition (e.g. Long, 1991, Long & Crookes, 1992, 1993; Doughty & Williams, 1998; Long & Robinson, 1998, Pica, Kanagy, & Falodun, 1993). Terms such as focus on form, focus on formS and focus on meaning have become the catch phrases in such debates. Confusions over these terms occur, especially concerned with focus on form. These confusions can be "traced to imprecise use of terminology" (Doughty & Williams, 1998, p.3). As focus on form will be one of the important theoretical bases for task design and evaluation in this research, it is necessary to clarify its meaning and boundary at the outset.

The clearest distinction of the three terms – focus on formS, focus on meaning and focus on form is discussed by Long and Robinson (1998). Table 2.2 reproduces Long and Robinson's (1998, p. 16) table, which summarizes three options in language teaching.

Table 2.2   Options in language teaching

Option 2	Option 3	Option 1
analytic	analytic	synthetic
Focus on meaning	focus on form	focus on formS
Natural Approach	TBLT	GT, ALM, Silent Way, TPR
Immersion	Content-Based LT (?)	
Procedural Syllabus	Process Syllabus (?).	Structural/N-F Syllabuses
etc.	etc.	etc.

Note: the order of the options in Table 2.2 follows the same order in the Long & Robinson's (1998, p. 16) table.
Source: Long & Robinson 1998, p. 16

Among the three options, *focus on meaning* stands out from the other two options and is seldom confused with the other two. It is the distinction between focus on form and focus on formS that often causes misunderstanding. The following discussion concentrates on this distinction.

As shown in Table 2.2, Option 1 – *focus on formS*, with a capital S, emphasizes its difference from *focus on form*, Option 3. The major difference between these two options lies in the way each treats the teaching of grammatical forms. *Focus on formS* breaks the language into various parts in teaching and synthesizes these parts in a linear and additive fashion. In Wilkins's (1976) words,

> Parts of the language are taught separately and step by step so that acquisition is a process of gradual accumulation of parts until the whole structure of language has been built up.... At any one time the learner is being exposed to a deliberately limited sample of language. (p. 2)

In other words, *Focus on FormS* breaks L2 down into "words and collocations, grammar rules, phonemes, intonation and stress patterns, structures, notions, or functions" (Long & Robinson, 1998, p. 15). These synthetic syllabi are often realized through a range of classroom practice such as repetition of models and error correction. Doughty and Williams (1998, p. 3) also point out that *Focus on FormS* "characterizes earlier, synthetic approaches to language teaching that have as their primary organizing principle for course design the accumulation of individual language elements".

(e.g. forms such as verb endings, or agreement features, or even functions such as greetings or apologies.)

In contrast, *focus on form* places the learning and teaching of grammatical elements in the context of negotiation of meaning. Long has defined and clarified *focus on form* on several occasions (e.g. Long, 1988a, 1991; Long & Crookes, 1992; Long & Robinson, 1998). For example, Long (1991, p. 45-46) defines focus on form as an occasion that "overtly draws students' attention to linguistic elements as they arise incidentally in lessons whose overriding focus is on meaning or communication". The 1998 definition by Long & Robinson is more operational, offering "researchers and practitioners greater direction for practical implementation" (Doughty & Williams, 1998b, p. 3):

> *Focus on form* refers to how focal attentional resources are allocated. Although there are degrees of attention, and although attention to forms and attention to meaning are not always mutually exclusive, during an otherwise meaning-focused classroom lesson, focus on form often consists of an occasional shift of attention to linguistic code features – by the teacher and or one or more students – triggered by perceived problems with comprehension or production. (p. 23; emphasis in original)

This "occasional" shift of attention to the linguistic code within a meaning-focused activity or interaction is what marks *focus on form*, and differentiates it from *focus on formS*. Long and Robinson (1998, p. 40) further maintain that "in an important sense, focus on form is learner-initiated, and it results in noticing".

Three important points arise from the above definitions. First and foremost, focus on form happens in a meaning-focused lesson, entailing "a prerequisite engagement in meaning before attention to linguistic features can be expected to be effective" (Doughty & Williams, 1998b, p. 3). In other words, focus on form happens in the process of negotiation of meaning, and is an integral part of negotiation of meaning. Indeed, Long and Robinson (1998, p. 22) point out that focus on form is "motivated (although by no means exclusively so) by the so-called Interaction Hypothesis (Long, 1981, 1983b, 1996), which holds that "SLA is a process explicable by neither a purely linguistic nativist nor a purely environmentalist theory". Long and Robinson (1998, p. 22) further discuss focus on form in the context of Interaction Hypothesis and emphasize that "[p]articularly important is the negotiation for meaning that occurs more or less predictably in certain interactions…". They continue that negotiation for meaning elicits interactional modifications, negative feedback, including recasts and noticing that "increase input comprehensibility without denying learners access to unknown L2 vocabulary and grammatical forms". Chapelle (2001, p. 48) further elaborates this understanding of focus on form by stating:

> The examples that best fit Long and Robinson's definition occur in communication tasks (Pica, Kanagy, & Falodun, 1993) in which learners' attention is on the meaning of the language, except for instances in which communication breakdowns occur. Communications breakdowns shift attention to the language until the breakdown is sufficiently resolved in a process referred to as negotiation of meaning. (Long, 1985)

The second important point arising from Long's definitions of focus on form is that the attention to linguistic code is not prescribed but triggered by the occasional appearance of problems in the process of negotiation for meaning. As a result, linguistic code features can be learned in a meaningful context, rather than in isolation.

Third, the purpose of learner's occasional shift of attention to linguistic forms is to aid comprehension or negotiation of meaning. In other words, the purpose of linguistic explanation is to help the flow of the interaction in the target language, not for the learning of linguistic forms *per se*. In Doughty and Williams (1998b, p. 4) words, the most important thing that we should keep in mind is that "the fundamental assumption of focus-on-form instruction is that meaning and use must already be evident to the learner at the time that attention is drawn to the linguistic apparatus needed to get the meaning across".

Doughty & Williams (1998b, p. 4) best summarize the three options by saying that "focus on form *entails* a focus on formal elements of language, whereas focus on formS is *limited* to such a focus, and focus on meaning *excludes* it" (Italics in original). In other words, focus on form happens in a meaning-focused interaction while focus on formS happened in a form-focused interaction. Thus the definition of *focus on form* adopted in this research can be summarized as *an occasional shift of attention to linguistic forms while the learner's primary attention is directed to the meaning of the language during the completion of a meaning-focused task.* This definition places focus on form in the process of negotiation of meaning and reflects the current understanding of focus on form in the literature.

Through this process of clarification and redefinition of the term *focus on form*, in a sense, the misconception of Communicative Language Teaching discussed by Thompson (1996) – that CLT means not teaching grammar – has been readdressed. Focus on form has been operationalized in language learning, especially in task-based learning and has become a guideline for implementing effective task-based instruction suggested by Skehan (1998), as discussed in section 2.2.8. In fact, in the recent L2 literature, the trend is leaning heavily towards focus on form. A very good example in CALL is Chapelle (2001, p. 47), who claims that "conditions directing learners' attention to linguistic form during tasks requiring meaningful language use are believed to be among the most important for learners' acquisition of target language structures". How to manage focus on form in task-based learning has remained a topic of research, and will be one of the issues to be examined in this research. Long (1996, p. 454) contends that "tasks that stimulate negotiation of meaning may turn out to be one among several useful language-learning activities in or out of classrooms, for they may be one of the easiest ways to facilitate a learner's focus on form without losing sight of a lesson's (or conversation's) predominant focus on meaning".

2.2.7 Task-based approaches in communicative L2 learning

The task-based approach is another influential L2 methodology stemming from communicative language learning theory and practice. It is generally maintained in the literature that a specially designed task can generate more opportunity for negotiation of meaning than spontaneous conversation alone because it encourages the learner to deal with difficulties in comprehension and language production (Long, 1996). This is also why this research adopts a task-based approach to the examination of oral-visual interaction via videoconferencing. Bygate et al. (1998, p. 1) point out that "research into pedagogic tasks is one of a growing number of areas of empirical research which have emerged since the early 1980s".

The popular position has long been that the impetus for task-based learning originated from the Bangalore Project (Prabhu, 1987), "which reacted both against the traditional form of EFL [English as a Foreign Language] used in India and against the type of communicative teaching then practised" (Cook, 2001, p. 221). Cook (2001, p. 221) further elaborates the background against which the task-based learning approach was born: "communicative language teaching started to recognize the importance of the classroom itself as a communicative educational setting in its own right and to organize the activities that occurred there in terms of educational tasks rather than tasks that necessarily relate to the world outside the classroom".

One of the earlier definitions of the task-based approach came from Richards et al. (1985), which emphasizes the successful completion of the task rather than the production of the target language.

> [a task is] an activity or action which is carried out as the result of processing or understanding language (i.e., as a response). For example, drawing a map while listening to a tape, listening to an instruction and performing a command, may be referred to as tasks. Tasks may or may not involve the production of language. A task usually requires the teacher to specify what will be regarded as successful completion of the task. The use of a variety of different kinds of tasks in language teaching is said to make language teaching more communicative…since it provides a

purpose for a classroom activity which goes beyond the practice of language for its own sake.
(p. 289)

This definition places task completion as the objective of learning, not language practice and production.

Breen (1987, p. 23) places more weight on the language itself in a task-oriented activity by defining task as "a range of work plans which have the overall purpose of facilitating language learning – from the simple and brief exercise type, to more complex and lengthy activities such as group problem-solving or simulations and decision making". Breen therefore treats the facilitation of language learning as the primary objective of a task.

A more comprehensive and thought provoking definition of task is proposed by Nunan (1989, p. 10), who defines task as "a piece of classroom work which involves learners in comprehending, manipulating, producing or interacting in the target language while their attention is principally focused on meaning rather than form". To Nunan, communicative language use in a classroom activity means that the language learner's attention should be guided more toward meaning than linguistic structures so that interaction will not be interrupted. At the same time, Nunan (1989, p. 10) also articulates that meaning and form are "closely interrelated", and that we "use different grammatical forms to signal differences in meaning". He also maintains that even the so-called "non-communicative" aspects of the tasks such as grammar exercises should be approached in both a meaningful and communicative manner.

Following Candlin (1987), Nunan (1989). Long (1988), and others, Skehan (1998) proposed the following definition of task within the task-based approach:

- ◆ meaning is primary;
- ◆ there is some communication problem to solve;
- ◆ there is some sort of relationship to comparable real-world activities;
- ◆ task completion has some priority;
- ◆ the assessment of the task is in terms of outcome.

This definition summarizes the current work on and understanding of the task-based approach to L2 learning. For a comprehensive review of the task based approach, also see Bygate et al. (1998). The most important characteristic of this approach is its emphasis on directing learners' attention more to meaning than to linguistic forms during task completion. This understanding of task-based approach will provide a theoretical basis for the task design, performance and evaluation conducted in this research. In other words, this research will depart and build on this definition of the task-based approach.

2.2.8   Task design principles

The issue of task design that maximizes conditions for L2 acquisition has been extensively addressed in literature (e.g. Long, 1996; Skehan, 1998; Chapelle, 2001). This section will first examine Nunan's (1989) framework for communicative tasks in order to understand each component of a task. This examination will then lead to a discussion of Skehan's (1998) task design principles so that a theoretical foundation can be laid for the task design in this research.

Nunan's framework for analyzing communicative tasks

In Nunan's framework, tasks are composed of goals, input, activities, setting and roles. (see Figure 2.1)

Figure 2.1   A framework for analyzing communicative tasks

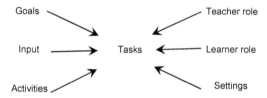

Source: Nunan, 1989, p. 11

Goals: "Goals are the vague general intentions behind any given learning task" (1989, p. 48). A task can involve a range of goals, which are not necessarily mutually exclusive. Goals can be categorized as different types, e.g. communicative, socio-cultural, learning-how-to-learn, and language and cultural awareness.

Input: "Input refers to the data that form the point of departure for the task" (1989, p. 53). Such data can be obtained from a great variety of sources ranging from authentic materials such as postcards or recipes, to materials written specifically for language learning, e.g. textbooks.

Activities: Activities are instructions specifying what the learner should do with the input data (1989, p. 59). Nunan proposed three general ways of characterizing activities: rehearsal for the real world, skills use, and fluency/accuracy.

Roles: Role here refers to "the part that learners and teachers are expected to play in carrying out learning tasks as well as the social and interpersonal relationships between the participants" (1989,

p. 79). The roles of the teachers and learners are closely related, and in many ways complement each other because asking the learners to play a different role "requires the teacher to adopt a different role". (1989, p. 87)

Settings: Settings here refer to "the classroom arrangements specified or implied in the task" (1989, p. 91). When deciding on settings, consideration should also be given to whether the task is to be carried out wholly or partly outside the classroom, such as in a community, or in an industrial or occupational setting.

As demonstrated in the above definitions of the different components of a task, Nunan's framework mainly concerns traditional classroom tasks and so does not deal with the problem of technology-mediated interaction in DLE. Consequently, in guiding the task design of this research, this framework is adopted with a certain degree of modification in order to take into account the technology involved, namely, that of videoconferencing (see Section 3.3.6).

Optimal conditions for task design for Second Language Acquisition (SLA)

How to create conditions that maximize the potential of each component of a task is an important issue to pursue when the components of tasks are determined. This has been a central issue in SLA research. The most influential work can be found in Spolsky (1989), Larsen-Freeman & Long (1991), Pica (1994), Long (1996) and Egbert, Chao & Hanson-Smith (1999). Skehan (1998, p. 132) summarizes current research findings in the task-based approach and proposes the following five guidelines for creating optimal conditions for SLA:

1. choose a range of target structures;
2. choose tasks which meet the utility criterion;
3. select and sequence tasks to achieve balanced goal development;
4. maximize the chances of focus on form through attentional manipulation;
5. use cycles of accountability.

Chapelle (2001, p. 46)) discusses these five guidelines in great detail and points out that "these suggestions summarize what can be gleaned from the current research based on instructional tasks and are therefore worth considering in an evaluation of CALL". The following discussion on the five guidelines provides a theoretical foundation for the videoconference-based task design that optimizes oral and visual interaction in this research.

(1) Choose a range of target structures

Central to this guideline is the belief that acquisition occurs only when the learner is instructed to follow the sequence of development for target structures. "The research on sequences of development implies that language far beyond or beneath learner's abilities or needs is not useful for acquisition" (Chapelle, 2001, p. 46). Skehan (1998, p. 133) stresses the need for "systematicity" in language learning and "keeping track of interlanguage development, but not in narrow specific terms". In other words, the choice of a wide range of target structures should be a systematic endeavour to ensure active interaction and language acquisition.

(2) Choose tasks which meet the utility criterion

Linking with principle (1), which concentrates on the target structures, this principle specifies the conditions for appropriate tasks that offer a favourable environment for the use of systematically chosen target structures, "without their being compulsory" (Skehan, 1998, p. 133).

(3) Select and sequence tasks to achieve balanced goal development

Skehan (1998) sees the goal development of L2 acquisition as a three-dimensional one: fluency, accuracy and complexity. Others (e.g. Cook, 2001) disagree, and perceive more L2 goals than Skehan's three dimensions. This research will limit its concern to the three goals only because of the spoken modality of its tasks. Skehan (1998, p. 5) further defines the three dimensions as follows: fluency (often achieved through memorized and integrated language elements); accuracy (when learners try to use an interlanguage system of a particular level to produce correct, but possibly limited, language); and complexity (a willingness to take risks, to try out new forms even though they may not be completely correct). To Skehan (1998), only a balanced development between these goals can ensure continuing interlanguage growth.

(4) Maximize the chances of focus on form through attentional manipulation

Whether and how to flag the learner's attention to forms during a meaning focused task has been a central concern in L2 acquisition (see Doughty & Williams, 1998; Pica, Kanagy, & Falodun, 1993; Long & Robinson, 1998; Long, 1988b; Chapelle, 2001). As shown in the discussion contained in Section 2.2.6, the general consensus is that, for L2 acquisition to occur, learners' attention should be directed to linguistic forms occasionally in the process of negotiation for meaning when there is a communication breakdown. Learner's attention should then be brought back to meaning when the communication breakdown is repaired. These breakdowns can be triggered by unknown linguistic forms or functions, or even problems in listening comprehension, and can be repaired through modified interaction and/or modified output. In Table 2.3, Chapelle (2001, p. 49) charts the following potential contributors to the manipulation of learner's attention in task completion.

Table 2.3   Conditions that may influence allocation of attention during L2 tasks

Attention affected by...	Definition	Reason
Modified Interaction	Interruption of a communication exchange due to a breakdown in comprehension and subsequent attempt to recover from breakdown.	Breakdown draws attention to unknown linguistic forms and recovery helps make unrecognized input comprehensible, and therefore makes it potential material for acquisition.
Modified output	Learners' correction of their own errors – either self-correction or correction prompted by something else.	Identification and correction of errors draws attention to linguistic form and accuracy.
Time Pressure	An urgency in achieving communication caused by one's own anxiousness or external factors.	When no time pressure exists, attention to form is more likely.
Modality	Whether the language is spoken or written.	Written communication typically affords more opportunity for attention to form, whereas spoken language often occurs under time pressure to achieve fluency.
Support	Cues or information available to the learner to help in constructing meaning during task completion.	When learners have help with some aspects of the language, their attentional resources are more free to be devoted to form.
Surprise	Introduction of an unexpected element during task completion.	The surprise element might be expected to decrease attention to form because of the interruption of plans and need to focus on the surprise, but these hypotheses would depend on the nature of the surprise.
Control	Who makes decisions about the directions that the task is to take.	Control of various aspects of the task by the teacher or the learner may help to prompt focus on form, but research is need to investigate questions about control.
Stakes	Learners' perception of the importance of accurate performance.	Tasks perceived as high stakes are likely to prompt more attention to form.

As shown in Table 2.3, modified interaction or interactional modification has been recognized as a potential contributor to L2 acquisition. Larsen-Freeman and Long (1991, p. 144) regard it as "a candidate for a necessary (not sufficient) condition for acquisition", and further contend that "[t]he role it plays in negotiation for meaning helps to make input comprehensible while still containing unknown linguistic elements, and hence, potential intake for acquisition". While recognizing the importance of interactional modification, this study modified the definition of interactional modification contained in Table 2.3, and expanded its scope. In Table 2.3, breakdowns are attributed only to incomprehension, whereas when defining occasions of interactional modification, this research encompasses another kind of breakdown, those caused by lack of vocabulary to maintain the horizontal movement of the interaction (Wang, 2006; for further discussion, see Section 3.3.9). This inclusion was motivated by data analysis in Chapter 5, when instances of interactional modification were identified and analyzed.

Modified output constitutes another indicator of L2 acquisition, and it is therefore another important point of analysis when discussing the language learning potential of the videoconferencing tasks designed for this research.

Support is defined in Table 2.3 as cues or information available to the learner to help in constructing meaning during task completion. In a videoconferencing-supported learning environment, such cues or information have their own distinct features, such as the use of the whiteboard and the function of video for negotiation of meaning (Wang, 2006). Instances of employing such cues or information were also discussed when evaluating the language learning potential of the tasks in Chapter 5.

(5) Use cycles of accountability

Cycles of accountability are a stock-taking measure, in which learners should be asked to examine regularly what they have learned and what remains to be learned. Skehan's (1998, p. 132) position is that such cycles enable "a balance to be struck between the inevitable freedom that is necessary for acquisition arising out of communication, and the need to be able to track progress and develop plans for the future which are more precise than believing that any structure may emerge simply through interaction".

The above-discussed five principles of task-based language learning all relate to the optimal conditions for interactive language learning and thus form a basis for the task design for this research.

2.2.9   Task evaluation – Chapelle's criteria for evaluating CALL tasks

Linking with optimal conditions for interactive language learning and task design is the issue of how to evaluate the success of interactive language learning and the appropriateness of the task. The CALL literature has never lacked in proposals for criteria for evaluating CALL tasks. However, only Chapelle's criteria will be discussed here because these criteria are largely drawn from the above-discussed five principles of task design proposed by Skehan (1998), and therefore fit (with modification) the design approach adopted for the empirical aspects of this study. Table 2.4 charts Chapelle's six criteria:

Table 2.4   Criteria for CALL task appropriateness

Language learning potential	The degree of opportunity present for beneficial focus on form.
Learner fit	The amount of opportunity for engagement with language under appropriate conditions given learner characteristics.
Meaning focus	The extent to which learners' attention is directed toward the meaning of the language.
Authenticity	The degree of correspondence between the CALL activity and target language activities of interest to learner out of the classroom.
Positive impact	The positive effects of the CALL activity on those who participate in it.
Practicality	The adequacy of resources to support the use of the CALL activity.

Source: Chapelle, 2001, p. 55

Language learning potential

As Table 2.4 demonstrates, *language learning potential* of a task can be determined by the extent to which the task promotes focus on form. Chapelle (2001, p. 55) further points out that "characteristics among those Skehan identified as relevant for promoting focus on form – interactional modification, modification of output, time pressure, modality, support, surprise, control, and stakes – need to be considered in an argument for language learning potential". Chapelle (2001) regards this criterion the most important among the six criteria.

Learner fit

Learner fit requires the linguistic level of task difficulty meet the learner's linguistic ability and non-linguistic characteristics. To be more specific, a beneficial balance should be maintained between the task level of difficulty and the learner's L2 competence so that the learner can benefit linguistically from performing the task. At the same time, task design should take into consideration other characteristics of the learner, such as age and learning style.

Meaning focus

According to Chapelle (2001, p. 56), meaning focus "denotes that the learner's primary attention is directed toward the meaning of the language that is required to accomplish the task", not to the linguistic forms. A meaning-focused task requires the learner to interact with each other in the target language in order to achieve the goal (s) of the task, goals such as making a decision or solving a practical problem.

Authenticity

The criterion of authenticity is largely derived from the communicative approach to L2 learning. This criterion stresses the importance of choosing tasks that the learner can associate with in real life so that the learner can use the language in a real world situation.

Positive impact

Positive impact refers to a range of effects a CALL task can produce on learners, aside from its language learning potential. These impacts can include the development of learner's metacognitive strategies, pragmatic abilities, interest in learning the target culture, and/or willingness to communicate in the target language.

The criteria discussed above will form a basis for the proposal of criteria for evaluating the videoconferencing tasks designed in this research. A more detailed discussion of these criteria is contained in Section 3.4.2.

2.3 Part Two – CMC: The provision of interaction in the 21st century

As the research question of this study aims to investigate the CMC-based, or more precisely, videoconferencing-based, oral and visual interaction, it is essential that we have a good understanding of what CMC entails and the kinds of interaction supported by CMC for L2 acquisition at a distance. The importance of CMC in language learning has been increasingly recognized. By updating the evolving features of CMC and addressing some confusion over the definition of CMC, this section will propose a new taxonomy of CMC-based interaction, as a contribution of this study to CMC research. This proposal is followed by a review of what has been achieved in CMC-based interaction in the area of DLE, and the importance of oral-visual interaction via videoconferencing in distance language learning. (see Wang, 2004a)

2.3.1 CMC – towards a definitional framework

As CMC is a key issue of this study, it is helpful to clarify its meaning at the outset so that a foundation can be laid for later discussion. It is also necessary to address some confusion over the extensive scholarly use of this term as its content and scope have evolved over time along with the development in computer and Internet technology.

It is commonly believed that the earliest history of CMC research can be traced back to 1978 when the book *The Network Nation* by Starr Roxanne Hiltz and Murray Turoff was first published. Since then scholarly interest in CMC has grown steadily in many disciplines such as psychology and business studies. "Surprisingly, although text-based CMC is constructed almost exclusively from linguistic signs, linguists have been slow to consider computer-mediated language a legitimate object of inquiry" (Herring, 1996, p. 2). However, in the late 1980s, linguists and L2 professionals began to research CMC and the interest has been mounting. CMC has been approached and evaluated from social, linguistic and cultural perspectives. (see Herring, 1996)

Of the various 1990s definitions, Santoro (1995), for example, defines CMC as the use of computer systems and networks for the transfer, storage, and retrieval of information among humans. Although the transfer of information is too broad a term to suggest explicitly the inclusion of communication and interaction between humans, this definition does indicate that CMC is computer network based. However, for Herring (1996, p. 1), CMC is the "communication that takes place between human beings via the instrumentality of computers". In Herring's definition, the word "network" is missing. The definition by Warschauer (1997) is more specific, distinguishing five features of CMC:

1. text-based and computer-mediated interaction,
2. many-to-many communication,
3. time-and place-independence
4. long distance exchanges, and
5. hypermedia links. (p. 470)

However, obvious questions arise such as: Aren't these just the features of e-mail or IRC (Internet Relay Chat)? Is e-mail communication or IRC equal to CMC? Indeed, it seems that in the 1990s, the perception that CMC is text-based was accepted almost unquestioningly in the field. Garrison (1997, p. 3) is another example. He defines CMC as an "asynchronous text-based (written) communication in a one-to-one or one-to-many context". Examples cited are e-mail, electronic bulletin boards, news groups, databases, electronic journals and computer conferencing. Although Garrison suggests the possibility of synchronous CMC communication, his understanding of synchronous conferencing is still that of a text-based and non-oral discourse.

Nothing in the term CMC suggests that it should be text-based or asynchronous, but in the 1990s, CMC was defined in an unnecessarily restrictive way to infer a text-based asynchronous communication. Such a perception was no doubt influenced by the technology prevalent at the time, which most people thought capable of providing only computer mediated written communication, such as e-mail, text chat and Web-based reading activities.

However, CMC in the 21st century embraces much more content and depth than text-based asynchronous interaction alone. In fact, CMC now offers improved scope and quality of interaction. To date, although technologies (e.g. Internet-based synchronous audio and videoconferencing) providing oral and oral-visual discourses are not sufficiently explored for language learning purposes, their existence and potential warrant the inclusion of at least these two discourses in CMC. To my knowledge, only Levy (2000) and Harrington & Levy (2001) have included videoconferencing in their definition of CMC.

On the basis of the above discussion, CMC is inclusively defined in this study as *"communications between human beings via a computer network"* (Wang, 2004, p. 75). It encompasses the following characteristics:

♦ It is computer network-supported.

♦ It can be text-based, oral and/or visual.

♦ It can be either synchronous or asynchronous.

♦ It can be one-to-one, one-to-many or many-to-many.

♦ It can be learner-to-learner, learner-to-instructor or learner-to-native speaker.

♦ It can be time and place dependent or independent.

Clearly, definitions need to reflect developments in a fast-changing field. This is the basis for rethinking the taxonomy of interaction in CMC.

2.3.2 A new taxonomy of interaction in CMC

In line with this understanding of CMC and interaction, I propose a new taxonomy of interaction in the context of CMC in terms of its potential for language learning and different L2 learner goals. This new taxonomy is based on the sociocultural perspective which regards language learning as a process of social communication and interaction.

It is proposed here that in a CMC context, interaction can be further categorized into written, oral, and oral-visual interaction in view of specific learner goals (see Wang, 2004a; Figure 2.2). These three types of interaction are distinct from the traditional non-computer mediated oral, written and face-to-face interaction both in terms of their linguistic and interactional functions and features. Established theories and empirical studies on the traditional forms of interaction can only shed light on CMC-based interaction, but cannot encompass the entirety of this emerging activity. New theories and empirical studies are needed in order to understand CMC-based interaction.

Figure 2.2   Three types of interaction in CMC

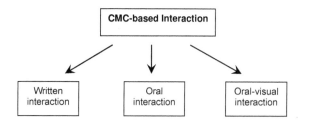

Written interaction in a CMC context

In a CMC learning environment, written interaction as a social activity can be both synchronous and asynchronous. Written interaction can be one-to-one, one-to-many or many-to-many between learners, learners and native speakers and/or learners and instructors. It can be either time and place independent or dependent.

Asynchronous written interaction can be achieved through e-mail and other Internet tools such as bulletin boards and listservs (for examples of this category of studies, see Schwienhorst, 1997, Warschauer, 1998). Towards the end of the 1990s, the trend was to place and interpret text-based communications within an oral discourse. These types of Internet tools are often evaluated against their potential in improving the learner's "conversation-like forms of written language exchange" (Lamy & Goodfellow, 1999, p. 43), through communication with native speakers or the instructor. Despite the fact that such discourse was still text based, the analysis is often conducted from a conversation analysis perspective (e.g. Negretti, 1999, Kitade, 2000), and this kind of written interaction is delineated as "reflective conversation" by Lamy & Goodfellow (1999, p. 43).

Synchronous written interaction is mostly generated by online chats using tools such as IRC (Internet Relay Chat) and Moo, MOO, Webchat, MSN etc. In recent years, research has increasingly moved towards this direction to investigate the nature of the discourse generated within such environments (see Negretti, 1999; Shield et al., 1999; Kitade, 2000). The potential of this type of interaction is again often interpreted using theories pertaining to oral discourse such as conversation analysis (e.g. Negretti, 1999 and Kitade, 2000) because of the communicative nature of such interaction. These kinds of views indicate that technology supporting written interaction is more mature than that supporting oral and oral-visual interaction. (For discussions on the use of Internet technology to improve text-based interaction, see Appel & Gilabert, 2002; Barnes, 2000; Chun, 1994; Kötter, 2003; Lee, 2004; Lamy & Goodfellow, 1999; Negretti, 1999; Pennington, 1999.)

Existing literature on CMC-based interaction mostly concentrates on its written rather than oral form. These studies concentrate on the similarities between CMC supported written interactions and face-to-face interactions, and regard written interaction such as text chat as a bridge to face-to-face interaction, which provides an optimal environment for SLA. (e.g. Chun, 1994; Kern, 1996; Pellettieri, 2002; Sotillo, 2000; Smith, 2003; Tudini, 2003)

Oral interaction in a CMC context

Oral interaction in a CMC context refers to real-time speaking interaction that can be realized through Internet audio conferencing tools, such as I-phone, NetMeeting, HomeMeeting and audio chat rooms. Despite the fact that visual input does not exist in such interaction, it is a step closer towards face-to-face interaction, providing the learner with a new venue for the improvement of oral communicative competence. At the same time, used effectively, these Internet conferencing tools can generate interaction that is richer, in some respects, than face-to-face interaction both in terms of its content and scope. For example, through an audio conferencing tool, an authentic conversation can be easily achieved between a learner in one country and a native speaker in another country where the target language is spoken.

There are at least two kinds of interaction in this category: time and place independent; and time and place dependent. PalTalk is a good example of network based conferencing tools providing time and place independent interaction in which students can join a chat group anywhere and anytime. They can use the computer's microphone to talk to native speakers or join a group with the same interest. Such an approach provides a good practice venue for students with an intermediate or higher level of proficiency in the target language. Skye, I-phone and NetMeeting (MSN) are good examples of time and place dependent network-based audio conferencing tools, which need to be set up with the party that one wants to talk to. Time and place dependent conferencing tools can be effectively used for planned tutorials with the goal of improving learners' speaking skills.

Probably because most of the available audio conferencing tools (e.g. Skype and MSN) are not specifically designed for language learning purposes, there is little work to date which investigates the use of these commercially or freely available audio-conferencing tools in language learning. The Open University (OU) develops its own Internet-based audio conferencing tool called Lyceum, the use of which has been reported in a series of articles (see Kötter et al., 1999; Hauck & Haezewindt, 1999; Shield et al., 2001; Hewer et al., 1999; Kötter, 2001; Hampel & Baber, 2003; Hampel & Hauck, 2004, Hampel & Stickler, 2005; Rosell-Aguilar, 2005, 2006a, 2006b). The OU project trialled audio conferencing software and e-mail to provide real-time tutorials. According to Hampel and Hauck (2004, p. 70), "students and tutors use headsets and microphones (which they have to provide themselves) to work together in real-time, an approach which enables them to simultaneously hear each other and talk to each other, but not to see each other". Lyceum also incorporates such tools as an on-screen whiteboard, shared document and a text-chat box to supplement the voice conferencing.

Another attempt to provide oral interaction can be found in Project MERLIN. This project, developed by the University of Hull and British Telecommunications plc and released in September 1996, had a different technical approach. It linked telephone conferencing facilities to the Web browser so that learners could interact with one another in small groups over the phone. Although the audio-conferencing was still telephone based, it differed from conventional telephone conferencing in that students' participation could be monitored through a window of the computer. (Marsh et al., 1997)

These two projects provide students with a higher level of interaction in that students can speak with one another spontaneously in the target language. However, without visual input, many conversational cues (e.g. eye contact and nods) are lost, rendering conversations less natural and communicative than in real life situations. (Wang, 2004a)

Oral-visual interaction in a CMC context

Oral-visual interaction in a CMC context refers to a much higher level of interaction, similar to but much richer than that of face-to-face interaction in some respects. It can be described as a potentially effective real-time learning environment in which language learners can not only interact orally with one another in the target language, but also use paralinguistic cues such as facial expressions and body movements. The visual input weighs heavily, according to Thompson (1996, p. 24):

> Where the teaching and learning do not incorporate visual elements the loss of the visual channel is less likely to be prohibitive but it is still significant. Although the telephone amplifies sound and hence spoken language, in its elimination of body language and physical context, important sources by which meaning is constructed are denied. While written text is fixed, oral discourse is fluid, ongoing and ever-changing. For this reason, there is general recognition of the importance of non-verbal features and contextual elements to support the communicative experience.

Besides, without visual input, the language learning environment is far removed from real-life situations, thus compromising an ultimate goal of language learning according to communicative methodologies, that is, to communicate and interact in the target language in an authentic environment. The importance of visual input and interaction may be even more essential to distance language learners in that it can help reduce isolation and anxiety and build confidence.

In a distance-learning environment, the best place for oral-visual interaction to occur is in front of a personal computer, where students talk to one another via a Web camera with a headset or microphone (see Figure 2.3). The multimodal nature of oral-visual interaction supported by CMC offers language learners the richest and most authentic learning environment, with the combination of the visual, oral, and written modes (see Kress & van Leeuwen, 2001). This is the highest level of interaction that distance language professionals can provide to the learner at this stage of technological development, although it is often time and place dependent. Nevertheless, this is the kind of interaction that distance learners need most, and Internet-based desktop videoconferencing tools now allow it to be achieved. For example, the combination of a Web camera and MSN provides potential for oral-visual interaction. (see later discussions on NetMeeting)

Figure 2.3   Example of a videoconferencing learning environment

Although Internet-based videoconferencing has been around since the 1990s, its capacity to support good quality interaction has been overshadowed by the poor video and audio quality of the pioneering videoconferencing facilities. Few attempts have been made to test the technological and pedagogical values of Internet-based desktop videoconferencing since, generally speaking, the technology required had not reached a stage at which it was sufficiently stable and reliable. However, the recent rapid development in computer network technology justifies a re-evaluation of Internet-based videoconferencing tools in terms of their technological and pedagogical capabilities. This is because:

- ♦ The computing power of the PC (Personal Computer) has increased. The memory of most present-day PCs is large enough to support highly interactive language tutorials and most computers have built-in sound and video cards. This means that the only additional hardware needed for network-based videoconferencing is a Web Camera and headphone, which cost around US$50.

- ♦ A variety of videoconferencing tools is also readily available. Some can be freely downloaded from the Internet. (e.g., MSN and Skype)

- ♦ Limited Internet bandwidth invariably represents the most fundamental problem in network-based videoconferencing, resulting in poor audio and video quality. However, the providers of videoconferencing tools are constantly reducing the bandwidth requirements of their products for faster performance.

- ◆ The network bandwidth has also been greatly improved since the 1990s.

- ◆ The interface of videoconferencing tools is under constant improvement to make it more user friendly.

Despite the above mentioned development, empirical research reporting on the use of videoconferencing for oral-visual interaction in distance mode is rarely found in the literature. However, there are three notable exceptions: the report on HIPERNET, LEVERAGE and ReLaTe projects.

McAndrew et al. (1996) described the HIPERNET (short for "HIgh PERformance NETworked multimedia for distributed language learning") which used a Bitfield H261 conferencing card with customized software. Instead of making use of the Internet, the system operates over the GRANTA Backbone Network, which connects the different institutions of Cambridge University. The results from the trials of the system suggested that "collaborative task-based learning is adequately supported by videoconferencing, with the important implication that such methods may be appropriate for distance learning". (McAndrew et al., 1996, p. 211)

LEVERAGE (LEarn from Video Extensive Real Atm Gigabit Experiment) was a three-year project from 1996-1998 researching the use of multimedia broadband technology to support language learning at a distance (see http://greco.dit.upm.es/~leverage/about.htm; Wong & Fauverge, 1999; Zähner et al., 2000). This system supported oral-visual interaction among the three sites participating in the project: University of Cambridge, Insitut National des Telecommunications, and Universidad Politinica de Madrid. The ATM LANs of the three sites were interconnected by using ISDN dial-up access routers and the Internet as a fallback path.

Learners from the three countries used LEVERAGE to assist one another in language learning. For example, a native student from Paris played the role of tutor to a learner of French from Madrid. Three field trials have been reported so far and the overall responses from the students have been very positive. Its multipoint and point-to-point videoconferencing feature allows the learners to see each other in the window, and is regarded by the students as "the most important tool" and "the best of the sessions" (Ibañez & Duque, 1999, p. 2). These results come from the third trial of the LEVERAGE in 1998. A search of the available literature does not suggest an extensive use of the LEVERAGE system so far.

ReLaTe (Remote Language Teaching) was originally developed by the University of Exeter and University College, London, in 1994 (see http://www-mice.cs.ucl.ac.uk/multimedia/projects; Buckett, Stringer & Datta, 1999). After several years of development, its videoconferencing interface can now support up to eight participants conferencing simultaneously. Extensive trials of

ReLaTe in teaching started in 1995 and since then several language courses and other subjects have been taught through ReLaTe. Feedback from both tutors and their distant students was "extremely positive". The results of these trials have also shown that "the use of Internet videoconferencing is a feasible proposition for language tuition and that with current software and hardware, small to medium sized groups can be taught cost-effectively". (see http://www.ex.ac.uk/pallas/relate/papers/peg99/stringer.htm)

The use of MBone (short for Multicast Backbone) and RAT (short for Robust Audio Tool) is the most innovative contribution from the ReLaTe project to Internet-based videoconferencing. "The MBone is an overlay network consisting of portions of the Internet which support a technique known as multicasting" (Buckett & Stringer, 1997a, p. 3). This technique can effectively reduce congestion on the Internet by selectively sending out only one stream of data to the participants, unlike other Internet-based videoconferencing, which duplicates data streams resulting in congestion because of the limited Internet bandwidth. The limited capacity of bandwidth is the most serious technical problem with the present generation Internet-based videoconferencing, because congestion caused by the limited bandwidth affects the audio and video quality of the conferencing. This problem is aggravated in the case of many-to-many videoconferencing.

To provide reliable sound quality, which is crucial to the success of language learning by videoconferencing, ReLaTe uses RAT (Robust Audio Tool) to send a duplicate copy of all the audio files. This is to ensure that the second copy backs up when the first one gets lost or delayed. (Buckett, Stringer & Datta, 1999)

ReLaTe seems to promise immense potential for distance language learning although experiments have so far been restricted to European universities using UK high-bandwidth SuperJANET academic computer network. The software is freely available on the Internet, but setting up and maintenance can be resource demanding. In this respect, freely or commercially available videoconferencing tools such as MSN and Skype clearly enjoy advantages because of their ease of installation and zero maintenance cost.

The HIPERNET, LEVERAGE and ReLaTe projects may represent the beginning of efforts to find a way of offering oral-visual interaction in distance language learning, but such efforts have so far been restricted to Europe and to the mid 1990s. Since then little substantial achievement has been reported that is sufficient to conclude that videoconferencing offers qualitative oral-visual interaction to distance language education.

The relationship between written, oral and oral-visual interaction in CMC

As discussed above, written interaction in CMC can be of both a synchronous and asynchronous nature. Research on the effectiveness of CMC-based written interaction (e.g. Nagretti, 1999; Kitade, 2000; Tudini, 2003) indicates that such interaction has the potential to improve students' writing skills and to prepare the student for the other two types of interaction (i.e. oral and oral-visual interaction). Most Internet chat facilities can be used for such preparation because students can carry out synchronous written conversations with one another. Although written interaction can achieve a certain degree of spontaneity and fluency, such spontaneity is often delayed.

Oral interaction in a CMC context offers more spontaneity and fluency than written interaction, but accuracy may be at risk because students do not have time to prepare what they wish to say in a real-time situation. Furthermore, without visual cues, the negotiation of meaning can take a longer time or can be difficult in some circumstances, such as when the learner's proficiency is low.

Oral-visual interaction in CMC should improve both fluency and accuracy because of its synchronous nature and visual input. This is because learners can more accurately negotiate meanings with the help of paralinguistic cues, thus improving the quality of interaction and the degree of interactivity. However, while this level of interactivity can be technically achievable through technologies such as videoconferencing, it is often technically problematic due to problems such as limited Internet bandwidth and delay in transmission.

It has to be pointed out that each tool in CMC has its own embedded feature that supports a specific aspect of interaction in language learning. For example, e-mails only support written interaction, while videoconferencing helps to ease the problem of lack of oral-visual interaction. The important thing is to determine firstly the needs of the learner and then the capabilities of the tool and design the tasks to meet the learning objectives.

2.3.3   *The importance of video-mediated interaction*

The central debate in using videoconferencing in the present time is probably whether video-mediated interaction is necessary or whether audio interaction itself is sufficient for task-based instructions. A review of the literature reveals a number of conflicting arguments, especially when CMC based interaction becomes the focus of the debate.

A generally held belief is that there are obvious advantages for seeing a person's face when interacting. Research from cognitive and social psychology identifies a number of potential benefits. Cognitively and linguistically, it is generally maintained that paralinguistic cues such as head nods and facial expressions reduce ambiguity in speech and improve understanding (see Bruce, 1996). As a result, there are more turn takings, shorter turn length and more interruptions than audio-only interactions (e.g. Cook & Lalljee, 1972; Rutter & Stephenson, 1977; Cohen, 1982; O'Conaill et al., 1993). Sproull & Kiesler (1986) present an even stronger argument that lack of nonverbal information reduces social cues and impairs interaction. Trevino et al. (1987, p. 557) hold that the level of ambiguity of a given message often gives rise to diverging interpretations and that different media choice can increase or decrease such ambiguity. They further conclude that face-to-face communication "is the richest medium because it has the capacity for immediate feedback, multiple cues, and natural language. Therefore it has the potential for decreasing ambiguity more quickly than other media".

Boyle et al. (1994) report that when performing a collaborative task, subjects produced shorter exchanges of speech and less problematic dialogues when they could see each other than when they could only hear each other. Summerfield (1992) also reports that, compared with only hearing, seeing the face allows a listener to tolerate an additional 4-6 dB of noise to obtain the same level of intelligibility, and that each decibel of signal-to-noise ratio gained can enhance intelligibility by 10–15 per cent. Bruce (1996) comments on Summerfield's finding by saying:

> These figures indicate that at certain levels of noise, seeing the face can allow a listener to 'hear' otherwise unintelligible speech. Information from vision may therefore be particularly important for speech perception when the auditory channel is noisy, as it can be during telecommunication, either because of signal limitations or because of competing noise from the external environment in which the communication is taking place. Information from vision neatly complements that available by hearing alone. (p. 172)

The issue of lack of body language and of depersonalization of communication in CMC has been recognized by scholars such as Lecourt (1999), Kress & van Leeuwen (2001) and Hampel & Hauck (2004). The findings from Hampel & Hauck (2004, p. 78) support the above arguments from a participant's point of view. They point out that when "tutors do not receive visual clues and body language, it is easier for students unsure of what is going on to sit quietly without participating and without getting help or encouragement".

Many of the above-discussed arguments have been generated around the disadvantages of text-based CMC such as e-mails and Internet Relay Chat. The general consensus seems to indicate that lack of access to nonverbal and paralinguistic information in the text-based media filters out rich information important to comprehension and performance.

From a sociocultural perspective, the impact of video on building a learning community, increasing confidence and reducing isolation is also largely recognized in the literature (see

Bloomfield, 2000; Kitao, 1999; Shield, 1999; Lake, 1999; Stacey, 1999; Hampel & Hauck, 2004; Lee, 2007). These issues are especially typical of the distance learners, who have been physically isolated from one another, and the video is perceived as even more crucial in reducing the impact of the distance.

In contrast to this view, some scholars believe that there are no demonstrated advantages for video-mediated communication vis-à-vis audio-only interaction. In fact, Walther et al. (1994, p. 465) argue that the critical difference between face-to-face and text-based CMC is "a question of rate, not capability". O'Malley et al. (1996, p. 177) conducted a series of experiments in which pairs of subjects performed collaborative tasks at a distance via video and audio links or audio links only. Their data indicates that "users of video links produced longer and more interrupted dialogues than those who had audio links only, although there were no differences in performance" and that "[p]erformance was affected when the video links were of low bandwidth, resulting in transmission delays".

These conflicting findings need to be further investigated through empirical studies. It is argued here that the end results of interaction (e.g. task completion) may be the same with or without visual signals, but the process of the interaction can be vastly different. It is not surprising that, without non-verbal signals, interaction may suffer, but at the same time, we can still get our message across, just as we have managed to do so well with telephone conversations. This is because "we have a flexible repertoire of strategies which allow us to compensate for missing channels of communication" (Bruce, 1996, p. 167). With language learning, the important issue is whether the visual and non-verbal component is helpful in language acquisition during the process of interaction. However, it is certain that, with visual input, a sense of realism and authenticity will be added to enhance the language learning tasks. The issue of oral-visual interaction constitutes a focal point in this research, and data will be collected to verify its importance in language acquisition at a distance.

2.4 Part Three – The provision of interaction in distance language education

What has been achieved in the distance language arena as far as the provision of oral-visual interaction is concerned? The following section will examine this issue from a historical perspective. Given the critical importance of interaction to the quality of distance language learning, this section traces how the nature and scope of interaction have changed and developed as DLE has moved through its main developmental stages. Such an examination serves the purpose of providing a historical insight into the problem we are facing today – the lack of provision of oral-visual interaction in DLE. By examining the different stages in DLE, the main purpose of this section is to gain insight into the following critical issues confronting language learning at a distance. In terms of the provision of interaction, what has been achieved so far with learning languages in distance mode? With the aid of advanced computer technology, what can be achieved in this field? What is the future of this mode of language learning and teaching? In a word, what are the major implications of advanced computer technology for distance language education? A re-examination of the development of DLE and the implications of technology for language learning at a distance should provide insight into the potential of the distance-learning mode, especially for language learning. (Wang & Sun, 2001)

In order to better understand the provision of interaction in DLE, it is necessary to probe the nature of distance education. In this research, distance education is regarded as a field and distance language education as a sub-field of distance education. "Distance" defines the field. Thus, to a large extent, the nature of distance education reflects the nature of distance language education.

2.4.1 The nature of distance education

The "distance" in distance education clearly indicates that interaction is not face-to-face. The problem, therefore, is that classroom interactive learning is not (or only minimally) present. So what, historically, has distance education had to offer learners, and how has its nature evolved since its conception? What can it offer learners at the start of the 21st century with the use of cutting edge technologies? I turn to definitions of DE in this section as it is central to the argument in this book.

The definitions of distance education prior to the 21st century

Keegan (1991) believes that there is sufficient consensus on the definition of distance education, both in theory and in practice, to consider distance education as a distinctive field of study. Reviewing the definitions of distance education over time, one perceives an evolution in thinking and an ongoing refinement of previous definitions as distance education has developed. One reflection of this evolution is the fact that Keegan has twice (1983 & 1996) synthesized the definitions of distance education by various scholars. In his 1983 synthesis, he discusses earlier definitions by Dohman (1967), Mackenzie, Christensen & Rigby (1968), Moore (1973) and Holmberg (1977), and on the basis of his own definition of 1983, proposes six "interdependent elements" of distance education (see Table 2.5). Rapid development in the 1990s led him to improve his previous definition. On this occasion, his synthesis added more recent definitions by Garrison & Shale (1987), Baker et al. (1989), Moore (1990) and Portway and Lane (1994). Consequently, he proposed the five basic defining elements of distance education contained in Table 2.6.

Table 2.5   Keegan's 1980 definition (1983, p. 30)

♦   The separation of teacher and learner which distinguishes it from face-to-face lecturing.

♦   The influence of an educational organization which distinguishes it from private study.

♦   The use of technical media, usually print, to unite teacher and learner and carry the educational content.

♦   The provision of two-way communication so that the student may benefit from or even initiate dialogue.

♦   The possibility of occasional meetings for both didactic and socialization purposes.

♦   · The participation in an industrialized form of education which, if accepted, contains the genus of radical separation of distance education from other forms within the educational spectrum.

Table 2.6   Keegan's 1996 definition (1996, p. 50)

♦   The quasi-permanent separation of teacher and learner throughout the length of the learning process; this distinguishes it from conventional face-to-face education.

♦   The influence of an educational organization both in the planning and preparation of learning materials and in the provision of student support services; this distinguishes it from private study and teach-yourself programs.

♦   The use of technical media, print, audio, video or computer, to unite teacher and learner and carry the content of the course.

♦   The provision of two-way communication so that the student may benefit from or even initiate dialogue; this distinguishes it from other uses of technology in education.

♦   The quasi-permanent absence of the learning group throughout the length of the learning process so that people are usually taught as individuals and not in groups, with the possibility of occasional meeting for both didactic and socialization purposes.

In comparison with Keegan's 1980 definition, his 1996 definition contains a number of refinements, which reflect subsequent developments in the field of distance education. For example, *quasi-separation* of teacher and learner further defines the realm of separation in the 1980 version, "in recognition of the fact that face-to-face teaching is part of many distance programs"(Verduin & Clark, 1991, p. 10). The influence of the educational organization is further clarified with an emphasis on its influence on "planning and preparation of learning materials and in the provision of student support services" (Keegan, 1996, p. 50). Thus distance education appears to be a more organized education system than merely self-study. Another important improvement of the 1996 definition is the inclusion of audio and video technologies, and more importantly, computer technology in the media, which was not mentioned in the 1980 definition. This is a significant improvement in that it recognizes the importance of computer technology in today's distance education. The fifth element in the 1996 definition is elaborated to stress individual teaching as opposed to group teaching. However, the sixth element in the 1980 definition is deleted from the 1996 definition. Keegan (1996, p. 50) regards "the presence of more industrialized features than in conventional oral education" and "the privatization of institutional learning" as two "social-cultural determinants which are both necessary pre-conditions and necessary consequences of distance education".

Holmberg's concept of "guided didactic conversation" provides us with another angle from which we can examine the nature of distance education. Interaction is central to this concept. The approach portrays distance education as a "conversation-like interaction between the student and the distance education provider, including the instructor, the counsellor, the author, and so on" (Holmerg, 1986, p. 55). There have been numerous further attempts to define this mode of education, although without unanimity. Nevertheless, drawing on the work of scholars, the nature of distance education can be summarized as follows:

- physical separation of learner and educator, that is, there is a physical distance preventing face-to-face education; (Holmberg, 1977, p. 9; Keegan, 1983, p. 15; Cunningham et al., 1998, p. 23);

- mediated subject-matter presentation (Holmberg, 1995);

- mediated student-tutor interaction (Holmberg, 1995) or student-tutor relationship (Dallos, 1984). Keegan refers to this as the provision of two-way communication (Keegan, 1983, p. 15);

- use of technical media. (Keegan, 1983, p. 15)

Throughout the development of distance education, the fundamental nature of physical separation of the learner and distance education provider has remained unchanged, despite the occasional face-to-face teaching. This physical separation is still true today when real-time Internet technology enters the scene of distance education, offering oral-visual interaction. The two basic constituent elements of distance education, as suggested by Holmberg (1995, p. 47): mediated subject matter presentation and mediated student-tutor interaction, also remain unchanged. However, the content and scope of these have been constantly enriched as distance education has moved from one generation to another.

Definition of distance education in the 21st century

The above-discussed definitions describe the nature and development of distance education up to the 1990s. Since then, the field of distance education has experienced tremendous development both in terms of the use of advanced educational technology and the scope of distance language education. This development warrants the following five modifications to these earlier definitions of distance education.

First, the earlier definitions only stress the separation of the learner and educator in a distance-learning environment (see above discussions). The separation of learners does not receive enough attention. The importance of emphasizing the latter separation in the start of the 21st century lies in the recognition of the capabilities of Internet technology in providing learner-learner interaction in distance education.

Second, the term "real-time "should be added to the earlier definition of mediated subject-matter presentation and student-tutor interaction. Along with rapid developments in information technology, the content and scope of the two basic constituents of distance education (Holmberg, 1995) have undergone qualitative changes, from asynchronous to synchronous and from non-real time to real time.

Third, n-way (multiple-way) synchronous interaction should be specified, as two-way communication defined by scholars such as Keegan (1983) is no longer adequate to encompass the scope and quality of real-time technology mediated interaction between the teacher and the learner, and among learners. Real-time interaction can now be generated not only between the tutor and the learner, but also between learners and native speakers anywhere in the world.

Fourth, learner characteristics should be a defining element in distance education. In distance education most learners are adults. In both of Keegan's definitions, this element of learner and learner characteristics was not mentioned. I argue that the learner constitutes the most important part of distance education, and should not be overlooked.

Fifth, the impact of social distance on learning should be acknowledged, as none of the earlier definitions have dealt with such impact. Social distance here refers to the isolation and lack of communication between learners due to physical distance between them. Research shows that such social distance can affect learners' confidence in learning and create frustration due to lack of support from their peers and education provider (see Brown, 1996; Williams & Sharma, 1988). Social distance is typical of distance education and has a contingent relationship with physical distance.

On the basis of these points, six defining elements of distance education in the 21st century can now be summarized:

- The physical separation of teacher and learner, and learner from learner.
- The influence of an educational organization both in teaching and in the provision of student support services.

- The use of technology and media such as print, audio, video or computer to present subject matter both synchronously and asynchronously.

- The provision of both two-way and n-way communication and interaction through media and technology.

- The majority of learners are adults.

- The existence of social distance due to physical separation.

The above discussion leads to the conclusion that "distance" defines distance education especially in terms of lack of provision of two-way and n-way interaction. In other words, the provision of interaction is a core problem in DE and DLE, and is a major indicator of to what degree the problem of "distance" has been eased in each generation of DLE. Interaction, to some extent, determines the characteristics of each generation.

2.4.2 The definition of "generation"

This study not only situates itself within the latest generation of DLE, but also proposes the emergence of a fourth generation of DLE as a contribution to the literature (Wang & Sun, 2001). To justify the creation of a new generation, it is therefore important that we clarify the definition of "generation" at the outset. In the context of distance education, few scholars have attempted to define the term "generation". One of these is Garrison (1985), who argues that

> Generation is used to suggest the building upon previous capabilities. The development of the generations of distance education represents, in systems terminology, a hierarchical structure with an increasing differentiation of technological capacity for integrating unique delivery systems. In other words, new media can be combined with older media to provide a greater range of choice for the design of effective distance education delivery systems. (p. 236)

This book has adopted the above definition to determine when one generation progresses to the next. Essentially, the dividing line for each generation occurs when technology fundamentally improves the mode of subject-matter delivery and learner-instructor and learner-learner interaction both in terms of its quantity and quality. These improvements do not change the fundamental nature of distance education (that is, the physical separation of education provider and learner), but instead create a qualitatively more favourable and more flexible environment for interactive language learning. In other words, technology has brought revolutionary changes in distance education in the sense that it has constantly advanced the evolution of distance education. The term "generation" has been discussed in the general context of distance education. However, it is argued here that the term applies equally to language learning at a distance because it constitutes a subfield of distance education, but one with its own set of teaching and learning characteristics.

2.4.3   The first generation of distance language education

Mediated subject-matter presentation

The first generation of distance learning did not see much of language teaching and learning, but it is important historically. In fact, until 1965 distance education as a separate discipline had remained virtually unexplored because it was not considered as part of mainstream education (Peters, 1994, p. 1). The first advertisement offering distance courses to learn a "new method of short hand" appeared in *The Boston Gazette* on 20 March 1728 (Battenberg, 1971, p. 1). However, more conclusive evidence of teaching of the distance nature was found a 100 years later (Holmberg, 1995). The generally accepted origin of distance education can be traced back to 1833, when an advertisement appeared in Sweden offering an opportunity to study "composition through the media of the post" (Baath, 1980, p. 13; 1985, p. 62). In 1840, Issac Pitman began teaching shorthand by correspondence in Bath England (Dinsdale, 1953). The University of London was the first University to found correspondence colleges such as Skerry's College and University Correspondence College in 1880 (Curzon, 1977). Following this, distance-learning courses began to appear in England, Germany, the United States and Japan (see Holmberg, 1995). The earliest distance language school, documented by Noffsinger (1926, p. 4), was established by Charles Toussaint and Gustav Langenscheidt in Berlin in 1856, in which language curricula and learning outcomes were undocumented.

Printed materials and the postal system were used almost exclusively to present and deliver the teaching, which is why this period is also known as "the correspondence generation" (Garrison, 1985). The area or distance covered by such an education was limited due to the restrictions of the then communication system.

Mediated student-tutor interaction

Limited data is available which match the primitive nature of the technology in terms of "guided didactic conversation". The combination of printed matter and the postal system could hardly offer any direct interaction between the student and the education provider, despite the existence of two-way communication. In Nipper's (1989, p. 63) words, "[s]tudent-teacher and teacher-student feedback processes are slow, sparse, and mostly restricted to the periods when the learners submit scheduled assignments".

The first generation of distance education lasted nearly a century, the longest generation in the history of distance education. However, "until 1965 distance education had very seldom been an object of scientific research or scholarly work" (Peters, 1994, p. 1). As a result, scholars "lacked reliable, impartial information about the practice of distance education, let alone theoretical explanations of its extraordinary methods and approaches with relevant empirical data" (Peters, 1994, p. 1). Few languages were offered then, probably largely due to the lack of technical support to foster interaction and the communicative nature of language learning. As a result, distance education for languages in this generation did not develop as fast as other disciplines in distance mode and remained a relatively neglected area.

2.4.4   The second generation of distance language education

Technological advances are the motor for generational changes in distance language education as Boyle (1995) states:

> The obvious characteristics of this second phase of development in distance learning are the technological ones, with the telephone being used increasingly, and with radio, television, and audio- and video-cassettes supplementing the printed material and bringing the teacher and student closer together. (p. 284)

This second generation is also known as "multimedia distance education" (Nipper, 1989), in which language learning became core content. When technologies such as telephone conferencing, television broadcasting, radio and audio-visual cassettes, were brought into distance education in the 1970s, the presentation of learning materials and the interaction between students and tutors underwent revolutionary changes. This generation witnessed a wealth of different modes of delivery of language learning materials, particularly in improving listening and speaking skills. Improving listening and speaking skills had been a century-long problem facing distance educators, because the distance between the learner and the instructor, and the limitations of the then technology, had prevented spontaneous and effective interaction. In the second generation, distance language educators attempted to tackle these hurdles by capitalizing on advanced educational technologies.

Changes in mediated Student-tutor interaction

The quality of interaction between the learner and the instructor greatly improved in the second generation DLE. In a telephone conferencing learning environment, learners may have real-time interaction with each other and with the teacher. With audiocassettes, they can send their taped speeches for the instructor to check and compare their pronunciation with either the instructor's or the taped authentic pronunciation. During a live television broadcast, learners may hear and watch the language being spoken at home. The use of technology not only improves students' language proficiency, but also reduces the sense of isolation common to most distance learners.

Despite the fact that technologies used in this generation are all single-medium technologies, they had a revolutionary impact on distance language learning. Distance language learning proliferated in this phase. The founding of the British Open University in 1969 is generally regarded as a landmark in distance education. This is because it marks the beginning of a new period in which distance education is institutionalized with full degree courses, systematic systems evaluation and new media (Rumble and Harry, 1982). This development distinguishes distance education from self-study. More languages were being offered than ever before. In Australia, as well as European languages, Asian languages such as Indonesian, Japanese and Vietnamese became popular distance-learning subjects (Williams & Sharma, 1988).

The second phase of distance language learning enjoys a closer link with electronic and telephonic technology. With the availability of more advanced communication technologies such as the television and telephone, the second generation model offers a more effective language learning environment in that it caters, to a certain degree, for more synchronous oral interaction.

2.4.5   The third generation of distance language education

Justification of a new generation

While the first two generations are generally accepted divisions in the scholarly research, existing literature does not offer a convincing dividing line between the second and the third generations. The term "computer generation" has been used by scholars, such as Garrison (1985), to describe the third generation, but this term is too broad and vague to define precisely the features of this generation. The definition by Chacon (1992), cited in Boyle (1995, p. 289), is even broader: "[t]he second model of distance learning gave way to the third generation when access to computers changed the way in which teachers and students were able to process information, interact with, and communicate with one another". It would be too simplistic to say that the third generation has been marked by the use of computers in distance education, not only because computers were employed in education as early as the 1960s, but also because the use of computers in distance education has a complex and evolving history.

Although Garrison (1985, p. 238) does not provide a distinctive commencement point for the "computer generation", he mentions that 25 years of research has proven that computer assisted learning (CAL) "can be a more efficient or effective means of instructional delivery than traditional face-to-face instruction". It can be argued that the third generation of distance language learning started in the early 1980s, and its characteristics can be best summarized by the acronym of CALL (Computer-Assisted Language Learning). This acronym indicates that in this period, computers have acted as an aid to the main teaching framework, not as the principal media of learning material presentation. Multimedia has become the catch phrase of this generation.

Changes in mediated subject-matter presentation

In addition to printed materials, this generation has witnessed two major delivery modes in language learning at a distance: off-line delivery and on-line delivery.

Off-line delivery refers here to delivery of course materials through multimedia software usually consisting of a multimedia package (e.g. a CD Rom) and a personal computer. *On-line delivery* refers here to the use of the Internet and the Web technology to present learning materials.

Multimedia packages

Multimedia packages have been the most popular off-line media for course presentation in the third generation. Using CD ROMs, distance learners have had greater freedom in choosing course materials that suit them best. For some languages, the whole course is presented on a CD ROM, for others CD ROM is used to store supplementary material for learning a specific part of the target language, such as a multimedia package for learning Chinese characters, and a Kanji package for learning Japanese characters (Wang, 1999). Numerous multimedia packages, ranging from exercises and tests to simulations and games using the target language, are being produced each year. The use of multimedia has enriched the language learning environment and has been readily accepted by learners.

Computer Mediated Communication (CMC)

Computer Mediated Communication (CMC) is another mode of delivery popular in this generation. Through e-mail, chat and other on-line tools, the Internet can provide an interactive and collaborative learning environment for learners around the world. (For more reading on Web-based instruction, see Khan, 1997; Jafari, 1997; Kubala, 1998; Kötter, 2003.) Although it is still asynchronous at this stage, Poon (1993, p. 65) believes that CMC "has emerged as a viable method to support distance education because it is low cost and readily accessible".

In the early stage of this period, the Web has been used mainly by distance education administrators to publicize course information such as course outlines and notices to students. In the early 1990s, distance educators realized the potential of the Web for teaching as well, and began to move the whole or part of their courses on to the Web.

A major advantage of using the Web over CD ROM lies in the flexibility the Web offers. For example, the course materials and information presented on the Web can be updated easily at any time. It is also low-cost and user-friendly, both to the instructor and the learner.

The Internet is also constantly employed by distance educators and learners. E-mail has proved to be a very effective and efficient means of learning and communicating (Peterson, 1997). Students can use e-mail to contact their instructor or communicate with a native speaker in the target language to improve their writing skills. A wealth of authentic learning materials and language learning courses is freely available on the Internet, and advanced language learners in particular, can benefit enormously from these online materials and courses.

More access to information

Learners can access online libraries and authentic materials (e.g. newspapers, magazines and radio programs in the target language) from home, unconstrained by barriers of time and distance.

Changes in mediated student-tutor interaction

Interaction between learners and tutors is more direct, varied and lively. Through video clips, sound and animation, learners can now visualize the teacher's instructional intentions, and thus feel closer to the teacher than with printed media or tapes. Although e-mail communication is not synchronous, it does provide reliable and fast communication between learners and the instructor. More important, the scope of interaction has been expanded to include learner-native speaker, learner-computer and learner-learner interactions. The learner, not the teacher, has become the centre of learning activities, thereby making learning a more effective and enjoyable process. The roles of both the learner and the teacher have therefore undergone a substantial change. The learner has changed from passive information receiver to active knowledge seeker and from silent learner to "noisy" learner. On the other hand, the teacher has now become more of a learning facilitator and moderator than an information provider.

To summarize, in this generation, interaction in DLE has been further improved both in terms of quality and scope. For the first time in the history of distance education for languages, interaction between the learner and education provider has become more direct, spontaneous and multi-modal. Students could enjoy a degree of freedom in choosing course materials and in managing their learning discourse. In this period, distance educators have explored various forms of computer-assisted learning and teaching in an attempt to create a more authentic and interactive language learning environment. Furthermore, interaction now embraces learner-educator, leaner-learner and learner-native speaker communication. Socially, advanced computer technology has brought students into closer contact with the real world and their peers. Learning is no longer as isolated as before. Last but not least, the Internet has broadened the physical boundary of distance education. Distance education can now reach more learners than ever before.

2.4.6   The emergence of a fourth generation DLE

Justification for a new generation

As discussed in section 2.4.2, generational changes happen when both the quantity and quality of interaction in distance language learning have been improved. It is on the basis of this understanding of the term "generation" that this research argues for the emergence of a fourth generation in distance language education. Beginning in the mid-1990s when the Internet and Web technologies grew and matured, the advent and more extensive use of Internet-based real-time technology in learning have ushered in this fourth generation of distance language education. The significant changes that computer technology has brought to distance education justify the creation of a new generation. Two reasons underlie this justification: (1) the use of advanced computer technology, such as real-time technology, has enabled distance education to achieve the highest level of interaction that present day technology can offer, that is, real-time oral-visual interaction, and (2) distance education is predicted to develop along a new path. This argument is fundamentally different from the three-generation theory popular among scholars such as Garrison (1985), Chacon (1992) and Boyle (1995). Tables 2.7 and 2.8 provide an overview of the difference between the four-generation and three-generation theories.

Table 2.7   Four-generation theory

Generations	Technologies
1st (1800s – 1970s)	Printed media, postal system
2nd (1970s – 1980s)	*Older media*: printed media, postal system; *New media*: broadcasting, television, radio, telephone, audio-cassettes, video-cassettes, cable television, etc.
3rd (1980s – 1990s)	*Older media*: printed media, post system, broadcasting, television, radio, telephone, audio-cassettes, video-cassettes, cable television, etc.; *New media*: Word processors, multimedia packages, e-mail, the Web, the Internet, etc.
4th (1990s –)	*Older media*: printed media, postal system, broadcasting, television, radio, telephone, audio-cassettes, video-cassettes, cable television, word processors, multimedia packages, e-mail, the Web, the Internet, etc.; *New media*: Internet-based real-time technology, such as desktop videoconferencing, Internet telephoning, virtual reality, etc.

Table 2.8   Three-generation theory

Generations	Technologies
1st (1800s – 1970s)	Printed media, postal system
2nd (1970s – 1980s)	Broadcasting, television, radio, telephone, audio-cassettes, video-cassettes, cable television
3rd (1980s – 1990s)	Computer

On the basis of Tables 2.7 and 2.8, it is evident that my theory of the fourth generation conforms with the commonly held three-generation theory with respect to the first and second generation. The differences appear in the divisions of the third and fourth generation. The fourth-generation theory also differs from the third-generation theory in that it stresses the combination of older media with new media in each generation.

Of the innovations and changes that distinguish the fourth generation from the third, asynchronous to synchronous communication is the most significant. In this process, "guided didactic conversation" has become real-time for the first time. This change is especially crucial to learning languages at a distance since synchronous communication technologies facilitate virtual interactions that are truly conducive to communicative language learning. In this generation, technology is no longer simply an add-on medium, instead "it touches the very substance of the university". (Tsichritzis, 1999, p. 93)

In the context of education, globalization now has a twofold meaning: the globalization of distance learning and the globalization of education as a whole. In response to this trend, we hear repeated calls to "reengineer", "redefine" and "reshape" modern education. In his 1996 article, Dede's (1996) speculation about how emerging technologies may reshape distance as well as face-to-face education generated a heated dialogue among the reviewers of his article. He depicts a new education system called distributed learning, consisting of knowledge webs, virtual communities and shared synthetic environments. Today, this speculation has been widely accepted as the future of education. Scholars are even announcing a historical convergence of distance education and traditional campus-based education toward a networked education based on research in the potentials of network technologies (Dede, 1996; Hall, 1998; Cunningham et al., 1998; Tsichritzis, 1999). The above-mentioned changes indicate a whole new kind of distance education system with fundamentally improved capability. Judged by Garrison's (1985) definition of generation, it can be argued that Internet-based real-time technology has pushed distance education into a new generation.

Changes in mediated subject-matter presentation

The Internet and Web are still the media underlying this generation of DLE. Different from the previous generation, Internet-based real-time technology has become the trademark of this fourth generation. To present an overall picture of the computer technology used in this generation, Figure 2.4 compares the Internet and Web technologies used in the third and fourth generations.

Figure 2.4   A comparison between CMC in the third and fourth generation

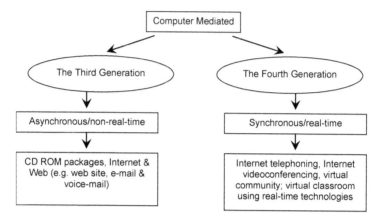

In fourth generation technologies, on-line delivery becomes more popular than in the previous generation with a variety of real-time media available to both the instructor and the learner. A combination of asynchronous and synchronous presentation of materials constitutes the major form of computer delivery. Although virtual reality is receiving more attention than before, real-time technologies, such as Internet telephoning and network-based desktop audio and videoconferencing, are more mature and less expensive to use.

A more authentic learning environment

At this early stage of the fourth generation, only limited data is available on Internet-based real-time language learning. However, a great number of studies in the area of CMC indicates the direction of language learning at a distance (see Cuskelly & Gregor, 1994; Bullen, 1998; Peterson, 1997; Chun & Plass, 2000; Hampel, 2003; Hampel & Hauck, 2004; Lee, 2007; Wang & Chen, 2007). Learners may have spontaneous conversations in the target language with other learners, teachers and even native speakers of the target language. For example, through network-based desktop videoconferencing or Internet telephoning, students can be exposed to virtual interpreting situations in which they can hear the target language being spoken, observe the body language of the speaker, and use the target language to communicate. Similarly, students can carry out simulated business negotiations in the target language with a native speaker. More importantly, language learning now takes place in a social context and has become more meaningful than ever. Students are exposed to a variety of dialects and accents in the target language and have an opportunity to develop language spontaneity and reflexiveness. In such a learning environment, better retention of learning material can be expected.

A wider coverage

Since real-time technologies use the Internet as their communication medium, the coverage of the subject-matter presentation is bounded only by the reach of the Internet. Moreover, since CMC also supports real-time multi-user learning environments, an unprecedentedly high level of student involvement and cooperation in learning can be achieved. This wider exposure to the target language is instrumental to increased proficiency in the target language.

Multimode of subject-matter delivery

It should be noted that, although Internet-based real-time technology has become increasingly popular and is an important delivery mode, it is not the only mode used by distance educators. In the fourth generation, as in most other generations, much language learning and teaching still retains technologies used in previous generations. These technologies include printed matter, audiovisual cassettes, telephone and e-mail.

Changes in mediated student-tutor interaction

With the use of Internet-based real-time technologies, the effect of physical distance on the interaction between learner and instructor can be reduced to a minimum. Some early projects investigating real-time technology (e.g. the LEVERAGE project; see discussion in Section 2.3.2) have demonstrated its potential to facilitate interactions nearly as effectively as those of face-to-face communication. Such interactions are real-time interactions with spontaneity (though sometimes delayed) as their defining feature. As a result, much less time is lost during the communication and interaction. On the other hand, some studies have shown that Internet-based real-time technology provides learners with numerous opportunities to engage in meaningful language learning. (see Section 2.3.2)

In the previous generation, on-line reading materials and e-mail messages helped the student improve their reading and writing skills, but not their listening and speaking skills because of the limitations of the then technology. In other words, a serious deficiency in distance education for second languages has been the incapacity to expose learners to spontaneous speaking activities. In the fourth generation, Internet-based real-time technology can foster such spontaneous communication and interaction, which aligns it more closely with modern conceptions of language learning and teaching, emphasizing communicative task-based learning models and learner autonomy.

Most importantly, the fourth generation also witnesses the merging of the presentation of subject matter and interaction into an interactive presentation of subject matter. Different from the previous generations, presentation of subject matter may be no longer separated from interaction. This merging means language learning at a distance can become interactive and spontaneous, which is particularly important to language learning at a distance, because modern language learning is a process of communicating and interacting.

In summary, as far as teaching languages at a distance is concerned, the first three generations had provided flexibility at the expense of quality. In the fourth generation, with the use of Internet-based real-time technology, this disadvantage can be neutralized, and the highest level of interaction can be ensured for learners. This improvement is most significant because it meets the special needs of distance language learners, that is, cultivating listening and speaking skills. Real-time technology, effectively facilitating the development of these skills, removes the most serous constraints imposed by the physical distance in learning languages at a distance. At the same time, it supports interactions similar to those of face-to-face communication, and a virtual social context in which the use of the target language occurs most naturally. Thus real-time technology brings the distance learner into the real world, both in the sense of reality and in the realm of the virtual learning environment. Further, advanced technology is leading modern education to an immersion of learning at a distance and on campus. All these improvements justify the conceptualization of a new generation.

It should be pointed out that the fourth generation is still in its infancy; advanced educational technology and the possibilities it has opened are only comprehended or explored by a few. The majority of distance education institutions still remain in the second or third generation. Since the pedagogical capabilities and soundness of real-time technology are yet to be fully discovered, refined and evaluated, distance language educators will need to further explore the use of this technology as it becomes more mature and widely used.

In summary, the employment of Internet-based real-time technology is revolutionary in that it has led to improvements in the presentation of course materials and further promotion of student-teacher interaction. The capacity and quality of distance education have been improved, compared with those of the previous generation. As a result, real-time technology, while building upon the capabilities of the previous generation, opens a new era in the history of distance education. This generation can be summarized as a new learning environment with increased interaction through collaboration, and with networked learning as its defining features.

Bates predicted (1993) that

> By the year 2010, this [print based delivery of distance teaching] will have changed in most developed countries, and in many of the newly emerging economic 'dragons' of South-East Asia. In particular, telecommunications-based technologies will have become the primary

means of delivery of distance teaching. The main reasons for the increasing importance of technology in distance education can be summarized as follows:

- A much wider range of technology is becoming more accessible to potential distance education students;
- The costs of technological delivery are dropping dramatically;
- The technology is becoming easier to use, both by teachers and learners;
- Technology is becoming more powerful pedagogically;
- Distance education institutions will find it increasingly difficult to resist the political and social pressures of the technological imperative. (p. 213)

The creation of a new generation advances and challenges the three-generation theory commonly held by members of the profession. This new division categorizes more precisely the roles played by different computer technologies in the provision of interaction to distance education for languages. The next section will examine in further detail the improved interaction in the fourth generation DLE, generated by computer and information technology, especially in terms of CMC.

2.5 Summary

The literature on interaction, CMC and the development of DLE confirms the significance of the investigation of oral-visual interaction via videoconferencing for distance language acquisition. The significance emerged through a step-by-step discussion of the nature of interaction and an evaluation of its importance to communicative language learning. Following this, the review of the present use of CMC to support interaction in DLE further reveals the importance of the research question. Last but not least, this chapter has critically reviewed the developmental stages of DLE in providing improved interaction for L2 acquisition.

This chapter has made a number of contributions. It has enriched some of the concepts and definitions by including recent developments in the field, for example, the definition of interaction and distance education. At the same time, this chapter has also addressed some confusion over the term CMC, emphasizing its inclusive nature rather than the text-based nature alone.

In the discussion of the evolutionary changes in the provision of interaction in distance language education, this research put forward a theory of an emerging fourth generation in DLE with synchronous real-time oral-visual interaction as its defining feature, challenging the commonly held three generation theory. The significance of this contribution lies in its more accurate identification of the impact of real-time Internet technology on DLE in the 21st century, and in its prediction of a historical convergence of campus-based education and distance education into a global education (Wang and Sun, 200). The discussion contained in this part of the chapter has partly answered the first subsidiary research question – *What are the needs of distance learners in terms of L2 acquisition*. One answer is their need for an improved platform for the provision of oral-visual interaction in their L2 learning.

Another contribution of the research in this chapter is its development of a new taxonomy in CMC-based interaction – written, oral and oral-visual interaction, each catering for different learning and learner goals. This new division classifies more precisely the roles played by and the technologies needed in each type of interaction. It is hoped this new taxonomy will provide some guidelines for future research, thus bridging a gap in DLE research. I have discussed this new taxonomy elsewhere. (see Wang, 2004a)

The improved provision of oral-visual interaction in distance language learning today is further investigated and evaluated in the empirical study of this research. The methodology for this investigation and evaluation is discussed in detail in the next chapter, Chapter 3.

Chapter Three

Preliminary studies, methodological approaches and criteria for evaluating videoconferencing

3.1 Introduction

The previous chapters have identified the need for improved provision of oral-visual interaction in distance language education, and have discussed the importance of oral-visual interaction in distance language learning both theoretically and historically. This chapter and the chapters that follow will investigate this issue through empirical studies in order to answer the central research question:

in what ways oral-visual interaction via videoconferencing is able to facilitate L2 acquisition at a distance?

The chapter consists of three major parts. Part One reports the findings from two preliminary studies. The first preliminary study investigates learning problems in DLE and reveals that synchronous speaking practice is urgently needed, further answering the first subsidiary question – *what are the needs of distance learners in terms of L2 acquisition?* As discussed in Chapter 2, the most recent and sophisticated forms of technology-mediated interaction are supported by videoconferencing. Thus the second preliminary study evaluated the commercially available desktop videoconferencing tools and finds that NetMeeting (see Section 3.2.2) emerged as a tool worthy of further exploration. This second preliminary study provides the basis for answering the second subsidiary research question – w*hat are the benefits and limitations of oral-visual interaction via videoconferencing forL2 acquisition at a distance?*

Following the two preliminary studies, a more in-depth evaluation of NetMeeting was designed in response to the central research question. Part Two of this chapter deals with the methodologies adopted for the two-stage evaluation of NetMeeting. This discussion presents such details as the objectives of the evaluation, a synopsis of each phase of the evaluation, the formative, qualitative and task-based approaches, data sought and methods of data collection and analysis.

Part Three of this chapter further discusses data collection and analysis methods. The emphasis is on the two sets of criteria developed in this research for evaluating videoconferencing tools and tasks. Both sets of criteria are crucial for later phases of this research in that they determine (1) the mode of data presentation and (2) criteria for data analysis. Lastly, the limitations of this research and the issue of obsolescence of technology are discussed.

3.2 Part One – Preliminary studies

3.2.1 Preliminary study 1 – a survey of the difficulties in learning Chinese

This preliminary study focuses on learning problems experienced by Chinese language students. To substantiate my identification of the problem with DLE – the lack of exposure to oral-visual interaction – a qualitative survey of both the students from the Open Learning Chinese language program and of on-campus first year Chinese students at Griffith University was administered in late 2000. This survey solicited students' views on the problems that they experienced in their Chinese language learning. A total of 35 completed questionnaires were collected. The distance group comprised eight students who were then in the second and fourth study period, equivalent to first-and second-year on-campus students as far as their length of study was concerned. The on-campus group was approaching the end of their second semester of learning the Chinese language. In other words, both groups had considerable experience with learning Chinese and should have a better understanding of the problems they had encountered than would new students. Most of them were native English speakers with only a few of the on-campus students from a Japanese background.

In order to solicit unbiased responses and to avoid leading questions, the survey posited only three general questions. In the survey with the Open Learning students these three questions were:

1. Why did you enrol in this Chinese course in distance mode?
2. What are your main problems with this course? Please comment on the four skills: speaking, listening, reading and writing.
3. What improvements would you suggest?

For the purpose of comparison, with the on-campus group, these questions remained otherwise exactly the same with the exception of question one. The wording of "in distance mode" was deleted as it was inappropriate to the on-campus students, and the question becomes "Why did you enrol in this subject?".

Discussion of survey results

This discussion will focus on the data provided by the distance group, while replies from on-campus students will only be used selectively to support the discussion on data collected from the distance group. Furthermore, to provide qualitative evidence of the lack of oral-visual interaction in DLE, this section will concentrate on replies from Question 2 of the survey – *what are your main problems with this course? Please comment on the four skills.* (for data from Questions 1 and 3, see Appendix A)

It was discovered that 100 per cent of the distance students felt strongly that they had experienced great difficulties in acquiring speaking skills. The distance group provided quite lengthy and specific comments on why speaking imposes a great difficulty in a distance-learning situation. Table 3.1 summarizes the major areas of difficulty identified by both the Open Learning and on-campus students, in terms of acquiring speaking skills.

Table 3.1   Difficulties in acquiring speaking skills (PCS1 – OLQ2 & PCS1 – OCQ2)

Areas of difficulty identified	Open Learning students (%)	On-campus students (%)
Lack of opportunity to speak with others	87.5	3.7
Pronunciation and tones	25	44.4
Speed of the speaker	0	11.1
Fluency	0	14.8
Lack of help from the tutor	37.5	0
Other	0	25.9

From the above table, it is evident that the great majority (87.5 per cent) of the distance learners ascribed the difficulty in speaking to the lack of a Chinese speaking environment. The following comments (in participants' own words) showed that most distance students understood the nature of their problems and believed that face-to-face interaction was vitally important to language learning.

♦ Obviously not attending a class makes the practice of responding verbally quite difficult.

♦ Lack of opportunities to practise speaking with native speakers. The thought processes involved in responding, as in normal conversation i.e. translating in your head and replying. (I hope you understand what I mean)…

♦ Because I am not exposed to Chinese environment most of my speaking is done to shop keepers and the occasional Chinese that I met. So it is therefore make it hard to use it in everyday life at this stage. I hope to go to China again, say for a few months so I am forced to use it.

♦ As I have no lecturer or tutor, I have no one I can actively practise my speaking skills with. A large part of my previous study was focused on speaking, so I feel that am now seriously disadvantaged in this particular area.

♦ No problems with the course itself. (My problem is that I have no Chinese speakers to practise with.)

♦ I feel difficult to learn speaking without tutor's help.

♦ I am finding tones and some of the initials quite difficult to master, and find it hard to concentrate on speaking (reading aloud) when making assignment tapes. I have not had time or opportunity to practise speaking with others and I am sure this would fasten improvement.

In contrast, lack of opportunity to speak with others was only mentioned by one on-campus student, but nearly half of them held that the mastery of tones and pronunciation was difficult. This difference may not indicate that the Open Learning students found tones and pronunciation easy to learn. On the contrary, it may mean that they considered the lack of someone to practise speaking with more of an obstacle than difficulties with tones and pronunciation. It could also be interpreted that the on-campus students had received more immediate feedback regarding their pronunciation and tones, and as a result, they were more conscious of these problems than the distance group who had never been corrected on the spot with regard to their pronunciation and tones.

Lack of help from the tutor was another area specifically indicated by the distance students, while none of the on-campus student mentioned this. The reason for this contrast is self-explanatory.

Fluency presented a difficulty to some on-campus students, but none of the distance students mentioned this. Again, this may mean that the need for interaction with others was more urgent to them than their improvement in fluency. Without an environment to interact in the language, fluency is out of the question.

Summary

To summarize, the distance group was overwhelmingly specific about their difficulty in attaining speaking skills – the lack of interaction with others. Data from this survey appeared to be consistent with those in Williams and Sharma's 1985 survey of DLE in Australia. They identify student dissatisfaction with their achievement in the four macro skills, which was distributed in the following percentages. "Thirteen per cent of responses indicated reading, 17% writing, 26% listening and 44% speaking" (Williams and Sharma, 1988, p. 143).

My search of the DLE literature failed to find any substantial improvement in speaking skills, despite the fact that some attempts have been made to utilize CMC (see Section 2.5.2). The question therefore is: what technological tools can be used and how can they help mitigate the distance factor and improve learner's speaking skills? This question led to the preliminary investigation of suitable videoconferencing tools detailed in the next section.

3.2.2 Preliminary study 2 – the investigation of four videoconferencing tools

A comparison of the four videoconferencing tools

In an attempt to find a solution to the problem of lack of provision of oral-visual interaction in DLE, this research proceeded to examine the capabilities of the present generation of videoconferencing tools by first comparing the available choices and then trialling the chosen one. My initial search of the CNET user evaluation revealed that there are four most popular Internet-based desktop videoconferencing tools – NetMeeting 3.01, CUseeMe 5.0, Video VoxPhone Gold 2.0 and ICUII 4.9 (Version 5.5 was released on 26 November 2001). Initial evaluation of the four videoconferencing tools started in July 2001, by the author and four computer specialists, in order to determine the most suitable tool to provide oral-visual interaction in DLE. Table 3.2 provides an overview of the four videoconferencing tools.

Table 3.2   Summary of the four videoconferencing tools

Name	Publisher	Number of downloads	Minimum requirements	Cost
NetMeeting 3.01	Microsoft	1,593,506	Windows 95/98/Me/NT	Free*
CUseeMe 5.0	CUseeMe	26,680	Windows Me/2000, 64MB RAM	$39.99 for downloadable version; $49.99 for CD; 15 day free trial.
ICUII 4.9	Cybration	299,481	Windows 95/98/Me/2000/XP	$39.95; 21 day free trial
Video VoxPhone Gold 2.0	E-Tech Canada Ltd.	20,992	Windows 95/98/MT/200, 32MBRAM	$31.99; 30 day free trial.

Notes:
1. Information on the videoconferencing tools was obtained from the following web sites, all accessed on 19 December 2001: http://download.cnet.com/downloads/1,10150,0-10001-103-0-1-7,00.html?tag=srch&qt= NetMeeting&cn=&ca=10001
http://download.cnet.com/downloads/0-3364651-100-5976507.html?tag=st.dl.10001-103-1.lst-7-6.5976507
http://download.cnet.com/downloads/0-3364651-100-7978697.html?tag=st.dl.10001-103-1.lst-7-1.7978697
http://download.cnet.com/downloads/0-3364652-100-4538974.html?tag=st.dl.10001-103-1.lst-7-1.4538974
*2. *The freeware version only supports one-to-one video and /or audio conferencing, but a server supporting multi users is commercially available at US$4000. (see* http://www.netmeet.net/nm3_faq.asp; *accessed on 10 August 2001)*

Table 3.2 demonstrates that NetMeeting had by far the largest number of users (1,593,506 downloads), in comparison with ICUCC (299,481), CUseeMe (26,680) and Video VoxPhone Gold (20,992). It is also shown in Table 3.2 that NetMeeting was the only tool that could be freely downloaded from the Internet.

The major features of the above-discussed four videoconferencing tools are summarized in Table 3.3.

Table 3.3   Comparison of major features of the four videoconferencing tools

Name	Video-conferencing	Audio-conferencing	White-board	Document sharing	File transfer	Text chat	Remote desktop sharing
NetMeeting 30.1	One to one	One to one	√	√	√	√	√
CUSeeMe 5.0	Many to many	Many to many	X	X	X	√	X
ICUII 4.9	Many to many	Many to many	X	X	X	√	X
VideoVoxPhone Gold 2.0	Many to many	Many to many	X	X	√	√	X

It is apparent in Table 3.3 that, except for NetMeeting, the other three are more or less just video chat tools, which are not easily adapted for learning *per se*. Although NetMeeting is also not specifically designed for language learning, it offers many useful functions (e.g. the whiteboard and Document Sharing) that the other three do not have, making it a more appropriate tool for language learning. Table 3.3 also indicates that NetMeeting can only support one-to-one videoconferencing, while the other three claim to support many-to-many videoconferencing. However, our trials revealed that none of the many-to-many videoconferencing tools could be used for language learning due to their poor audio and video quality – slower frame rate, poor resolution, muffled sound, etc. The usual occurrence was, as soon as the third party joined the conferencing, these videoconferencing tools either crashed or the video images of the participants froze and the sound became distorted. The audio transmission was also much delayed. This is because these videoconferencing tools used centralized servers for message propagation, which introduce extra communication latency and can easily become a communication and computation bottleneck.

The second search of CNET user evaluations of the four videoconferencing tools was conducted in November 2001 (for CNET user evaluation results and comments on these videoconferencing tools, see Appendix B). These evaluations further confirm the findings from my investigation and support my argument that among the four videoconferencing tools evaluated, NetMeeting appeared to be the most suitable for providing oral-visual interaction. The comparison was very brief as, after the sound and video quality of the later three was found to be unsatisfactory for language teaching, they were quickly abandoned.

The trial use of NetMeeting

NetMeeting is an Internet-based desktop conferencing tool developed by Microsoft. NetMeeting 3.01 was the latest version at the time this research was undertaken. It was included in the Windows 2000 suite. It integrates audio, video and data conferencing into a single package. In NetMeeting 3.01, "[m]any performance improvements have also been made, including lower bandwidth requirements for faster performance, support for 24-bit true colour, enhanced security, and, on faster multimedia machines and high-speed networks, NetMeeting can now achieve up to 30-frames-per-second video performance". (see http://download.cnet.com/downloads/0-3364652-100-911418.html?tag=st.dl.10001-103-1.lst-7-1.911418)

This research holds that it is imperative that computer experts be involved in the initial phase of the evaluation of a new videoconferencing tool for the simple reason that the technological capability of the videoconferencing tool under investigation can be more precisely determined. Thus, together with four computer experts, we trialled NetMeeting for approximately five months from July to November 2001, with a focus on the investigation of its technological capabilities. NetMeeting was extensively investigated in both LAN (Local Area Network) and the Internet environments, in terms of five criteria: user friendliness, audio and video quality, other features of pedagogical value, reliability, and cost. Performance against the criteria is discussed below.

User friendliness

The trial started with the setting up of NetMeeting. It was discovered that the set up of NetMeeting was not complicated, although there are a few steps to follow. As far as its interface is concerned, NetMeeting offers the most user friendly interface design of the four videoconferencing tools. The layout of the interface is simple with only a few icons (see Figure 3.1). The participants became familiar with it almost immediately.

Audio and video quality

Our trials confirmed that NetMeeting offered the best audio and video quality among the four videoconferencing tools tested. In a LAN environment the sound quality proved to be nearly as good as that of the telephone. No sound distortion was detected. The sound proved to be clear and consistent enough for interactive language learning. For example, NetMeeting can be used to perform a role-play or interactive pronunciation drills to detect the subtle differences between z, c, s, and zh, ch, sh in Pinyin.

During the two-month trial, with the exception of occasional video images blurring for about a second, probably due to temporary congestion in the network or too much body movement, the video image on the whole was found to be clear and continuous. Conversational cues such as a nod and a smile were all presented almost in real-time. When showing how to pronounce certain words, lip movements could be seen clearly enough for the learner to notice the difference in pronunciation. There was no significant delay in the synchronization of sound and video image. As expected, both the audio and video quality of NetMeeting in a LAN environment was better than that using the Internet. Nevertheless our trials indicate that the audio and video quality of NetMeeting has reached an acceptable level of performance for the provision of oral-visual interaction in distance language learning.

Figure 3.1   The interface of NetMeeting

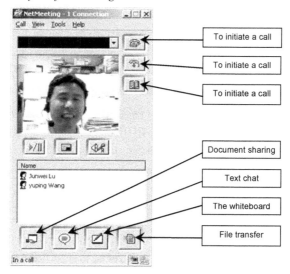

Other features of pedagogical value

The whiteboard

Figure 3.2   Whiteboard in NetMeeting

Among the four videoconferencing tools, NetMeeting is the only one that offers the facility of an on-screen whiteboard (see Figure 3.2). It was found to be a valuable tool for language learning as it allows you to review, create, and update information collaboratively in real-time. For example, you can cut, copy and paste information from any Windows-based application onto the whiteboard. Both parties can view, write, edit and draw simultaneously. This will be especially useful for teaching how to write Chinese characters online for the simple reason that the stroke orders can be shown step by step in real-time. It is also a good platform for negotiation of meaning, because the learner can write the characters and draw pictures on it to paraphrase their intended meaning. Furthermore, the whiteboard contents can be saved for future reference.

File Transfer

Figure 3.3   File Transfer in NetMeeting

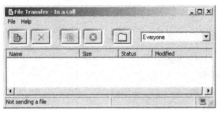

Only NetMeeting and Video VoxPhone Gold 2.0 offer this function. Used in a language learning situation, this function enables the learner or teacher to send files (e.g. video clips or text files) to other people during a conference so that a lively interaction can be generated around the video clips or text files (see Figure 3.3). It was found that the transfer of text file was instant and of the highest quality in both LAN and the Internet environment, but transfer of videos took longer when using the Internet.

Document Sharing

Figure 3.4   Document Sharing in NetMeeting

Again, although important to language learning, the function of Document Sharing is only offered by NetMeeting (see Figure 3.4). With this function, you can share multiple programs opened in the background during a NetMeeting conference. The difference between Document Sharing and shared whiteboard lies in that, when sharing a program, the other party cannot edit your file. In other words, you have greater control of your files. This function is useful in presenting a prepared document, be it a PowerPoint slide, a scanned photo, or a Web page. This function was employed extensively to share photos and Web pages with the participants during the trials to facilitate spontaneous discussions.

<u>My Video</u>

Figure 3.5   Self-view window

NetMeeting also offers a picture-in-picture function called My Video, a self-view window, which was found to be very useful for teachers to watch their teaching and to modify their paralinguistic cues (see Figure 3.5). The My Video window can be placed anywhere on the computer screen.

Reliability of NetMeeting

In our investigation of videoconferencing tools, reliability was treated as an essential issue and was one of the most important criteria in determining the appropriate tools. When using a LAN, NetMeeting never crashed. And the audio and video maintained constant good quality during the videoconferencing sessions. When used in an Internet environment, a crash never occurred, although the video and audio quality was, to a degree, affected by the low bandwidth of the Internet resulting in background noise and unstable sound quality. However our investigation indicates that NetMeeting could still be used to provide good quality oral-visual interactions if conferences were conducted at a time when the Internet was less congested. (e.g. during weekends or early in the morning)

Cost of NetMeeting

Point-to-point videoconferencing version of NetMeeting was free and could be downloaded from the company's web site. The cost of the group version of the program was $US4,000 (see Table 3.2 and notes above). Because NetMeeting was a Microsoft product, users had no maintenance cost to bear. The only required purchase for learners was a web camera with headphones, around US$50. Compared with the costs of some textbooks, most students should be able to afford NetMeeting, especially since it could be used over the entire course of their studies.

To summarize, my investigation shows that among the four videoconferencing tools, NetMeeting represented state of the art in videoconferencing tools and was the most viable one for the provision of oral-visual interaction in DLE at the time of the trials (in 2001). This conclusion is based on the following results from our evaluation:

+ The audio and video quality of NetMeeting was acceptable for language learning.

+ NetMeeting was reliable both in terms of its sound and video quality and its network transmission.

+ NetMeeting was easy to use and to set up. Its interface and other features were more refined and user friendly than other videoconferencing tools.

+ NetMeeting also offered features such as the Whiteboard and Document Sharing that were indispensable to interaction and language acquisition at a distance.

+ NetMeeting was free. Neither the students nor the educational institutions needed to invest in anything except a Web Camera and headphone.

+ Because it was a Microsoft product, it is expected to be updated regularly.

3.3 Part Two – Methodology

3.3.1 Introduction

In relation to its central and subsidiary research questions, this study aims to examine, firstly, whether NetMeeting was technologically capable of assisting the distance learner to reach the goal of effective oral-visual interaction, and secondly, whether the process of oral-visual interaction via NetMeeting provided for students' learning needs to be met. Thus a more in-depth evaluation than the preliminary investigations discussed previously was conducted. This investigation was completed in two stages: Stage One by on-campus students in an intranet environment, and Stage Two by distance students in an Internet environment. Although each of the two stages of the evaluation had its own specific objectives, the general objective of this evaluation was to answer the second subsidiary research question:

What are the benefits and limitations of oral-visual interaction via videoconferencing for L2 acquisition at a distance?

It was hoped that data in relation to the second subsidiary question could be drawn to answer the third subsidiary research question:

What are the implications and potential of oral-visual interaction via videoconferencing for L2 acquisition in distance mode?

This second part of the chapter details the methodology to achieve the above objectives. Firstly, it outlines the objectives, procedure, participants and the network environment of each stage of the evaluation. Secondly, the formative, qualitative and task-based nature of this research is discussed. This is then followed by a specification of data collected from the evaluation, and methods of data collection and analysis.

3.3.2   Stage One – evaluation by on-campus students from Griffith University

Objectives

The evaluation of NetMeeting was approached in a progressive way, that is, the results from Stage One informed Stage Two, which constituted the core stage of the evaluation. Thus the main purpose of this first stage was to gather information on what actually happened in each videoconferencing session so that the advantages of videoconferencing could be further explored and the pitfalls avoided in Stage Two. This investigation was to provide data on both the technological and pedagogical capabilities of videoconferencing in supporting spoken interaction in task completion.

Thus, the purpose of this stage of the trial was to gather data in relation to on-line/real-time oral-visual interaction generated by videoconferencing, with particular emphasis on effective task designs and the possible technological strengths and constraints of videoconferencing. This was also a process of debugging the technology and task design. In this respect, this phase of the research was of an exploratory nature, with the understanding that the more data obtained from the experiment, the better the next stage would be prepared for the trial with the distance students.

Procedure

As the trial of NetMeeting with the on-campus students was scheduled during the summer holidays, that is, between November 2001 and February 2002, expressions of interest in participating in the trial were called for in October 2001, and four students offered to help. Following that, a computer room was booked for the experiment in the Language and Linguistics building at Griffith University.

This trial consisted of two parts – the installation of NetMeeting by the participants and the task-based tutorial sessions using NetMeeting. A Student Handbook was prepared and provided to each participant prior to the trial in order to assist the participant's understanding of and preparation for the trial. The handbook contains information such as the objectives of the trial, the task description and requirements for preparation, the manual for setting up NetMeeting, etc. (see Appendix C)

After NetMeeting was installed by the participants, five one-to-one NetMeeting sessions were conducted with each participant separately. To simulate a distance-learning environment, the participants and the teacher (author) were stationed at separate locations: the participants were in the Computer Lab while the teacher was in her office. They communicated via NetMeeting, but a telephone was provided at each end in case of the failure of NetMeeting.

Participants

Due to personal reasons, one student could not participate in the trial, reducing the number of participants to three, two females and one male. The three participants had just completed their first year of Chinese in conventional face-to-face mode. This means their level of Chinese proficiency was still basic. Although none of them had studied Chinese prior to their studying at Griffith University, their proficiency levels varied from one another. In comparison, Student 2 had the highest level of proficiency, Student 3 the lowest, and Student 1 was in the middle.

The network environment

In this phase of the evaluation, both the students and the teacher communicated through NetMeeting, using a LAN. This means that the trial took place on campus via its local area network without using a modem (see Figure 3.3). The choice of LAN was made on the basis that it was easier to debug the technology and revise the task design in a controlled environment such as a LAN. A controlled environment was deemed imperative when evaluating a new technology for teaching and learning because such an evaluation involves many unfamiliar factors. This is especially true when the investigation relies on the Internet, which is often unreliable. Apart from the unreliability of Internet transmission, another factor taken into consideration was the lack of on-site technical support for distance students. In a LAN environment, when encountering a problem, the author could easily go over to the participant's site and investigate the situation. Furthermore, technical support was always readily available on campus. In fact, during the sessions, although not always physically present, a technician was usually on standby in his office in case of unpredicted technical problems. All these would be impossible in the Internet environment where students are at different remote locations.

Figure 3.6   The LAN environment in Stage One of the evaluation of NetMeeting

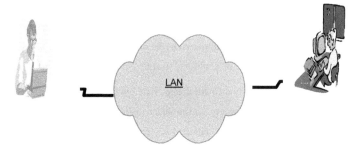

3.3.3   Stage Two – evaluation by the Open Learning students

Objectives

The trial of NetMeeting with distance language students from the Open Learning Chinese Program at Griffith University constituted the final and core stage of this formative evaluation. (For details on this Chinese program, see section 1.3.) This final phase further examined the technological and pedagogical capabilities of videoconferencing, but this time, in a real distance language learning situation. Although informed by the results from the previous stage, this stage confronted two new frontiers – *the Internet environment* and *the distance language learners*. It was hoped that much data could be obtained from this stage so that recommendations for future incorporation of videoconferencing tools into distance language programs could be proposed.

Procedures

The trial started in March 2002 and was completed in August 2002. A pre-trial survey was first e-mailed to the 11 students enrolled in Study Period 2 of the Open Learning Chinese program. The objective of the survey was twofold – inviting participation in the trial and soliciting information on the availability of student computer resources. (For results of this survey, see Section 4.3.1.) Five students expressed interest in taking part in the trial. Following the survey, a parcel containing the following items was posted to each participant:

1. a WebCam and the set-up CD ROM,
2. a pair of headphones,
3. a copy of the Student Handbook containing general information about the trial, task description and manual for setting up NetMeeting, etc., and
4. a gift pack to thank the students for their participation.

The participants were asked to set up NetMeeting by themselves after receiving the parcel. A toll free number was provided for the participants to reach me in case of difficulties in the installation process. Following completion of the installation, a trial schedule was negotiated between each participant and the teacher by e-mail.

Participants

Of the five participants, two were from Victoria in Australia (approximately 2,000 kilometres away from Griffith University, where the tutor was based), one was from New South Wales (more than 200 kilometres away), one was from Queensland, (nearly 100 kilometres away) and one was from Adelaide (about 2,000 kilometres away from the tutor). By the time of the trial, all participants had completed CHN10 and CHN11, an equivalent of two semesters of study in on-campus education, in terms of length of study. However, due to lack of speaking practice, their level of Chinese proficiency was much lower than that of the participants in Stage One, that is, the on-campus participants. Soon after the trial started, it became evident that some students possessed neither the linguistic resources nor the interactional skills to conduct comparatively continuous conversation in Chinese. Only one student who had previous experience of studying Chinese was fluent enough to carry out less interrupted dialogues with the teacher. This finding further confirms the urgency of finding a solution to the problem of lack of oral-visual interaction in DLE.

The network environments

The trial went through three network environments: the modem-Internet-modem environment (see Figure 3.7), the LAN-Internet-Modem environment (see Figure 3.8) and the LAN-Internet-LAN environment. (see Wang, 2004b, Figure 3.9)

The modem-Internet-modem environment

When the trial first started, there was a firewall at Griffith University blocking the access of NetMeeting from outside the University. As a result, the person outside the University could see and hear me, but no sound and video signal from the person outside the University was allowed to reach me. In an attempt to bypass the firewall, I had to install a modem on my computer to dial into the Internet, while the participants had to dial into an ISP (Internet Service Provider), also through a modem, as illustrated in Figure 3.7.

The LAN-Internet-modem environment

Half-way through the trial, an access to NetMeeting in the firewall at Griffith University was obtained for the purpose of this experiment. Thus, while the participants were still using the commercially available Internet service provider via a modem, on the teacher's end, the LAN was used to connect directly to the Internet without having to go through a modem, as demonstrated in Figure 3.8.

Figure 3.7   The modem-Internet-modem environment in Stage Two of the evaluation of NetMeeting

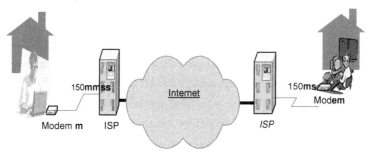

Figure 3.8   The LAN-Internet-modem environment in Stage Two of the evaluation of NetMeeting

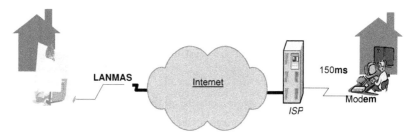

The LAN-Internet-LAN environment

The trial of NetMeeting was carried out in this environment only with Participant E, who was able to use a LAN to connect to the Internet in the computer laboratory at Deakin University. No modems were used in this environment. Figure 3.9 illustrates such an environment.

Figure 3.9   The LAN-Internet-LAN environment in Stage Two of the evaluation of NetMeeting

3.3.4 A formative evaluation approach

This research adopts a formative evaluation of a videoconferencing tool and its capability to support task-based spoken interaction in L2 learning. Brown (1989) argues that "formative evaluation occurs during the development of a program; the purpose of gathering information is to improve the program. Summative evaluation occurs at the end of the program, and the purpose of gathering information is to determine whether the program was successful." Palloff & Pratt (1999) take a similar view:

> Formative evaluation is an ongoing process that can occur at any point throughout the course; it can surface gaps in course material or in learners' ability to grasp that material. Formative evaluation gives instructors a way to shift focus if the course is not proceeding according to plan. Summative evaluation assesses the completed course and is most often the model of evaluation used in academic institutions. (p. 144)

Brown (1995, p. 227) further defines language program evaluation "as the systematic collection and analysis of information necessary to improve a curriculum, assess its effectiveness and efficiency, and determine participants' attitudes within the context of a particular institution".

Thus formative evaluation is crucially important, especially with the fast pace of technological development, in that it can provide up-to-date information on the advantages and disadvantages of new technology. Palloff & Pratt (1999) point out that evaluating:

> an online course using only summative methods serves to ignore many of the important concepts we have been discussing that are related to this form of teaching and learning. If instructors are truly establishing a collaborative, transformative process, then formative as well as summative evaluation must be used. Formative evaluation helps determine to what extent instructors are successfully facilitating reflection on the course material under study, reflection on this means of learning, and reflection on self as a learner as the course progresses. Summative evaluation helps us know how well we have achieved the goals and learning outcomes we established going into the course. (p. 145)

Translated into the evaluation design and data collection in this research, formative evaluation was realized through the following constant adjustments:

♦ on a macro level, the evaluation of NetMeeting was carried out in two-stages: Stage One informs Stage Two, the main stage of the evaluation;

♦ on a micro level, on-going improvements occurred at many points during the two stage evaluation. For example, the installation manual of NetMeeting was improved to include more details and screen layouts in Stage Two (see Section 4.3.2). The videotaped NetMeeting sessions were reviewed after each session for reflection and necessary adjustments in later sessions. As a result, a three-stage progressive improvement was made to the task designs (see Section 3.3.6). Furthermore the researcher constantly improved the task performances by adjusting task difficult levels in accordance with individual participants' Chinese proficiency (see Section 5.2.2).

These adjustments and improvements were considered essential to ensuring the accuracy of data collection and analysis, and were done through both regular and instant participants' reports (end of session written surveys and interviews and end of evaluation written surveys and interviews) and the researcher's observation. This research project thus gathered learners' experiences in an immediate and ongoing way throughout the course of the project, and adjustments made to research design, the implementation of teaching and learning strategies.

3.3.5   A qualitative approach

The formative evaluation was approached using a qualitative methodology. The qualitative approach is gaining importance in today's SLA and CALL research due to a recent move towards the investigation of learning processes. According to Negretti, (1999) and Seliger & Shohamy (1989), this trend is due both to the fact that "it is not easy to apply to classroom learning (the main SLA context) the controls necessary for good experimental research" (Negretti, 1999, p. 76), and to the growing awareness of the distorting influence of the research settings (Tarone, 1982).

As defined by Strauss and Corbin (1998, p. 10), qualitative research refers to "any type of research that produces findings not arrived at by statistical procedures or other means of quantification" and can be used to "obtain the intricate details about phenomena such as feelings, thought processes and emotions that are difficult to extract or learn about through more conventional research methods". Stern (1980) also believes that qualitative research can be employed to investigate substantive areas about which little is known or to explore areas about which much is known to obtain new understandings.

The ultimate goal of qualitative research is, according to Seliger and Shohamy (1989, p. 120), to discover phenomena such as patterns of second language behaviour not previously described and to understand these phenomena from the perspective of the participants in the activity.

Larsen-Freeman and Long (1991, p. 11) also define the qualitative methodology as "an ethnographic study in which the researchers do not set out to test hypotheses, but rather to observe what is present with their focus, and consequently the data, free to vary during the course of the observation". The attributes of the qualitative paradigm are summarized in Table 3.4:

Table 3.4   Attributes of the qualitative paradigm

	Attributes
Qualitative Paradigm	Advocates the use of qualitative methods.
	Phenomeonologism and verstehen: 'concerned with understanding human behaviour from the actor's own frame of reference'.
	Naturalistic and uncontrolled observation.
	Subjective.
	Close to the data; the 'insider' perspective.
	Grounded, discovery-oriented, exploratory, expansionist, descriptive, and inductive.
	Process-oriented.
	Valid; 'real', 'rich', and 'deep' data.
	Ungeneralizable; single case studies.
	Holistic.
	Assumes a dynamic reality.

Source: Larsen-Freeman & Long, 1991, p. 12

Thus, a qualitative approach was adopted throughout the phases of the evaluation, not only in view of the above-mentioned goal and nature of qualitative research but also in recognition of the multi-dimensional nature and objectives of the evaluation planned for this research. As the objective of the evaluation was to clarify the extent to which videoconferencing is an effective tool for the provision of oral-visual interaction, such an investigation needed to examine what actually happens during the learning process of individual learners (e.g. how the learners interact and their reception of videoconferencing tools). It is generally believed that understanding of the learning process benefits more from qualitative measures such as interviews and questionnaires than from quantitative evaluations. Negretti (1999, p. 76) comments that "the development of the rigorous methods for conducting qualitative research and collecting SLA data allows good results and good reliability and validity".

Qualitative investigation consists of three major components (Strauss & Corbin, 1998): data collection, coding (data interpretation) and oral/written presentation of the findings. The data collection, analysis and presentation in this research are of a qualitative nature.

3.3.6 A task-based approach for evaluating videoconferencing

Introduction

The issue raised in the central research question – the ways in which oral-visual interaction facilitates L2 acquisition – motivated the adoption of the task-based approach in the evaluation. Thus the overall objective of the tasks designed in this research was to provide an environment that fosters oral-visual interaction and eventually facilitates language acquisition. The successful completion of such tasks is regarded as an indicator of the capabilities of NetMeeting to support oral-visual interaction in distance language learning.

Description of tasks designed for this research

The task analysis follows Nunan's framework. As detailed in Section 2.2.8, tasks are composed of goals, input, activities, setting and role. For ease of reference, Figure 2.1 is reproduced below:

Figure 2.1   A framework for analyzing communicative tasks

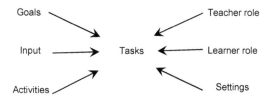

Source: Nunan, 1989, p. 11

For guiding the task design in this research, this framework has been adopted with a certain degree of modification where technology, namely, videoconferencing is concerned. These modifications were deemed necessary because Nunan's framework mainly concerns traditional classroom tasks.

Goals of the tasks

The goals of the tasks are closely related to the research question identified in earlier chapters – to investigate optimal task design for facilitating effective language learning interaction through an oral-visual CMC technology, in this case, NetMeeting, a videoconferencing tool. Thus it has a communicative and interactive nature. To be more specific, the tasks were intended to design a communicative language learning environment, where students, through the use of videoconferencing, could engage in natural conversations with the teacher in the target language. Care was taken to ensure that such tasks would help the students to improve their listening and speaking skills, e.g. clarification request, confirmation checks and spontaneous responses. On the other hand, the tasks were also designed in such a way that the students could associate them with their own experiences and could benefit from them later in their professional life. Furthermore, such tasks were designed to provide the students with a sense of reality and authenticity. In other words, these tasks were not far removed from the students' real life. Specific learning goals were also embedded in each subtask. (see Table 3.8)

Input of the tasks

There are a variety of input sources in the tasks. A combination of authentic and non-authentic materials was employed in the subtasks, in recognition of the features of videoconferencing. It should be noted that some of the inputs were largely determined by the capabilities of a videoconferencing tool. (see Table 3.5)

Table 3.5   Input of the tasks

Type of input	Authentic materials	Non-authentic materials
Input	The video provided by Webcam	A job advertisement
	The whiteboard in NetMeeting	A menu
	File Transfer in NetMeeting	
	Document Sharing in NetMeeting	
	My Video in NetMeeting	
	Photos	
	Resumes	

Activities

Tasks were planned in advance and given to the students at the beginning of each stage of the evaluation of NetMeeting. Tasks were so designed that they only required a general preparation. To achieve spontaneity, the teacher took care to embed "surprises" in the tutorials, in order to avoid too many prepared speeches from the students.

The task design in this empirical study went through three stages of progressive improvement, resulting in the evaluation of three sets of tasks with five subtasks to each set. Task Set 1 (see Table 3.6 for its contents) was evaluated by the on-campus students in Stage One. Informed by the results from this stage, Task Set 2 (see Table 3.7) was then designed to include a component called "free conversation" and was tested with the distance participants in Stage Two. The third set of tasks (see Table 3.8) was then developed in response to the specific needs of the distance learners as identified in the course of the trial.

Table 3.6   Task Set 1 – An overview of the activities for NetMeeting sessions with on-campus students

Sub-tasks	Task description	Aim	NetMeeting feature used
1	You are to play the role of an applicant. You saw an advertisement in the Courier Mail about a part time job at LELE in Chinatown. You want to know more about the job, so you ring the shop and ask to speak to the manager. You will need to first introduce yourself and then find out: ♦ what kind of person they are looking for; ♦ how many hours the applicant would be required to work every week; ♦ what the hourly rate is; ♦ when the applicant would be required to work, (e.g. in the morning, afternoon or weekend); ♦ when the job starts. The manager will ask questions about the applicant such as age, language abilities, likes and dislikes.	1. To practise making a phone call 2. To practise introducing oneself	Videoconferencing and whiteboard
2	Being very nervous about the application, you decide to ring your friend, Linda, who used to work at LELE as a shop assistant. You arrange to meet at a café in the city the next day. You will need to ♦ tell Linda what happened the previous day about the job inquiry; ♦ ask Linda what it was like working at LELE; ♦ arrange to meet Linda at a cafe in the city (You will suggest a newly opened Cafe in the City Mall and heap praise on it); ♦ draw a map on the whiteboard to show Linda the location of the cafe.	1. To practise again making a phone call 2. To practise making an appointment. (time, place, etc.) 3. To practise giving directions	Videoconferencing and the whiteboard
3	You and Linda meet at the cafe. You will need to ♦ discuss with Linda what drinks and food to order; ♦ comment on the price; ♦ place an order; ♦ ask Linda's opinion about working at LELE; ♦ tell Linda why you are nervous about working at LELE; ♦ tell Linda that you will ring her and tell her your decision; ♦ Linda shows a photo of the people who used to work with her at LELE and introduces those people in the photo.	1. Practise ordering food and drinks 2. Practise talking about price. 3. Practise describing people.	Videoconferencing and the Document Sharing function
4	After much deliberation about the job, you decide to ring LELE and ask for an interview. The first time you ring, you only hear a message on an answering machine asking you to leave a message. The manager returns the call later and you arrange to meet at Griffith University the next day. You will	1. Practise again making a telephone conversation, 2. Practise making an appointment.	Videoconferencing, whiteboard Document Sharing and File Transfer

Sub-tasks	Task description	Aim	NetMeeting feature used
	need to ♦ remind the manager of who you are; ♦ ask for an interview; ♦ make sure where and how to find LELE; ♦ confirm time and place for the interview.	3. Practise talking about directions.	
5	You and the manager meet at Griffith University bus stop. You first show the manager around Griffith University. Later at the interview, you give a copy of your resume to the manager and try hard to sell yourself. You will need to ♦ prepare a "resume" (You can save an existing resume onto a floppy disk and bring the disk to this session. Or you can type a new one in Chinese); ♦ talk about why you want to apply for this job; ♦ tell the manager your qualifications (what you have learned, what you are learning and your language abilities etc.); ♦ elaborate on your previous work experience; ♦ ask if you get the job, what you are expected to do; ♦ inquire about your pay, how many hours you are expected to work and if you need to work during weekends or evenings and what is the rate for working in evenings and weekends; ♦ accept or refuse the job offer.	1. Practise describing places. 2. Practise talking about one's experiences. 3. Practise talking about one's likes, dislikes, capabilities, etc. 4. Learn how to accept or refuse an offer.	Videoconferencing, Document Sharing and File Transfer

Task Set 2 is more or less a duplication of Task Set 1 with a few minor alterations and additions. First, a component called "Free Conversation" was added to serve as a prelude to the major task that follows. This inclusion was made in response to the observation that during task completion, the participants in Stage One tended to talk about themselves instead of the role they were playing. Another reason for adding this free chat was to create a relaxing atmosphere before the major task starts. Second, to suit the distance-learning environment and the characteristics of the distance students, the place of the clothes shop was changed from Chinatown to the city, in case students in remote areas of Australia cannot relate to the idea of Chinatown. Third, the last scene at Griffith University was moved to the manager's office because the distance students might find it hard to imagine a specific university environment.

*Table 3.7   Task Set 2 – An overview of the activities for NetMeeting sessions with the Open
             Learning students*

Sub-tasks	Task description	Aim	NetMeeting feature used
1	1. **Free conversation (5–10 minutes)** 2. You are to play the role of an applicant. You saw an advertisement in the Courier Mail about a part time job at LELE in Chinatown. You want to know more about the job, so you ring the shop and ask to speak to the manager. You will need to first introduce yourself and then find out: ♦ what kind of person they are looking for; ♦ how many hours the applicant would be required to work every week; ♦ what the hourly rate is; ♦ when the applicant would be required to work, (e.g. in the morning, afternoon or weekend); ♦ when the job starts. 3. The manager will ask questions about the applicant such as age, language abilities, likes and dislikes.	1. To practise making a phone call 2. To practise introducing oneself	Videoconferencing and whiteboard
2	1. **Free conversation (5–10 minutes)** 2. Being very nervous about the application, you decide to ring your friend, Linda, who used to work at LELE as a shop assistant. You arrange to meet at a café in the city the next day. You will need to ♦ tell Linda what happened the previous day about the job inquiry; ♦ ask Linda what it was like working at LELE; ♦ arrange to meet Linda at a cafe in the city (You will suggest a newly opened Cafe in the City Mall and heap praise on it); ♦ draw a map on the whiteboard to show Linda the location of the cafe.	1. To practise again making a phone call 2. To practise making an appointment. (time, place, etc.) 3. To practise giving directions	Videoconferencing and the whiteboard
3	1. **Free conversation (5–10 minutes)** 2. You and Linda meet at the cafe. You will need to ♦ discuss with Linda what drinks and food to order; ♦ comment on the price; ♦ place an order; ♦ ask Linda's opinion about working at LELE; ♦ tell Linda why you are nervous about working at LELE; ♦ tell Linda that you will ring her and tell her your decision; ♦ Linda shows a photo of the people who used to work with her at LELE and introduces those people in the photo.	1. Practise ordering food and drinks 2. Practise talking about price. 3. Practise describing people.	Videoconferencing and Document Sharing

Sub-tasks	Task description	Aim	NetMeeting feature used
4	1. **Free conversation (5–10 minutes)** 2. After much deliberation about the job, you decide to ring LELE and ask for an interview. The first time you ring, you only hear a message on an answering machine asking you to leave a message. The manager returns the call later and you arrange to meet at Griffith University the next day. You will need to ♦ remind the manager of who you are; ♦ ask for an interview; ♦ make sure where and how to find LELE; ♦ confirm time and place for the interview.	1. Practise again making a telephone conversation, 2. Practise making an appointment. 3. Practise talking about directions.	Videoconferencing, whiteboard Document Sharing and File Transfer
5	1. **Free conversation (5–10 minutes)** 2. You and the manager meet at Griffith ♦ University bus stop. You first show the manager around Griffith University. Later at the interview, you give a copy of your resume to the manager and try hard to sell yourself. You will need to ♦ prepare a "resume" (You can save an existing resume onto a floppy disk and bring the disk to this session. Or you can type a new one in Chinese); ♦ talk about why you want to apply for this job; ♦ tell the manager your qualifications (what you have learned, what you are learning and your language abilities etc.); ♦ elaborate on your previous work experience; ♦ ask if you get the job, what you are expected to do; ♦ inquire about your pay, how many hours you are expected to work and if you need to work during weekends or evenings and what is the rate for working in evenings and weekends; ♦ accept or refuse the job offer.	1. Practise describing places. 2. Practise talking about one's experiences. 3. Practise talking about one's likes, dislikes, capabilities, etc. 4. Learn how to accept or refuse an offer.	Videoconferencing, Document Sharing and File Transfer

Task Set 3 was developed in response to the preferences and level of proficiency of the Open Learning participants. While the basic requirement for linguistic input and output remained similar, the activities in subtasks 1–3 were heavily oriented towards talking about one's own life experiences such as family members and one's daily activities. The last two subtasks were quite similar to subtask 2 and 3 in Task Set 1 and 2.

Table 3.8   Task Set 3 – An overview of the activities for NetMeeting sessions with Open Learning students

Task no.	Task description	Aims	NetMeeting features to be used
1	**Talking about myself.** A: You can tell your teacher anything about yourself, e.g. 1. a brief self- introduction, 2. your work, 3. your study, 4. what you do everyday, 5. where you live etc. B: Be prepared to ask about your teacher.	Linguistic: Practise using the present continuous tense (zai). Functional: Self introduction How to ask a question politely (*qingwen*). Interactional: How to check understanding in Chinese	The Whiteboard
2	Talking about family members A: You can use a photo as a prompter to describe each family member: 1. their name, 2. age, 3. birthday, 4. likes and dislikes. B: You also need to prepare to ask your teacher about her family members.	Linguistic: Practise how to use *you* (there is/are) Functional: 1. Practise the different ways of asking about one's age. 2. Practise how to say age and dates. 3. Practise talking about one's habits. Interactional: 1. Practise how to clarify meaning using Chinese. 2. Practise how to check understanding using Chinese.	The Whiteboard and Document Sharing
3	**What I did yesterday** A: Prepare to tell the teacher about the major events that happened yesterday such as where you went, what you did and why you did it etc. B: You will also need to ask your teacher about the things she did yesterday.	Linguistic: 1. Practise the use of *le* to indicate completion of an action. 2. Practise the use of *you* (again). Functional: Practise asking questions regarding what happened. Interactional: 1. Practise how to clarify meaning using Chinese 2. Practise how to negotiate meaning using Chinese	The Whiteboard

Task no.	Task description	Aims	NetMeeting features to be used
4	**Going out together** *Part one:* You are to ring your friend Linda (your teacher) to invite her for coffee. After a chat, tell Linda that you just found a very good cafe in town and invite her to have coffee with you there. You also need to draw a map to show Linda the location of the cafe.	<u>Linguistic:</u> 1. Practise expressing preferences by using *xiang, yao, xihuan* and *ai*. 2. Practise the use of *li* to express distance between two places. 3. Practise the use of *guo* to talk about past experience. <u>Functional:</u> 1. Practise conducting a telephone conversation. 2. Practise inviting people. 3. Practise giving directions. <u>Interactional:</u> 1. Practise how to clarify meaning using Chinese 2. Practise how to negotiate meaning using Chinese.	The Whiteboard
5	**Going out together** *Part two:* You and Linda are at the coffee shop. You can start the conversation by apologizing for being late, and then ask Linda how and when she came. You will then discuss with Linda what to order and comment on the prices and the food and drinks. You can end the meeting by saying that you have to go because you have to meet someone at Hoyts cinema.	<u>Linguistic:</u> Practise the structure of *shi ... de* <u>Functional:</u> 1. practise apologizing. 2. practise ordering food and drinks 3. practise talking about money 4. practise taking leave of someone. <u>Interactional:</u> 1. Practise how to clarify meaning using Chinese 2. Practise how to negotiate meaning using Chinese 3. Practise how to check understanding in Chinese.	The Whiteboard and File Transfer

As shown in the above table, the aims in each task were set out more specifically than in the previous two sets of tasks. These aims were categorized into linguistic, functional and interactional objectives. Such specifications were deemed necessary in Stage Two of the evaluation due to the emerging traits of the distance participants. After the first sessions with the participants, it became apparent that most of the participants were lacking linguistic, functional and interactional skills for completing the tasks. It was hoped that such specifications would raise the participants' awareness of these aims.

Roles

For task set 1 and 2, the students were asked to assume the role of an applicant for a shop assistant position at a clothes shop. The teacher played the role of the shop manager and the applicant's friend, Linda. In Task Set 3, there was no role-playing for the students, who were only required to talk about themselves and their experiences, while the teacher only assumed the role of the participants' friend, Linda, in the last two subtasks of task set 3.

Settings of the tasks

The setting was limited to the environment generated by videoconferencing, that is, in front of the computers, although the tasks prescribe different scenes, e.g. in a cafe, in the manager's office or at the university.

Design principles underpinning the tasks to be evaluated

The design principle of the tasks in this research and the implementation of the task-based learning approach regard language learning and teaching as a discipline with the same academic standing as any other disciplines such as computer science and biochemistry. That is, language learning should be treated as the understanding of a complex intellectual system, not just learning how to order a coffee or read a map.

This principle is manifested in the design of the tutorial style of the videoconferencing sessions in this research, where a teacher and learner engage in the prescribed tasks, instead of learner-learner interaction. This decision was made in view of the following three factors. First, a tutorial with the teacher is a process of both learning the systems of the language and applying the language to interaction, which is qualitatively different from simply using the language. The learner can find many occasions to put the target language into use in real life. For example they can talk to waiters and patrons in a restaurant or a cafe. However, a teacher can guide the learner through the scene of ordering coffee to understand the linguistic and cultural values of the language in a more comprehensive and systematic way. Furthermore, learners can receive instant feedback regarding their progress. The impact of interaction involving the teacher has also been documented in the literature. Studies such as Tanaka's (1991, cited in Ellis, 1994) confirmed that teacher-learner interaction results in better comprehension, more linguistic forms being learnt and better retention than either baseline input or premodified input. Second, in the case of the participants in this evaluation, the students' proficiency in Chinese was not adequate for unsupervised interaction in the target language. Third, videoconferencing could be used more effectively with the guidance of the teacher because it was still a novel experience for the learners. Of course, when the students become familiar with the technology and have acquired a considerable level of proficiency to conduct conversations in the target language, nothing would stop them from using videoconferencing to chat in the target language among themselves or even with native speakers.

The goal of the tasks was to design an environment in which learners would have sufficient opportunities to engage in activities that would both improve their speaking skills and explore the potential of videoconferencing. Thus, the task design, on the one hand, closely followed the five guidelines proposed by Skehan (1998) for designing effective task-based instruction. (See Section 2.2.8 for detailed discussion of the five guidelines.) On the other hand, as Skehan's guidelines only concern effective task-based instructions in a general sense, without taking into consideration the implications of the technology used to fulfil the tasks, this research extended Skehan's guidelines by adding a sixth dimension – incorporating the features of the technology used, in this case, the videoconferencing tools. Thus the following six principles underpinned the task design for this research:

- ♦ choose a range of target structures (Skehan, 1998, p. 132);
- ♦ choose tasks which meet the utility condition (Skehan, 1998, p. 132);
- ♦ select and sequence tasks to achieve balanced goal development (Skehan, 1998, p. 132);
- ♦ maximize the chances of focus on form through attentional manipulation (Skehan, 1998, p. 132);
- ♦ use cycles of accountability (Skehan, 1998, p. 132);
- ♦ incorporate the features of the technology used.

The six guidelines will now be discussed in reference to the task design in this research.

(1) Choose a range of target structures

As discussed in section 2.4.1, choosing a range of target structures is deemed imperative to language development. In this research, the choice of target structures was determined by the learner's level of proficiency in Chinese. In other words, care was taken to expose learners to the level of difficulty of the task that was within their grasp.

The target students would eventually be the distance language learners who, because of the lack of a Chinese learning environment, had only acquired a basic level of Chinese proficiency. Therefore first year (CHN11 & CHN12) textbooks for the Open Learning Chinese program offered at Griffith University were used as a basis for the level of difficulty and sequences of the tasks designed for this experiment. Also taken into consideration in task designs was the level of proficiency of the on-campus participants. My experience with both the first year Open Learning and on-campus students led to the conclusion that the first year on-campus participants generally had a higher level of proficiency than the distance participants, at least as far as speaking skills were concerned. So within the same task frame, I would guide the conversation to a slightly more sophisticated level with the on-campus participants. For example, I may ask a simple question to a distance participant, such as "how old are you", while with the on-campus students, the same question would be extended to "could you please tell me how old you are this year". Thus a smooth performance of the tasks by both groups of participants could be maintained. A short glossary was provided whenever deemed necessary.

(2) Choose tasks which meet the utility condition

Chapelle (2001, p. 46) describes utility as a "category in a classification of L2 tasks" which distinguishes "among the degrees of likelihood that a particular structure will be used by learners as they perform a task". (See section 2.2.8 for more detailed discussion on this principle.) The task design in this research ensures that a range of structures have "utility in the task". For example, in Task Set 1, there are three telephone conversations in the subtasks, in which participants could open and close the conversation with a variety of structures, instead of specifying the use of one particular structure. Although the learners were not always required to employ any number of prescribed structures in task completion, the task conditions often set the boundary of the range of structures to be used. For example, subtask 3 in Task Set 3 requires the learners to talk about what happened yesterday, then the use of "*le*" indicating completion of action became inevitable.

(3) Select and sequence tasks to achieve balanced goal development

Skehan (1998) sees the goal development of L2 acquisition as a three-dimensional one: fluency, accuracy and complexity. Fluency has been a serious problem facing distance language learners due to their solitary and isolated learning environment. In view of this problem, the tasks were designed in such a way that they not only required the students to use what they had learned before, but also provided them with an opportunity to use that linguistic repertoire to improve their fluency. To be more exact, recycling of certain language uses and situations is embedded in the tasks so that students would have opportunities to reuse what they have learned. For example, structures for introducing oneself, describing people, giving directions and making a phone call and so on were reused in different subtasks.

As fluency was treated as the priority in task performance, accuracy was only dealt with when necessary, that is, when misunderstanding occurred. Five to ten minutes were allocated at the end of each task to focus on troubleshooting and accuracy, such as problems in tones, pronunciation, or linguistic explanations not dealt with during task performance. E-mail was used on a number of occasions after NetMeeting sessions to clarify certain structures and grammatical points.

Due to the low level of Chinese proficiency, complexity was only encouraged among learners of higher proficiency in Chinese.

(4) Maximize the chances of focus on form through attentional manipulation

Section 2.4.1 defines the term *focus on form* as an occasional shift of attention to linguistic forms while the learner's primary attention is directed to the meaning of the language during the completion of meaning focused tasks. Chapelle (2001, p. 48) believes that "sufficient evidence exists to suggest that it is worthwhile to attempt to get learners to focus on form during engagement in meaning-based tasks".

The tasks designed for this research were all meaning-based tasks of a communicative nature. In Chapelle's (2001, p. 48) words, "[c]ommunication tasks are chosen on the basis of the meaning that learners are expected to practise, and no metalinguistic explanation is included as part of the task". In this research, videoconferencing was employed mainly for creating an environment for students to interact in the target language and improve their interactional skills, not for the purpose of solely teaching new forms. However, this does not mean a complete exclusion of linguistic explanations. Linguistic explanations did occur during the process of negotiation of meaning, especially when a breakdown in comprehension happened. Such breakdowns are inevitable due to the inclusiveness of meaning-based tasks, especially when learners only possess a basic level of proficiency.

During the performance of the tasks, participants were encouraged to use only Chinese for completing the tasks. However, when a breakdown occurred due to an unknown word or grammatical point, explanations in English were sometimes attempted for accuracy and effectiveness in understanding.

(5) Use cycles of accountability

According to Skehan (1998), cycles of accountability is a stock taking measure, in which learners are asked to regularly examine what they have learned and what remains to be learned. In the case of distance language learning, where the major part of language learning is done by the students themselves, videoconferencing sessions are deemed to be more important to raise the awareness of such stock taking by simply designing into the task what they have learned and what they should be learning. Such stock taking is exhibited in the task design process of this research by way of using their textbook as a basis for the linguistic requirements of the tasks (also see Section 2.2.8).

(6) Incorporate the features of the technology used

In this study, the technology is videoconferencing, to be more specific, NetMeeting. The task design takes into consideration the following features of NetMeeting:

- ♦ the one-to-one nature of the freely downloadable version of NetMeeting;
- ♦ the function of the video;
- ♦ the function of the Whiteboard;
- ♦ the function of the File Transfer;
- ♦ the function of the Document Sharing;
- ♦ the function of My Video.

In view of the fact that NetMeeting only supported one-to-one conferencing, role-plays between the participants and the teacher formed the backbone of each session. This one-to-one nature of NetMeeting also allowed the learner to be treated as an individual with his or her own needs and interests, and provided with immediate and appropriate feedback about each individual's progress. These are the two task design principles advocated by McKay (1996, p. 25).

The task design in this research also embraced the effective use of the whiteboard (for detailed description of the whiteboard, see Section 3.2.2), e.g. drawing diagrams to show directions and writing Chinese characters on the whiteboard for both parties to view. Also designed into the tasks were occasions for use of File Transfer and Document Sharing to view prepared documents or photos, Websites etc. The teacher had also planned to utilize the function of My Video to monitor her teaching and to show objects such as a photo or a book during task completion.

3.3.7   Data collected

In accordance with issues raised in the central and subsidiary research questions (see Section 1.2), this evaluation sought two sets of data – data relating to the technological capabilities of NetMeeting and data relating to the pedagogical values of a videoconferencing-supported distance language learning environment, with the emphasis on the latter set. Recommendations were made on the basis of this data. (see sections 6.2, 6.3, 6.4, 6.5 and 6.6)

Determining the technological capabilities of NetMeeting

The attempt to determine the technological capabilities of NetMeeting involved personal observation and participants' feedback with an emphasis on the video and audio quality of NetMeeting. The major issue here was whether Internet-based desktop videoconferencing is an adequate tool that can technically support oral-visual interaction between distance learners and the instructor. Thus data was obtained during the course of the evaluation to respond to the following issues:

1. Is NetMeeting user friendly?
2. Is the video and audio quality of NetMeeting adequate for supporting oral-visual interaction?
3. Does NetMeeting have other features of pedagogical value besides its video and audio features?
4. Is NetMeeting reliable and stable?
5. Is videoconferencing an economically viable tool?

Criteria for evaluating the above data were proposed in Section 3.4.1 and were used for the analysis of this data.

Determining the pedagogical values of a videoconferencing-supported learning environment

While confirming the technological capabilities of videoconferencing, the evaluation concentrated on the ways in which oral-visual interaction supported by videoconferencing facilitates L2 acquisition in distance education. Scholars (e.g. Salaberry, 2000; Bates, 1995; Higgins, 1998; Künzel, 1995; Price, 1987; Romiszowski, 1990) have identified a gap in the evaluation design of CALL or CMC research by pointing out that "previous pedagogical claims focused primarily on the technological capabilities of the new medium and neglected to analyze the pedagogical design of instructional activities" (Salaberry, 2000, p. 29). In recognition of this gap, this research went well beyond evaluating the technological capabilities of videoconferencing. It placed considerable weight on the pedagogical values of the videoconferencing-supported learning environment. When proposing his model of a Web-based university of instruction, Duchastel (1997, p. 225) pointed out that evaluation should be at a task level and allow for diversity and production. He goes on to say that this is "best achieved by aligning evaluation not with knowledge, but with task accomplishment that utilizes knowledge". Thus the pedagogical values of the videoconferencing-supported interaction were evaluated through task performance by the participants. The following concrete data was sought and examined in the evaluation of NetMeeting:

1. What is the language learning potential of the videoconferencing-supported tasks designed for the evaluation? To be more exact, do the tasks provide opportunities for focus on form during negotiation for meaning in task completion? What is the frequency of interactional modification, and in what ways do they contribute to L2 acquisition?

2. What are the *perceptions* of the participants in regard to the improvement in their language proficiency through the five videoconferencing sessions?
3. Do the tasks suit the participants' Chinese proficiency level?
4. Do the tasks relate to the participants' life and experiences?
5. What are the positive impacts of the videoconferencing-supported interaction on participants, specially on the distance participants?

This data was evaluated using the criteria proposed in Section 3.4.2. The following recommendations were made in accordance with this data:

1. What types of tasks are appropriate to videoconferencing-based DLE?
2. In what ways can videoconferencing tools be incorporated into distance language learning?
3. What are the implications of this research for videoconferencing-based task design and performance?

It has to be pointed out that students' improvement in the target language proficiency was not quantitatively assessed. This is because of the complicated and open-ended nature of the issue of learner language proficiency. There are numerous factors influencing proficiency level; it is thus hard to provide an accurate assessment of the extent of one's improvement in a certain skill within a limited period of time. Thus there were no skill assessments at the end of the evaluation to show the effectiveness of videoconferencing-supported learning, as such an exercise would be far from conclusive and could be misleading. Furthermore, as Von der Emde et al. (2001, p. 222) point out: "Measuring all students against the same proficiency goals may not provide an accurate picture of language learning success, many of which are more intellectual and cultural than practical". However, the language learning potential (i.e. the provision of focus on form during negotiation of meaning) of the tasks was treated as a major indicator of L2 acquisition and thus proving the effectiveness of the videoconferencing-supported interaction. In view of the importance of this data, the process of negotiation of meaning was analyzed in detail using the model proposed by Varonis and Gass (1985). (see Section 3.3.9)

3.3.8 Methods of data collection

In view of the nature of the above mentioned data collection, this evaluation was approached from a formative and qualitative methodology. Thus a combination of data collection methods of an interpretive and exploratory nature was deemed more effective than one method only. This approach is also in line with the trend of current qualitative data collection. In view of the innovative and fast changing nature of computer technologies, scholars (e.g. Murray, 1999) have begun to explore, not a particular method, but a configuration of methods to investigate and document learning experiences. Murray, et al. (1989, p. 99) argue that "the impact of the material on the students' motivation, interest, and general cognitive and linguistic abilities will have to be assessed in ways approximating more the method of the social sciences (students' reports, teacher diaries, think aloud protocols, etc.) than those of the natural sciences". Thus a combination of methods of an interpretive nature was adopted for data collection in this experiment. These include personal observations, videotaped sessions, teacher's diary, pre-trial written surveys, post-session and post-trial written surveys and post-session and post-trial interviews. These methods are discussed below.

(1) Personal observations

Brown (1989) compares diary writing and personal observation and concludes that they are compatible data collection methods. As I personally conducted these sessions with each participant, my observation was a first-hand experience, and a diary was kept to record immediately after each session such details as the date and time, the quality of the connection, video and sound, technical and linguistic issues or problems that occurred during each session (see Appendix K for content and format of the diary). As each session was videotaped, this diary was not kept to record the actual interaction in task completion for fear of imprecision in documenting such a dynamic process. Instead, this diary only documents the reflections of the teacher immediately after each session and information useful for data coding.

(2) Videotaped sessions

Videotaping is growing in importance, especially with studies involving the investigation of a learning process. Goldman-Segall (1991) points out that videotaping enables the researcher to capture the interplay of many details, which otherwise might be overlooked. Heath's (1997) contention is to the point:

> As some ethnomethodological and conversation analytic researchers become increasingly concerned with talk and interaction, it has been found that audio and audio-visual recordings provide useful resources with which to subject *in situ* practical action and activities to detailed analysis. (p. 183)

In the trial with on-campus students, because both parties wore headphones to avoid feedback from the speakers, the audio signal of the other party would be lost if only one video camera was used to videotape the sessions. Therefore, two cameras were employed, one on the participant's side and the other on the teacher's side, to record the screen and audio signal from both sides.

In the case of the distance students, it was impractical to request the participants to videotape the sessions at their end. Therefore only one video camera was used on the teacher's side to record the whole session. On the teacher's side, the speakers were used instead of the headphones in order to catch the audio signals. To reduce feedback from the speakers, a dual socket was used to connect both the headphones and the speakers. This was to ensure that the sound from the speakers could be recorded with minimum feedback. An amplifier was placed near the speakers and connected to the video camera in order for the video recorder to pick up the sound clearly. Despite this, the videotaped sound of the participants was not as clear as it was during the actual sessions. The function of My Video was employed to show on the same screen the image of the teacher and the participants' image. The videotaped sessions were later transcribed for analysis, using common transcription conventions. (see Schiffrin, 1994, p. 422-433)

As expected, video recording of a computer monitor produced poor results due to the difference in scanning frequencies between the computer monitor and the video camera. The quality of the taped video image supported by videoconferencing lost considerably during videotaping.

(3) Pre-trial survey

A short survey was conducted by e-mail prior to the trial with the distance students with two objectives – to invite participation in the trial and to determine the students' availability of computer resources for the trial.

(4) Post-session survey

This survey was only carried out with the on-campus participants. At the end of each session, each participant was requested to complete a short written survey seeking his or her feedback for each videoconferencing session. A total of 15 questionnaires was collected. Similar questions were asked of the distance students in the post-session interviews, which were used instead of written surveys, in order to save the students the trouble of sending in their replies after each session.

(5) Post-trial surveys

In order to provide the participants with an opportunity to reflect on their learning experience with videoconferencing, a comprehensive written survey was carried out when each participant had completed all five sessions, in the trials with both the on-campus and distance students. A total of four completed questionnaires were collected and analyzed. (see Appendix D)

(6) Post-session interviews

In our "interview society" (Silverman, 1993), the interview is by far the most widely used method of data collection in the social sciences. Its importance and effectiveness have been well documented in the qualitative research literature (e.g. Holstein & Gubrium, 1997; Miller & Glassner, 1997). Due to the qualitative nature of this research, this data collection method was employed extensively and became the major data collection method in this research. All interview questions are open-ended. In both the trials with the on-campus and open learning students, immediately following the completion of each session, an in-depth interview was conducted in order to determine particular aspects pertaining to each individual session, such as the quality of the video and sound, and the appropriateness of the tasks for each session. Immediate adjustments were made following the participants' feedback (e.g. adjustments to the task designs as discussed in Section 3.3.6). In total, 40 such interviews were conducted and taped using a cassette recorder. These interviews were transcribed employing the commonly used conventions for conversation analysis. (see Atkinson and Heritage, 1984, p. ix-xvi and Appendix L – Transcription Notations)

In these interviews and surveys, Haastrup's (1987, p. 204) "researcher-controlled and informant-initiated" methodology was adopted. In other words, the researcher posed general questions to initiate the conversation and followed with more specific questions in response to the participants' comments.

Each of the six methods of data collection yielded abundant and useful data about different aspects of the evaluation. In combination, they allowed in-depth qualitative feedback on both the technological and pedagogical values of videoconferencing supported DLE.

3.3.9   Methods of data analysis

Two sets of criteria

Following data collection and subsequent transcriptions of the interviews and videotaped sessions, a more detailed analysis of the data was undertaken using the criteria detailed in Sections 3.4.1 and 3.4.2 below. The criteria discussed in Section 3.4.1 were employed to ascertain the technological benefits and limitations of NetMeeting, whilst the pedagogical benefits and limitations of a videoconferencing-supported learning environment were analyzed using the criteria elaborated in section 3.4.2.

The Varonis and Gass Model

The process of oral-visual interaction characterized by negotiation of meaning was a focal point in the data analysis. This analysis was approached using the discourse model proposed by Varonis and Gass (1985). The utility of models that account for discourse structure has been recognized in the literature. (see Ellis, 1994; Stenström, 1994)

As discussed in sections 2.2.9 and 3.4.2, the language learning potential of the tasks designed for this research were determined by identifying opportunities for beneficial focus on form. For example, participants may experience problems in understanding due to a variety of reasons, such as unknown or unfamiliar words or structures. To solve these problems, participants often engaged in negotiation of meaning, in which interactional modifications occurred. Such modifications are believed to be beneficial to language acquisition because they lead to shared understanding (Varonis & Gass, 1985; Pica, Kanagy & Falodun, 1993; Pica, 1994; Long, 1983b, 1988a). The frequency of interactional modifications that occurred during task completion by each participant was tallied and samples of such modifications were analyzed using Varonis and Gass's model.

Varonis and Gass's model treats spoken interaction as a discourse that moves in a horizontal fashion, whereas occasions of non-understanding are regarded as vertical deviations. According to Varonis and Gass's model, these occasions of non-understanding can be solved through vertical levels of negotiation before the conversation pops back to the horizontal movement. It has to be pointed out that Varonis and Gass's (1985) model is limited to the analysis of instances of non-understanding. Non-understanding was operationally defined by Varonis and Gass (1985, p. 73) as "those exchanges in which there is some overt indication that understanding between participants has not been complete". However the use of their model in the current research has been extended to include the analysis of occasions of interactional modification. An occasion of interactional modification is defined here as a period from a breakdown in interaction to the resumption of the interaction. Such breakdowns can be caused by a non-understanding or simply a request for new words or phrases due to lack of vocabulary (Wang, 2006). The following two examples illustrate the difference between a breakdown due to non-understanding and a breakdown due to a request for new words.

An example of non-understanding:

      A: Do you have many colleagues who speak Chinese?

→   B: Colleagues? What does colleague mean?

An example of request for new words

      A: Do you have many friends who speak Chinese?

→   B: No, but I have a…What is the word for describing people who work with you?

      A: Colleagues

The first example shows that Person B does not understand the meaning of the word "colleagues", whereas in the second example, Person B understood the question, i.e. there is no non-understanding. The breakdown occurs only when Person B does not know how to say 'colleagues'. In the current research, Varonis and Gass's model was used for analysis of interactional modifications caused by both kinds of breakdown. Thus the discourse of spoken interaction in videoconferencing-based task completion is characterized by the model contained in Figure 3.10.

Figure 3.10 A model for analysing an occasion of interactional modification during task completion

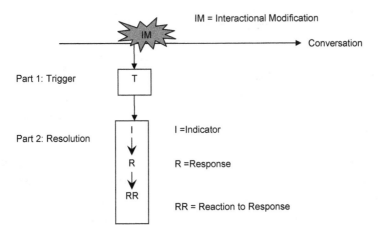

Note: This figure presents a modified version of the Varonis and Gass's (1985, p. 74) model with the negotiation routine shown vertically; this better represents the negotiation process of an occasion of interactional modification (Wang, 2006)

Figure 3.10 shows that an occasion of interactional modification consists of two parts – a trigger and a resolution, and that there are four functional primes in the model. "Simply put, the trigger [the first prime] is that utterance or portion of an utterance on the part of the speaker which results in some indication of non-understanding of the part of the hearer" (Varonis & Gass, 1985, p. 74). The second part of the model, the resolution, consists of the other three primes: an indicator (I), a response (R), and a reaction to the response (RR). An indicator (I) is an "utterance on the part of the hearer that essentially halts the horizontal progression of the conversation" (Varonis & Gass, 1985, p. 75). A response (R) is initiated by the speaker to the indicator, acknowledging the non-understanding. The last prime is an optional element, a reaction to the response (RR). When a resolution is reached, a negotiation routine is considered completed and the conversation resumes its horizontal movement. In order to better understand this model, Table 3.9 reproduces the model with an example.

Table 3.9   Discourse model of an occasion of interactional modification with an example R = Researcher, S = Student 2; Session Three, Stage One

	Utterance		Function
R:	Gangcai wo xia che de shihou, bu zhidao yinggai wang zuo guai haishi wang you guai	When I got off the bus just now, I didn't know whether I should turn left or right.	Trigger
S:	'Zuo guai' shi shenme yisi ?	What does 'zuo guai' mean?	Indicator
R:	'Zuo', zhidao ma?	Do you know 'zuo'?	Response
S:	Zhidao, zhidao.	I know, I know.	Reaction to Response

Table 3.9 shows that the first turn initiated by the researcher, in retrospect, serves as a trigger to the start of a negotiation of meaning. The second utterance is an explicit request for the meaning of "*zuo guai*", thus indicating a non-understanding triggered by the previous utterance, and functioning as an indicator. The third turn, "do you know '*zuo*'" is a response to the indicator, and the last turn. "I know, I know" constitutes a reaction to the response.

Varonis and Gass (1985, p. 74) further identify the various types of each of the four primes. For example, either a question or a statement can function as a trigger. An indicator can appear in the form of an echo, an explicit statement of non-understanding, a non-verbal response or an inappropriate response. Types of responses can include repetition, expansion, rephrasing, acknowledgement and reduction.

The significance of this model lies in its identification of the important "players" in the process of interactional modification, thus "allowing us to measure and compare the depth, i.e. the complexity of these non-understandings" (Varonis & Gass, 1985, p. 81). It was with this understanding of the model that the current research employed it in its data analysis in regarding to the language learning potential of the videoconferencing tasks.

3.4   Part Three – Criteria for evaluating videoconferencing tools and tasks

The need for this research to develop criteria for evaluating videoconferencing-supported language learning stemmed from the fact that well-established criteria have not been found in this field. This is because interaction enabled by videoconferencing has not been sufficiently explored in distance language education. Two sets of criteria are discussed below: *criteria for evaluating the technological capabilities of videoconferencing tools* and *criteria for evaluating the pedagogical values of videoconferencing-based interaction in task completion.* Both data collection and analysis followed the two sets of criteria in the process of fulfilling the objectives in the central research question:

In what ways is oral-visual interaction, enabled by videoconferencing, able to facilitate L2 acquisition at a distance?

3.4.1   Criteria for evaluating the technological capacities of videoconferencing tools

Introduction

As Internet-based videoconferencing is still new to distance language learning, criteria for selecting appropriate videoconferencing tools are not readily available in the literature. General guidance for developing such criteria appears in Levy's (1997) argument that there be a fit between the demands of learning objectives and the capabilities of technology. In other words, it is very important to "adopt the available technologies to the pedagogy rather than the pedagogy to the technology". (Hewer, et al., 1999, p. 382)

For the purpose of this study, the point of departure in developing criteria for selecting appropriate videoconferencing tools lies in the identification of the need for such a tool. In other words, for what learning goals do we use it? In this instance, the learning objective of using such a tool is to provide a synchronous interactive learning environment where distance learners can improve their communicative speaking skills in the target language through oral-visual interaction. Thus, there are three major aspects that determine criteria: the synchronous and interactive nature of the learning environment, the distance between the learner and education provider, and oral/aural-visual interaction. On the basis of the above consideration and drawing on the findings in the two preliminary studies discussion in Section 3.2, the following criteria are proposed: user friendliness, acceptable video and audio quality, other features of pedagogical value, reliability, and low cost.

User friendliness

The main concerns here are the ease of setting up the videoconferencing tools and the effectiveness of the interface. As distance language students do not have ready access to technical support, user friendliness is an important factor in the choice of videoconferencing tools. The interface layout should be uncomplicated and effective (e.g. with few icons and buttons). The ease of setting up is judged by whether learners can set up everything by themselves following written instructions.

Acceptable video and audio quality

Findings from the preliminary studies (see Section 3.2) indicate that there is still room for improvement as far as the video and audio quality of the present generation of videoconferencing is concerned. This is because Internet-based real-time audio and videoconferencing is "a low-cost, low-bandwidth alternative to these expensive forms of communication, and must look for the minimum quality (that is, requiring a low amount of bandwidth) necessary to support a multimedia conferencing application" (Watson & Sasse, 1996, p. 258). It would consequently be unrealistic to expect a television broadcast quality from such videoconferencing. Criteria for audio and video quality in videoconferencing should then aim at a level acceptable to both the learner and the instructor so as to facilitate interactive language learning. Too much sound distortion and too many freezing and jittery images disrupt the flow of interaction and will frustrate the learner.

The synchronization of sound and video images should also be taken into consideration in the choice of technology. Summerfield (1992) (discussed by Bruce, 1996, p. 173) believes that with a delay of up to 80 msec. the sound and image can still be perceived to be synchronous, given that sound travels slower than light. Longer delays can be tolerated if the audio transmission lags behind the video transmission than vice versa. Therefore a delay of a little more than 80 msec. in a language learning situation can be accepted as long as it does not cause miscomprehension or ineffective and inefficient language reproduction.

For the purpose of interactive distance language teaching, reasonable clarity and continuity of the video image and sound should be the minimum requirements for supporting interaction. Watson & Sasse (1996, p. 273) point out that "[e]stablishing the minimum quality required for adequate task performance will lead to guidelines towards which applications are viable under certain bandwidth constraints". Such an assessment of audio and video quality often tends to be subjective rather than objective, that is, it is often a perceived quality. To make matters more complicated, the quality of audio and video that each participant receives is likely to be different due to many factors, such as different network conditions and different hardware (e.g. computer processing power, sound and video cards). Therefore the assessment of audio and video quality in Internet-based conferencing is of a more subjective and experimental nature than objective and instrumental.

Other features of pedagogical value

Other features of pedagogical value refer to features beneficial to language learning, other than video and audio functions. For example, a videoconferencing tool with a whiteboard can better facilitate interaction and language acquisition than a video chat alone.

Reliability

Reliability here refers to the stability of the videoconferencing tools (e.g. whether or how often they crash), crucial for maintaining the flow of interaction. As distance students and teachers are often physically separated and access to technical support is not readily available, reliability is imperative in ensuring the success of CMC based interaction. Of course, an ideal videoconferencing tool should never crash. Findings from the preliminary investigation of NetMeeting indicate that more than one crash during a videoconferencing session will deter the learner from using it.

Low cost

Cost here consists of the initial set up and ongoing maintenance cost. These include costs to both the institution and the learner. Although this is not a pedagogical criterion, it is obviously an important factor influencing the choice of a particular technology. The less it costs the learner, the more acceptable it will be.

The above technical criteria must be complemented by pedagogical values of a videoconferencing tool to produce an appropriate assessment methodology.

3.4.2 Criteria for evaluating the pedagogical values of videoconferencing-supported interaction in task completion

As employing videoconferencing in distance language education is still a new experience, comprehensive criteria for evaluating the appropriateness of tasks in such an environment are absent from the literature. In this research, the six criteria (see Table 2.4) for CALL task appropriateness developed by Chapelle (2001) will be referred to as guidelines when attempting to propose criteria for evaluating videoconferencing tasks. Drawing on Skehan's (1998) principles for task design and adapted from Chapelle's criteria, the following criteria have been developed for evaluating meaning-based tasks in a videoconferencing situation (see Wang, 2007; Table 3.10). These five criteria are discussed below in reference to Chapelle's (2001) six criteria.

Table 3.10 Criteria for evaluating meaning-based videoconferencing tasks

Practicality	The fit between the task and the capability of the videoconferencing tool(s) to support task completion.
Language learning potential	Two conditions are under investigation: the extent to which task conditions present opportunities for focus on form, and learners' perceived improvement in the target language
Learner fit	The fit between the characteristics of the learner and the task characteristics (e.g. the fit between the level of difficulty of the tasks and the level of proficiency of the learner).
Authenticity	The degree of correspondence between the videoconferencing activities and target language activities of interest to the learner out of the classroom.

Positive impact	The positive effects of the videoconferencing tasks on those who participate in it, e.g. the impact of the video, the impact on the learner's confidence in learning etc.

In reference to the above criteria, the following questions in Table 3.11 can be asked in evaluating videoconferencing-based tasks. Some of the questions are adapted from Chapelle's (2001, p. 59) questions. The questions are:

Table 3.11 Questions in relation to criteria for evaluating videoconferencing-based tasks

Qualities	Questions
Practicality	Is the videoconferencing tool technologically sufficient to support oral-visual interaction in task completion?
	Does the videoconferencing tool offer an appropriate environment for the accomplishment of the tasks?
Language learning potential	Do task conditions present sufficient opportunity for beneficial focus on forms?
	Has the learner's target language proficiency been improved?
Learner fit	Is the difficulty level of the targeted linguistic forms appropriate for the learner to increase their language ability?
Authenticity	Is there a strong correspondence between the task and second language tasks of interest to learners outside the classroom?
	Will learners be able to see the connection between the videoconferencing tasks and tasks outside the classroom?
Impact	Will learners have a positive learning experience with oral-visual interaction via videoconferencing?
	How important is the video in videoconferencing to distance language learners?
	Will the learner's confidence be improved through the use of the tasks?

(1) Practicality

Different from Chapelle's list of criteria, practicality occupies the first place in the above table. This is not because practicality is regarded here as more important than the other criteria, but because practicality is the precondition for task performance. To be more specific, in this research, the evaluation and analysis of technological capabilities of the videoconferencing tool provide the necessary background for the discussion of the appropriateness of the tasks. Thus the discussion on practicality lays the foundation for the analysis on the other four criteria.

The fit between the technology and the task is considered imperative in evaluating videoconferencing-based tasks. This is because videoconferencing tools determine the successful completion of tasks in DLE. This fit addresses issues on the two sides of the coin – whether the technology is capable of assisting the completion of the task and whether the task design is beyond the capability of such technology. Criteria for evaluating the practicality have been extensively addressed in Section 3.4.1.

(2) Language learning potential

As shown in Table 3.10, language learning potential in this research incorporates two constituents: opportunities for focus on form and learner's perceived improvement in the target language. The evaluation of NetMeeting will provide data on these two aspects to prove if videoconferencing can successfully support such language learning potential.

Focus on form

It has to be pointed out that focus on form does not mean metalinguistic explanations of any prescribed grammatical items. Rather, learners' attention is brought to certain linguistic forms occasionally and temporarily for the purpose of negotiation of meaning in the process of completing a meaning-based task. These opportunities for focus on form usually happen irregularly when communication and interaction in the target language break down due to unfamiliar or unknown linguistic forms. Communication and interaction resume when the breakdowns are repaired, usually through linguistic explanations and/or negotiation of meaning in the target language. It is argued here that occasional focus on form is beneficial to language acquisition in a meaning-based task, and a high density of frequency of focus on form in a meaning-based task could be disruptive to task completion. Major factors relevant for promoting focus on form were identified by Chapelle (2001) and are listed below:

- ◆ international modification
- ◆ modification of output
- ◆ time pressure
- ◆ modality
- ◆ support
- ◆ surprise
- ◆ control
- ◆ stakes

For definition and discussion of each of the above elements, see Table 2.3. In this research, due to the real-time and synchronous nature of the tasks, the emphasis of the evaluation concentrated on interactional modification, modification of output, support and the spoken nature of the modality.

Improvement in the target language

In addition to focus on form, the language learning potential of the tasks is also measured by the participants' improvement in the target language proficiency, be it observed or self-perceived improvement. In this research, due to the spoken nature of the modality of the tasks, participants' improvement in listening and speaking is closely examined.

(3) Learner fit

Learner fit refers to the fit between the learner characteristics (e.g. the learner's language proficiency, age, willingness to communicate) and the task characteristics such as the difficulty level, the settings and activities of the task. Taken from Chapelle's (2001) definition, learner characteristics here take two appropriate conditions into consideration – the linguistic level of the learner to accomplish the task and the characteristics of the learner as an individual. It is generally believed in the SLA literature that language either below or above the grasp of the learner will not promote acquisition (Chapelle, 2001). This corresponds with Skehan's (1998) suggestion that a range of target structures be selected for task-based instruction, in order to cater for different linguistic abilities and levels of the learner. Learner characteristics, such as willingness to communicate, age and learning styles, play a much more crucial role in distance language learning than in face-to-face language learning.

(4) Authenticity

According to Chapelle (2001, p. 56), authenticity refers to "the degree of correspondence between a L2 learning task and tasks that the learner is likely to encounter outside the classroom". This relevancy to real life situations is important for at least two reasons. First, the closer the task is to real life, the more it should help the learner to engage in language use and improve the learner's willingness to participate. Second, a task relevant to a real life situation is believed to be important in acquiring real life skills. Nunan (1993) believes that the authenticity of a task promotes more meaningful interaction in the target language, which in turn encourages the production of comprehensible output and provides learning objectives and personal involvement. This demand for authenticity applies equally to videoconferencing task design, which needs to "identify 'viable' rather than 'artificial' purposes for electronic interaction amongst students and staff". (Selinger & Pearson, 1999, p. xii)

(5) Positive impact

In essence, to Chapelle (2001), positive impact includes any improvements the learner obtains from performing the task beyond language learning potential, be it the learner's improved knowledge or interest in the target culture or their improved pragmatic abilities. It is argued here that in the case of videoconferencing in distance language learning, such impact is a combination of the task and the technology used to realize the task. In this research, because the task completion is supported by videoconferencing, visual impact realized through the function of the video on establishing a personal link with others, will be one of the key criteria for judging the values of oral-visual interaction. Positive impact on affective factors such as confidence building and reduction of isolation in the case of distance learners will also be underscored and evaluated.

The criteria in Table 3.10 are different from Chapelle's criteria in a number ways. The first difference lies in the scope of these two sets of criteria. In other words, the scope of the criteria developed by this research has been narrowed down to just the criteria relevant for evaluating meaning-based tasks in a videoconferencing-supported learning environment, not for all the tasks in CALL.

Second, because these criteria are for evaluating meaning-based tasks, meaning focus is the obvious goal of the task, which is already embedded in the task activities. Therefore, the term "meaning focus" is not specified in the criteria developed here. Furthermore, in Table 2.4 Chapelle summarizes language learning potential as "[t]he degree of opportunity present for beneficial focus on form", and meaning focus as "the extent to which learners' attention is directed toward the meaning of the language". I argue that the two criteria proposed by Chapelle, that is, language learning potential and meaning focus, are in fact one and the same criterion for evaluating meaning-based tasks. This is because focus on form is understood as an occasional shift of attention to linguistic forms while the learner's primary attention is directed to the meaning of the language during the completion of meaning-focused tasks (see Long & Robinson, 1998, p. 23). In other words, focus on form happens in a meaning-based context, and focus on form and meaning focus are inseparable.

3.5 Assumptions and limitations

Due to the difficulties in attaining interactive learning in DLE, enrolment in DLE programs is usually much lower than that in other disciplines in the distance mode. This was one of the problems experienced in this research when recruiting participants for the empirical dimension of this research. In Stage Two of the evaluation, only 11 students enrolled in the distance program in the third study period (CHN21). Of these, five volunteered to participate in the evaluation. Although in a qualitative investigation such as employed in this research the number of participants is not crucial, this issue was still taken into consideration when designing the evaluation. For example, it had originally been planned to carry out 3–4 sessions with each participant if a larger number of participants had been recruited. The number of sessions with each participant was thus increased to five when only five distance learners volunteered, in order to compensate for the small size of the evaluation population. Furthermore, participants were treated as unique and specific in recognition that each individual has his or her own language learning background, proficiency level, learning strategies and language aptitude, and that there are many factors influencing their perceptions of a new medium such as NetMeeting. Finally, when discussing contributions and implications of this research, established L2 acquisition theories and empirical studies in CMC-supported distance language learning are drawn on to avoid over generalization from the small case study sample.

As the researcher, I conducted the NetMeeting sessions, interviews and surveys with each participant. I strove for systematic recording of the research, the application of criteria, and analysis of the data. Care was taken to ensure that, in the interviews and written surveys, my attitudes did not intrude excessively by asking general and open ended questions, such as "what do you think of the video quality in this session?". Such questions do not predetermine participants' responses. As both of the two stages of evaluation were unrelated to their language programs, the participants did not have to please the researcher in order to obtain better grades. In this regard, my presence might be considered to have a minimum impact on the participants' performance in and perception of these videoconferencing sessions. Furthermore, issues which were unclear in my observations were invariably taken up in the interviews with the participants, and my observations were cross-checked with the participants' perceptions. In addition, all NetMeeting sessions were videotaped and interviews were audio taped for accurate data transcription and analysis, and for subsequent data validation. While I recognize that, as an active participant in the research procedure, there existed the possibility of intrusion of my values and assumptions, I strove to ensure that these would not skew the results. I did this in three ways: firstly, by being conscious of my role as a participant observer and "reflective practitioner" (Schön, 1983), who constantly reflected on the research methodology and practice; secondly, by scrupulous and systematic application of the criteria employed in the research procedure; and thirdly, by taking great care in drawing any conclusions from what the participants said in the surveys and interviews. I believe I was successful in these objectives, and that the data collected has veracity sufficient to draw conclusions about the utility of a videoconferencing-supported learning context for L2 acquisition in distance mode.

The choice of precisely which videoconferencing tool to use is another complication facing this research at a time when information and Internet technology is advancing rapidly. At the time that this research was undertaken, as can be seen in Section 3.2, NetMeeting was definitely the strongest product available. Inevitably, however, developments occur, and it might be replaced by more advanced products when this research is completed. In fact, NetMeeting 3.01 is the last version and

Microsoft has now incorporated the video and audio functions into MSN, which was originally a text chat tool.

3.6 Dealing with obsolescence

The issue of obsolescence of technology was recognized when selecting the appropriate videoconferencing tool for this research. As mentioned above, one of the distinctive difficulties and challenges involved in research with technology is its rapid replacement, often mid-stream. This is especially true with computer technology. However, inevitably, I had to conduct my research with a particular videoconferencing tool. The issue of obsolescence was dealt with in the following three ways. First, when deciding on a particular videoconferencing tool for this research, two issues were examined closely: the state-of-the art quality and capability of the technology, and its general applicability. In this way, a longer shelf life can be preserved. In this case, NetMeeting was chosen not only because of its cutting edge technology but also because it represents the future of Internet-based desktop videoconferencing. In fact, the basic technology of all Internet-based desktop videoconferencing tools is quite similar. The differences lie primarily in the video and audio quality and built-in features such as the Whiteboard and Document Sharing. In other words, the quality of a particular videoconferencing tool can be improved constantly, e.g. better video or audio quality, but the basic functionality of Internet-based desktop videoconferencing tools will not change dramatically in the near future. Second, when discussing NetMeeting, I endeavour to discuss general principles to ensure their general applicability when NetMeeting becomes obsolete.

Last but most importantly, there is a significant pedagogical concern at the heart of this research. This research only utilizes videoconferencing as a tool to achieve its pedagogical objectives, that is, to inform distance language professionals of the advancement in technology supporting oral-visual interaction, as well as the appropriate task design and performance supported by videoconferencing. In so doing, this research aims to fill a gap in videoconferencing task design and performance, and will serve as an icebreaker for distance language learning and research in terms of the use of Internet-based desktop videoconferencing. It also aims to provoke a change in thinking, that is, that language professional should utilize what is available to maximize the potential of distance language learning.

3.7 Summary

This chapter focuses on the methodological approaches relating to the investigation of *the benefits and limitations of oral-visual interaction via videoconferencing forL2 acquisition at a distance.* It first reported the findings from two preliminary studies – the survey on the learners' difficulty in L2 learning, and the initial evaluation of the four Internet-based desktop videoconferencing tools. The first preliminary case study confirmed that the lack of oral-visual interaction was still the most urgent problem facing learners in DLE, while the initial investigation of the four videoconferencing tools revealed the potential of NetMeeting in supporting the much-needed oral-visual interaction. Drawing on these findings, a two-stage formative evaluation of one particular videoconferencing tool, NetMeeting, was designed. This chapter then outlined the general methodological approaches to this evaluation. The interactive nature of the research problem determines the formative and qualitative nature of this investigation. Such qualitative nature, in turn, determined the adoption of a task-based approach in assessing the pedagogical values of videoconferencing-enabled interaction. The qualitative nature of the research also determines the data collection and analysis methods. Two sets of criteria were then developed for evaluating the technological capabilities of videoconferencing tools and the pedagogical values of videoconferencing-based interaction in task completion in the distance mode. These criteria bridge a gap in CMC research. Moreover, these two sets of criteria set the framework for the next three chapters, which present the data and analysis from the two-stage evaluation in the following two broad contexts: technology fit – the technological capabilities of NetMeeting in supporting oral-visual interaction in DLE – and task fit – the pedagogical values of videoconferencing-supported interaction in task completion.

Chapter Four

Results: The technological capabilities of NetMeeting in supporting oral-visual interaction

4.1 Introduction

The preliminary studies reported at the beginning of Chapter 3, especially the investigation of the four most popular videoconferencing tools, directed this research to the technological and pedagogical potential of one videoconferencing tool, NetMeeting. In order to examine its potential, a two-stage evaluation of NetMeeting was designed, involving on-campus Chinese language learners in Stage One and distance Chinese language learners in Stage Two. Criteria for evaluating the **technological** and **pedagogical** capabilities of videoconferencing-supported interaction were also developed (see Section 3.4.1 and 3.4.2). This chapter focuses on the extensive empirical investigation of the **technological** capabilities of NetMeeting in supporting oral-visual interaction to distance language learners, while Chapter 5 will concentrate on reporting the findings in regard to the **pedagogical** values of NetMeeting in the provision of oral-visual interaction to distance language learning. A more in-depth discussion on the findings presented in this chapter and Chapter 5 will be conducted in the discussion chapter, Chapter 6.

The presentation and preliminary discussion contained in this chapter followed the criteria (developed in Section 3.4.1) for selecting videoconferencing tools. These criteria are briefly summarized here:

- ◆ User friendliness
- ◆ Video and audio quality
- ◆ Reliability
- ◆ Other features of pedagogical value
- ◆ Cost (This issue will not be discussed here again as it has been dealt with in Section 3.2.2)

Data in relation to the above five criteria answered the second subsidiary research question from a technological perspective:

What are the benefits and limitations of videoconferencing-supported oral and visual interaction in the process of L2 acquisition?

As discussed in Chapter 3, Stage One (evaluation by on-campus students from Griffith University) was conducted between November 2001 and February 2002. Stage Two (evaluation by distance language students from the Open Learning Chinese Program at Griffith University) took place in March 2002 and concluded in December 2002. This chapter reports on the results from these two evaluations with an emphasis on Stage Two with the Open Learning students, as Stage One was planned and carried out as the preparatory phase for Stage Two.

4.2 The evaluation of NetMeeting – Stage One

4.2.1 Introduction

The results from this stage were mainly obtained from four sources: ongoing interviews carried out at the end of each videoconferencing session with each participant, a written survey at the end of each session with each participant, a journal recording my observations of the trial, and a final comprehensive interview at the end of the trial.

This stage of the evaluation of NetMeeting involved three on-campus students, who had just finished their first year Chinese in the face-to-face teaching mode. To model a distance-learning situation, the trial took place with me in my office at Griffith University and the participants at the Computer Lab in the School of Languages and Linguistics at Griffith University. It should be emphasized here that, although the teacher and the participants were situated at separate locations during NetMeeting sessions, this trial was performed in an **Intranet** environment, that is, the **Intranet** at Griffith University, not through the Internet. The objective of the trial was to test-run the NetMeeting sessions in order to debug the technology and the task design in a controlled environment before the final trial with the Open Learning students was launched in the Internet environment, which contains more variables. In other words, data collected from this trial was intended to inform the next phase of this research.

For ease of analysis and confidentiality, the participants in Stage One of the evaluation are referred to Student 1, Student 2 and Student 3. A total of 15 sessions were successfully conducted through NetMeeting with five sessions to each participant.

The length of each session ranged from one to one-and-a-half hours, excluding time for interviews. Data was presented in two formats – **personal observations,** as I personally conducted all the NetMeeting sessions, and **participants' perceptions** from the feedback contained in the written surveys and interviews. The personal and participant feedback on the technological capabilities of NetMeeting are largely positive, although there were a few problems. The feedback is discussed below under the five criteria for evaluating videoconferencing tools.

4.2.2　User friendliness

The examination of user friendliness entailed two dimensions: the ease of setting up the necessary components for NetMeeting-supported videoconferencing and the ease of use of NetMeeting. In a distance education context, where virtually no on-site technical support is available, students have to install NetMeeting by themselves. The lack of on-site support thus requires a clear and accessible instruction manual to be written for the success of the installation. In view of this necessity, I wrote an instruction manual (hereafter known as the *Manual*), which is contained in the *Student Handbook* (see Appendix C). The accuracy and clarity of the instructions in the *Manual* were then tested in this stage.

Ease of installation

Personal observations

The first thing each participant did was to set up NetMeeting following the *Manual*. Before the start of the first NetMeeting session, I went through the whole process of installing on the participants' computer the various components to support NetMeeting following the *Manual*, and tested the running of NetMeeting with a computer specialist. This was done for two reasons. First, I needed to ascertain that all of the system requirements were available, such as the connection to the Intranet and the necessary software on the computer. Secondly the clarity and accuracy of the *Manual* needed to be tested.

During the installation by the first participant, two computer experts and I were physically present in case any unexpected technical problems emerged. However, as this trial simulated a distance-learning environment, no further instruction or assistance was provided during the installation unless a problem occurred. I was the only person on site when students 2 and 3 set up NetMeeting. I observed that only Student 3 needed to be guided as to where to plug in the headphones. Students 1 and 2 both completed the whole process following the *Manual*, without the necessity of assistance.

On the whole the installation went very smoothly, even though none of the participants had used NetMeeting before. Table 4.1 shows the length of time each participant needed for completion of the whole installation process.

Table 4.1　Length of installation of NetMeeting in Stage One

Student 1	Student 2	Student 3
20 minutes	15 minutes	50 minutes

It is apparent from Table 4.1 that Students 1 and 2 took much less time than Student 3. On observation, Student 2 only followed the *Manual* at the beginning. She then set up everything following the instructions without looking at the *Manual*. She glanced quickly at the messages popping up during the installation and then clicked the right buttons. In contrast, Student 3 had to refer to the *Manual* constantly and read every message that appeared during the installation carefully before proceeding to the next step.

Participants' perceptions

A short evaluation form was administered at the end of the installation. Only two questions were contained in this survey:

1. How easy or difficult was it to set up NetMeeting?
2. Were the instructions for installing NetMeeting easy or difficult to follow?

Both were multiple-choice questions with five choices – very easy, easy, OK, difficult and very difficult. Table 4.2 summarizes the results for the two questions.

Table 4.2   Post-installation survey results in Stage One

	Student 1	Student 2	Student 3
Ease of installation	Very easy	Very easy	OK
Ease of instructions	Easy	Very easy	Easy

The interviews with the participants immediately following the installation also confirmed the results contained in Table 4.2 and revealed that Students 1 and 2 considered themselves quite good with computers; Student 3 mentioned that she only had basic computer skills.

All participants believed that they could set up NetMeeting by themselves following the *Manual*. However, the following improvements were suggested (in their own words).

♦ Instructions could be more detailed. (Student 1)

♦ …. But for some people I think you might need to put down more steps. Every step if there's more windows. Even if you just have to click 'accept' or 'OK', just to tell them that's coming up, for some people may not think it's normal and then they may not click but just cancel it without knowing. (Student 2)

♦ It might take some time for the programs to load on different people's computer because if they have a lot of information on the hard drive, it might take a while. If you let them know on the instruction sheet, they would be more patient. (Student 2)

- Probably you need some levels of understanding of computers before you start....(Student 3)

- Just probably the equipment.... You know plugging into the back, figure out which one to go to.... (Student 3)

To summarize, both my observation and the students' feedback indicate that the installation of the various components of NetMeeting by the students was not beyond their capability. Anyone with basic computer skills could install NetMeeting following well-written instructions, although it may take a longer time for students with inadequate computer skills. Furthermore, an accurate installation manual proved to be vital for the successful completion of the installation. This is especially true with students of lower computer literacy who do not have on-site technical support. These findings suggest that in the next stage of NetMeeting evaluation, more details and steps should be included in the *Manual*. Important screen layouts should be captured and inserted in the instructions to provide the participants with more visual information about the different components so that they would know what to expect.

Ease of use

Personal observations

As NetMeeting offers a simple interface design (see Figure 3.1) with far fewer functions than a word processor, participants became familiar with the few functions almost immediately. Figure 3.1 is reproduced here for ease of reference.

Figure 3.1   The interface of NetMeeting

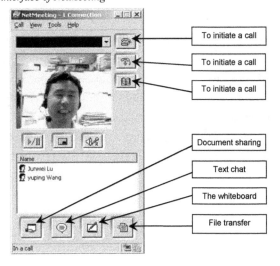

Little time was spent on teaching the participants how to use the program because all the icons were self-explanatory. The only problem observed was that some participants tended to forget to activate the video at the beginning of the NetMeeting sessions. However the problem was quickly solved by reminding them through the audio function. In fact, after the audio and video channels were established, few actions were needed unless one wanted to make use of other features such as the Whiteboard or File Transfer. A simple click on the icons of these features would activate them. After using these functions once, all participants knew how to use them. In fact Student 3 initiated the use of the whiteboard in every session after the first session.

Participants' perceptions

At the end of session five, the last session, a comprehensive interview was conducted with each participant. When asked if NetMeeting was easy to use, all participants confirmed its ease of use. For example, Student 2 said: "Yeah, I think it is very easy".

To summarize, the ease of use of NetMeeting was both observed by the researcher and commented on by the participants. The simple and distinctive layout and the fewer icons in the interface created a less intimidating atmosphere for language learning. NetMeeting proved to be a tool for any user with or without experience with videoconferencing tools. These findings further supported the results from the preliminary studies regarding NetMeeting's user friendliness.

4.2.3   The audio and video quality

The audio quality

Personal observations

The sound quality in the Intranet environment was found to be more or less the quality of an international call. Although the sound was slightly muffled at times, it was sufficiently clear and continuous for interacting in the target language. Conversations generally flowed thanks to the consistency of the sound quality. As expected, a delay of 1 to 2 seconds was noticed in the transmission of sound from one end to the other, although it generally did not affect the flow of interaction. It was also noted that, at the start of some sessions, the sound could be expected to fade in and out for a period varying from a few seconds to a minute, but became steady soon afterwards. However, breakdowns occurred more because of unknown linguistic elements than problems with the sound. Focus on form was successfully achieved (see Section 5.2.2). The sound quality was also tested through correction of the participants' pronunciation and they could distinguish the differences in the pronunciation.

Participants' perceptions

In regard to the sound quality of NetMeeting, two issues were discussed with the participants: what the sound quality for each session was like and whether it reached a satisfactory level for learning Chinese. Table 4.3 summarizes the participants' responses in regard to the sound quality of each session as reflected in the post-session interviews.

Table 4.3 Results from post-session interviews in Stage One – responses to the question regarding sound quality

	Session 1	Session 2	Session 3	Session 4
Student 1	Could be better Occasional fading in and out	Better today	OK Occasional fading in and out	OK, occasional fading in and out
Student 2	It's not too bad	Very good	Really good	Good
Student 3	Good	Much better	OK	Very good

Note: Only 4 post-session interviews for each participant were conducted because at the end of the fifth session, a comprehensive interview was performed in regard to the whole trial.

A number of indications can be derived from Table 4.3. Firstly, Table 4.3 seems to reflect a pattern in the participants' perceptions, that is, as the sessions progressed, the participants seemed to grow more accustomed to and more receptive of the sound quality. The following two factors might have affected this perception. As these on-campus participants had been accustomed to face-to-face lectures and tutorials, and none of them had had any previous experience with videoconferencing, they used the quality of face-to-face teaching as their point of reference when judging the quality of the sound of the first few sessions. Furthermore, participants grew accustomed to the sound quality after the first sessions. The following excerpt from the interview with Student 3 at the end of Session One supports this trend.

> It's not too bad. At first it's like "oh it's not that good". You don't think it's that good.
> But when it's all you're hearing, then it becomes fine. You get used to it.

The second implication derived from Table 4.3 is that the sound quality was generally considered to be good throughout the 12 sessions despite its occasional fading in and out.

Students' responses to the question soliciting their opinions on whether the sound quality was good enough for learning Chinese also confirm the acceptability of the sound quality for language teaching. In fact, all participants believed that the sound quality was good enough for language learning. (extracts of the interviews are contained in Appendix E)

The video quality

Personal observations

It was observed that the quality of the video reached a satisfactory standard for language learning despite the fact that it was still not up to the quality of a television broadcast in terms of image stability and resolution. The resolution was acceptable for language learning with the normal video window size but was reduced when the video window was enlarged. (There are four window sizes to choose from – 100%, 200%, 300% and 400%.) At the same time a slight delay in the synchrony of sound and video was also experienced, with the video transmission lagging behind the sound by less than 1 second. However, such delay did not cause any disruption to interaction as discussed earlier because "the sound and image can still be perceived to be synchronous" with a delay of less 80 msec. (Bruce, 1996, p. 173). Furthermore, there was no eye contact similar to that experienced in face-to-face interaction. When one party was looking at the video window depicting the other party on the screen, the perception was that the person on the other end was looking down and not directly at the other party. This was caused by the position of the camera on top of the computer. Subtle movements of the lips could not be seen clearly unless the student's attention was brought to those movements by slowing them down to show the differences in pronunciation. Body movements were mostly confined to above the shoulders, unless one sat further back from the Web Cam.

Despite the above imperfections, it can be concluded that the video quality had reached a satisfactory level for language teaching in an Intranet supported videoconference. This is because the video transmission, on the whole, was continuous with insignificant delays. Furthermore, facial expressions, such as a smile, a surprised or a puzzled look, or a nod, were all present synchronously. These visual cues are all important for negotiation of meaning in distance language learning.

Participants' perceptions

Data from the interviews and surveys show that the video quality was generally considered to be satisfactory and good enough for language learning, despite the emergence of several problems.

First, the above-mentioned lag between the sound and video was also noticed by the participants. Although this delay was not considered by Student 1 to have a disruptive impact on negotiation of meaning during task performance, it was believed to have rendered the conversation less natural, as Student 1 expressed in the interview at the end of Session One.

Student 1:	[...]. Ah there is a little bit of delay between the facial expression and the speech.
R:	So that affected your understanding?
Student 1:	It doesn't affect the understanding but it can affect the situation.

R:	Situation?
Student 1:	Just the feeling of the situation. You were talking, by the time they hear, it's maybe already too late.
R:	Did that make you misunderstand something?
Student 1:	I guess not.
R:	Do you think it's good enough for teaching?
Student 1:	Yeah.

Secondly, as observed, the video image was reported to be unstable. A blurry image could occur if the person moved too much in front of the Webcam. Student 1 also reported, at the end of Session Two, that the video image actually "blacked out" once or twice during the session. It was discovered later that this occasional disappearance of video was caused by activating the My Video function by the other party. It was a normal occurrence lasting about one second every time the My Video function was initiated.

In spite of these problems, participants still reported that the video was clear enough to show paralinguistic cues. Student 3 commented at the end of Session Four as follows:

[the video quality was] really good. Like I could tell when I said "bu yinhang"(not, bank), and you sort of went like "hm"....and I could tell by the look on your face that I said something really wrong there.

All participants believed that the quality of the video attained a satisfactory level for language learning. For example, Student 2 commented on the video quality at the end of Session One:

Student 2:	Very good.
R:	So you could see me clearly?
Student 2:	Yeah.
R:	[...] And did you think it's good enough for teaching?
Student 2:	Yeah.

In summary, data from both my observations and the students' feedback confirms the high quality of the video – continuous, instantaneous, and clear with good resolution. Furthermore, the video and sound were sufficiently synchronized with no significant delays that would interrupt the flow of interaction. All participants held that the quality of the video was good enough for learning Chinese.

4.2.4 Other features of pedagogical value

Apart from audio and video, four other major features of NetMeeting were tested for their pedagogical values: the Whiteboard, Document Sharing, File Transfer and My Video. (For detailed discussion on the functions of these features, see Section 3.3.)

The Whiteboard

Personal observations

The on-screen whiteboard was used in this trial in a similar way to the use of the whiteboard in a face-to-face lecture. It was employed for two main purposes: to write unknown or unfamiliar Chinese characters for the participants and to draw maps demonstrating locations and directions. (see Figure 4.1)

Figure 4.1   Whiteboard content of Session Three with Student 2

Although the use of the whiteboard was originally designed for only two sessions, it was used in every session. There were several occasions in which students initiated the use of it when they wanted to show something in writing. In fact, Student 3 activated the whiteboard first at the beginning of each session following Session One. It was observed that usually students with lower language proficiency relied more heavily on the use of the whiteboard for negotiation of meaning and for ensuring understanding.

Participants' perceptions

Data from the post-session surveys confirms that the whiteboard was considered very useful for language learning. Of the six responses received, five were 'very useful' and only one was 'useful'. No one responded that the whiteboard was not useful. (see Appendix M)

In the Post-trial interviews, all participants rated the whiteboard as the most useful feature compared to File Transfer and Document Sharing. Responses to the question about the feature that they **enjoyed** most also point to the whiteboard, as shown in the following extract from the post-trial interview:

Student 3: Sharing, the whiteboard. I love it.

R: Comparing sharing and the whiteboard, which one did you enjoy most?

Student 3: Whiteboard.

On the whole, the above-discussed data demonstrates the participants' strong preference for the Whiteboard over Document Sharing and File Transfer in terms of its pedagogical usefulness. This positive perception of the whiteboard further confirms the crucial nature of the visual in terms of audio-visual kinetics.

Document Sharing

Personal observations

The Document Sharing function was tested on two occasions so that each participant could view the documents on my computer. It was first used to share and view a photo (240kB) found on the Internet. The second occasion was to look at a menu (a 32 kB Word document) prepared by the teacher beforehand in a Word document. It was found that both the photo and the Menu could be shared with the other party almost instantly and with the same quality as in the original documents. The participants were pleasantly surprised to see the photo and the menu suddenly appearing on their screen. As a result, lively discussions in the target language occurred around these shared documents.

Participants' perceptions

The post-session surveys show that of the six responses received, four chose "very useful" and two "useful" (see Appendix M for results). The post-trial interviews yielded the same results – the function of Document Sharing was very useful, second only to the Whiteboard. Student 1 commented that: "Sharing is useful too" because "it's as close as you can get to face-to-face contact."

File Transfer

Personal observations

This function enables the teacher or the learner to transfer prepared files of multi pages or segments to the other party so that the receiving party can view it immediately or save it for later use. This function was also under evaluation on two occasions to facilitate interactions between the two parties during task completion. A video clip of 2.41MB was sent to the students via File Transfer, simulating an answering machine with a recorded message for the participant to listen to. The participants were also requested to send me a Word document through this function. Both files were transferred instantly with the original quality retained. The participants were instructed through NetMeeting on how to transfer their files to the teacher and the transfer went smoothly.

Participants' perceptions

Results from the post-session surveys show that File Transfer was perceived to be useful for language learning with responses ranging from 'very useful' to 'OK'. For details of the survey results, see Appendix M.

My Video

No special use of My Video was planned in these sessions apart from using it to monitor my teaching. Without the interference from the network, the video was of high resolution with superb clarity and consistency. I found it very useful in adjusting my expressions for negotiation of meaning. For example, when I did not understand the participants' input, I could quickly monitor my expression and adjust it to one of a puzzled look.

4.2.5   Reliability of NetMeeting

No videoconferencing session failed because of a crash of NetMeeting itself. Neither did its functions such as the audio and video, the Whiteboard, File Transfer and Document Sharing fail to perform during this stage of the trial. In fact, every session was successfully completed, although three had to be rescheduled due to problems irrelevant to the reliability of NetMeeting (see Section 4.2.6). The reliability of NetMeeting has profound implications for language learning in that it ensures the success of videoconferencing sessions. NetMeeting proved to be a mature and reliable tool for language learning.

4.2.6   Technical problems unrelated to NetMeeting

Among the completed 15 sessions of videoconferencing, three sessions had to be rescheduled due to technical problems. The first instance occurred when the sound volume was accidentally muted on my computer resulting in no sound coming through my computer. The session was rescheduled because I could not pinpoint the muted sound volume as the source of the problem at the scheduled time for the NetMeeting session. The second session was aborted because the Intranet was down for maintenance, unbeknown to me at the time of the session. The third failure was caused by access denied to MSN. It was later discovered that to sign into MSN, I needed to first sign into NetCheck, an Internet accounting and management system newly installed by Griffith University at the time of the trial. I was not aware of its function at that time.

The examination of the causes for the three failed sessions indicates that these problems were minor and not insurmountable. However they did affect teaching plans and may have had an adverse effect on the learner's perceptions of videoconferencing tools and their learning experience. Thus, when using a technology, one should be prepared for the appearance of unexpected technical problems. Sometimes a minor problem, technical or non-technical, can abort a videoconferencing session if one cannot pinpoint the problem at the time of the session. This is especially true for users with basic computer skills at a time when Internet technology is developing rapidly.

4.2.7 Summary and implications for Stage Two evaluation of technological aspects of NetMeeting

Data from the Stage One evaluation of NetMeeting strongly confirms the technological capabilities of desktop videoconferencing tools in supporting oral-visual interaction in language learning. The trial on the whole was a success. Despite the relatively small number of participants, this evaluation thoroughly examined the capabilities of videoconferencing and participants' perceptions of this new medium. In the Intranet environment, NetMeeting proved to have reached a satisfactory level of quality and sophistication for supporting one-to-one interaction in real-time synchronous language learning. The most important finding is that both the video and audio were synchronized to a real-time standard with sufficient clarity and minimum delays. In contrast to most commercially available desktop videoconferencing tools, which are often chat tools, other features of NetMeeting also proved to be pedagogically valuable and mature enough for language learning, e.g. the Whiteboard, File Transfer and Document Sharing. The whiteboard was especially favoured by all participants, and its indispensability to language learning was strongly emphasized in the interviews and surveys. Furthermore, NetMeeting's user friendliness offered a relaxing environment for language learning. NetMeeting performed reliably with a crash rate of zero. Without a high level of reliability, videoconferencing would be impossible.

These results have profound implications for distance language learning, as this research is essentially concerned with the provision of oral-visual interaction, an indispensable and key component in communicative distance language learning. For the first time in DLE history, the high performance standard of NetMeeting promises a viable and economical solution to the urgent problem facing DLE – the lack of oral-visual interaction. This means we may now be able to provide distance language learners at home with much needed oral-visual interaction that would have been otherwise unavailable to them. The distance between the learner and education provider may be minimized through desktop videoconferencing tools, which have now proved to be mature, sophisticated and affordable. At the very least, the results from this phase of the evaluation qualify the possibility and necessity of the next stage – the evaluation in the Internet environment with distance language learners.

4.3 The evaluation of NetMeeting – Stage Two

This section reports firstly the results from a pre-trial survey, which was considered as a necessary precondition to the launch of the Stage Two evaluation of NetMeeting. It then presents the results from this stage with preliminary discussions.

A total of 29 tutorial sessions of NetMeeting were attempted in this stage, with 19 successful sessions and 10 unsuccessful ones. Data consists of my personal observations of these sessions, results from the post-session interviews and post-trial written survey results. Findings are presented following the same criteria employed in Stage One of the evaluation, and are summarized as follows:

- user friendliness
- audio and video quality
- other features of pedagogical value
- reliability

Results are discussed in comparison with the findings from Stage One wherever it is applicable so that a more detailed analysis can be achieved on the technical capabilities of NetMeeting. To distinguish from those in Stage One, the participants in this trial are referred to Participants A, B, C, D, and E. It should be noted that Participant C only completed the first three sessions and withdrew from the trial due to personal problems. She did not complete the post-trial survey either.

Prior to the start of the trial, the following additional resources were provided by the researcher to the participants, to minimize their costs:

1. a WebCam (a web camera) and the set up CD ROM,
2. a headphone,
3. a copy of the Student Handbook containing information for the trial and the Manual for setting up NetMeeting (see Appendix G),
4. a gift pack to show my appreciation for the students' participation.

4.3.1 Pre-trial survey

The pre-trial survey was conducted through e-mail in March 2002. A total of 11 e-mails with survey questionnaires attached were sent out to all students enrolled in CHN21 in the Open Learning Chinese program offered at Griffith University (see the questionnaire in Appendix H). There were two objectives of the survey. One was to invite students' participation in the trial and the other was to determine whether the students possessed the necessary computer resources to enable their participation. The issue of access to computer and Internet resources had been discussed in the CALL literature and regarded as an area of concern. (see Williams and Sharma, 1988)

For those who had expressed interest in participating in the trial, the survey also asked them to explain why they wanted to take part in the trial. The major reason for participating in the trial was to improve their spoken Chinese, as shown in the following replies.

- ♦ I find it very difficult having nobody to speak Chinese with.

- ♦ I would like to improve my spoken Chinese. I am a little apprehensive about it all, as I have never used Webcam before, and also seem to have a mental blank when I try to speak Chinese! But I suppose if I can get over that initial fear, then I will improve heaps.

- ♦ Hopefully to gain an additional medium to help me with my Chinese studies and the opportunity to contribute to the development of new ways of instruction that would benefit all students that study Chinese through Open Learning.

- ♦ [...] I would welcome the opportunity to have some ongoing conversation practice, because I find learning at home a little like learning in a vacuum – I long to have someone to talk to in Chinese, to develop some confidence, spontaneity and skill. I find now that I tend to "freeze" when someone uses Chinese to address me. Another reason is to develop a more personal relationship with you, because of your role in my learning. Finally I am so enthusiastic about my studies that I try to take up any opportunity offered.

As shown in the above replies, confidence building through these NetMeeting sessions was another major incentive for participating in the trial.

Survey results also show that the five participants all had computers, varying from IBM, Pentium 1, Pentium 2, and Pentium 3. They all used up-to-date operating systems with three Windows 98 and two Windows 2000. All five used Internet Explorer, with three having version 5.0, one version 4.0, and one version 6.0, which are all adequate to support NetMeeting. This simple survey informed the research that all the participants possessed the basic resources needed for this trial.

Therefore my concern that the learners might have problems in accessing computer resources and the Internet was not borne out.

4.3.2   User friendliness

The main concerns in this criterion are the ease of installing NetMeeting and the effectiveness of its interface design. Data presented here were obtained from two surveys – a post installation survey and a post-trial survey.

Ease of Installation

Personal observations
In this trial with the distance participants, I was unable to observe personally the installation process by each participant due to the distance between us. However, the participants were instructed to set up NetMeeting following the *Manual* contained in the Student Handbook (see Appendix G) as soon as they received the above-mentioned package. A Wednesday was set aside for enquiries concerning the installation, and an 1800 toll-free number was provided for such enquiries. However, all five participants set up NetMeeting without requesting any assistance from me, although I later learned that some of them obtained various degrees of help in installation from their family members or technicians at work.

Participants' perceptions
A brief post-installation survey was e-mailed to each participant to determine the level of difficulty of the installation (see Appendix I). Question I-Q1 asks the participants to choose from five choices – very easy, easy, OK, difficult and very difficult – in regard to the level of difficulty of installation. In comparison with the responses from the on-campus students, in this phase, participants' responses on installation are more diverse ranging from very easy to difficult, as shown in Appendix I.

Answers to question I-Q2 regarding the clarity of the *Manual* were more positive, ranging from very easy to OK. A consensus was reached that the *Manual* was written with sufficient clarity and accessibility. This finding corresponds with the responses from the on-campus participants.

Question I-Q3 is an open-ended question requesting the participants to write down the length of time that they took to install NetMeeting. (see Table 4.4)

Table 4.4 indicates that the Open Learning participants seemed to have taken a longer time to complete the installation, averaging around one hour, in contrast to most on-campus students who took less than half an hour. A number of factors contributed to the lengthy time spent by the Open

Learning students. First, they had to download NetMeeting from the Internet if they used a Windows program lower than Windows 2000, while on-campus students all used Windows 2000, in which NetMeeting was incorporated. Second, the on-campus students used the Intranet, which offers much faster downloading speed when they downloaded other programs, such as MSN Messenger, while most Open Learning participants had to download through a modem, which usually slows down the downloading speed.

Table 4.4   Survey on installation in Stage Two – length of time for setting up NetMeeting

Participant A	Participant B	Participant C	Participant D	Participant E
1 hour	1.5 hours	1 hour	20 minutes	A few weeks *

*Note: * Participant E had a faulty Webcam that had to be replaced.*

Again, similar to the response from the On-campus students, there is a correlation between the time the participants took to set up NetMeeting and their perception of how easy the installation was. To be more specific, the longer it took, the more difficult the installation seemed to the participants.

I-Q4 invited students to comment on the whole installation process, and answers to this question can be summarized as follows (see Appendix I for original replies):

♦ The installation itself was a straightforward process.

♦ The *Manual* was a useful reference.

♦ Some basic information, such as where to plug in the microphone and speakers and how to adjust the Webcam, should be included in the *Manual*.

Ease of use

Personal observations

The participants seemed to be very confident in operating NetMeeting during our sessions, thanks to the simple interface design. When we were connected, the sound and video was automatically on. However, it was often in the initial connection that we experienced difficulties. Although most of the time the connection was straightforward, sometimes we could not hear or see each other or, if we invited each other at the same time, the system would become too confused to launch NetMeeting. However, once the initial connection was set up, the conference usually went smoothly.

Participants' perceptions

In the post-trial survey, question PTS-2.12 asked the participants to rate the ease of use of NetMeeting on a 10 point scale. (see Figure 4.2)

Figure 4.2   Results from Stage Two evaluation – the ease of use of NetMeeting (PTS-2.12)

Very easy								Very difficult	
1	2	3	4	5	6	7	8	9	10
x (A)		x (B)	x (E)	x (D)					

Note: 1. x represents the choice of the participants.
2. Participant C did not complete the survey.

Figure 4.2 shows that participants' responses concentrated on the "very easy" end of the scale. Participant D's choice was a function of the difficulties that he experienced during the evaluation, such as a faulty headphone and a firewall in his Internet Service Provider. (see Section 4.3.6)

PTS-2.12 further invited the participants to comment on their choices on the scale, and the following explanations were offered:

- ◆ Netmeeting [NetMeeting] was very easy to use, as the program is user friendly, and simple to follow. (Participant A)

- ◆ […] the actual Netmeeting [NetMeeting] program is very user friendly, and easy to operate. My low rating is due to the initial connection difficulties. (Participant E)

- ◆ The visual layout of the program window and the conveniently arranged buttons for the ancillary features (whiteboard, file share etc) were not too numerous and complex…. (Participant B)

The issue of user friendliness was also discussed with the participants in the post-session interviews. All responses concurred that NetMeeting was very user friendly. For example, at the end of Session Five, Participant B commented:

Oh I found it easy enough. You know, it's not too overloaded. There's not a lot of functions in the tool bar. It's easy enough to handle.

In conclusion, although the participants only had a basic level of computer literacy, none was unable to set up NetMeeting. As expected, some students found it easy and others found it less easy, all depending on the individual student's computer skills and knowledge.

4.3.3   The audio and video quality

The audio quality

As mentioned in Section 3.3.4, Stage Two of the evaluation was conducted in three network environments: modem-Internet-modem, LAN-Internet-Modem and LAN-Internet-LAN. Data from this phase of the evaluation is presented separately on each environment so that a precise account of what happened in each environment can be depicted.

The audio quality in the modem-Internet-modem environment

<u>Personal Observations</u>

As reported in Section 3.3.4, at the beginning of Stage Two, it was discovered that there was a firewall blocking the access of NetMeeting from an outside party. To bypass this firewall, a modem was used instead of a LAN. This meant that a longer delay could be expected. Findings from sessions in this network environment confirm the existence of a longer delay and the detrimental influence of the Internet traffic.

A total of nine out of the 29 sessions were conducted in the modem-Internet-modem environment. On average, the sound quality of the successful sessions was generally clear and continuous enough for accomplishing the planned tasks, if the timing of the sessions was right. However, it was still not as consistent as that in an Intranet environment, and a delay in transmission was more noticeable than in an Intranet situation, but not prominent enough to hinder the general flow of the interaction. A major issue in the sound quality was its instability. In some sessions, the sound quality was quite similar to that in an Intranet environment, but in others the sound was unreliable – sometimes clear and continuous and sometimes jammed and lost. Similar to the sound quality in Stage One, it was also observed that during the first 10 to 20 seconds, the sound was usually unstable and of poor quality, but it subsequently improved.

One of the most notable discoveries in this stage of the evaluation was the timing of the NetMeeting sessions. It became clear that, with the present generation of Internet bandwidth, choosing a less congested Internet time was crucial to the success of NetMeeting sessions. In the Intranet environment, timing was never an issue. No noticeable difference in video or audio quality had been detected between different times of the day. However, timing became an essential issue when using the Internet. At a time when the Internet was less congested, the video and audio quality could almost reach the Intranet quality. It was discovered that early in the morning (before 8:00 o'clock) and weekends were the best times for NetMeeting sessions. Other times could make videoconferencing impossible. For example, Session Two with participant B took place between 8:30 and 9:30 o'clock on a Wednesday evening. This was probably a time when there was heavy usage of the Internet. Both the sound and video quality were so bad that we could hardly communicate. Often half of a sentence was lost and the sound seemed to become stuck a few times resulting in a loss of words or unintelligible sounds with echoing. However, when the sound did come through, it was quite clear although sometimes it became intermittently very loud and faint. The video image was much delayed and froze from time to time.

Participants' perceptions corresponded largely to my observations – the sound was good enough for interacting in the target language but unstable at times. Table 4.5 summarizes the feedback on the sound quality of the nine sessions in the modem-Internet-modem environment.

Table 4.5   Results from the post-session interviews in Stage Two – all participants' responses regarding the sound quality in the modem-Internet-modem environment

Participant	Session 1	Session 2	Session 3	Session 4	Session 5
	Wed. 5:00–6:00pm	Wed. 5:00–6:00pm			
A	Sometimes it was really good, sometimes it broke into little segments.	A lot better first but became a bit fuzzy towards the end. On the whole, a little bit better.			
	Sat. 6:50pm–7:20pm	Wed. 8:25pm–9:20pm	Sat. 10:30pm–midnight	Wed. 7:30pm–8:30pm	Sat. 9:30pm–11:00pm
B	Good.	Very bad, disconcerting, distracting.	Good, definitely better than the previous session.	Quite good, better than last session at the start, but broken up a bit at the end.	Very good, the best out of the five sessions.
	Sun. 10:00am–11:30am	Sat. 10:00am–1:00am			
C	Very good and continuous with only a few occasions when the sound got stuck.	When it's running alright, very clear, but getting worse towards later in the morning.			

Note: Participants' feedback was only solicited on the successful sessions in the modem-Internet-modem environment. Participants D and E did not use this Internet environment.

These responses in Table 4.5 suggest that the sound quality was generally acceptable – continuous and clear if the sessions were conducted early in the morning before 8:00 o'clock or weekends. The following transcript of the post-session interview at the end of Session Five provides a more detailed account of the participants' perceptions of the sound quality. This session was conducted between 9:30am–11:00am on a Saturday.

Participant B: It was quite good until the end, it started to sort of break up a little bit.

R: [...] So at first it was OK, was it?

Participant B:	Yeah, it was quite good actually.
R:	Quite good. So compared with the last session, was it getting better or worse? Or the same?
Participant B:	I remember our last session was not too bad either. I think the quality, if anything, was a bit better early on.

To summarize, while timing was never an issue in Stage One in the Intranet environment, with no noticeable difference in video or audio quality between different times of the day, timing became a crucial factor in the Internet environment. Internet conditions such as bandwidth and latency became critical. Nevertheless, the sound quality in this environment reached a satisfactory standard for language learning, corresponding with the results from Stage One of the evaluation.

The audio quality in the LAN-Internet-Modem environment

Personal observations

In this network environment, LAN was used instead of a dial-up modem at my end, but on the participants' side, a modem was still used for the connection to the Internet. Of the 29 completed sessions, 13 were carried out in the LAN-Internet-modem environment with five successful sessions. Eight sessions failed, not because of this environment or NetMeeting itself, but because of such problems as the firewall. (A detailed discussion of these problems is contained in Section 4.3.6.) In this network environment, a faster transmission was experienced on my side resulting in clearer sound and more continuous video images.

Participants' perceptions

On the participants' side, the judgment of the improvement in sound quality was mixed. Their feedback is provided in Table 4.6.

Participant A did not seem to have noticed an obvious improvement on her side when asked about the sound quality of Session Three, Four and Five in the post-session interviews (see Appendix F). Unlike Participant A, Participant C noticed better sound quality even at 3:00 o'clock on a Friday afternoon, a comparatively busy Internet time, compared with her two previous sessions on weekends.

Participant C:	It was good today. We had a little bit um [echo at time, but that wasn't too bad.
[...]	
R:	Do you think it's better than before?
Participant C:	Oh yeah, yeah.

The difference between the sound quality experienced by Participants A and C may be caused by the different quality of the sound cards on their computers.

Table 4.6   Results from the post-session interviews in Stage Two – all participants' responses regarding the sound quality in the LAN-Internet-modem environment

Participant	Session 1	Session 2	Session 3	Session 4	Session 5
A			Really bad for about 20 seconds in the beginning, but for the majority of the lesson, it was very good.	Very good, but a little bit worse than normal.	Good, same as the last session.
C			Really good and clear.		
D					Quite good
					It crackled a bit. A little bit delay.

* Note: Participants' feedback was only solicited on the successful sessions in the LAN-Internet-modem environment.

The audio quality in the LAN-Internet-LAN environment

<u>Personal observations</u>

In such an environment, with the exception of the Internet section in the middle, data travelled through a much wider cable (LAN) at both the teacher's and the participants' ends without using a modem. The seven sessions with Participant E were conducted in this environment because Participant E was able to use both her school Intranet and a computer laboratory at Deakin University. All seven sessions with her were carried out at a distance of more than 2,000 kilometres and on weekdays between 2:00pm to 6:00pm, a peak period for Internet traffic. Of the seven sessions, two failed because of the existence of a firewall in either her school's Intranet or in Netspace, their ISP (Internet Service Provider). During the two failed sessions, I could see and hear her with absolute clarity during all the sessions in this stage of the trial. Unfortunately, she could not hear and see me at all. Every time I invited her to start NetMeeting, a message would appear on my computer screen saying that the person was unable to accept NetMeeting calls. This occurrence seemed to suggest a firewall blocking my access to her.

The five successful sessions were all completed at Deakin University. It was observed that the audio was consistently clear and continuous with delays up to one second. Occasional background noise did occur but, on the whole, the sound was as constantly stable and clear as in an Intranet environment on my side. In fact, I had the best audio quality among the 19 successful sessions with the distance participants.

In contrast to my observation, the sound quality on the Participant's side was not reported to be as good as it should be. Table 4.7 summarizes Participant E's comments on the audio quality of NetMeeting in the interviews immediately following each session.

Table 4.7   Results from the post-session interviews in Stage Two – all participant's responses regarding the sound quality in the LAN-Internet-LAN environment

Participant	Session 1	Session 2	Session 3	Session 4	Session 5
E	Good, but with crackly interference.	Not so good, Fading in and out.	Much better than the previous two sessions.	Sometimes it was good, sometimes it was worse. Second best.	Same as Session 4

Note: Participants' feedback was only solicited about the successful sessions.

The computing power of her laptop may have been a determining factor in her critical assessment of the audio quality, because many functions of laptops are compressed, limiting the power to support quality audio or video transmission. This also explains the crackling sound she heard at times.

The following excerpt from the post-session interview at the completion of Session Four further explains her perception of the sound quality.

Participant E: OK. Well it wasn't wonderful quality.

R: So you heard some crackling sound?

Participant E: I did.

R: Apart from that, what else did you...

Participant E: Apart from that, it wasn't bad. It was, the major thing that happens is when you are saying a sentence, I get crackles that have the effect of stopping me from hearing a few of the words in the sentence.

[...]

Participant E: [...]. But sometimes it's good, sometimes it's worse. It varies a lot in the course.

To summarize the findings in relation to the three network environments, the best video and audio quality was achieved in the LAN-Internet-LAN environment and the most uncontrollable environment was the modem-Internet-modem one. On the whole, in the Internet environment the audio quality was not as good as that in an Intranet environment, with more problems experienced in the Modem-Internet-modem environment. The main difference in sound quality lies in its instability – at times, it could be as clear and continuous as that using a LAN, but sometimes it could be broken and lost. However, 19 NetMeeting sessions with the distance students were successfully completed and the participants were all very positive about this learning experience.

The video quality

Again findings in relation to the video quality of NetMeeting are categorized into three network conditions: modem-Internet-modem, LAN-Internet-modem, and LAN-Internet-LAN. Two issues are covered in the findings and discussions: what the quality of video was like in the three environments and whether it was adequate for supporting oral-visual interaction in distance language learning.

The video quality in the modem-Internet-modem environment

Personal observations

The video on my side, though not as clear as in the Intranet environment and often more delayed, was usually continuous and presented paralinguistic cues accurately and spontaneously. Signs of comprehension, frustration, nervousness and enjoyment were all evident in real time. Through the video, I demonstrated how to pronounce a word or how to position the tongue when producing a sound. Delays in transmission were not quite as obvious during continuous speech but became noticeable during turn takings, sometimes causing start up collisions or false starts.

A major problem with the video was the freezing of the image caused either by congested Internet traffic or the limited capacity of participants' computers. The length that the image was frozen could vary from one to ten seconds with the exception of Session Two, in which the image of Participant B was frozen for the entire session.

Participants' perceptions

Again, the video quality varied from participant to participant and from session to session, although the participants' perceptions of the video were always positive as far as its pedagogical values were concerned. Feedback is summarized in Table 4.8.

Participant B seemed to have good video images throughout the sessions except for Session 2. When asked to compare the video quality in Session Four and Session Three (which he said was quite good), he offered:

Participant B: It [Session 4] was better actually initially, and again towards the end, I guess the Net gets busier, it started to sort of you know break up the image. But in, in the beginning, it was very good, very good quality I feel.

R: So when I showed you how to write the character with my finger, could you see it clearly?

Participant B: Yes.

R: Good enough for learning Chinese?

Participant B: Yes, definitely.

Again, although the video quality was not ideal in this environment, all participants perceived it to be adequate for language learning.

Table 4.8   Results from the post-session interviews in Stage Two – all participants' responses regarding the Video quality in the modem-Internet-modem environment

Participant	Session 1	Session 2	Session 3	Session 4	Session 5
A	OK. Sometimes there was a delay.	Good. Better than last session with fewer delays and less freezing.			
B	Quite good.	Better than last session.	Quite good.	Very good at the beginning but the image broke up a bit towards the end of the session.	Very good.
C	Good.	Most of the time, it's very good.			

Note: Participants' feedback was only solicited on the successful sessions in the modem-Internet- modem environment.

The video quality in the LAN-Internet-modem environment

Personal observations

Similar to the sound quality, the video quality was noticeably better on my side with clearer and more continuous images and less delays. Again, similar to participants' comments on the sound quality, quite dissimilar opinions on the improvement of the video quality were offered by the participants.

Participants' perceptions

Participant A did not notice any obvious improvement in comparison with the previous sessions. However, Participant C observed a difference in the video quality between the modem-Internet-modem and LAN-Internet-modem environments. Table 4.9 summarizes participants' comments.

At the conclusion of Session Three, Participant C commented on the improved quality of the video as follows:

Participant C: It was go:od. And I got the picture through well, and I could see you and the whiteboard was, was clear. So there was no problem.

[...]

R:	Compared with the previous sessions?
Participant C:	Oh I think compared with the last one, it was much better. The picture last time, your, your video was very a stop starting. This time, it was fairly continuous. I got the picture all the time.

Despite the difference they saw in the improvement of the video quality, both Participant A and C believed that the video quality reached a satisfactory level of performance for supporting language learning at a distance. For example, at the interview following the completion of Session Five, Participant A commented that the video quality was good enough for learning Chinese and that "it's good to see facial expressions" and "have that facial contact". Participant C also confirmed the capability of the video in supporting distance language learning by saying that she could see the movements of my lips and so on when she needed to. (see Appendix F for detailed transcripts of the interview at the end of Session Three)

Table 4.9   Results from the post-session interviews in Stage Two – all participants' responses regarding the video quality in the LAN-Internet-modem environment

Participant	Session 1	Session 2	Session 3	Session 4	Session 5
A			Fine. It was probably better than previous sessions. Quite continuous.	Good. A few little delays. A little bit worse than previous sessions.	Good. Just a delay in the first 20 seconds.
C			Very good. Much better than the last session.		
D					Very good. Sometimes it froze for half a second.

Note: Participants' feedback was only solicited on the successful sessions in the LAN-Internet-modem environment.

The video quality in the LAN-Internet-LAN environment

Personal observations

On my side, I enjoyed the highest and most consistent quality of the video transmission among the sessions with the distance group, similar to that in the Intranet environment. The video was synchronized with superb clarity, good resolution and continuity throughout all the sessions in this network environment. Such consistently high quality videos were not found in the other two network environments.

However, the video quality on the participant's side was reported to be not as satisfactory. Table 4.10 lists Participant E's comments.

Table 4.10   Results from the post-session interviews in Stage Two – all participant's responses regarding the video quality in the LAN-Internet-LAN environment

Participant	Session 1	Session 2	Session 3	Session 4	Session 5
E	Very good, but could not see facial expressions clearly.	Not clear at all. Blurred and pixilated but continuous.	A bit better than last session but still blurred and pixilated. Occasionally clear.	Similar to the previous session, still blurred and pixilated.	Sometimes clear but blurred 55% of the time.

Participant E further commented at the completion of Session Three:

> It [the video quality], it still wasn't good. It's still what I call pixilated. Sometimes it's clear and I can see quite well. I could see that you had your hair tied back today, and you had black and white on. But a lot of times it was still not that clear. Not as clear as I see myself in that corner box [the My Video window].

This poor video quality on the participant's side was probably caused by the low computing power of her laptop. Thus a powerful desktop computer can be a crucial factor in generating a quality video transmission.

In summary, despite the fact that the video quality in the three network environments varied one from the other, the Open Learning students were genuinely delighted to see me, especially on the first occasion and they watched the video much more continuously than did the on-campus students. The importance of the video will be further discussed in Chapters 5 and 6.

4.3.4   Other features of pedagogical value

Other features of NetMeeting (the Whiteboard, Document Sharing, File Transfer and My Video) proved to be of particular pedagogical value. In the post-trial survey, the participants were asked (Question PTS-2.1) to rank the features of NetMeeting according to their usefulness to language learning. Table 4.11 demonstrates the participants' preferences.

Table 4.11 shows that all four participants ranked audio No. 1 in terms of its importance to supporting interaction in communicative language learning, for obvious reasons. Without auditory input, no interaction can be generated. For distance language learners, although the video quality was not great, three out of four responses indicate video as the second most important feature. This is another indication of the importance of visual interaction to distance language learners. Closely following the video was the whiteboard. In fact, Student E ranked the whiteboard as equally important as the audio function.

Table 4.11 Results from the post-trial survey in Stage Two – the rankings of features of NetMeeting (PTS-2.1)

	No. 1	No. 2	No. 3	No. 4	No. 5	No. 6
Audio	4					
Video		3	1			
File Transfer		1		1	2	
Document Sharing				2		
Whiteboard	1		3			
My Video					2	2

N = 4
Note: Participant E put No. 1 for both audio and the whiteboard. Sharing was not rated by Participant D and E.
No. 1 represents most important and No. 6 the least important. The numbers 1–4 represent the number of entries to each ranking.

The Whiteboard

Personal observations

The whiteboard was mostly used for character writing, linguistic explanations and showing directions during task completions. (see Figure 4.3 for an actual example of the use of the whiteboard)

Figure 4.3   The Whiteboard contents of Session Three with Participant A

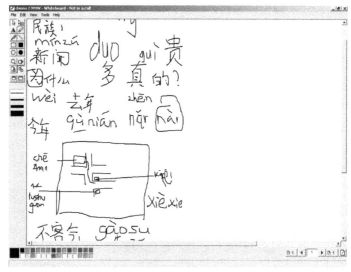

It was observed that the whiteboard was used in every session, although only two occasions were originally intended. In many instances, it was the participants who initiated the use of the whiteboard. It was generally reliable with only two crashes. On one occasion, NetMeeting crashed immediately the whiteboard was clicked on. Another happened when the two parties were moving the whiteboard at the same time, and in one session, the whiteboard could not be activated at all. These problems had never happened in Stage One. The crashes and failure to start may be caused by the low capacity of the students' computers.

Participants' perceptions

Again, as with the on-campus students, the whiteboard was greatly favoured by the distance participants. Question PTS-2.10 in the Post-Trial Survey further solicited participants' opinions about the features of NetMeeting. The whiteboard attracted the most attention. Participant E wrote: "I loved learning new characters via the whiteboard". And Participant A was also very positive about the whiteboard:

> Yeah the whiteboard helped heaps. When I could not understand a word my tutor could write it on the board. (Well at first the character, which I was none the wiser with!), but writing the pinyin was good, as sometimes I thought I was hearing a totally different sound. The more this happened though, the more I got used to the way my tutor pronounced the words (the correct way as opposed to my incorrect way!).

Participant B summed up neatly:

> We used all those features at times and they were largely useful for specific purposes e.g. video in conjunction with audio gives the opportunity to see body language and facial expressions which contribute to the communication process.

> The whiteboard proved useful for instant demonstration of written language w.o. [without] Having to go to cumbersome keyboard input methods [the use of the mouse to write characters].

More discussion on the pedagogical values of the whiteboard is contained in Section 5.2.2.

Document Sharing

Personal observations

The use of the Document Sharing function was originally designed for use in the tasks on two occasions: to share a menu and to show a digital personal photo. With some participants, the sharing of the menu (a 32 kB Word document) or a lecture note appeared on the participants' screen almost instantly with excellent quality. With others, it took somewhat longer to share a document. For example, it took about one minute to load onto Participant B's computer screen. However, the photo (240 kB) could not be shared successfully, and only a frame of the photo could be seen on the participant's screen. This failure may have been caused by the slow Internet transmission speed or the limited capacity of the participant's computer, because in Stage One in the Intranet environment the sharing of the same documents was instant with the quality equal to the original documents. To rectify this situation, the photo was replaced by a family photo of a much smaller size (32kB) captured by Logitec Webcam and shared with the participants with success. (also see discussion in Section 5.2.2)

Participants' perceptions

As shown in Table 4.11, Document Sharing was considered by the participants to be useful, occupying the fourth position in terms of its importance to the support of interaction in language learning. When answering question PTS-2.10, Participant A commented:

> We used the sharing files feature to talk about family photos. But this feature could be used for endless conversation possibilities.

File Transfer

The function of File Transfer was planned for two occasions for each participant – the transfer of a video clip with sound and transfer of a word document. The 2.41MB video clip was the same clip transferred instantly in Stage One of the evaluation in the Intranet environment. However, in this phase of the evaluation the size of the video clip was too big for the Internet to transfer within a reasonable time frame. For example, in Session Four with Participant B, the transfer was still going when the session finished. I had to abort the transfer and sent the video clip by e-mail. To further test the function of File Transfer, a small digital family photo was sent through this function to the participant and the transfer was found to be generally quick, varying from one to three minutes. Thus it can be concluded that this function was useful for transferring small documents, be it a Word document or a photo. Different from the function of Document Sharing, documents transferred can be kept by the other party for future reference (also see discussion in Section 5.2.2).

Participants' perceptions

As shown in Table 4.11, no consensus was reached regarding its position of importance to language learning in reference to other features, with one participant ranking File Transfer as the second one, one as the fourth and two as the fifth.

My Video

As discussed in Section 3.22, My Video is a self-image window where one can see oneself while watching the video of the other party. This function was always used to ensure that the researcher's image on the other side of the conference was still on the screen and, more importantly, to adjust paralinguistic cues to assist the flow of interaction and negotiation for meaning. For example, when the researcher could not understand a participant's Chinese, she tended to look frustrated. A quick glance at the My Video image of herself would remind her that a puzzled look should be more appropriate and encouraging for inviting further explanations from the participant. The My Video function is also an important source of information when using a recording device (such as Camtasia) to capture the screen activities (also see discussion in Section 5.2.2).

Participants' perceptions

All participants considered this function as the least useful feature in NetMeeting. This is probably because its potential was not sufficiently explored, apart from its use in monitoring one's own performance during the sessions.

4.3.5 Reliability

Personal observations

Reliability here refers to the stability of NetMeeting in terms of its crash rate during a videoconferencing session. While it never crashed in Stage One of the evaluation, in this phase, NetMeeting crashed five times of the 19 successful sessions, resulting in an average of 0.26 crash per session. In other words, NetMeeting was very reliable even in the Internet environment. One of the crashes happened in Session Four, when Participant E attempted to enlarge her video size. In Session Three, when Participant B tried to use My Video while I was clicking on the whiteboard, NetMeeting froze. Two other crashes occurred when I tried to write on the whiteboard. On another occasion, a message appeared saying an illegal operation had been performed, when Participant A (in Session Three) clicked on NetMeeting, and NetMeeting shut itself down.

Participants' perceptions

In the Post-trial Survey, Question PTS-2.4 asks the participants to mark on a scale of 1 to 10 the reliability of NetMeeting, where 1 represents 'very reliable' and 10 'not reliable'. Figure 4.4 gives the results for this question.

Figure 4.4   Survey results from Stage Two – reliability of NetMeeting (PTS-2.4)

Very reliable								Not reliable	
1	2	3	4	5	6	7	8	9	10
	x (A)	x (B)						x (D)	
	x (E)								

The participants were also required to explain their choices of the positions. They offered:

♦ I have marked 2, basically very reliable, as even though the system froze a couple of times, it was quickly remedied by either inviting the person to netmeet again, or a quick restart of the computer. As I say, it only happened a few times, but was easily fixed. (Participant A)

♦ The problems I experienced were not due to the Netmeeting [NetMeeting] program itself, but more to the connection between my school and Griffith University. Once we had established successful contact the meetings were very smooth. (Participant E)

♦ Seemed quite reliable in terms of program stability, I can only remember having to re-boot it once or twice during the sessions. (Participant B)

While most participants were able to differentiate the problems with NetMeeting itself from those non-NetMeeting problems such as the instability of the Internet transmission and hardware problems, Participant D (who marked 9 on the scale) blamed NetMeeting for his unsuccessful attempts to have videoconferencing sessions:

My net meeting [NetMeeting] trial had a lot of problems. Beyond the hardware problems, there was difficulty with the Internet connection and its speed, the netmeeting [NetMeeting] application.

Both my observation and the participants' feedback demonstrate that NetMeeting itself was basically very reliable. Problems mostly occurred due to factors other than the program itself, such as Internet connections, ISP and inadequate hardware.

4.3.6   Problems unrelated to NetMeeting

In contrast to the Stage One evaluation in the Intranet environment, this phase uncovered many problems unrelated to NetMeeting, which nevertheless directly affected its performance. Some factors even determined the success of a videoconferencing session and thus are worth documenting here.

Limitation of computer skills

The teacher

As a language teacher, my computer skills were sufficient in using NetMeeting and its various functions properly, and I consider myself to be familiar with the operation of NetMeeting. However, when a problem arose unexpectedly (e.g. when the audio or video was not available), my computer knowledge and skills proved to be insufficient to pinpoint the cause or causes of an emerging problem and find a solution on the spot. I often became panicky and had to rely on the expertise of computer specialists. This inability to cope with emerging technical problems might be common among language teachers who are not specialists in computer technology.

The learner

Generally speaking, once the participants were instructed clearly, they could manage NetMeeting and its various functions with ease. However, a general apprehension of the new technology caused by lack of confidence in their computer skills could be observed during the sessions, especially in the first few sessions. Whenever a problem materialized, the participants easily became panicky and frustrated. For example, Participant C kept restarting her computer when she could not hear me at the beginning of a conference. Once it took us 30 minutes to find out that she had plugged her speaker into the wrong socket, resulting in no sound coming through to her. When the audio was not available, most participants knew how to use the MSN text chat function to communicate with me, but Participant C did not know how to use this function.

Limitations of the technology

Difficulties in initial connections

Most of the problems that we encountered in this stage were related to the initial connections at the beginning of the videoconferencing sessions. Of the 19 successful sessions, 12 sessions were instantly connected between the two parties at the beginning of each session while the initial connections of the other seven were problematic. The usual occurrence was no sound or video coming through. We had to quit NetMeeting and restart it. Sometimes, we had to restart our computers to establish a connection. This is typical of many Microsoft Windows-based applications, which have never been bug-free.

Limited computer power

Most participants had reasonably up-to-date computers, such as Pentium 2 and Pentium 3, with the exception of Participant D, who had a Pentium 1. As the sound card on his computer was unable to support videoconferencing, a Pentium 3 computer was lent to him for this trial.

It was found that an overloaded computer could affect the quality of the conferencing in a number of ways. For example, the computer could be very slow to respond to the instructions if many files were open on the screen, or features of NetMeeting could not be activated, or the activation of a certain feature (e.g. the whiteboard) could cause crashes of NetMeeting. The video and sound quality could be reduced if the computer power was limited as shown in the case of Participant E, who used a laptop.

Problems with Internet Service Provider (ISP)
All participants were connected to the Internet through commercially available Internet Service Providers (ISP) with the exception of Participant E, who used both a LAN and a commercial ISP. Some ISPs were found to offer excellent audio and video quality when the Internet was not very busy. However, it was discovered that some had longer latency and more limited bandwidth. For example, in the two failed sessions with Participant E using a commercial ISP, we could see and hear each other but the sound was too broken to be comprehensible and the video was not clear at all. We tried both on a Friday afternoon between 4:00 and 5:00 o'clock and a Saturday morning between 8:00 and 8:30, but there was no significant improvement in the sound and video quality. Some Internet Service Providers may deliberately install a firewall to block videoconferencing in order to reduce cost, as in the case of Participant D.

The issue of firewalls
Usually between commercially available networks, there is no firewall blocking the sound and video of a videoconferencing tool. However, if it is used in an institutional setting, users can experience a blockage from a firewall.

Griffith University in Australia, where this research took place, erects a firewall, which blocks most of the videoconferencing tools from entering the University's Intranet. In an attempt to find a way to solve this problem, Yahoo Messenger was investigated and found to be able to run through the University's firewall. It was tested for a few days but discovered to be unsuitable for language teaching for the following reasons:

1. The sound and video quality was acceptable, but not as good as that of NetMeeting. This was especially true with the video quality, which was not as clear and continuous.
2. Yahoo messenger was only a chat tool without the useful features that NetMeeting offers, such as the Whiteboard, Document Sharing etc.
3. The most serious problem with Yahoo was its loss of sound when both parties spoke at the same time. Although this could be avoided by watching the movements on the sound volume chart before one spoke, it is a very time-consuming procedure and takes a great

amount of practice and patience. One has to wait to ascertain that the other party has finished speaking before proceeding to take a turn. This renders the conversation less natural and full of false starts, thus negating in some ways the whole point of this research.

The dial-up function using a modem was then tried, and I found that NetMeeting could run through the University firewall without any blockage. However my initial testing revealed that the audio and video quality was slightly affected by the latency in the modem. This was confirmed in Stage Two of the evaluation with the Open Learning students. (see Sections 4.3.3)

A firewall could also be encountered on the students' side if he or she uses a LAN, as discovered in the case of Participant E. Future researchers should be aware of the issue of firewalls when using a LAN or ISP to connect to the Internet.

Faulty equipment

The problems with some hardware that Participant E and D encountered are not problems inherent to NetMeeting and are not typical of the problems encountered by other students. However it is worth documenting them here for future reference.

When Participant E first started to install NetMeeting, she could not install her Webcam due to a problem with the installation software. The Webcam had to be posted back for repair. Our schedule for the trial was thus affected.

When Participant D could not hear me for the first time, I thought the sound card of his computer might be inadequate since he was using a Pentium 1 computer. After I replaced his computer with a Pentium 3, he still could not hear me. After numerous testing of various software on his computer, we discovered that the problem was caused by his headphones, which were faulty.

Although these technical problems were incidental, they did reveal the vulnerability and unpredictability of the Internet-based videoconferencing environment. Future users of videoconferencing should be made aware of these problems.

4.4 Summary

This chapter has presented and discussed the results from the two-stage evaluation of NetMeeting in terms of its **technological capabilities** in supporting oral-visual interaction in distance language education. The results from Stage One informed Stage Two. On the basis of the data from these two stages of the evaluation of NetMeeting, it can be safely concluded that NetMeeting is a reliable and appropriate tool for supporting oral-visual interaction in distance language learning, despite the limitations in the Internet service standard. This conclusion has profound implications for the use of Internet-based desktop videoconferencing in DLE. First, the findings in this two-stage evaluation not only confirm the technological capabilities of the present generation of videoconferencing tools in supporting real-time oral-visual interaction, but also identify the limitations in Internet technology, namely, the problems of narrow bandwidth and long latency. Second, these findings direct the attention of distance language professionals to videoconferencing as a potential solution to the problem of lack of oral-visual interaction in DLE. Third, the findings demonstrate the potential and promising future of videoconferencing with improved Internet bandwidth and reduced latency. This chapter has therefore answered the technological aspect of the second subsidiary research question: *What are the benefits and limitations of oral- visual interaction via videoconferencing for L2 acquisition at a distance?* More thorough discussion of the technological capabilities of NetMeeting appears in the discussion chapter, Chapter 6.

Chapter Five

Results: The pedagogical values of oral-visual interaction via videoconferencing for L2 acquisition at a distance

5.1 Introduction

In contrast to most published studies which only investigate the technological capabilities of new educational technology, the two-stage evaluation of NetMeeting in this research examines two aspects of a videoconferencing tool – its technological capabilities and pedagogical values. The technological capabilities of NetMeeting in supporting oral-visual interaction have already been extensively reported in Chapter 4. This chapter moves a step forward to investigate the pedagogical values of videoconferencing through an examination of the process of oral-visual interaction in this context.

According to communicative L2 learning methodology, interaction in meaning-focused task-based learning facilitates language acquisition (Vygotsky, 1978; Hall, 1995; Lantolf, 1994; Ohta, 1995; Swain & Lapkin, 1995; Long, 1996; Mitchell & Myles, 1998; Kitade, 2000; Gass, 2003; Hampel, 2003). Consequently, in this chapter, the presentation of the evaluation results covers what occurred in the process of oral-visual interaction, and what the participants perceived in regard to their improvement in language proficiency and achievement in task performance and completion. In this regard, this research does not attempt to investigate the participants' improvement in their spoken Chinese proficiency in a quantitative manner.

Data is presented in the form of a comparison between findings from stages one and two, with an emphasis on those obtained in Stage Two, for the obvious reason that this research concerns itself with interactive language learning in distance mode. Data presentation will follow the criteria developed in Chapter 3 in keeping with the amended version of Chapelle's (2001, p. 55) framework, which has been adjusted to cater for the requirements of this study (see Section 3.4.2). These criteria are:

- practicality
- language learning potential
- learner fit
- authenticity
- positive impact

As the first criterion, practicality, has been extensively discussed in Chapters 4, this chapter will concentrate on the presentation of data following the last four criteria, with a focus on the language learning potential of the tasks as this criteria is the most important of the five criteria. This data is crucial for the investigation of the second subsidiary research question:

What are the benefits and limitations of oral-visual interaction via videoconferencing for L2 acquisition at a distance?

While data contained in Chapter 4 provided insight into the benefits and limitations of videoconferencing-supported interaction from a technological perspective, data presented and discussed in this chapter further answered the second subsidiary research question, but this time, from a pedagogical angle. It is hoped that this chapter will contribute to our understanding of appropriate task design and performance in terms of Internet-based desktop videoconferencing-supported DLE.

5.2 Presentation of findings

5.2.1 Introduction

Participants

As mentioned in Chapters 3 and 4, three participants, who had just finished their first year Chinese at Griffith University, were involved in Stage One. For ease of analysis and confidentiality, these on-campus participants are known in this research as Student 1, Student 2 and Student 3. Stage Two evaluation saw the participation of five students from the Open Learning Chinese program offered at Griffith University (i.e. the distance students), who were designated as Participants A, B, C, D and E. They had just completed two study periods of Chinese learning in distance mode, an equivalent of one year of studying Chinese in face-to-face mode in terms of length of study. In other words, their Chinese proficiency level should theoretically have been similar to that of the on-campus participants. Part one of the Post-Trial Survey (PTS) collects some background information of the participants in Stage Two, collated in Table 5.1.

As shown in Table 5.1, with the exception of Participant B, who had learnt Chinese at an institution other than Griffith University and possessed a much higher proficiency level, and Participant E who had also learnt Chinese previously and was a fluent speaker, the other three all began their Chinese study with the Open Learning Chinese program at Griffith University, and their spoken proficiency was quite low. Table 5.1 also demonstrates that most of the students did not have much exposure to any Chinese speaking environment, apart from cassettes and video tapes. The lack of exposure to oral-visual interaction in the target language further explains my observation during the trial that their interactional, listening and spoken skills were almost non-existent. Their level of spoken proficiency in Chinese was indicative of the general proficiency level of the distance learners in the same study period of the Open Learning Chinese program.

Table 5.1   Background information of Participants in Stage Two of the evaluation of NetMeeting (PTS-1.1, PTS-1.2 and PTS-1.3)

Participants	Length of learning Chinese	Ways of practising speaking Chinese before this trial	Place of Residence	Level of proficiency in Spoken Chinese
Participant A	10 months	Never practised	Queensland	Very low
Participant B	Started in the 1970s and continued intermittently	With tapes, Rosetta Stone (an online course)	South Australia (Adelaide)	Fluent speaker, the best
*Participant C	10 months	With tapes	Victoria	Very low
Participant D	10 months	With tapes and Chinese speakers	New South Wales	Medium
Participant E	2 years	With tapes and colleagues	Victoria	Quite fluent

*Note: * Participant C withdrew from the trial after completing 3 sessions and did not complete the post-trial survey. Her information contained in this table was obtained from the post-session interviews with her.*

Tutorial sessions

Five videoconferencing sessions were conducted between the teacher and each participant with the aim of completing various tasks in Chinese, the target language. (For content and requirements of each task, see Section 3.3.6.) A total of 44 sessions were carried out, with 15 (all successful) in Stage One and 29 in Stage Two. Of the 29 in Stage Two, 19 were successful, thus making a total of 34 successful sessions. All these sessions were conducted through either an intranet or Internet supported NetMeeting while, as stated, the teacher and the participants were at different locations from one another.

5.2.2   Language learning potential

As shown in Table 3.10, two issues in this criterion are under close examination: the provision of focus on form in oral-visual interaction; and the perceived participants' improvement in their target language proficiency, especially in terms of their interactional, listening and speaking skills. The central question in focus on form is whether task conditions provide the opportunities for directing the learner's attention temporarily towards linguistic forms during the student's primary engagement in learning the meaning of the language (Long & Robinson, 1998, p. 23). Thus, closely investigated here are such indicators of focus on form as interactional modifications, modifications of output and support. Instances of interactional modification were tallied and tabulated, and samples of such instances were presented and analyzed using the Varonis and Gass's (1985) model discussed in Section 3.3.9. Varonis and Gass's model is reproduced here for ease of reference. (see Figure 3.10)

Figure 3.10 A model for analysing an occasion of interactional modification during task completion

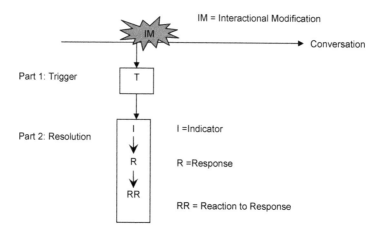

Note: Modified version of Varonis and Gass's (1985, p. 74) model.

Examples of the various types of trigger, indicator, response and reaction to response were selected from the data collected during the two-stage evaluation and analyzed. In addition, support is also a crucial factor for promoting negotiation of meaning in a videoconferencing-supported learning environment. Support is defined in Section 2.2.8 as cues or information available to the learner to help in constructing meaning during task completion. As such, cues or information typical of oral-visual interaction enabled by videoconferencing were also presented and discussed.

As far as improvement in Chinese is concerned, because of the spoken nature of the modality of the tasks, the emphasis of the investigation is on the improvement in interactional, listening and speaking skills that the researcher and the participants themselves perceived. Due to book length limitations, data presented in this section will be selective and concentrate heavily on data collected from the Stage Two evaluation in order to better evaluate the learning process of the distance learners.

Focus on form in oral-visual interaction

Findings from Stage One – evaluation by on-campus participants

As discussed in Section 2.2.8, interactional modifications and modifications of output are factors promoting focus on form in a meaning-based task. Given the primary objective of these videoconferencing sessions was to provide a venue for language learners to improve their spoken proficiency, no metalinguistic explanation was designed into these tasks. Instead, from the very beginning of each task, the learner and the instructor engaged in a role-play or a conversation in the target language for the purpose of completing the task. The two-way interactive conversations were only interrupted when there was an unknown or unfamiliar linguistic element. On such occasions, focus on form in Chinese or English took place to ascertain the understanding of vocabulary or a grammatical structure. Role-plays resumed after a breakdown was repaired. Such occasions of focus on form were characterized by interactional modification which constitutes a focal point of the data analysis in relation to the language learning potentials of the tasks. It was observed that focus on form happened a few times in every session, varying from three to ten, when the participants could not understand certain sentences or words. Such occasions often occurred when either the participants forgot the words they had learned or the teacher deliberately used new vocabulary to create opportunities for focus on form. Interactional modification and modification of output were clearly evident in this process, as shown in the following transcript of the videotaped Session Three with Student 2.

R = Researcher, S = Student 2 – Session Three

R:	Ni zai zher deng le duo chang shijian le?	R:	How long have you been waiting here?
S:	[paused and looked puzzled] Duo chang shijian?	S:	[paused and looked puzzled] How long?
R:	Duo da, ni zhidao ma?	R:	How old, do you know?
S:	Duo da? ((nodding))	S:	How old? ((nodding))
R:	Ni jinnian duo da?	R:	How old are you this year?
	Ni zai zher deng le duo chang shijian le?		How long have you been waiting here for?
S:	[looked as if she realized]. Wo... bu tai duo chang.	S:	I... not too much long.
R:	Bu tai chang?	R:	Not too long?
S:	Bu tai chang.	S:	Not too long.

As shown in the above negotiation routine, on this occasion of interactional modification, the researcher's question, *Ni zai zher deng le duo chang shijian le*, triggers a non-understanding and thus functions as a trigger. Student 2 paused to think and repeated *duo chang shijian* to indicate her non-understanding of this phrase. Her puzzled look also revealed to the researcher that a problem in understanding was encountered. As such, this turn acts as an indicator, and indicates specifically the source of non-understanding. The researcher perceived that the non-understanding might be caused by the word '*duo*'(how), and thus responded with an example '*duo da*'(how old), which the students had learned in class. In this response, comprehension check occurred when the researcher asked *ni zhidao ma* (do you know). In the next turn, Student 2 reacted positively by nodding to the researcher's response, confirming that she knew '*duo da*'. Following this, the researcher made the second comprehension check by comparing '*duo da*'(<u>how</u> old) with '*duo chang*'(<u>how</u> long). Student 2 reacted by using '*duo chang*' to answer the researcher's previous question, *Ni zai zher deng le duo chang shijian le*(How long have you been waiting here for). However, she made a grammatical mistake, which was corrected by the researcher in the next turn. In the last turn, Student 2 modified her output by repeating what the researcher said, thus nicely tying up this occasion of interactional modification. There were quite a few occasions in which modification of output such as the one in the above segment happened during the 15 NetMeeting sessions with the on-campus students. (see Appendix J)

Support is defined in Table 2.3 as cues or information available to the learner to help in constructing meaning during task completion. Features (e.g. the Whiteboard, Document Sharing, the function of the video, etc.) offered through NetMeeting were found to be useful in negotiation of meaning. For example, the Whiteboard was used regularly in every session to show the forgotten characters or to explain the meanings of new words. Students could remember or understand the meaning of the words more easily when they saw the characters, as many Chinese characters are pictographic. The whiteboard was also used to draw pictures in an attempt to get the messages across. For example:

R = Researcher, S = Student 2 – Session Three)

R: Gangcai wo xia che de shihou, bu zhidao yinggai wang zuo guai haishi wang you guai.

R: When I got off the bus just now, I didn't know whether I should turn left or right.

S: 'Zuo guai' shi shenme yisi ?

S: What does 'zuo guai' mean?

R: 'Zuo', zhidao ma?

R: Do you know 'zuo'?

S: Zhidao, zhidao.

S: I know, I know.

((The teacher began to draw on the whiteboard as shown in Figure 5.1.))

Figure 5.1   Whiteboard content of Session Three with Student 2

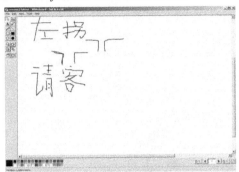

R: Ni kan wo hua de tu. Wang zuo guai,   R: Look at the picture I am drawing. Turn
wang you guai. ((drawing a left and right   left, turn right. Do you understand?
turn on the whiteboard)) Dong le ma?

S: ((found the whiteboard and looked at the   S: ((found the whiteboard and looked at the
drawing I made))   drawing I made.))

R: ((drawing the picture again.))   R: ((drawing the picture again.))

S: Zhidao. Zhidao le.   S: I know. Now I understand.

Visual cues through the function of video were another source of support to aid negotiation of meaning, as shown in Example 1. Facial expressions such as a puzzled look and nod were all available. The function of the video was also deliberately employed in the process of negotiation of meaning. When Student 2 asked if the teacher knew this café they were in, the researcher said '*ting shuo guo*' (I've heard about it). Seeing the student did not understand, the researcher pointed her index finger to her ear and repeated '*ting shuo guo*' with a stress on '*ting*' (hear) and added '*danshi, mei lai guo*' (but I have not been here before).

As this stage is a preparatory phase for Stage Two, only the above instances were selected for comparison with data in Stage Two. More examples of focus on form can be found in Appendix J. Among the 15 sessions conducted in Stage One, instances of interactional modifications happened occasionally varying from three to ten. This forms a contrast to the findings from Stage Two.

Findings from Stage Two – evaluation by the distance participants

Occasions of interactional modification that occurred during Stage Two were tallied and tabulated to provide a general picture of instances of focus on form during each task completion by each participant. This was followed by analysis of specific examples of interactional modifications in accordance with Varonis and Gass's model (see Wang, 2006; Figure 3.10).

In comparison with Stage One, Stage Two witnessed a higher frequency of focus on form. For example, during an approximately one-hour session, modification of interaction could happen on approximately three to ten occasions with an on-campus participant in Stage One, but on around 20 occasions with a distance participant. The frequency of interactional modification (IM) in each session for each participant is tallied and presented in Table 5.2.

Table 5.2   Occasions of interactional modification in Stage Two

Session		1	2	3	4	5	Means
Participant	Time: (mins)	33:43	40:10	50:15	47	47:51	**44:04**
A	No. of IM	17	15	28	24	23	**21.4**
Participant	Time: (mins)	19:14	*	27:16	25:10	28:44	**25:36**
B	No. of IM	5	*	7	6	11	**7.25**
Participant	Time: (mins)	40	35	51	**	**	**40:33**
C	No. of IM	23	21	31	**	**	**25**
Participant	Time: (mins)	58	***	***	***	***	***
D	No. of IM	19	***	***	***	***	***
Participant	Time: (mins)	44	45	71	22.30	60	**48:46**
E	No. of IM	22	20	52	10	23	**25.4**

*Notes: * Session Two with Participant B was successful. However, due to bad sound quality, there were many occasions of breakdown in conversation, the cause of which could not be clearly identified as technical or linguistic. Thus tallying such occasions was given up for fear of data inaccuracy.*
** Participant C withdrew from the trial after the first three sessions for personal reasons.
*** Only one successful session was conducted with Participant D, due to technical problems.

It has to be pointed out that the length of time recorded in Table 5.2 was the actual time spent on completing each task, not the whole videoconferencing session which often lasted approximately one to one and a half hours, because of the free chats, grammar explanations at the end of task completion and technical difficulties. In addition, no graphic was generated from this table because it is difficult to generalize a tendency with only five participants. We cannot confidently conclude that the longer it took to complete the task, the more occasions of interactional modification there would be. This is because some interactional modifications could be very lengthy, while others were brief. On the whole, it was the Chinese proficiency level of each participant that determined the variety in number, length and quality of interactional modification. By the same token, neither can we generalize that the longer the session lasted, the more target language output would be produced in the session. We have to take into consideration factors, such as the number of repetitions and explanations of sentences, due to differences in participants' Chinese proficiency. However, the aim of the tabulation is to record what happened to each participant, providing a foundation for individual case analysis.

Table 5.2 indicates that Participant B had the lowest number of occasions of interactional modification, a mean of 7.25 per session. This means that during each session, the role-play broke down only occasionally to allow temporary focus on linguistic forms, which was to be expected. Table 5.2 also indicates that Participant B's sessions were the shortest of all the participants', averaging approximately 25 minutes per session, while the average length of session for most participants was between 40–50 minutes. This means he completed his tasks faster than others. However, it was observed that he produced the largest amount of output during these short periods of time. All these were due to the fact that Participant B enjoyed the highest Chinese proficiency among the distance participants; he had little difficulty in understanding what he heard or in expressing himself in Chinese. As a result, the researcher sometimes had to deliberately create occasions of focus on form at the task performance level by using words that Participant B had not learned before (see Example A (6)). This was to ensure that he would be provided enough occasions for beneficial focus on form. In turn, according to the criteria for evaluating the language learning potential of a task proposed by Chapelle (2002) and developed by this research, these occasional instances of focus on form establish the language learning potential of the task designed for this evaluation, at least, as far as Participant B is concerned.

The case of Participant E is quite extraordinary. Table 5.2 demonstrates that Session Three with Participant E lasted 71 minutes and the number of interactional modification reached 52. This was the longest session with the greatest number of interactional modifications of all sessions. However, these results do not imply that Participant E's Chinese proficiency was low. In fact her proficiency was in between that of Participant B and participants A and C. The main reason for the lengthy session was her strong interest in Chinese food. A great amount of output was generated when she deviated from the task to talk about the variety of Chinese cuisine and requested for new vocabularies to convey her meaning. Consequently, numerous occasions of interactional modification emerged, in which modified output occurred frequently. This trend was quite consistent with the length and number of occasions of interactional modification in her other sessions with the exception of Session Four. She just enjoyed speaking Chinese so much that she deviated from the tasks frequently. However, in Session Four, the researcher had deliberately confined the course of the conversation to what was required of for completing the task. Thus both the length of the session and number of interactional modifications were less than other sessions and quite similar to those by Participant B. This similarity can probably be attributed to the fact that both participants' Chinese proficiency was quite high.

In comparison with Participant B, whose average session length was approximately 25 minutes, participants A, C, and D averaged at over 40 minutes per session, doubling the length by Participant B. However, this difference does not signify that participants A, C and D produced more output in the target language than Participant B. This is because, due to their low Chinese proficiency, it took a much longer time and more repetitions for participants A, C and D to understand what had been said or to finish an instance of interactional modification. Table 5.2 also shows that the number of occasions of interactional modification by participants A, C, D reached an average of 21.6 per session, about three times of that by Participant B. By the same token, nor can we confidently conclude that more language acquisition occurred because of the increased occasions of interactional modification. It was true that more linguistic features were dealt with on these occasions, but how much had been retained or acquired was not certain. However, what can be ascertained is the improvement in these participants' listening and speaking skills. This is because most of these occasions of interactional modification were caused by participants' low listening ability or lack of familiarity with what they had learnt before. Usually after some repetition, the participants could understand what the researcher said previously, as shown in examples D (1) and (2) below. This is not to say that the vocabulary and sentence structures required to complete the tasks were beyond what the participants had learned. On the contrary, frequent non-understanding occurred due to lack of listening practice and rare opportunities to apply what they had learned. This was especially true with the first few videoconferencing sessions. However, an increase in the quality of focus on form happened towards the last few sessions as the participants' communicative competence was improving. Interactional modifications and modifications of output were generated more naturally and with better quality.

For distance learners with better proficiency in spoken Chinese, focus on form was achieved mainly in the target language, while for less proficient learners, Chinese explanations were usually followed by English clarifications. The one-to-one nature of NetMeeting proved to be able to allow teaching to cater for learners of various levels of language proficiency.

Further analysis of individual instances of interactional modification covers the two parts of the negotiation routing (the trigger and the resolution), and the various types of the four primes (trigger, indicator, response and reaction to response) as discussed in Varonis and Gass's model (see Figure 3.10). Examples of different categories of the four primes are selected on the basis of their high frequency of appearance in the data to ensure that a range of representative data is discussed. Emphasis is given to examples not covered in Varonis and Gass's model. Some of the examples are reproduced in order to demonstrate that in one instance of interactional modification, all four types of primes existed. (Wang, 2006)

A. Triggers

Triggers are turns in the conversation that activate occasions of interactional modification. According to Varonis and Gass (1985, p. 75), triggers can come from a question, an answer to a question or neither a question or an answer. Data in the current research reveals all three kinds of triggers, but the majority of triggers are from questions.

Triggers – as questions

In the distance group, especially with Participants A, C and D, whose general Chinese proficiency was lower than Participants B and E, the great majority of occasions of non-understanding was caused by their low listening ability, as shown in Examples A (1) – (3). Triggers are indicated by an arrow.

Example A (1)

R = Researcher, P = Participant C – Session Three

→	R:	Zuotian ni zuo shenme le?	R: What did you do yesterday?
	P:	(9 secs) ((Busy writing down something))	P: (9 secs) ((Busy writing down something))
	R:	Dong le ma	R: Do you understand?
	P:	((Looking at her notes)) Qing ni zai shuo yibian.	P: ((Looking at her notes)) Please say it again.
	R:	Hao. Zuotian ni zuo shenme le?	R: OK. What did you do yesterday?
	P:	(3 secs) Zuotian wo shangban.	P: (3 secs) Yesterday I go to work.

Example A (2)

R = Researcher, P = Participant A – Session One

→	R:	Ni jintian zenme yang?	R: How are you today?
	P:	((looking puzzled)) Sorry?	P: ((looking puzzled)) Sorry?
	R:	Ni jintian zenme yang?	R: How are you today?
	P:	((still looking puzzled)) I didn't get the first bit. I heard 'zenmeyang'.	P: ((still looking puzzled)) I didn't get the first bit. I heard 'zenmeyang'.
	R:	Uh, jintian, jintian.	R: Uh, today. Today.
	P:	((still looking puzzled))	P: ((still looking puzzled))

R: Jintian>	R: Today.
P: ((still looking puzzled)) (3 secs)	P: ((still looking puzzled)) (3 secs)
R: Today.	R: Today.
P: Oh, jintian, jintian, yeah. ((nodding))	P: Oh, today, today, yeah. ((nodding))

Example A (3)

R = Researcher, P = Participant D – Session Five

→ R: Ni zai daxue de shihou, xuexi shenme? Xue le shenme?	R: What did you study when you were at university? What did you learn?
P: Eh, qing ni zai shuo yi bian.	P: Please say it again.
R: Ni zai daxue de shihou, xuele shenme?	R: What did you study when you were at university?
P: Wo zai daxue xue le (3 secs) Guoji Maoyi, dui ma?	P: I studied International Trade, is it correct?

Triggers in the above three examples were initiated by questions directed to the participants. It has to be pointed out that these questions are simple sentences containing no words or structure that the participants had not learned in their distance programs. In Example A (2), Participant C could not understand the word "*jintian*" (today), a word she had learned before. After she was told the meaning in English, she finally comprehended the meaning of the question. In both examples A (1) and (3), after the researcher repeated the question, both participants understood the questions. In fact, Participant A became so frustrated that she explained her inability to comprehend in English during the role play:

> It's very hard for me to hear. I have the difficulty of understanding spoken Chinese. I
> can, if you write the words, I can try to understand, but I find it very hard to listen.

In Session Two when the same question was asked, Participant A understood it instantly.

Triggers as answer

This type of trigger was also common in the data. In Example A (4), when answering the question about what she did yesterday, Participant C's turn was not understood. The researcher could not make out *jiawushi*. It was not until the participant explained *jiawushi* (house work) in English that the researcher realized that the non-understanding was triggered by the participant's incorrect pronunciation of *jiawushi*, as shown in Example A (4).

Example A (4)

R = Researcher, P = Participant C – Session Three

→   P: Zuotian wo gan jiawushi.   P: Yesterday I did house work.

      R: Um, qing ni zai shuo yibian. Qing ni...   R: Please say it again. Please….

      P: House work. Is it house work?   P: House work. Is it house work?

      R: Oh, zuotian wo zuo jiawushi le   R: Yesterday I did house work.

Triggers as neither question nor answer

In Example A (5), the trigger comes from neither a question nor an answer, when Participant C was trying to describe her family members.

Example A (5)

R = Researcher, P = Participant C – Session Two

→   P: Wo you erzi.   P: I have a son.

      R: You shenme? Dui buqi.   R: What do you have? Sorry.

The non-understanding in Example A (5) was again caused by the participant's incorrect pronunciation of *erzi*. However, breakdowns caused by unknown words or phrases in the triggers were not as common as those in Varonis and Gass's study. This category of triggers in the current study only happened when the researcher deliberately used a word knowing it would lead the participants to negotiate its meaning. Example A (6) illustrates this category of triggers.

Example A (6)

R = Researcher, P = Participant B – Session Five

→   R: …ni yiqian gongzuo de shihou jingchang   R: You often came into contact with
            he guke da jiaodao.   customers in your previous job.

      P: (5 secs) ((not replying))

      R: Xue guo ma?   R: (Have you learned it?)

      P: Hai mei xue guo. Qing ni xie, zai   P: Not yet. Could you please write, on the
            whiteboard xie gei wo, hao ma?   whiteboard to show me?

The trigger, *da jiaodao*, in Example A (6), was deliberately embedded by the researcher to raise Participant B's awareness of this phrase, anticipating that the participant would negotiate the meaning of the phrase. Seeing no immediate reaction from the participant, the researcher checked the participant's understanding by asking if he had learned the phrase before. Participant B confirmed that he had not leaned it before and requested the researcher to write it on the whiteboard. The researcher only employed this kind of trigger occasionally with participants at a higher level of Chinese proficiency for the purpose of creating occasions for beneficial focus on form during task completion.

B. Indicators

Indicators are the second prime in Varonis and Gass's model, signalling the start of a breakdown in the interaction. Varonis and Gass (1985, p. 76) identified four types of indicators: echo, explicit statement of non-understanding, non-verbal response and inappropriate response. In data collected in this evaluation, explicit statements of non-understanding are more frequent than others. Furthermore, visual indicators of non-understanding constitute another type of indicator which stands out from the rest and which is not covered in Varonis and Gass's study. Examples of the most frequent two types of indicators are discussed below.

Explicit statements of non-understanding

Explicit statements of non-understanding were abundant during the role plays. There were two types of such statements if categorized according to their sources: breakdowns due to participants' low listening skills and breakdowns due to unknown linguistic elements. Data in regard to the former type of breakdown corresponds with triggers as questions (see examples A (1) – (3)). At the start of the trial, such non-understanding was usually expressed in English as shown in Example B (1). After the researcher emailed the participants a list of frequently used phrases, the participants started to indicate their non-understanding in Chinese as with examples B (2) and (3).

Example B (1)

R = Researcher, P = Participant A – Session One

→ R: Oh, OK. Ni jintian zuo shenme le?   R: What have you done today?

      P: ((Looking puzzled and trying hard to   P: ((Looking puzzled and trying hard to
          understand)) (3 secs) I don't understand.   understand)) (3 secs) I don't understand.

Example B (2)

R = Researcher, P = Participant A – Session One

→ R: Zhongwen nan xue ma?   R: Is Chinese difficult to learn?

      P: Bu dong.   P: I don't understand.

Example B (3)

R = Researcher, P = Participant D – Session Five

→ R: Ni zai daxue de shihou, xuexi shenme?   R: What did you study when you were at
     Xue le shenme?   university? What did you learn?

    P: Eh, qing ni zai shuo yi bian.   P: Please say it again.

The second type of breakdown in the role-play often occurred when the participants attempted to answer the researcher's questions. This type of indicator often emerged when participants found they did not have the vocabulary to finish their turns, as demonstrated in examples B (4) to (9).

Example B (4)

R = Researcher, P = Participant E – Session One

→ R: Ni you hui shuo Zhongwen de pengyou   R: Do you have any friends who speak
     ma?   Chinese?

    P: ((Shaking her head again)) Wo you yi ge,   P: I have a, a colleague…
     uh, yi ge colleague…

Example B (5)

R = Researcher, P = Participant B – Session Four

→ R: Uh, ni, ni zhao wo you shenme shi ma ?   R: You, what can I do for you?

    P: Uh, wo, wo xiang "apply", 'apply for a   P: I, I want to, how do you say "apply for a
     job', zenme shuo?   job"?

Example B (6)

R =researcher, P = Participant A – Session Two

→ R: Jintian ni zuo shenme le?   R: What have you done today?

    P: (2 secs) Wo jintian zuo, uh ((looking at   P: (2 secs) I have done today, uh ((looking
     her notes)) 'cleaning the house' yong   at her notes)) How do you… 'cleaning the
     zhongwen zenme…   house' in Chinese?

Example B (7)

R = Researcher, P = Participant D – Session Five

→ R: Ni xihuan zuo shenme gongzuo?   R: What kind of job do you like to do?

    P: Eh, wo xihuan… (7 secs). Wo bu hui shuo   P: I like… (7 secs). I can't speak Chinese.
     Zhongwen. Eh, I don't know how to say it   Eh, I don't know how to say it in Chinese.
     in Chinese.

As shown in examples B (4) to (7), the participants' turns broke down because they did not know how to say certain words in Chinese. In these breakdowns, participants explicitly expressed their need for help either in Chinese or English. This type of breakdown is the typical by-product of meaning-based tasks, which require the learner to convey meaning using resources, sometimes beyond what they have learned, thus creating opportunities for focus on form.

Visual indicators

Through the function of video in NetMeeting, another type of indicator emerged: non-understanding visualized through facial expressions. Often a puzzled or blank look indicated that incomprehension was experienced. Again this type of indicator was not present in Varonis and Gass's study (see examples B (8) and (9)).

Example B (8)

R = Researcher, P = Participant A – Session One

R: Ni jintian zenme yang?	R: How are you today?
→ P: Um, ((looking puzzled again, not answering)) (5 secs).	P: Um, ((looking puzzled again, not answering)) (5 secs).
R: Ni jintian mang bu mang?	R: Are you busy today?
→ P: ((looking puzzled and trying to work out the meaning)) (15 secs). I'm a bit nervous. Can you say it again? […]	P: ((looking puzzled and trying to workout the meaning)) (15 secs). I'm a bit nervous. Can you say it again? […]

Example B (9)

R = Researcher, P = Participant A – Session Five

R: Ni xie shenme wenzhang le?	R: What article did you write?
→ P: ((Looking puzzled (2 secs) and then understood)) Zhongwen 'literature' zenme shuo?	P: ((Looking puzzled (2 secs) and then understood)) How to say 'literature' in Chinese?

The above two examples also demonstrate the importance of visual cues in negotiation of meaning, and the capability of NetMeeting in the provision of such visual information to aid understanding.

C. Responses

Response is a turn that reacts to the cause(s) of the breakdowns expressed in the indicator. According to Varonis and Gass (1985, p. 76), there are different types of response: repetition, expansion, rephrasing, acknowledgement and reduction. All these types were found in the current study, with an additional type, direct Chinese equivalent of the unknown phrases or words requested in the indicators. Examples of the above mentioned types of responses are provided below to demonstrate the variety of responses.

Repetition

As a large number of triggers resulted from participants' low listening ability, repetition of what had been said in the triggers became the logical response. This type of response materialized more frequently in the first few sessions with participants of lower Chinese proficiency. Very often, the participants explicitly requested the repetition. Here are some examples:

Example C (1)

R = Researcher, P = Participant C – Session Three

R:	Zuotian ni zuo shenme le?	R:	What did you do yesterday?
P:	(9 secs) ((Busy writing down something))	P:	(9 secs) ((Busy writing down something))
R:	Dong le ma?	R:	do you understand?
P:	((Looking at her notes)) Qing ni zai shuo yibian.	P:	((Looking at her notes)) Please say it again.
→ R:	Hao (OK). Zuotian ni zuo shenme le?	R:	OK. What did you do yesterday?

Example C (2)

R = Researcher, P = Participant D – Session Five

R:	Ni zai daxue de shihou, xuexi shenme? Xue le shenme?	R:	What did you study when you were at university? What did you learn?
P:	Eh, qing ni zai shuo yi bian.	P:	Please say it again.
→ R:	Ni zai daxue de shihou, xuele shenme?	R:	What did you study when you were at university?

Usually after the repetition, comprehension could be achieved. It was also discovered that as the sessions went on, repetitions became less frequent.

Expansion

In order to explain certain words or sentences, expansion sometimes occurred in the researcher's turns. In Example C (3), the researcher tried to explain the sentence, *Ni jia hai you shenme ren* (who else is there in your family), in the context of mentioning other members of the family.

Example C (3)

R = Researcher, P = Participant C – Session Two

R: Ni jia hai you shenme ren?	R: Who else is there in your family?
P: ((looking at her notes)) Qing ni zai shuo yibian.	P: ((looking at her notes)) Please say it again.
→ R: Hao. Ni jia hai you shenme ren? Ni you yi ge erzi, liang ge nu'er, hai you shenme ren?	R: OK. Who else is there in your family? You have one son and two daughters, who else?

Rephrasing

Rephrasing is another type of response used by the researcher to get the meaning across. Usually the words in the rephrased sentence were those that the researcher was certain that the participants had learned (see the following example).

Example C (4)

R = Researcher, P = Participant A – Session One

R: Ni jintian zenme yang?	R: How are you today?
P: Um, ((looking puzzled again, not answering)) (5 secs)	P: Um, ((looking puzzled again, not answering)) (5 secs)
→ R: Ni jintian mang bu mang?	R: Are you busy today?

In Example C (4), when realizing that *zenme yang* (how) might be causing the non-understanding, the researcher replaced it with *mang bu mang* (busy or not busy).

Acknowledgement

Acknowledgement of what the participants said was correct often occurred when a comprehension check was received. Such comprehension checks could appear in words or visually through the function of the video in NetMeeting.

Example C (5)

R = Researcher, P = Participant D – Session Five

P: Wo zai daxue xue le (3 secs) Guoji Maoyi, dui ma? ((Looking at the researcher for confirmation of his use of	P: I studied (3 secs) International Trade, is it correct? ((Looking at the researcher for confirmation of his use of International

International Trade, a phrase he had just   Trade, a phrase he had just learned))

learned))

→   R: Dui, dui.   R: Correct, correct.

Reduction

Reduction of the trigger sentence often occurred when the researcher realized that a certain part of the sentence was causing the non-understanding (see Example C (6)).

Example C (6)

R = Researcher, P = Participant A – Session One

R: Ni jintian zenme yang?   R: How are you today?

P: ((still looking puzzled)) I didn't get the   P: ((still looking puzzled)) I didn't get the
first bit. I heard 'zenme yang'.   first bit. I heard 'How are… '.

→   R: Uh, jintian, jintian.   R: Uh, today, today.

In Example C (6), when realizing that the word *jintian* (today) was not being received, the researcher reduced the whole sentence to *jintian* and repeated. As the teacher of the distance Chinese program, the researcher was certain that the participant had learned *jintian*, but probably forgot it.

Target language equivalent

As a response to indicators expressed by participants' requests for unknown Chinese words, an equivalent in Chinese was provided by the researcher immediately following the indicator. This is probably because this type of responses often came from the researcher, who is a native speaker of the target language. Varonis and Gass' study does not cover this category of responses (see examples C (7) to (10)).

Example C (7)

R = Researcher, P = Participant B – Session Four

P: Uh, wo, wo xiang (2 secs), how do you   P: I, I want to (2 secs), how do you say
say 'apply', zenme (how), 'apply for a   'apply for a job'?
job', zenme shuo?

→   R: Shenqing ((seeing the participant did not   R: Apply for ((seeing the participant did not
react)) (2 secs), shenqing.   react)) (2 secs), apply for.

P: Shenqing?   P: Apply for?

165

Example C (8)

R = Researcher, P = Participant D – Session Five

	R:	Ni xihuan zuo shenme gongzuo?	R:	What kind of job do you like to do?
	P:	Eh, wo xihuan… (7 secs). Wo bu hui shuo Zhongwen. Eh, I don't know how to say it in Chinese.	P:	I like… (7 secs). I can't speak Chinese. I don't know how to say it in Chinese.
→	R:	Just say, you can ask […]. Zhongwen zenme shuo?	R:	Just say, you can ask […]. How do you say it in Chinese?

Example C (9)

R = Researcher, P = Participant A – Session Five

	R:	Ni xie shenme wenzhang le?	R:	What article did you write?
	P:	((Looking puzzled (2 secs) and then understood)) Zhongwen 'literature' zenme shuo?	P:	((Looking puzzled (2 secs) and then understood)) How to say 'literature' in Chinese?
→	R:	'Literature' zhongwen shi 'wenxue'.	R:	The Chinese for 'literature' is *wenxue*.

Example C (10)

R = Researcher, P = Participant E – Session One

	R:	Ni you hui shuo Zhongwen de pengyou ma?	R:	Do you have any friends who speak Chinese?
	P:	((Shaking her head again)) Wo you yi ge, uh, yi ge colleague…	P:	((Shaking her head again)) I have a colleague…
→	R:	Tongshi.	R:	Colleague.

D. Reaction to Response

Reaction to response was treated as an optional element in Varonis and Gass' study (1985, p. 77). However, it was found in the current study that reaction to response is an important prime, often indicating that some degree of acquisition has occurred as the result of a breakdown. Two major types of reaction to response dominate data in this evaluation: understanding and modifications of output.

Understanding of what had been said in the triggers sentences occurred often following the repetition in responses. Examples are as follows

Example D (1)

R = Researcher, P = Participant D – Session Five

R: Ni zai daxue de shihou, xuexi shenme?   R: What did you study when you were at
      Xue le shenme?   university? What did you learn?

P: Eh, qing ni zai shuo yi bian.   P: Please say it again.

R: Ni zai daxue de shihou, xuele shenme?   R: What did you study when you were at
                                                university?

→ P: Wo zai daxue xue le (3 secs) Guoji   P: I studied (3 secs) International Trade, is it
      Maoyi, dui ma? ((Looking at the   correct? ((Looking at the researcher for
      researcher for confirmation of his use of   confirmation of his use of International
      International Trade, a phrase he had just   Trade, a phrase he had just learned))
      learned))

R: Dui, dui.   R: correct, correct.

P: ((smiled))   P: ((smiled))

Example D (2)

R = Researcher, P = Participant A – Session Two

R: Ni changchang kan zhongguo dianshi   R: Do you often watch Chinese TV?
      ma?

P: Mm, changchang shi shenme yisi ?   P: What's the meaning of 'changchang'?

R: Oh, changchang, changchang, um…   R: Often, often, um…

→ P: Changchang, changchang, I know that   P: Often, often, I know that ((laughing and
      ((laughing and thinking hard))   thinking hard))

R: Ni zhidao meitian…   R: You know everyday…

→ P: Often!   P: Often!

In Example D (1), after the researcher repeated the same question, asking him what he learned at the university, Participant D understood the question and proceeded to answer that he learned International Trade. However, Example D (2) illustrates a different kind of understanding. At first, Participant A could not understand *changchang* (often) but she was sure that she had learned it before. After the repetition in the researcher's turn, Participant A finally recalled that it meant 'often'. It is evident that her initial non-understanding was brought about by the lack of use of what she had learned before.

Examples D (3) to (5) best illustrate how reaction to response facilitated modified output in the exchanges.

Example D (3)

R = Researcher, P = Participant C – Session Three

R: Hao. Zuotian ni zuo shenme *le*?	R: OK. What did you do yesterday?
P: (3 secs) Zuotian wo shangban.	P: (3 secs) Yesterday I go to work.
R: Hao. Zuotian wo shangban *le*.	R: OK. I went to work yesterday.
→ P: Shangban *le*.	P: went to work.

Example D (4)

R = Researcher, P = Participant E – Session One

P: Tongshi. [...] Ta jiehun Aodaliya ren. ((looking at the researcher for confirmation of her grammar))	P: Colleague). [...] She/he married an Australian. ((looking at the researcher for confirmation of her grammar))
R: Ta he yi ge Aodaliya ren jiehun le.	R: She/he married an Australian.
→ P: Aha ((realized)). Ta he yi ge Aodaliya ren jiehun le.	P: Aha ((realized)). She/he married an Australian.

Example D (5)

R = Researcher, P = Participant B – Session Four

P: Shenqing, qing, qing, wo qing ni de qing?	P: Apply, qing, qing, as the qing in wo qing ni?
R: Dui, qing ni gaosu wo de qing.	R: Yes, as the qing in qing ni gaosu wo.
→ P: Um, Na, shenqing, shenqing gongzuo?	P: Um, then, apply, apply for a job?

Participant C's interactional and listening skills were almost non-existent when the trial first started, and she appeared to be very nervous in the first two sessions. Although listening was still a problem for her in Session Three, Example D (3) shows that she could detect her grammatical error after the researcher stressed the *le* in *Zuotian wo shangban le (went to work)*. Participant C quickly modified her output by repeating *shangban le*. In the latter part of the session, Participant C became conscious of the use of *le* and used it later in "*wo zuo le rou*" (I cooked meat) and "*wo hai zuo le qingcai*" (I also cooked some vegetables).

The same learning process happened to Participant E in Example D (4), who corrected her structure immediately after hearing the correction in the researcher's response. Participant B's turn represents a slightly different modification of output, in which he reacted by applying *shenqing* (apply), a phrase he had just learned from the researcher's response, in *shenqing gongzuo* (apply for work). This application of what he had learned indicates, to a certain degree, that acquisition was happening.

Support

As defined in Table 2.3, support refers to cues or information available to aid negotiation of meaning during task completion. Data from this research indicates that NetMeeting-supported distance learning environment offered many types of support to the participants, which proved to be crucial for their successful negotiation of meaning. Examples of five major types of support are presented and discussed below: the function of the video, the Whiteboard, Document Sharing and File Transfer.

The most valuable support was found in the video. Body movements above the shoulders were all present during the videoconferencing sessions (also see discussion in Section 4. 3.3.) Facial expressions such as an expectant look or raised eyebrows conveyed the intended message accurately during focus on form as shown in Example E (1).

Example E (1)

R = Researcher, P = Participant A – Session Five

R: Nimen jidian dao jia de?	R: What time did you get home?
P: Please say it again.	P: Please say it again.
R: ((looking at the Participant with a mock puzzlement and raising her eye brows)	R: ((looking at the Participant with a mock puzzlement and raising her eye brows)
P: Oh, hahaha. I'll get my note (looking at her note).	P: Oh, hahaha. I'll get my note (looking at her note).
R: Hahaha. Wo bu dong, wo bu dong Yingwen.	R: Hahaha. I don't understand, I don't understand English.
P: Qing ni zai shuo yibian.	P: Please say it again.

In Example E (1), Participant A asked the researcher to repeat what she had said, but the participant rendered her request in English. To encourage her to speak Chinese, the researcher pretended that she did not understand the request in English by putting on an expression of incomprehension and raising her eyebrows in anticipation. Through the real-time video transmission, the participant immediately understood the researcher's intention and laughed, saying she would consult her notes and see how to make the request in Chinese. The last turn in the example shows that she eventually made her request using Chinese. Instances of the video in transmitting facial expressions in real time during negotiating of meaning were abundant in the data collected (also see examples B (8) and (9)).

The function of the video was also used to demonstrate hand gestures to aid negotiation of meaning, usually deliberately by the researcher. For examples, when talking about numbers, the researcher would put up three fingers in from of the Web camera to indicate the number three. However, in Session Four, it was Participant B who requested the researcher to write characters using finger movements in front of the Web camera. To show his understanding of how the characters were written, the participant also wrote with his index finger in front of the camera following the researcher's finger movements.

The video was also employed to show objects in promoting the authenticity of the tasks. For example, in Session Four, Participant A showed pictures of her family and her dogs through the video when completing the task on talking about family members.

The linguistic benefits of the video were also highly appreciated by the participants, and the importance of video was generally viewed in terms of its support to communicative language acquisition. For example, in the interview at the completion of Session 2, when asked how often he looked at the video, Participant B replied:

> I, I looked at the image all the time. I think it's quite import, quite important, you know, form. You want to see the, the a, reaction, the facial expressions, because that's part of the communication.

To Participant B, facial expressions were an indispensable component of interaction and communication. Question PTS-2.8 (Appendix D) asked the participants to indicate on a 10 point scale the importance of video to the improvement of listening and speaking skills, 1 representing 'important' and 10 'not important'. Participant A marked 1, and explained her choice as follows:

> ... Silence is not a problem while you think of a response, because your tutor can see that you are thinking (very hard!). You can see facial expressions which are very important to try and guess what on earth your tutor just said when you can't understand any of the words!...

Participant B, who indicated 2 on the scale, also commented on the importance of video to language learning:

The importance of the video image lies in the fact that one gets the dialogue with the appropriate body language and facial expression, which do not only aid in understanding meaning but are part of the message itself. More specifically it seems to me that to achieve accurate pronunciation the opportunity of seeing the actual sound being formed by a native speaker is very helpful. It also would allow the teacher to do on the spot correction of mistakes through sound and visual demonstration.

Apart from the video, the whiteboard was the second most frequently used function offered through NetMeeting. Data discussed here corresponds with findings in Section 4.2.4. This on-screen feature functions similarly to the whiteboard in traditional classrooms, and was frequently utilized in almost every session for character writing and picture drawing to aid focus on form. The pictographic nature of the Chinese characters may contribute to the frequent use of this function as it is easier to figure out the meaning when seeing the characters than hearing them. This is perfectly exemplified by the following instance of interactional modification:

Example E (2)

R =researcher, P = Participant A – Session Four

R: Ni qu guo Zhongguo jici?

R: How many times have you been to China?

P: Ni qu guo Zhongguo shenme?

P: You've been to China what?

R: Jici (writing on the whiteboard).

R: How many times (writing on the whiteboard).

P: (Reading the whiteboard and realized) Ah, wo yici quguo Zhongguo.

P: (Reading the whiteboard and realized) Ah, I've, once, been to China.

Example E (2) shows that Participant A did not understand *jici* (how many times) until she saw it written on the whiteboard. She had obviously learnt this phrase because she showed her understanding of it by saying *yici* (once) in her reply, although she put it in a wrong place.

The function of Document Sharing was another type of support available through NetMeeting. During task performance, this function was employed to show documents such as a menu in a café and some lecture notes prepared beforehand. It was discovered that this function complemented the whiteboard in that, through Document Sharing, more organized information of large volume could be made available to the students immediately, while the whiteboard can be used for spontaneous explanations of linguistic codes. For example, when explaining how to ask about one's age in Session Four with Participant A, the lecture note clearly outlining the three ways of asking one's age was shown to the participant through the function of Document Sharing. It saved online time to write them one by one on the whiteboard. For more discussion on Document Sharing, see Section 4.2.4.

The function of Document Transfer also supported authentic task performance in that it transferred authentic documents to the other party for either in class or out of class reviewing. For example, when conducting the task on talking about family members, a family photo was transferred to the participants through this function, and abundant exchanges and lively discussions in Chinese were generated in relation to this photo. (also see discussion in Section 4.2.4)

My video is a picture-in-picture self-image window on the computer screen where one can see oneself while watching the video image of the other party. It was found that this function was extremely useful in monitoring the performance of oneself during task performance. The researcher utilized this function constantly in every session to ensure that her paralinguistic cues promoted negotiation of meaning, as shown in Example E (1). Participants only used it to watch their own images in the videoconferencing, with the exception of Participant A, who used it to adjust the photos she wanted to show me through the Web camera.

It is evident that these types of support afforded by NetMeeting are conducive to successful focus on form during task completion, and offered immense pedagogical values to L2 acquisition. The inter-relationship between the technological affordances and pedagogical values of videoconferencing is further discussed in Section 6.3.1.

In summary, this section has discussed in great detail the frequency of interactional modification that occurred during the 34 successful sessions of NetMeeting, with an emphasis on the 19 sessions conducted with the distance participants. Examples of such interactional modification have been analyzed using the Varonis and Gass's model. These examples demonstrate that videoconferencing allowed the participants to modify their interaction when there was a breakdown in task completion. It is also evident from these examples that videoconferencing-supported negotiation of meaning has its own distinct features in comparison to face-to-face or written interaction. A more in-depth discussion of the implications of these occasions of interactional modification will be conducted in Chapter 6. At this point in the discussion, the language learning potential of the tasks has been established as improvement in participants' proficiency is evident in the negotiation routines analyzed above. Such improvement was further attested below by what the participants think about their improvement through these videoconferencing sessions.

Perceived Improvement in Chinese proficiency

As discussed in Section 3.4.2, the evaluation of the language learning potential of a task captures two groups of data: the opportunities for focus on form and learners' perceived improvement in the target language. While the above section has presented data on opportunities for focus on form, this section will report an improvement in the target language. Improvement has been observed both by the teacher and by themselves.

Findings from Stage One – evaluation by the on-campus participants

Personal observations

On observation, the improvement in speaking skills appeared to be more obvious for those with lower Chinese proficiency than for those who had already obtained better speaking skills. It was also discovered that the on-campus participants regarded learning new linguistic elements such as a new phrase or grammatical structure more important than improving communicative speaking skills. This is probably because they had been provided ample opportunities to practise speaking in their face-to-face learning environment.

Participants' perceived improvement in their Chinese proficiency.

Question 2 in the Post-session Survey (PS-2) asks the participants to rate the usefulness of the **tasks** for improving their Chinese fluency. Figure 5.2 shows the number of entries for 'very useful', 'useful', 'OK', 'not very useful', 'not useful'.

Figure 5.2   Data from the post-session surveys in Stage One – the usefulness of tasks for improving fluency (PS-2)

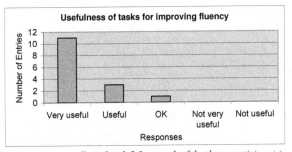

Note: N=15 (15 surveys were collected with 5 from each of the three participants)

It is obvious from the above figure that the overwhelming majority of the entries score the task as being very useful for improving the participants' fluency in Chinese.

To further determine the pedagogical values of videoconferencing in supporting the language potential of the tasks, PS-3 invites the participants to rate the usefulness of **NetMeeting** for the improvement of their fluency in Chinese, and the results are shown in Figure 5.3.

Figure 5.3   Data from post-session surveys in Stage One – the usefulness of NetMeeting for improving fluency (PS-3)

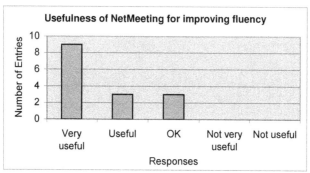

Note: N=15 (15 surveys were collected with 5 from each of the three participants)

In comparison with Figure 5.2, Figure 5.3 shows a slight disparity between 'very useful', 'useful' and 'OK', with a greater concentration still on 'very useful'.

PS-4 further solicits the particular aspects of perceived improvement in participants' Chinese proficiency. Figure 5.4 demonstrates the results.

Figure 5.4   Data from post-session surveys in Stage One – the aspects of improvement (PS-4)

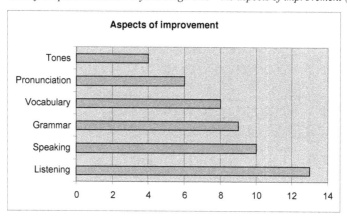

Figure 5.4 shows that listening (13) was the most improved skill through videoconferencing, closely followed by spontaneous responses (11) and speaking skills (10).

<u>Personal observations</u>

After the first sessions with each participant, it became evident that most participants only possessed a minimum level of interactional and communicative skills in Chinese. Such low proficiency in spoken Chinese was manifested in their poor listening ability, poor pronunciation and tones, and lack of spontaneous replies and interactional phrases for everyday conversations. Participants' low proficiency in listening constituted a major factor in conversation breakdowns. I often had to repeat a simple sentence a number of times before they could grasp the meaning. Due to lack of training in listening, they tended to listen for individual words, instead of listening to the meaning of the whole sentence. In other words, they did not know how to infer meaning according to the context. For example, Participant C kept writing down the sentences she heard and translating them in her mind before attempting an answer. The participants' incorrect pronunciation and tones also contributed to their listening difficulty. For example, a simple sentence, such as '*ni xihuan xue zhongwen ma*' (do you like learning Chinese), was lost on Participant A in Session One. She could not comprehend '*xihuan*' (like). But when I wrote the characters on the whiteboard, she recognized and understood them immediately. This indicates that she had learned the characters for '*xihuan*' but she had seldom heard it spoken, and thus was unfamiliar with its correct pronunciation. It was later discovered that she pronounced it as '*sheehun*'. Obviously her incorrect pronunciation and tones aggravated her difficulty in comprehension when the correct utterance was heard. However, it was also observed that, when the participants read the questions they had prepared beforehand, these questions were usually correct, and with a degree of sophistication. For example, when reading her prepared questions, Participant A looked much more relaxed and her sentences were mostly correct, with complicated structures learned in the course. However, when I replied to her questions in Chinese, she could not understand my answers, although I used the same structures and similar vocabulary. Sometimes she asked for clarification in English, other times she just ignored them because she could not understand.

Furthermore, when asked a question in Chinese, even if the participants understood the meaning after a number of repetitions from the teacher, they still did not know how to reply in correct Chinese, nor could they reply with reasonable spontaneity. Few verbal fillers or parentheses were used or understood, and little in the way of spontaneous replies could be generated.

To summarize, in the first videoconferencing sessions, with most participants, the role-play was accomplished with great difficulty. I had to control the conversation and speak English constantly to ensure understanding. To improve the quality of negotiation of meaning, a list of frequently used phrases was e-mailed to each participant at the end of the first session. The conversation became more natural and less interrupted in the following sessions because the participants learned to use these frequently-used phrases to maintain the flow of conversation. For example, in the second session, most participants could request clarification of meaning in Chinese, referring to the list of phrases e-mailed to them. Despite their low spoken proficiency, as the sessions progressed, the participants' interactional, speaking and listening skills improved rapidly.

Similar to the findings from Stage One, the distance participants with lower Chinese proficiency progressed with greater speed than those with a higher proficiency. And the average progress of the distance participants was much more obvious than that of the on-campus students. Very often, after the first two sessions, the participants were observed to be able to produce more quality output and were more at ease with speaking and listening to the language. More quality interactional modifications, modifications of output and spontaneous replies were generated towards the end of the trial. Data clearly demonstrates that with sufficient oral-visual interaction in the target language, learners' speaking skills can improve, even in a short period of time. Internet-based desktop videoconferencing proved to be capable of supporting such interaction.

Participants' perceived improvement in Chinese proficiency
The participants also confirmed that their Chinese proficiency, especially with regard to their listening and speaking skills, had improved throughout their five sessions. Participants' perception of their improvement was sought both in the post-session interviews and the post-trial surveys. The benefit of the spontaneous use of the language was favourably perceived by Participant A as early as in Session One:

> Eh, My Chinese isn't very good, and, when, when I'm sitting writing Chinese, it's fine. When I got my dictionary with me, it's fine. But then if I'm put on the spot, trying to remember the words, it's very, very difficult. Now this for me is a very good practice.

Participant C reported an improvement in her listening comprehension at the end of Session Three, even though she had the lowest listening skills when we first started the NetMeeting sessions and could not understand the simplest questions.

> Yeah, yeah. I can often, sometimes, need to hear it, maybe twice, three times, then I can pick up bits of it, as I was doing last time and sort of, as you suggested, sort of, get the context from what I am hearing.

With a similar level of listening and speaking proficiency before the videoconferencing sessions, when asked if she thought her listening was improved at the end of Session Five, Participant A affirmed with confidence:

Participant A:	Improved.
R:	Improved?
Participant A:	Like I could, I could understand most the words you were saying today, and trying...

Similar improvement was also perceived by participants with better Chinese proficiency. Although with the highest listening and speaking skills in Chinese among the distance participants, Participant B was also very positive about his achievement as early as in Session Three, as shown in the following excerpt of the interview.

Very useful [Session Three]. The last session would've been useful. It was just the technical difficulties that made it frustrating. But I really profited out of the first and this session, I profited an awful lot. If I had session like this on a regular basis, I think I would make, you know, considerable progress.

At the end of Session Four, he further explained his improvement as follows:

Participant B:	Em. Just, just the fact that I get a chance to use, to use the language in a direct conversation which I normally don't have. I...
R:	like spontaneous reply. Do you think you've improved in that way, when we have spontaneous conversations?
Participant B:	Yeah, I, I, definitely. You know it becomes easier to, to sort of, to spontaneously respond in Chinese. I don't have to, I don't have to grab as much for words any more as I did initially.

Similar improvement was also expressed by Participant E at the end of Session Five, who also enjoyed a better Chinese proficiency than most of the participants:

Yeah, I do. And actually I can just sense now, now that we have actually met a couple of times that had good connections, I can see each time you've taught me several new things. So yes I can. Now I can start to see well. If I were to be doing this regularly, I would be learning so many new things to say, plus having you correct me. When I spontaneously say something and get it wrong a little bit, you straight away say no *le*, or you add what I have done wrong. And I think it's a very good enforcement to have too.

Participants also enjoyed learning new grammatical structures and vocabulary, as manifested in the post-session interview following Session Three. For example, Participant E acknowledged her enjoyment of using and learning the language.

Yeah. I really did. What I enjoyed today was being able to practise some familiar things that I knew, plus learning some new phrases. As I said to you before I really enjoy learning new phrases. When they come up in conversations, and you point out something that I could say or a new word or phrase, I really enjoy that.

Participant A also expressed delight at learning something new with each task at the completion of Session Two:

[...] The kind of thing it's [the task] asking you should do is good because it, it. Um there's all sorts of vocabulary that you, that I'm learning. From all the little, from the things I have to work out what to say, I am learning all sorts of grammar, vocabulary. So yeah, I think it's really good.

Furthermore, participants' improved language proficiency was also discussed in the post-trial survey. For example, question PTS-2.2 requires the participants to indicate the strengths of NetMeeting for language learning. Table 5.3 demonstrates that the provision of instant feedback, spontaneous interaction and improvement in listening skills were perceived unanimously as the positive impact of videoconferencing on the participants' learning.

Table 5.3   Results from Stage Two evaluation of NetMeeting – strengths of NetMeeting for language learning (PTS-2.2)

Aspects of improvement		Results
(a)	Building my confidence in speaking Chinese	4
(b)	Reducing my anxiety in learning Chinese	2
(c)	Reducing isolation in learning in distance mode	3
(d)	Increasing my motivation in learning the language	3
(e)	Seeing the person I am talking to	3
(f)	Allowing instant feedback from the teacher	4
(g)	Allowing mistakes to be corrected on the spot	4
(h)	Providing me the opportunity to interact spontaneously with someone	4
(i)	Negotiating for meaning using Chinese	3
(j)	Allowing me to ask for more information using Chinese	4
(k)	Allowing me to clarify meaning using Chinese	4
(l)	Inferring meaning according to the context	3
(m)	Improving my listening skill	4

Note: N = 4

Almost all the participants believed that the impact of videoconferencing on the above aspects of language learning assisted their Chinese acquisition. In order to further determine the degree of improvement in their oral-visual interaction in the target language, question PTS-2.7 asks the participants to identify the specific aspects of improvement in their Chinese language learning after the five videoconferencing sessions with each participant (see Appendix D). Again, the results show that listening, speaking and conversational tactics were unanimously agreed upon as the most improved aspects corresponding with the results in question PTS-2.2 in Table 5.3.

It was hypothesized in Chapter 2 that the provision of oral-visual interaction supported by videoconferencing facilitates language acquisition. Already confirmed by the above-discussed improvement in participants' Chinese proficiency, this hypothesis was further tested in the Post-Trial Survey. Question PTS-2.11 asked the participants to rate the importance of oral-visual interaction to language acquisition on a 10-point scale. One participant marked '1' and the other three marked '2', suggesting that they unanimously believed that oral-visual interaction was essential to language learning. Participant B further commented on his entry by saying that such interaction is "important in providing visual cues involved in the communication process" and it is "useful also for demonstrating and correcting sound formation in establishing correct pronunciation". Participant D also explained his choice by saying:

> If you cannot speak with and see anyone while you are learning a language, it is very difficult to improve and to become fluent. It is integral that a student be able to practise what they are learning.

Participant E believed that oral-visual interaction "creates more of a classroom feeling which is a useful adjunct to all of the individual study that must be done by a distance education student".

Summary

This section has presented data in regard to the language learning potential of videoconferencing supported tasks, addressing issues such as the provision of focus on form and the improvement in the participants' target language proficiency. Data demonstrates that these tasks offer abundant language learning potential through videoconferencing-supported interaction, and that all participants believed that videoconferencing provided them with the much-needed opportunity to improve their listening, speaking and interactional skills. The lengthy and detailed presentation of data in this section can be justified by Chapelle's (2001, p. 58) contention that "the criteria of language learning potential should be considered the most important".

5.2.3   Learner fit

This section investigates the fit between the linguistic level of the participants and that required by the tasks. Different learner characteristics of the two groups of participants – the on-campus and the distance participants – is also examined for the judgment on the appropriateness of tasks for videoconferencing.

Participants' level of proficiency in Chinese

Theoretically speaking, the proficiency level of the on-campus and distance groups should be similar, as both groups had just finished the first two semesters of Chinese language learning. However, data revealed that, due to lack of speaking practice, the average level of general Chinese proficiency of the distance participants, was much lower than that of the on-campus students, despite the fact that the proficiency level varied from participant to participant. Among the three participants in Stage One, two had a comparatively higher level of proficiency and Student 3 possessed comparatively poor listening and speaking skills. In Stage Two, Participant B was a very fluent speaker, while Participant A and C could not conduct a basic conversation in Chinese at the start of the trial. Participant D and E were at a similar level as Student 3 in the on-campus group.

The level of difficulty of the tasks

As discussed in Section 3.3.6, when setting the level of difficulty of the tasks, the textbooks for both the on-campus and distance students were used as a reference. Care was taken to ensure that only basic grammar and limited vocabulary would be sufficient for completing these tasks.

Participants' perceptions on the level of difficulty of the tasks

Findings from Stage One – evaluation by on-campus students

All three participants confirmed that the tasks designed for each session were set at the right level of difficulty. Table 5.4 summarizes participants' responses at the post-session interviews in regard to the level of difficulty of the tasks.

Table 5.4   Results from Stage One evaluation – the level of difficulty of the tasks

Participants	Session One	Session Two	Session Three	Session Four	Session Five
Student 1	It's so so.	Just about the right level.	About the right level.	A bit difficult.	It's OK.
Student 2	A little bit difficult.	It was quite easy.	It's about the right level.	About the right level.	It was OK.
Student 3	No data available (The participant was not asked this question).	It wasn't too easy but it was fine.	Good. Not too easy but not too difficult either.	It's about the right level.	It was fine.

*Note: *For transcripts of some of the post-session interviews, see Appendix E.*

In the comprehensive interview at the end of Stage One, the participants' opinions on the level of difficulty of the task were sought from a different angle. They were asked if they thought their

Chinese proficiency was good enough to accomplish the tasks. The replies were all positive, confirming that the tasks were set at the right level of difficulty (see Appendix E).

Findings from Stage Two – evaluation by the distance students

Results from the evaluation by the distance participants, on the whole, support the findings from the evaluation by the on-campus students. At the end of each session, the participants were immediately interviewed by telephone to discuss their experiences during the session. Participants' responses in regard to the level of difficulty of the tasks are recapitulated in Table 5.5.

Table 5.5   Results from Stage Two evaluation – the level of difficulty of the tasks

Participants	Session One	Session Two	Session Three	Session Four	Session Five
Participant A	I'd say it was the level I am supposed to be on. It was OK.	I'd say about the right level. It would; it's definitely not too easy, but I don't think it's too difficult either.	It was about the right level for me.	I think about the right level for me.	About the right level.
Participant B	It was just right.	No it wasn't too difficult, but it was sort of stretched a little bit.	It was a bit demanding. But it was OK.	I didn't find it difficult. It was the right level.	Not too difficult, not too easy.
Participant C	It was not too difficult but not easy either.	It was OK.	It was about right. I don't think it was too easy. But I think it was a doable task.	*	*
Participant D	No data due to unsuccessful session.	No data due to unsuccessful session.	No data due to unsuccessful session.	No data due to unsuccessful session.	It was a good level.
Participant E	[The task was not difficult]. It was a very familiar territory. It's spontaneity I found difficult.	Good, I think it's good.	About the right level today.	A little bit difficult but very useful.	It was OK.

*Notes: *Participant C withdrew from the trial after the first three sessions.*
For transcripts of some of the post-session interviews, see excerpts in Appendix F.

The above data suggests that all participants believed that the level of difficulty of the Tasks was within their grasp. Such a level of agreement did not mean that they never encountered any difficulties in task completion. However, they could usually pinpoint the source of the difficulty as shown in the following excerpt from the interview at the completion of Session One:

Participant A:	I'd say, I'd say it was the level I am supposed to be on. It was, it was OK. I don't think it was too difficult. I think it was just the fact that I am a little bit nervous with Chinese.
R:	Mm Mm.
Participant A:	Yeah, but I don't think the content's too difficult.

Summary

Data from both stages one and two confirms the fit between the participants' level of proficiency in Chinese and the level of difficulty of the three sets of tasks, despite the fact that the proficiency level of the participants varied. The reasons for such consensus are manifold and will be discussed in Chapter 6.

5.2.4   Authenticity

Major issues under investigation in this section are whether the tasks designed for the NetMeeting sessions were perceived to be useful in and related to real life, and whether these tasks can help the students cultivate communicative skills.

Progressive improvement on the authenticity of the tasks

Findings from Stage One – evaluation by on-campus participants
As described in Section 3.3.6, there were three sets of tasks designed for the two stages of NetMeeting evaluation. The major theme of Set 1 (see Table 3.6 for its content) is a job application. It consists of five subtasks all relating to the major theme, although each has its own central topic(s) such as a telephone conversation enquiring about details of the job, inviting a friend to have coffee together and talking about the job, and a job interview, etc. Care was taken to include in the subtasks topics about everyday activities, such as food, price, directions and one's own life experiences. These topics were selected in consideration that they would be of interest to the participants while ascertaining that the linguistic structures and vocabulary were within the grasp of the participants.

It was discovered in Stage One that students tended to deviate from the main task and talk about themselves and their daily activities. Besides, some participants also suggested that a greater variety of topics be introduced in the tasks. For example, when asked about the limitations of the tasks at the end of Session Five, Student 1 mentioned:

> I guess the tasks are drawn by the teacher. If you want to talk about something else, the task
> might not let you do that, because they have the limitations of what the teacher put down for the
> tasks.

Student 2 also preferred topics about more everyday activities as she commented following Session Five:

I think it's very useful, the different situations. Probably would have preferred something more with shopping and buying things. And things like how to cook this or where to put this away.

Findings from Stage Two – evaluation by the distance participants

In view of the on-campus participants' tendency to talk about themselves, Set 2 of the tasks (see Table 3.7 for the contents of Set 2) was introduced in Stage Two. Set 2 retains all the contents in Set 1 but with the addition of a free chat at the beginning of each subtask, in order to relax the participants and provide them with an opportunity to talk about things of particular interest to them. Thus the first 5–10 minutes of each session were dedicated to this free chat, that is, no specific topic(s) were set. The teacher and the students could talk about anything they wanted to, for example, the weather, the food they had eaten that day, the movie they watched the week before or someone they both knew. Apart from putting the participants at ease, this free chat also served the purpose of mentally preparing them for thinking in Chinese. After the free conversation, they would then move to the main task for the session.

Set 2 was trialled with the distance participants and they all enjoyed the free chat. Furthermore, during the course of this stage of the evaluation, some improvements to the tasks were deemed necessary in view of the emerging characteristics of the distance learners.

It was found that role-plays with the teacher seemed somewhat awkward for some distance participants. For example, I found that Participant B constantly reverted to talking about himself during the role-plays. When interviewed on this, Participant B replied,

I just found it personally... difficult to go into role-plays like that. But it's probably useful tools to sort of, you know, introduce situations and vocabulary and so on. I can see the point but I found it difficult.

When asked what kind of tasks he would prefer, Participant B offered: "I personally would prefer a more informal way, you know, if you could just, you know, engage in a conversation, and introduce, you know, certain curriculum material you want to introduce". At the end of the trial with him, he also commented:

Participant B: I would prefer, you know, not as structured as this, you know what I mean?... we went through a set. In the five sessions we went through this procedure of me applying for the job... but I would prefer personally less structured in that way.

R: But would you prefer we have a topic for each session?

Participant B:	Yes a topic. Maybe just a topic. And then to loosely engage in dialogue around that topic, I think that would suit me better.

It also became evident after the first sessions with a few participants that some participants forgot many basic grammatical structures and vocabulary they had learned before, probably due to lack of practice. It was then deemed important to make the participants explicitly aware of these basic grammatical rules when preparing for and completing these tasks.

In view of the above findings, Set 3 (see Table 3.8 for the contents of Set 3) was then brought in to include a combination of *real-world* tasks such as talking about oneself and one's family, and *pedagogical* tasks such as role-plays. Care was also taken to design the tasks in such a way that basic grammatical rules and structures were specified in task descriptions and required to be used together with more complicated ones. When Set 3 was e-mailed to the participants in Stage Two, everyone chose it with the exception of Participant B, who by then had already completed his five sessions. Participant A opted for Set 3 after finishing the first two sessions in Set 2. She compared the two sets of tasks and commented:

Participant A:	Good. I, I, I actually enjoyed the task [Set 3, Task 1 – Talking about myself] a lot better than, than the previous task. Probably because it was easier, and, and more basic Chinese, kind of like talking about myself and asking you questions. It was probably more interactive than the last one [Set 2, Task 2 – A telephone conversation between two friends].
[...]	
Participant A:	... I think talking about yourself you can explore and you can start to look at new vocabulary as you think about what you do. You then start to look, looking for more Chinese and to explore a bit more where as in those role-plays, it was quite, it was difficult to imagine, and look for new words that way.
[...]	
R:	Um, did you think the task was useful in real life?
Participant A:	Yes! Yes.

Again, when asked what she thought of the task in Session 4, She replied:

Participant A:	Good!
R:	Good?
Participant A:	Yeah, I'm, I'm enjoying, I enjoyed your other subtasks as well, but I'm enjoying these tasks about, something about like myself and my family because it's, it's very basic Chinese and...

R:	Yeah.
Participant A:	... and I think I need this because I don't talk to anybody in Chinese. I'm getting this opportunity now with you, it's good just to talk about those basic things.
R:	Yeah, yeah.
Participant A:	So yeah, I enjoyed the task.

It was also observed that the participants were aware of the specified linguistic forms for each session and consciously used them in their conversations. For example, they made an effort to use *le* in the session focusing on the use of *le*.

Participants' perception on the authenticity of the tasks

Findings from Stage One – evaluation by the on-campus participants
The participants were interviewed after each session on the usefulness of the tasks in real life. All participants believed that the tasks were authentic and related to real life. For example, at the end of Session One, Student 2 was very positive about the authenticity of the task, and further explained:

Student 2:	Yeah it's [this session] very fun.
R:	Why did you say that?
Student 2:	Umm, talking about just everyday things.
R:	Yeah?
Student 2:	So it gives me a chance to practise the structure of my sentences as well.

At the completion of Session One, Student 1 also confirmed that "this task is more of real life situations" and that "if you have more real life situations in the speaking, speaking activities, it'll be very useful". The same positive feedback was also received from Student 3. (see Appendix E)

Findings from Stage Two – evaluation by distance participants
Responses from the distance participants in Stage Two also confirmed the relevancy of the tasks to the real world. Upon completing Session One, Participant B talked about such relevancy:

Participant B:	Oh, yes, obviously. I mean this is the sort of thing you want to do. I think this little task actually lacks in the other materials we are getting through Griffith.
R:	... So what do you think of this session as a whole?
Participant B:	I thought it was very useful. I don't get the opportunity to do something like this normally. I only listen to the audio tapes, that's you know, missing that dynamic and interaction.
R:	Yeah, did you enjoy it?

Participant B: Yes. Very much, want to do it again.

At the end of Session Four, Participant B again pointed out the authenticity of the tasks by saying that "it was a useful task" and that "I like most of the things we've done, something you do in everyday life". Participant E offered more detailed comments on the usefulness of the tasks after completing sessions Four and Five.

> ... I think both of the tasks today are really essential for anyone who wants to communicate in Chinese. They all are. They've all been really essential but, I think the sort of things we are talking about today would be often what you would ask some one, the first task, often you would ask someone each time you are meeting in the street, those sorts of questions about, where is something, how do you get somewhere. I thought that was really good. And tourism is often easy to talk about.

At the end of Session Two, Participant A also agreed that the task was closely related to every day life "because it's a phone call and you talk about directions" and because "the task involves a lot of daily activities". To Participant C, all the tasks she had completed were very beneficial in real life, as shown in the following remarks on the activities in Session Two:

> That was, well, I thought the activity was very good. What we did was useful.... it's really good to be able to hear and try to use some of the language.

Summary

Data in this section shows that the authenticity of the tasks underwent progressive improvement during the two stages of the evaluation in accordance with the participants' needs. While the participants' tendency to talk about their own life experiences as opposed to the prescribed pedagogical tasks was evident in the evaluation, they all believed that the pedagogical tasks were also relevant to and useful in real life, and they all enjoyed these tasks.

5.2.5   Positive impact

In essence, the positive impact of videoconferencing refers to any impacts apart from those discussed in language learning potential of the tasks (Section 5.2.2). In this section, four issues will be under close investigation here in view of their significant importance to this research – the impact of video, the impact of videoconferencing on the reduction of the sense of isolation, on confidence building and on enthusiasm in distance language learning. As these impacts of videoconferencing were more manifest among the distance participants than among the on-campus learners, data presented in this section centres on the perceptions of the distance participants from

Stage Two of the evaluation, while perceptions of the on-campus participants will be used as a comparison.

The impact of the video

In Section 5.2.2, the importance of video was perceived and discussed in terms of its linguistic benefits and its support for task completion. This section will examine the role that the real-time video played in establishing personal links and teacher-learner rapport during oral-visual interaction via videoconferencing. Being a major component of videoconferencing, this role should not be neglected. The video transmits in real time the facial expressions of the two parties and their body movements above the shoulders. During the videoconferencing sessions, participants were not explicitly required to watch the video, but the video was on their desktop throughout the sessions. The importance of the video was firmly confirmed by the participants, especially the distance participants.

Findings from Stage One – evaluation by the on-campus participants
In Stage One, it was observed that the participants only looked at the video at the beginning of each session for a few minutes and then they seemed to ignore the video and concentrate on listening and speaking. This observation was further confirmed by the participants in the post-session interviews. For example, Student 3 admitted that she did not pay much attention to the video in Session one.

> …I was like, oh my god, what's that word? you know like I was just trying to concentrate, I didn't even look at you really because (a) you were blurred and (b) I was more focusing on your voice than your face.

However, Student 2's perception of the importance of the video underwent a change from being positive to less positive. For instance, in Session 1, Student 2 believed that visual input was important for language acquisition.

Student 2:	[…]. I've used programs to just talk but not to see. It makes it a whole lot different, because you can see the person. Because we learn Chinese you can see the expression on the face.
R:	Is that important for learning language.
Student 2:	I think it's important. Yeah. Because you not only can see, but you sort of can see the rhythm of the speaker to try to correct yourself.

However, in Session 5, she seemed to look at the importance of video from a different angle:

| Student 2: | It [the video] may have been important, but to me I felt it wasn't that important as the previous sessions, like the first and the second. |

R:	Just imagine if we didn't have the video, how would you feel about that?
Student 2:	Not having the pictures at all?
R:	Yep, not at all.
Student 2:	Umm. I think it might, I think it might help. It might help take the distraction away.
R:	Oh? So it might be better?
Student 2:	Yeah. Umm maybe for the first time or the first two times it might be good to see your teacher and who you're talking to so you can match the face with the person's voice. But after that I think it might be more beneficial to just listen.

On the whole, the video was not perceived essential to language learning by the on-campus participants. This perception forms a distinct contrast to that obtained from the distance participants.

Findings from Stage Two – evaluation by distance participants

It was observed that, apart from looking down at their notes, the distance participants always kept their eyes on the video image. Although the video could be frozen or delayed at times, such quality did not seem to deter them from watching the video all the time. They were all delighted to see me, and a friendly and positive atmosphere was usually created. This observation was further supported by the participants' feedback in the end-of-session interviews. All participants confirmed that they constantly watched the video image in every session. Participant A reported that she watched the video all the time, apart from when she was looking down at her notes. She discussed the importance of video at the completion of Session Two by saying that "I think more than anything it helps just the fact that we can see each other", and that "it's a bit more personal than just talking on the phone".

As mentioned in Section 4.3.3, Participant E did not have good video quality due to her limited laptop power. However she still looked at the video all the time throughout the sessions because she enjoyed the personal contact with her teacher, as she indicated at the end of Session 1.

Participant E:	[...] I think my overwhelming impression that, is that it was really nice to have something personal, to feel like a personal contact. And that's, that's a really favourable impression that I got from the whole exercise.
R:	Because of the video or ?
Participant E:	Yeah, I really did feel like I had met you.

For Participant C, video was considered important for linguistic reasons as well as for the access to personal contact. She commented at the completion of Session Two that the video helped to "watch the mouth" and that "there were a couple of instances you were showing the different mouth positions" of some of the words.

Answers to the question (PTS-2.5 in Appendix D) about the aspects of NetMeeting that they liked also support the importance of video as perceived by the participants. Participant B commented:

> I liked the one on one nature of the medium which provided for very intensive lessons. Plus the features of Netmeeting [Netmeeting] that allowed for instant feedback (e.g. whiteboard), and introduction of other materials e.g.: documents (sharing) and video [...] relevant to the context of the face to face dialogue.

Question PTS-2.8 (Appendix D) required the participants to indicate on a 10 point scale the importance of video to the improvement of listening and speaking skills, 1 representing 'important' and 10 'not important'. Participant A indicated 1, and offered the following reasons for her choice:

> The video is very important, because it is more personal to speak to each other face to face than on the phone.... And again it is nice to have that face to face contact, and put a face to the name, both for student and teacher. The video can be a little scary at first, especially if you have not used netmeeting [NetMeeting] before in other situations. But like any new technology, it is also exciting, and any nerves of using the video quickly disappear!

Again, the above comment indicates that the provision of personal links was regarded as an important attribute of the video function. To Participant D, who marked 3 on the scale, to establishing a personal learning environment assists language acquisition:

> I think it is important, because it is helpful to 'see' your teacher. To have a telephone conference would not be as good. Seeing your teacher is more personal, and it makes you more comfortable, which assists with learning. Of course video is not as important as audio, but it is still significant.

Participant E chose 4 on the scale and explained that "the video quality I experienced was never good enough to allow me to see my tutor's lips clearly, but I still got a lot from my sessions". Because she used a laptop, the video quality was affected by the limited power of her computer. Participant B chose 1 on the scale and commented the importance of video from a linguistic perspective. (see Section 5.2.2)

In summary, a distinctively contrasting perception was obtained from the two-stage evaluation in regard to the importance of video. While the on-campus participants regarded video as an added value, the distance participants valued the video for its provision of personal links and paralinguistic cues, both being perceived as crucial to language acquisition.

The impact of videoconferencing on the reduction of isolation

Closely related to the impact of the video is the impact of videoconferencing on the reduction of isolation commonly experienced by distance language learners. The establishment, through the video, of personal contact between the teacher and the participants was genuinely appreciated and highly valued by the distance participants, as clearly evident in the interview segments presented above. Again, such enthusiasm did not surface among the on-campus participants, none of whom showed any enthusiasm for being able to see the teacher. On the contrary, the distance participants welcomed with great enthusiasm the opportunity to interact with another human being, despite the not-so-perfect sound and video quality. The participants' enthusiasm, tolerance of the technology and appreciation of the opportunity to interact with others are plainly manifested in the following excerpt from the interview with Participant A immediately following the first session:

> Participant A:... Like I've been studying Chinese now a little over six months and I haven't been able to talk to anybody really, so this communication is really good.
>
> [...]
>
> R: Yeah, because I think you don't have this kind of exercise.
>
> Participant A: That's right. Exactly, yeah. And this is what I need to do↑.
>
> R: Hm
>
> Participant A: Break that, to break that barrier. Now I've been a little bit more confident after today's session. So
>
> R: Yeah.
>
> Participant A: Next session may be a little bit better and then, hahh.

In the post-trial survey, question PTS-2.5 asked what the participants liked when using NetMeeting for learning Chinese. Participant A again showed her appreciation of such an opportunity to interact with the tutor.

> It was just so nice as a distant student learning a difficult language to have face-to-face tutor contact. Distance students normally are studying via distance ed because they are busy – so it was a bonus to be able to practise speaking Chinese with my tutor in my own home!

Such positive reception of videoconference was also manifested in question PTS-2.2 (see Table 5.3), which indicates that most participants believed that videoconferencing helped with the reduction of the sense of isolation in their language learning.

The impact of the videoconferencing on confidence building

Personal observations

Confidence building is another positive impact of videoconferencing that manifested itself strongly during the trial with the distance participants. In contrast, none of the on-campus participants even mentioned this issue. Due to lack of exposure to oral-visual interaction, a common feeling of apprehension among the distance participants existed even before the trial, as Participant C described in her e-mail:

> [...] I was still undecided as to whether I wanted to take part or not. I really do, but was a little apprehensive about it! Hopefully my fear will be overcome after I have tried it once!

It was also observed in the videoconferencing sessions, especially in the first sessions, that most participants were very nervous about speaking Chinese and often had a mental block when spoken to in Chinese because they had seldom had the opportunity to communicate with anyone in Chinese. Such apprehension was clearly evident in the case study with Participant A (see Section 5.2.2). However, as the sessions proceeded, it became apparent that they were gradually gaining confidence and could produce more quality output.

Participants' perceptions

Confidence building was cited by all the distance participants as one of the advantages of using videoconferencing to learn Chinese in distance mode. For example, Participant B admitted in the interview following Session Three that "every time I feel more confident that I can use the language". This kind of confidence-building process also happened to Participant C who had the lowest level of proficiency in spoken Chinese. She became more confident even as early as the second videoconferencing session.

Participant C:	A little bit [of improvement in speaking skills]. I probably wasn't quite nervous this time. [...] so each time it gets a little bit easier, I'm more prepared to have a bit of a go at it. hahh without feeling I am going to make terrible mistakes, hahh. So that's improving my confidence in that regard.
R:	Yeah, good, hahh. OK, so more of your confidence than speaking skills? Is it?
Participant C:	Yeah. Yeah. What it is actually being game enough to actually use it without feeling like, you know, I'm going to make a terrible blue or something.

In Session Three, she also mentioned that "it's good for my confidence to actually speak with you" and that "it's making me feel more confident about the language.

Participant A also stressed that she felt more confident as each session progressed. For example, in Session Four, when asked about her improvement compared with the previous session, she confirmed:

Participant A: Yes, a big improvement.

R: Big improvement. Like in what, in what area?

Participant A: Em, just the confidence with, and, and I suppose like I used to, whenever I tried to
                    think and say something in Chinese, I was just freeze. And even though I probably
                    knew the words, I couldn't think of them and couldn't put them together. Each
                    session I have been able to, eh, like it's not so scary anymore to try to be put on the
                    spot and asked the question. Yeah I am improving in that way.

In the post-trial survey, Participant A further confirmed her re-ignited motivation after completing the five videoconferencing sessions (PTS-2.5):

Before the sessions, I used to freeze when I tried to string a sentence together spontaneously!
Netmeeting [NetMeeting] has enabled me to overcome that initial fear of being asked a question
in Chinese, to only feel embarrassed that I cannot think of a response, even though I have
learned the words! I am not quite fluent yet (ha ha!), but I definitely have the confidence now to
take on further challenges in Chinese conversation!

In comparison with Participant A, Participant E had encountered a much greater range of problems both during the installation of NetMeeting and during the actual sessions (e.g. a faulty Webcam, a firewall and limited laptop capacity). Despite all these problems and frustrations she enjoyed the sessions so much that, after the trial, she was willing to meet me again online once her school technician had solved the problem of the firewall at her school. Her excitement about the chance to use Chinese and sense of achievement were clearly demonstrated in the following interview excerpt (Session Five):

R: I was surprised when I said "*wen ni duixiang hao*" (Say hello to your boyfriend).
                    And you said quickly "*yi ding zhuangao*" (I'll certainly pass it on). Very quickly.
                    Really. Just like we were in a, you know, real conversation.

Participant E: Hahh. I got very excited when those things happen. After Wednesday's meeting, I
                    went home on a real high. Hahh

R: Hahh.

Participant E:	I was so excited. Hahh, I was a bit excited today when I got back to school, I was bouncing upstairs and I ran into the technician who tried to help me, I said oh, I just had another NetMeeting, [...] So, Yeah, I still feel a bit on a high again. *Wo huijian yihou, yiding he yi da bei hong putao jiu* (After I get home, I must have a big glass of red wine).
[...]	
R:	To celebrate.
Participant E:	Celebrate, qingzhu. Yeah, definitely.
[...]	
R:	[...] And do you feel more confident [with your Chinese?
Participant E:	[Definitely, yeah. Definitely.

Replies to question PTS-2.2 (see Table 5.3) also demonstrate that all participants believed that they became more confident in speaking Chinese during the NetMeeting sessions.

Participants' enthusiasm in videoconferencing supported DLE

The distance participants' enthusiasm in videoconferencing supported learning was evident not only in their strong belief in the pedagogical and motivational values of videoconferencing, but also in their unanimous endorsement that videoconferencing be incorporated in distance language learning. In the Post-Trial Survey, question PTS-2.13 explicitly solicits participants' opinions on whether NetMeeting should be incorporated into the Open Learning Chinese program after the trial. All participants welcomed such a component in their learning. The advantages of the inclusion of videoconferencing were viewed from the following perspectives: linguistic benefits, the increase of motivation, reduction of isolation and the effective pedagogical values of the videoconference. For example, Participant A believed:

Yes I do think that netmeeting [Netmeeting] should be incorporated into the OLA Chinese Program, because of all the reasons above! The trial has been a great opportunity for me to improve my Chinese, and therefore using netmeeting [Netmeeting] as a set part of the course would obviously be nothing but advantageous for students and their results, and most importantly their enthusiasm and motivation by having fun learning Chinese!

Participant B appreciated the importance of videoconferencing in terms of its linguistic benefits to the learner, as shown in the following excerpt taken from the Session Two interview:

Participant B:	Speaking about suggestions, what I would feel, personally feel that this type of delivery would be really useful for pronunciation drills, because when you are

studying on your own, it's very hard, you know, to just pick it up off the tapes, because you can't, you don't get the, you need the visual as well, how the sound is formed. Also you need instant eh, instant feedback, specially for the still too…yeah. If you got mistakes, to correct them instantly so you don't form bad habits.

R: OK pronunciation drills.

Participant B: I thought it would be very good for that. In case… the camera setting is good as it is, fairly close up, you can see the face and how the sounds are formed. But when we do a, a you know, little role-play, it might be better, I don't know if the camera is good enough for that, if you could sit back a little bit, you see more of the body language.

In her reply to question PTS-2.13, Participant E emphasized both the provision of motivation and linguistic benefits through videoconferencing:

> […] I absolutely loved having the opportunity to converse with someone in Chinese. Apart from being exciting, it motivated me to continue studying, and gave me some much needed contact with someone. Therefore I think some kind of videoconferencing should be used. The very best thing would be for some opportunity to speak with small groups including other students on some occasions, and the opportunity to speak only with the tutor on other occasions. I think I learned a lot in a short time while talking with my tutor, and would like to see continued opportunity to develop spontaneous conversation skills in this way.

Participant D regarded the use of videoconferencing as a necessity in DLE (PTS-2.13):

> Although my trial had a lot of technical problems, I can certainly see the immense benefit in having NetMeeting in the Open Learning Chinese Program. Without it, Chinese is extremely difficult to learn without any other support. I think Netmeeting is almost a necessity.

The pedagogical values of videoconferencing were also recognized by the participants, as demonstrated in Participant B's reply to question PT2-2.13:

> Provided the technical problems related to unreliable and slow connection can be at least minimized, I would strongly support the incorporation of NetMeeting into the Chinese program. All the features of the program provide useful aids for the language learner, e.g.: sharing, video, whiteboard. Initially one might consider using NetMeeting as the preferred form of liaising with the tutor during the regular time slot provided for the purpose.

The last question in the Post-Trial Survey (PTS-2.14) offered the participants an opportunity to comment freely on their experience of the trial, and the following responses were collected:

♦ The trial really showed me that it is possible to learn a language through distance education. Although it is still difficult, and there are a range of technical problems, it is a great idea, and I would recommend it as a significant educative tool. (Participant D)

♦ Thank you very much. I have appreciated it very much! (Participant A)

♦ In my view, it is difficult to learn Chinese by distance education unless there is a component of conversation included. Netmeeting [NetMeeting] could be an effective way to build some regular conversation practice into Chinese studies. (Participant E)

To summarize the findings in this section, videoconferencing has profoundly impacted the participants, especially the distance participants in many positive ways. The video provided the participants with interactive learning opportunities that simulated face-to-face interaction. Most linguistic and social cues were present in real time during videoconferencing sessions, which reduces linguistic insecurity and the sense of isolation felt by most distance language learners. Consequently the participants' experiences with videoconferencing greatly added to their enthusiasm and confidence in speaking and continuing to learn the language. The incorporation of videoconferencing into distance language learning was strongly recommended by all distance participants.

5.3 Summary

This chapter has presented, with preliminary analysis, the findings from Stage One and Two of the evaluation of NetMeeting, in relation to the pedagogical values of videoconferencing. Such evaluation was approached from the perspective of the potential of videoconferencing for supporting oral-visual interaction in **task** completion. The following findings can be summarized from my observation and participants' feedback in regard to these two stages of evaluation:

♦ The language learning potential of the videoconferencing-supported tasks was confirmed based on its provision of focus on form in oral-visual interaction and a perceived improvement in participants' Chinese proficiency.

♦ The fit between the level of difficulty of the tasks and the participants' proficiency level was established.

♦ The authenticity of the tasks underwent phases of improvement during the evaluation and was perceived by all the participants to be relevant to and useful in real life.

♦ The most manifest sentiment that emerged in the evaluation was the positive impact of videoconferencing on participants' enthusiasm and confidence building, and reduction in the sense of isolation. The video was especially well received by the distance participants, who had been physically separated from a learning community, and needed a sense of connectedness to other learners and their education provider. They all believed that the five videoconferencing sessions were a rewarding experience in their learning.

On the whole, participants perceived the use of videoconferencing in a balanced way. On the one hand, they recognized the limitations of the Internet technology; on the other, they were very positive and enthusiastic about the technological and pedagogical potential of videoconferencing for the promotion of oral-visual interaction in their distance language learning. The findings in this chapter suggest that real-time oral-visual interaction via videoconferencing does indeed facilitate L2 acquisition at a distance. As this is the primary research focus of this study, further discussion in terms of both the evaluation data and the subsidiary research questions is conducted in the chapter that follows, Chapter 6.

Chapter Six

Discussion: The technological capabilities and pedagogical values of oral-visual interaction via videoconferencing for L2 acquisition at a distance

6.1 Introduction

This chapter develops the discussion in chapters 4 and 5, in order to provide more details on the central research question:

in what ways is oral-visual interaction, enabled by videoconferencing, able to facilitate L2 acquisition at a distance?

As the main concern of this research is the pedagogical value of videoconferencing-supported interaction, a large proportion of the discussion of its technological capabilities will be kept in the background except where it supports the analysis of its pedagogical potential. A recurring point of discussion is the pedagogical value of oral-visual interaction supported by videoconferencing, bringing together the theories in the literature and the data from stages one and two of the evaluation of NetMeeting. It is in light of this objective that the discussion in this chapter is developed and the conclusion in regard to the capabilities of oral-visual interaction via videoconferencing is reached.

The discussion in this chapter is organized in reference to the criteria developed in research for the evaluation of the technological capabilities and pedagogical values of videoconferencing in the support of meaning-based task completions:

- ◆ practicality
- ◆ language learning potential
- ◆ learner fit
- ◆ authenticity
- ◆ positive impact

Discussions on the findings will constantly draw on comparisons between the Stage One and Stage Two evaluation in order to achieve a more comprehensive analysis of the findings. Upon examination of the findings in regard to each of these criteria, recommendations will then be made for each criterion so that future research can take the best advantage of videoconferencing-supported oral-visual interaction.

6.2 Practicality

The analysis of practicality examines the data from the two-stage evaluation of NetMeeting in regard to the fit between the task and the videoconferencing tools used to realize the tasks. In other words, the emphasis of the discussion will be on the technological capacity of NetMeeting. This analysis will follow the criteria developed in this research for selecting videoconferencing tools. They are:

- ♦ user friendliness
- ♦ video and audio quality
- ♦ features of pedagogical values
- ♦ reliability
- ♦ cost

Following the discussion of each of the above criteria, recommendations will be suggested on how to take the best advantage of each of these features of NetMeeting.

6.2.1 User friendliness

The evaluation of the user friendliness of NetMeeting constituted two parts: the ease of installation and ease of use. Sections 4.2.2 and 4.3.2 indicate that in regard to ease of installation, both the on-campus and distance participants were very positive, although the distance participants' responses were slightly diverse.

Aside from the differences in individuals' level of computer knowledge, the following two factors might play a part in the diversity in the perception of the Open Learning students. First, without any technical assistance at hand, they might be overwhelmed by the steps contained in the *Manual*. In contrast, the presence of technical support at the installation of NetMeeting by the on-campus students might increase the students' confidence. Second, minor mistakes or the appearance of unknown elements in the installation would tend to disadvantage the distance participants because they did not possess enough computing knowledge to solve unexpected problems. Even a simple step such as plugging in the microphone in the right socket was a challenge for one student. These factors might have an adverse effect on the distance participants' perception. Thus a foolproof installation manual and uncomplicated installation procedures proved to be vital for the acceptance of a videoconferencing tool by a new user. Nevertheless, NetMeeting proved to be a tool that could be installed by anyone with basic computer knowledge.

As shown in Sections 4.2.2 and 4.3.2, ease of use was unanimously agreed upon by both the on-campus and distance participants. The simplicity in the interface design of NetMeeting ensured a smooth operation of NetMeeting during the trial sessions.

In conclusion, the user friendliness of NetMeeting was firmly established in both the trials with the on-campus and distance participants. NetMeeting proved to be easy to install and easy to use. It is a generic tool for any user with or without knowledge about videoconferencing. The user friendliness of NetMeeting greatly added to the participants' positive perception of videoconferencing.

Recommendation for setting up NetMeeting

It is suggested that a detailed manual for the steps involved in setting up NetMeeting should be written and given to the learner at least two weeks before the first videoconferencing session. A few time slots should be set aside for the learner's consultation during the set up period. An animated instruction manual can be provided on the Web or on a CD ROM.

Furthermore, as suggested by Participant B, following the installation of a videoconferencing tool, a tutorial session should be provided to familiarize the learner with the various functions of NetMeeting so that anxiety and apprehension about using the new technology can be reduced.

Last but not least, before using NetMeeting, it is recommended that other applications on the desktop be closed in order to save computer power for running videoconferencing. Too many applications will take up too much computer power resulting in poor video and sound quality, slow program response, or even crashes of videoconferencing and its functions. These recommendations are not NetMeeting specific and might also be applicable for other similar desktop videoconferencing products.

6.2.2 Audio and video quality

Data in sections 4.2.3 and 4.3.3 shows that there were some differences in the audio and video quality of NetMeeting between Stage One and Stage Two. In Stage One, both the sound and video quality in the Intranet environment reached an excellent level for language teaching and learning with an insignificant delay (up to one second) and excellent continuity. Such quality was consistent enough even for language testing because with a delay of less than 80msec, the sound and video can still perceived as synchronous, as specified in the criteria for selecting videoconferencing tools (see Section 3.4.1). In contrast, a variety of sound and video quality was experienced when the evaluation was launched in the Internet environment in Stage Two. An analysis of the relevant data reveals two major issues: the inconsistency of the audio and video quality and a delay in sound and video transmission.

The biggest issue in this stage was the instability of the sound and video quality, and the problematic sessions were mostly experienced in the *modem-Internet-modem* environment. Internet conditions such as bandwidth and latency became decisive as far as video and audio quality was concerned. In this environment, the success of each session relied heavily on the Internet traffic conditions at the time of the session. Thus timing became a crucial factor.

In the *LAN-Internet-modem* network environment, on my side, an obvious improvement in the video and sound quality was noticed with better continuity and clarity. However, on the participants' side, the judgment of the improvement in sound quality was mixed. This difference may be caused by the processing power or the quality of the sound and video cards on each individual's computer.

The *LAN-Internet-LAN* environment proved to be able to offer the best audio and video quality in comparison with the other two environments. My observation suggests that the audio and video quality was not much affected by Internet traffic even at peak Internet times. On the contrary, consistent audio and video quality could be achieved on my side. However such consistency was not experienced by Participant E, who did not report satisfactory sound and video quality. The poor audio and video quality was probably caused by the low computing power of her laptop, many functions of which are compressed. Thus a powerful computer with high capacity audio and video cards is another crucial factor in generating quality video and sound transmission. Similar problems were also reported by Hampel & Hauck (2004). Nevertheless, the findings regarding the excellent audio and video quality in the *LAN-Internet-LAN* environment are significant in that they promise videoconferencing with consistent quality audio and video when Internet bandwidth is broadened. At the very least, these findings suggest that inter-school/university desktop videoconferencing is viable and free. Collaboration between education providers and among learners is now easily and freely attainable through NetMeeting.

Data from this research supports Watson & Sasse's (1996) contention that the quality of audio and video is most likely to vary from one participant to another:

> This can arise for many different reasons: different local network loads, different hardware (e.g. headsets), different background noise and lighting, and loading on the individual's workstation. These differences mean that it is not easy to get inter-observer reliability for perceived quality over one conference. (p. 260)

Probing the causes of the inconsistency in video and sound quality in the Internet environment, this research confirmed that the limited bandwidth of the Internet and long latency lay at the heart of these problems. Bandwidth refers to how many bits per second a communication line can transmit. Inherent with the Internet, it has been a critical factor affecting the consistency and reliability of videoconferencing. This is because real-time transmission of high quality video usually consumes much larger amounts of network bandwidth than do audio channels only. The constraints of Internet bandwidth have long been recognized as a major detrimental factor affecting quality videoconferencing (see Kötter et al., 1999; McAndrew et al., 1996; Wong & Fauverge, 1999; Ibañez & Duque, 1999; Buckett & Stringer, 1997; Zähner et al., 2000; Hampel, 2003). Chou (2001, p. 9) points out, "desktop audio-videoconferencing systems are still very limited in their functions and constrained to network bottlenecks". The evaluation of NetMeeting confirms that this limitation still exists and determines the quality of videoconferencing. Attempts have been made by language professionals to minimize the impact of bandwidth. For example, Hearnshaw (2000, p. 221 & 227) assesses the effects of different levels of video channel quality on learning outcomes and points out that "increasing the quality of the video channel resulted in no measurable increase in the quality of dialogue within the tutorial". He concludes that desktop videoconferencing "can be used effectively with low video quality levels which only need consume modest amounts of bandwidth". While decreasing the quality of video might be a temporary solution, the use of broadband techniques can deliver a more fundamental and effective solution. Results from this research show that, at the time when this research was conducted, choosing a less congested Internet time was probably a more practical and economical option to deal with the constraints of Internet bandwidth. At a time when the Internet was less congested, the video and audio quality could almost reach the Intranet quality. However, it has to be noted that such a restraint on time may have an adverse implication for the actual implementation of videoconferencing, as Internet off-peak time may mean both the teacher and the learner would have to work at a time which may not be convenient to them.

As an important contribution of this research, the findings also direct our attention to the existence and impact of communication latency. Communication latency is the time interval for a message travelling from the source machine to the destination machine. Satyanarayanna (1996) emphasizes the detrimental effect of latency by saying that "the entire focus of the industry is on bandwidth, but the true killer is latency." The longer the latency is, the more delayed the transmission will be. Sun & Chen (2002) argue that the key to achieving quality interactivity is to use latency-hiding techniques that help create the illusion that the latency is lower than it really is. Computer specialists are working towards solutions to this problem.

Having discussed these problems, I do not suggest that language professionals wait for the improvement of the technology. Rather, language professionals should be informed of these problems and work to maximize the potential of videoconferencing and minimize the effect of the bandwidth and latency. Fortunately, with the rapid development in computer technology, and with more advanced videoconferencing tools, improved Internet bandwidth and reduced latency have been a reality.

To summarize, it was confirmed by both my observation and the participants' feedback that the audio and video quality in both the Intranet and Internet environment achieved a satisfactory level for supporting one-to-one language learning, despite the existence of problems such as unstable audio and video quality. This research argues that this is an accurate and fair assessment because it was derived from the experiences of both the participants and the researcher in the participation of these videoconferencing sessions. This is especially true when we take into account the fact that "learners of a foreign language do not possess the native speaker's facility for compensating for poor audio quality, and lip synchronization is required for at least some tasks" (Watson & Sasse, 1996, p. 266). At the same time this research also recognizes that this favourable assessment of audio and video quality is subject to individual perceptions and that it was unlikely that each participant received the same audio and video quality. Nevertheless, the audio and video quality required for adequate task performance had been established.

Recommendations for using the audio and video

1. A suitable timetable needs to be negotiated with the learner. Early mornings before eight o'clock or weekends appears to be the best time for videoconferencing.

2. To receive the best audio quality, it is suggested that users wear headphones instead of using the speakers of the computer. This is because speakers can produce feedback and echoes of one's own voice, thus frustrating the other party.

3. Be aware that the sound may fade in and out at the beginning of the conference but usually improves after 1 or 2 minutes, if the Internet is not too congested. It therefore pays to be patient.

4. If the Webcam has been used (e.g. to take a photo, or to make a video clip, etc.) before a videoconferencing session, it often takes the video away from NetMeeting. It is therefore suggested that the computer be restarted prior to NetMeeting sessions so that it reconfigures the video to NetMeeting.

5. It is also recommended to avoid too much or too quick movements in front of the Webcam because the video image may become blurred. It is advised to test the focus of

the Webcam before first use by adjusting the Webcam lenses. The quality of the image can be monitored through the function of My Video.

6.2.3   Other features of pedagogical value

The findings from the two-stage evaluation in relation to NetMeeting features (such as the Whiteboard, File Transfer, Document Sharing, and My Video) other than its audio and video functions indicate that NetMeeting is a pedagogically sound videoconferencing tool for supporting language learning. These features proved to be indispensable to effective distance language learning.

The Whiteboard

The whiteboard proved to be the favourite feature for both the distance and on-campus participants. On many occasions, it was the participants who initiated the use of the whiteboard. The frequent use of the whiteboard signifies its reliability with a zero crash rate in the Intranet environment and two crashes among the 19 successful sessions under the Internet condition. The participants' enthusiasm for the whiteboard also implies that some sort of shared writing space is valuable to effective negotiation of meaning in L2 learning. It is argued here that a video chat tool without the facilitation of the whiteboard is probably sufficient for just conversing in the target language. However for systematic and communicative language learning, the use of a writing tool such as the whiteboard is necessary for effective and efficient focus on form. Furthermore, the whiteboard was shown to be particularly helpful for writing Chinese characters because the stroke order of a character can be demonstrated stroke by stroke in real-time. Beginners of Chinese language will benefit enormously from such use of the whiteboard.

Recommendation for using the whiteboard

It is advised that moving the whiteboard on the computer screen by the two parties at the same time should be avoided. It was discovered in the trial of NetMeeting that manipulating the whiteboard simultaneously could trigger a crash. Pedagogically, the whiteboard can be used in a number of ways. Apart from using it to draw and write non-alphabetical languages, such as Japanese or Korean, it can also be used to copy information from another source, e.g. from the Web. It should also be noted that it may take some practice for both the learner and the teacher to become accustomed to writing with a mouse.

Document Sharing

The function of Document Sharing proved to be useful for sharing a prepared document with a participant, be it a PowerPoint document, a short lecture note, or a picture. These shared documents can act as a catalyst for discussion and negotiation of meaning in the target language. In an Intranet environment, the sharing of a document or a picture was instant with quality as good as the original documents. However in an Internet environment, it may take up to a few minutes for the shared document to be loaded on the computer screen of the other party. Again bandwidth and latency played a crucial role in the delay in transmission. Thus in the Internet environment, the success of sharing a document largely depends on the Internet traffic conditions, the size of the document and the capacity of the other party's computer.

Recommendation for using Document Sharing
It should be noted that the bigger the document, the larger the bandwidth needed to transmit it, and the slower the transmission will be. It is thus recommended that small sized documents be used for effective document sharing. It is recommended that the Document Sharing function should be employed only on occasions when it is considered that interaction can be promoted during task completion. Too frequent use of this function could interrupt the flow of interaction.

File Transfer

File Transfer can be used to transfer a larger document of multiple pages, such as an article, or a video clip for the other party to review. Different from the function of Document Sharing, the documents transferred can be kept by the other party for future reference. Again, Data in sections 4.2.4 and 4.3.4 shows that File Transfer was a useful tool if used properly. Similar to the function of Document Sharing, its transmission was instant in the Intranet environment but was subject to the Internet traffic conditions and latency devices when the Internet was involved.

Recommendation for using File Transfer
In view of the above-discussed limitations of the state-of-the-art technology, it is suggested that for future users of NetMeeting, the sending of large files through File Transfer should be avoided if the two parties' computers are connected to the Internet via a modem. E-mail can be a better choice when large files need to be sent. Again, in order to maintain a healthy flow of interaction during task completion, this function should only be used when absolutely necessary. Documents which are not essential to the promotion of interaction can be transferred at the completion of the task or after the videoconferencing session via e-mail.

My Video

Due to time constraints and the learning task requirements, there were not sufficient opportunities to explore the capabilities and functions of My Video. Data in sections 4.2.4 and 4.3.4 indicates that My Video was a valuable tool when teaching or learning is organized around the video, for showing objects or documents through the video and for monitoring self-performance in front of the

Webcam. The excellent video quality makes it particularly useful for the teacher to monitor his or her own teaching, for example, adjusting or controlling facial expressions in order to assist interaction in the target language.

Recommendation for using My Video
Future studies can design more tasks for the learner to utilize this function in the task completion. For example, through this function, the teacher and the learner can show certain objects for the purpose of generating language production and interaction in the target language, and monitor the demonstration.

Summary
In summary, all four functions performed well in both the Intranet and Internet environment. The combination of these features creates an authentic and rich multimodal environment for language learning that participants greatly appreciated. When discussing the advantages of NetMeeting, the first thing that came to the mind of Student A was the variety of tools that it offers to assist language learning:

> [...] there's a lot of ways you can transfer information – you can read, you can listen, you can speak, you can write, you can do all the things that you do in a normal Chinese class.

This view corresponds with the current theory in CMC that the multimodal nature of CMC contributes to language learning (see Kress & van Leeuwen, 2001), as Chun & Plass (2000) comment on networked hypermedia environments

> that not only present learners with information in various modes (visual, audio, and verbal/textual), but also require learners to engage in productive tasks and activities in a variety of modes, both synchronous and asynchronous methods of student collaboration, and they employ video, images, sound, and text for both the presentation and the negotiation of information. (p. 152)

6.2.4   Reliability

The reliability of a videoconferencing tool mainly addresses its crash rate per videoconferencing session. It is argued in this research that more than one crash during a videoconferencing session can discourage the learner (see Section 3.4.1). The zero crash rate in Stage One in the Intranet environment firmly established NetMeeting's reliability. Such reliability was further confirmed in Stage Two with a less than 0.4 crash rate per session.

However, regardless of the participants' positive attitude towards NetMeeting, the few crashes did become a matter of concern during the trial with the distance students in the Internet environment, while crashing was not an issue in the trial with the on-campus students in the Intranet environment. Although the issue of reliability only concerns the stability of the NetMeeting program itself, the examination of the causes for these crashes led this investigation to the discovery of many factors other than NetMeeting itself, which had directly affected the performance of NetMeeting. The following causes of the crashes have been identified:

1. When both parties attempted to initiate an action at the same time, for example, to move the whiteboard simultaneously, a crash of NetMeeting could be triggered due to insufficient computer power to support such movement;

2. When the computer power was limited (as in the case of Participant E, who used a laptop), NetMeeting could became frozen;

3. When the Internet was severely congested, causing NetMeeting to freeze; and

4. When the participants became panicky and kept shutting down the computer. (as in the case of Participant C)

These causes further proved the reliability of NetMeeting because none of the above factors is inherent to NetMeeting. In an open and dynamic environment such as the Internet, any of the above factors could make a videoconferencing session impossible. While most of the above problems can be solved with more practice and experience, the Internet presents a challenge to distance language educators, who have to accommodate themselves to its present capabilities.

Recommendation in regard to reliability

On the basis of the above discussion, it is suggested that initiating actions by both parties at the same time be avoided. For example, if both parties call each other at the same time, NetMeeting can become confused, resulting in crashes or lack of an immediate response. It is also recommended that a powerful desktop computer be used instead of a laptop, because many of the functions of a laptop are compressed.

6.2.5 Cost

The issue of cost has been extensively discussed by Wang (2004) and in Section 3.2.2. To summarize, NetMeeting is freely downloadable from the Internet, and the only cost involved is the purchase of a Webcam (US$50) and Internet connection. This research recognizes that the issue of affordability is as important as technological and pedagogical issues in distance language learning. In fact, affordability is the foundation of any innovative attempt in teaching. This was one of the reasons for the discontinuation of many grant-funded large-scale videoconferencing projects. When the grant money had been consumed, it was difficult to find the financial resources necessary to continue the maintenance of the systems. Since not every language professional can afford expensive and sophisticated videoconferencing systems, it is essential to find a ready-made product (e.g. NetMeeting, Yahoo messenger etc.) that is cheap or free.

6.2.6 Problems unrelated to NetMeeting program

No insurmountable problems emerged in Stage One. However, many unexpected problems surfaced from Stage Two. These problems fall into two categories – the human and the technological.

The human factors directly relate to the computer knowledge and skills that each individual possessed. Generally speaking, the levels of computer proficiency of the participants and the researcher varied, while none had any professional training in computer technology. Data from this research largely supports the findings by Chen & Willits (1999), who report a survey they conducted in 1997:

> [O]ther questions on the survey asked about students' access to computers and electronic communication software and about their skill levels in using these tools. More than two-thirds of participants rated these facilities as "readily accessible" (rating of 6 or 7 on a 7-point scale); less than 6% reported that they did not have ready access (codes 1 and 2 on the scale). About 40% rated their skill level as "very strong", while 20% felt it was "not at all strong". Thus, while access did not appear to be an important factor restricting electronic communication, student skill level may have inhibited such interaction. (p. 56)

While the learner's computer skills remain a constant variable, ongoing technical training for language professionals become imperative. Distance institutions should ensure that such training happens on a regular basis. Furthermore the problem of an individual's computer skills is not insurmountable with more practice and technical support, as Dias (1998, p. 24) optimistically predicts that "eventually, even the most technically inept teacher can learn to diagnose problems and give appropriate advice". After all, videoconferencing tools (similar to any computer program, such as a word processor) are mostly simple applications that do not require a professional level of computer knowledge. It is the non-human factor, the technology, that presents the challenge to the field of distance language learning in the fourth generation of DLE.

With the exception of the limitations in Internet bandwidth and communication latency, the technical problems (e.g. firewalls, faulty equipment, etc.) that emerged in Stage Two are all incidental and user-context dependent. However, future users of videoconferencing should be made aware of the fact that a range of things can go wrong in an Internet-based videoconferencing environment where so many factors come into play simultaneously.

6.2.7   Implications of the practicality of NetMeeting for future provision of oral-visual interaction in DLE

In a LAN environment

NetMeeting proved to have reached a satisfactory level of quality and sophistication for supporting one-to-one interaction in real-time synchronous language learning. Both the video and audio are synchronized to a real-time standard with minimum latency. The implication of such findings is significant in a number of ways. For traditional institutions with on-campus lectures, desktop videoconferencing can be established between campuses for a variety of purposes. For example, oral presentation from a different campus can be shown in real-time through NetMeeting on a bigger screen to a class on another campus. It can also be used to conduct speaking tests between campuses so that the lecturers do not have to travel to another campus to conduct the tests. It is true that there are more sophisticated videoconferencing facilities in many institutions, but NetMeeting is a more reliable and economical solution with no maintenance cost, in comparison with those more delicate videoconferencing facilities which have a higher crash rate.

In an Internet environment

When using the Internet, the video and audio quality was generally not as good as when using a LAN. Internet traffic conditions and the computing power of individual computers are crucial factors determining the quality of a desktop videoconferencing session. With this in mind, the present generation of Internet and videoconferencing tools should be used with detailed planning and appropriate time management. The quality of video and audio may not be of sufficient quality for language speaking tests due to inconsistency caused by Internet congestion, but it was sufficiently stable for regular consultations and tutorials in a distance mode. In addition, it is a confidence booster to establish a constant visual contact with the instructor and other learners. For example, a buddy system can be built between a native speaker and a distance language learner.

6.2.8   Summary of the practicality of NetMeeting

The evaluation of the technological capabilities of NetMeeting went through two stages involving both the on-campus and distance participants. It yielded a wealth of data strongly supporting the use of videoconferencing in DLE for the provision of oral-visual interaction.

The ease of installation and use makes NetMeeting a user-friendly videoconferencing tool, a merit that was unanimously agreed upon by both the on-campus and distance participants. While acknowledging three major constraints (the Internet bandwidth, latency and the computing power of the individual PC) on the quality of a videoconference, this research has successfully confirmed the capabilities of NetMeeting in supporting audio and video quality required for successful task completion on a one-to-one basis. This finding is a major contribution to the study of Internet-based desktop videoconferencing because, without good audio and video quality, videoconferencing would be impossible. Particularly significant is the high performance standard of NetMeeting in the LAN-Internet-LAN environment, which promises that with improved Internet bandwidth, quality videoconferences at a distance will be easily attainable. In contrast to most commercially available videoconferencing tools, NetMeeting lends itself well to supporting effective distance language learning by offering features of great pedagogical value such as the Whiteboard, Document Sharing and File Transfer. As far as its reliability is concerned, NetMeeting itself proved to be very reliable despite the fact that the Internet could pose potential problems due to limited bandwidth and latency. In addition, the fact that NetMeeting can be freely downloaded from the Internet and that there is no maintenance cost involved effectively reduces the cost to both educational institutions and the learner, making it a more economically viable and sustainable option. The above discussion not only confirms the technological capabilities of NetMeeting, but also provides useful references for the use of NetMeeting and guidelines for videoconferencing tool selection. In addition, this discussion has also laid the foundation for the following analysis of the pedagogical values of videoconferencing in terms of communicative task completion. The facilitating role of videoconferencing to successful real-time oral-visual interaction in the target language is seen as a benchmark for assessing the pedagogical values of videoconferencing.

6.3 Language learning potential

Data in Section 5.2.2 demonstrates that videoconferencing was able to adequately facilitate the planned tasks and realize their language learning potential. Supported by NetMeeting, focus on form occurred in the process of negotiating for meaning in both stages one and two, resulting in a noticeable improvement in the participants' listening and speaking skills, as shown in the following discussion. Following the criteria developed both by Chapelle (2001) and for this research, the language learning potential of videoconferencing-based tasks is further assessed below in terms of:

♦ focus on form

♦ participants' improvement in Chinese proficiency

Finally, recommendations are suggested for promoting the language learning potential of videoconferencing-support tasks.

6.3.1 Focus on form

With reference to L2 acquisition theories and research, this section further examines data collected from the two-stage evaluation, in terms of interactional modification, modification of output and support. These are important indicators of successful focus on form. During the 34 videoconferencing sessions with both groups of participants, though the participants' attention was primarily directed to the meaning of the tasks, focus on form was successfully achieved. In other words, "an occasional shift of attention to linguistic code features" (Long & Robinson, 1998, p. 23) was generally allowed to occur. However, data from this research further suggests that variations existed between the frequency of interactional modification by the distance and on-campus groups, and even between individual participants. It can be summarized that, during the five NetMeeting sessions with each participant, interactional modification happened occasionally in Stage One with the on-campus participants. For example, it only happened three times in the first session with Student 2. In contrast, in Stage Two, and especially in the first few sessions, there was a much higher (about ten times more) frequency of interactional modification with most participants. This was especially true with participants with lower Chinese listening and speaking skills. In the first few sessions, conversations often broke down or became awkward. As a result, English was used more frequently than in Stage One, in order to achieve comprehension. Further analysis of individual instances of focus on form uncovered several factors contributing to this high frequency.

First, the triggers of those instances of interactional modification revealed that most of the participants had a much lower level of listening and speaking skills compared with the on-campus students. This is because most of the distance participants only practised their listening and speaking with tapes without the opportunity to converse with other people, as shown in Table 5.1. Furthermore, as discussed in Chapter 1, teaching listening and speaking skills had never been part of the curriculum. The fact that Chinese is not a phonetic language whose pronunciation can be deduced from its spelling also makes listening and speaking harder to acquire without a sufficient amount of practice. The pronunciation of the Chinese characters needs to be memorized and practised constantly in order to achieve fluency. It was further discovered that most participants did not know how to infer meaning from the context. They often attempted to grasp every word and translate word for word in their minds as they listened, instead of listening to the whole sentence. Nunan (1989, p. 138) precisely describes this situation by saying that "[m]any low-level learners are traumatized when first exposed to authentic samples of language, and have to be taught that it is not necessary to understand every word for communication to be successful". The above factors were further compounded by the participants' poor pronunciation and tones, because they had become accustomed to their incorrect pronunciation and could not understand the correct pronunciation. (see examples A (4) and (5) in Section 5.2.2)

Analysis of the indicators of breakdown in role-plays further reveals the distance participants' low listening and speaking skills. While the on-campus participants indicated their non-understanding in Chinese, the average distance participants seemed to possess few interactional skills and phrases in Chinese, such as clarifying meaning and checking understanding in Chinese, especially in the first few videoconferencing sessions. Instead, they relied on English, and did not know how to use verbal fillers, parentheses, etc. This was also why interactional modifications happened more frequently in Stage Two, and more so with participants who had lower Chinese proficiency. Again, the poor interactional skills of the distance participants were the direct result of the lack of speaking practice and interactive and spontaneous use of the language. Spontaneity was another problem surfacing from the two stages of the evaluation. Again this problem was more acute with the distance participants. They did not possess a ready repertoire of linguistic input to enable them to produce spontaneous replies, nor were they accustomed to replying spontaneously in the target language. This does not mean that they had not learned the necessary vocabulary and structures for completion of the tasks, as the tasks were based on what they had been taught previously. Their lack of spontaneity resulted from the absence of opportunity to practise what they had learned in communicating with others; they consequently readily forgot previously learned vocabulary and structures. Spontaneity was lacking even though the topics were familiar. This was also why, when asked about the level of difficulty of the tasks, they responded that the tasks were set at an appropriate level, even though they experienced various degrees of difficulties in task completion (see Section 5.2.3). They blamed themselves for not being able to remember what they had learned.

Lack of vocabulary constitutes another type of indicator of breakdowns in conversation. Interestingly, this type of indicator occurred more with participants of higher Chinese proficiency than with those of lower proficiency. The following factors can explain why lack of vocabulary became an issue in breakdowns. First, this was determined by the open-ended nature of meaning-focused tasks. In completing such a task, learners are not restricted to the use of any vocabulary or sentence structures, because there is usually no predetermined linguistic requirement for the completion of the task. For example, when talking about what she did the day before, Participant E spent a long time talking about Chinese cuisine, a topic stemming from the dinner she cooked the day before. She requested a great number of vocabulary items relating to food and cooking in China, resulting in the longest session and the highest frequency of focus on form (see Table 5.2) among all sessions. In contrast, participants with lower Chinese proficiency level usually limited their output to what they had learned and never ventured too far away from the central topics of the tasks. The second factor contributing to the request for new vocabulary lies with the researcher's control at the task performance level. With more advanced participants, the researcher often guided the role-plays to a level that requested more complicated input and output, deliberately creating opportunities for beneficial focus on form (see Example A(6) in Section 5.2.2). However, with less advanced participants, the researcher placed more weight on helping the participants to complete the tasks by avoiding using new vocabulary and sentence structures.

Typical of the videoconferencing supported environment were the visual indicators emerging from the sessions. As this type of indicator was not covered in Varonis and Gass' (1985) study, it deserves some elaboration here. Similar to visual cues in face-to-face interaction, facial expressions such as a puzzled look, an expression of confusion, and signs of comprehension and enjoyment, were often received accurately by the other party in the conferencing. Cognitively and linguistically, it was generally maintained that paralinguistic cues reduce misunderstanding and ambiguity in speech (see Bruce, 1996, for a review, and Section 2.3.3). Data from this research indicates that, even with a varying degree of delay (see Section 4.3.3), these visual cues transmitted through NetMeeting promoted understanding and communication. In fact, the visual information became even more crucial when the sound quality of a videoconferencing session was imperfect. Parties at both ends of the videoconferencing often relied on the video transmission to confirm understanding or non-understanding as shown in examples B (8) and (9). This result corresponds with findings reported by Hampel & Hauck (2004, p. 78). Their study confirms the importance of visual clues and body language in the promotion of interaction between tutors and students.

Section 5.2.2 shows that a variety of responses can be found in the current data, including all the types discussed in the Varonis and Gass (1985) study, and with the additional type: target language equivalent. In analyzing these responses, it became evident that most of the responses came from the researcher. This is because, in most cases, indicators of breakdowns were initiated by the participants and the researcher was obliged to respond to these indicators. What is worthy of deliberation here are the reasons for the variety of responses. Here the advantage of the one-to-one nature of NetMeeting clearly manifested itself. In analysing the advantage of the one-to-one learning mode, we have to bear in mind the two distinct characteristics of the distance participants: limited listening and speaking skills and the varied Chinese proficiency levels. The one-to-one interaction allowed the researcher to provide immediate and specific responses to the indicators from the participants, thus catering for the differences in and special needs of individual learners. Hence it can produce more effective learner outcomes when the level of proficiency of the learners is varied.

Data analysis further indicates that repetition of the trigger sentences occupied a considerable portion of the responses, and resolution could often be reached after one repetition. Probing the causes of this type of non-understanding, it is obvious that participants' limited listening skills played a large part in their inability to comprehend. Another possible cause lies in the not-so-perfect sound quality, which interfered with their listening, as claimed by Participant E (see Section 4.3.3). In some cases, the combination of the two factors, that is, participants' poor listening skills and the sound quality, might have caused the non-understanding.

In Varonis and Gass's (1985) study, reaction to response was treated sparsely. They did not elaborate on the implications of reaction to response for language acquisition. In fact, they regarded reaction to response only as an *optional* prime in the negotiation routine, which ties up the negotiation routine before the horizontal movement of the conversation resumes. However, data in Section 5.2.2 proves that reaction to response is an indispensable unit in the negotiation routine when discussing L2 acquisition following negotiation of meaning in task completion. This is because reaction to response in the data collected for this research witnessed a great number of modified outputs, indicating successful focus on form. Thus, this fourth prime in the negotiation routine should be treated as an important indicator of L2 acquisition. These modifications of output often occurred following the specific responses from the researcher, which facilitated understanding and learning of new linguistic code features. Reaction to response happened in every instance of focus on form, again, thanks to the one-to-one nature of NetMeeting. In such interaction, the researcher's responses were directed more immediately and accurately to the specific needs of individual participants, who were "forced", to some extent, to react to the response. Thus the exchanges between the two parties were much more intensive than in a multi-way interaction. Furthermore, in view of the diverse proficiency levels of the distance participants, a multi-way discussion in the target language would waste a great deal of valuable online time. More interaction gaps, such as silence, could be expected, resulting in lower quality and less effective interaction. In fact, Hampel and Hauck (2004, p. 75) report that one of the improvements in audio conferencing activities suggested by their participants is that "more pair work and less whole group work could be done to increase the actual time people are speaking in the target language". The one-to-one nature of NetMeeting proved to be able to offer more effective and intensified negotiation of meaning than group interaction for distance participants of low target proficiency.

In fact, group size has become an issue in the literature on videoconferencing. O'Dowd (2000, p. 57) reports that participants in a larger group were less positive about the potential of videoconferencing in foreign language learning than those in a smaller group, because it was "difficult for all students to speak with their partners as much as they might have wished". This finding also supports my contention that with one-to-one interaction, more intensified interaction can be managed and retained. Thus it can be said that the one-to-one nature of NetMeeting is capable of catering for individual needs and fostering basic conversational skills and levels of language proficiency.

While preferring the one-to-one interaction, the participants also acknowledged the advantages of multi-way interaction, emphasizing that such interaction was more beneficial to advanced learners. As Participant E commented, "many-to-many would probably allow more variety of communication". (PTS-2.9)

Although no participant mentioned the resource and time consuming nature, and lack of collaborative learning of the one-to-one interaction, these two issues should not go without due attention. While videoconferencing can minimize the effect of distance in distance language education, the one-to-one mode does not solve the problem of the labour intensiveness of language teaching. For example, in instructor-moderated interaction, more tutors would be needed if the number of learners were to increase dramatically. Annand (1999, p. 51) discusses the economic implications of CMC for distance education and recognizes the "significant costs" in implementing electronic interaction. However, the fact that NetMeeting is freely downloadable from the Internet, and that no ongoing maintenance is needed, can offset some of the costs of employing more tutors.

Lack of collaborative learning potential is regarded by some (e.g. Buckett & Stringer, 1999) as a defect of one-to-one interaction at a time when collaborative learning is strongly advocated. It is argued here that collaboration in learning on a large scale (e.g. more than two people) is not universally needed. It is rather subject and learner dependent. In a certain subject or field of study, collaboration of more than two people at a time may prove to be essential and productive, while in other subjects and with other learners, such collaboration might deter progress and be less effective. As far as language learning is concerned, collaboration may mean a partnership between two students or between a student and a native speaker. It is also recognized here that advanced language learners may benefit more from many-to-many interaction because they have the linguistic repertoire to cope with such interaction and can learn from others' strengths and mistakes.

An optimal scenario for distance language education is to provide both one-to-one and many-to-many interaction, as suggested by Participant E. With the recent advancement in Internet-based desktop videoconferencing, many-to-many interaction is already a reality (see Wang & Chen, 2007), although little substantial research has been done to investigate this type of interaction.

To summarize, the above discussion inevitably directs our attention to the appropriate density of focus on form in a meaning-based task. In other words, a balance needs to be struck between occasions of focus on form and the horizontal movement of the conversation, a crucial issue in the language potential of a meaning-based task. The appropriate balance between the two and how to achieve this balance is a central debate among scholars (e.g. Doughty & Williams, 1998; Pica, Kanagy, & Falodun, 1993; Long & Robinson, 1998; Long, 1988b.). Pica, Kanagy, & Falodun (1993)'s balance is the most prevalent in L2 literature: learners should focus on meaning until communication breakdowns occur due to unknown linguistic elements, and learners' attention should be shifted back to meaning when breakdowns have been repaired. However they did not discuss the appropriate frequency of focus on form. Long (1988b) proposes an *occasional* shift of attention to forms while learners are primarily engaging in meaning-focused tasks. The findings from this research support Long's contention, and it is argued here that language learning potential and focus on form are not in a direct ratio – the more occasions for focus on form the more language learning potential a task provides. Instead, it is contended here that *occasional* focus on form promotes language learning and can help lay the foundation for higher quality interaction, while too much focus on form interrupts the horizontal movement of the role-plays and thus is detrimental to task completion. Thus a beneficial balance between the two needs to be determined in task design and adjusted at task performance level in accordance with the proficiency level of the learner. Such an endeavour will present an ongoing challenge to language professionals.

Varonis and Gass's (1985) model has proved to be a useful tool to reveal the instances of focus on form in negotiation of meaning and to characterize the complexity and depth of those instances. Moreover, this model has also assisted this research to identify the causes of these breakdowns. It can now be concluded that the above-discussed problems experienced by the distance participants are flow-on effects from the lack of exposure to oral-visual interaction in their distance language learning, confirming the validity of the first subsidiary research question – the distance language learners do need an improved platform for effective acquisition of listening and speaking skills through oral-visual interaction. In addition, Varonis and Gass's (1985) model unfolded the process of interactional modification and exposed the facilitating effect of videoconferencing-supported interaction to L2 acquisition, especially in the form of modifications of output in the target language.

Data in Section 5.2.2 further demonstrates that NetMeeting was able to offer valuable support in assisting negotiation of meaning in task completion. Despite some technical problems, a multi-dimensional learning environment was offered to the learners with the support of the video, the Whiteboard, File Transfer, Document Sharing and My Video. The multimodal nature of videoconferencing-based interaction has been regarded as beneficial to negotiation of meaning in L2 acquisition (see Chun & Plass, 2000) and was highly appreciated by the participants. Data in this research shows that paralinguistic cues (such as facial expressions and hand gestures) were all present in real time and almost synchronously. Furthermore, the learners could avail themselves of the whiteboard for character writing and for other purposes in the process of negotiation of meaning. Lecturers could share and transfer prepared documents or lecture notes to the learners in order to assist language acquisition. All these types of support proved to be conducive to task completion. Thus the compatibility or the fit between the task and the technology was confirmed. The issue of choosing the appropriate technology to realize the focus of the task has gained increasing attention from CMC research. (see Levy, 2004)

The language learning potential of the tasks – realized through of oral-visual interaction – was further established by the improvement in participants' interactive proficiency as the trial unfolded. This was especially the case with the distance participants in Stage Two. It was observed that the flow of the conversation became more continuous and the intervals between interactional modifications became longer. Data in Section 5.2.2 indicates that after the five NetMeeting sessions with each participant, improvement in the participants' communicative competence was clearly manifest to the researcher and the participants. (also see discussions in Section 6.3.2)

6.3.2   Participants' improvement in Chinese proficiency

The facilitating effect of negotiation for meaning in interactive language learning has long been recognized in the L2 literature. As Long (1996, p. 451) suggested, "*negotiation for meaning*, and especially negotiation work that triggers *interactional* adjustments by the NS [Native Speaker] or more competent interlocutor, facilitates acquisition because it connects input, internal learner capacities, particularly selective attention, and output in productive ways"(italics in original). Although it was not possible to measure the exact degree of improvement in each participant's Chinese proficiency during the short time in which the trial was conducted, qualitative data (presented in Section 5.2.2.) suggests improvement of various degrees by every participant in this study.

In summary, listening, speaking (especially fluency) and interactional competence were the most improved aspects brought about by videoconferencing for both the on-campus and distance groups. This is not surprising as these aspects were identified as a deficiency in the DLE literature and by the preliminary study participants in this research. (see Section 3.2. 1)

It was discovered in the trial that the listening competency of the distance group was very low, but the improvement in listening was highlighted both in the end of session interviews and the post-trial survey (see PTS-2.2, PTS-2.7 and Figure 5.4). The low listening competency was mainly caused by lack of exposure to the target language being spoken, coupled with incorrect pronunciation and tones of the participants, which interfered with their understanding of the correct pronunciation and tones. This is a problem typical of non-phonetic languages such as Chinese, which can only be overcome with continuous exposure to listening exercises in the target language.

The improvement in participants' speaking was mainly manifest in their improved fluency, and this improvement was evident in both groups of participants. Figure 5.2 and Figure 5.3 illustrate that both the task conditions and capabilities of NetMeeting were perceived to be very useful in improving the participants' fluency in Chinese because of the presence of constant negotiation of meaning. According to Long (1996, p. 452), "[n]egotiation of meaning by definition involves denser than usual frequencies of semantically contingent speech of various kinds (that is, utterances by a competent speaker, such as repetitions, extensions, reformulations, rephrasing, expansions and recasts), which immediately follow learner utterances and maintain reference to their meaning". Although the distance participants, who had been deprived of such interaction, found it hard to negotiate meaning in Chinese at the beginning of the trial, they quickly became accustomed to it.

Generally speaking, it appeared that the improvements of the participants with lower proficiency were more obvious than of those who already had a higher proficiency level in Chinese, and that the improvement of the distance participants manifested more strongly than that of the on-campus group. This is especially the case in terms of the improvement in conversational tactics and interactional skills, which can be more easily obtained through conscious awareness.

However, it is equally the case that more intensive and quality language production was generated by participants with higher proficiency during task completion. More quality interactional features which are conducive to language acquisition (e.g. negotiation for meaning, and clarification and repetition requests in the target language) emerged during these videoconferences. To summarize, both groups of participants enjoyed qualitative improvements of various degrees and aspects in their language learning.

The fact that both the on-campus and distance groups benefited linguistically from these videoconferencing sessions indicates the importance of oral-visual interaction to L2 acquisition, particularly in distance mode. Thus, the research question – **in what ways oral-visual interaction via videoconferencing facilitates L2 acquisition at a distance** – is partially answered.

6.3.3   Recommendations for language learning potential

The first videoconferencing session should be geared more towards familiarizing the students with the various functions of a videoconferencing tool than dealing with linguistic content. Teachers can instruct students to try out different functions in the target language and encourage students to perform small tasks presenting minimum linguistic challenges.

As discussed above, a critical issue that should be taken into consideration when designing a videoconferencing task is the density of the frequency of focus on form. It has to be stressed again that too many occasions of focus on form in a task intended for learners of low level of target language proficiency can interrupt the interaction, resulting in discouragement for the learner and difficulty in task completion on time. Thus when designing a speaking task for this group of learners, unknown linguistic elements, such as new words or structures, should be avoided because learners would have plentiful opportunities to deal with unfamiliar linguistic and interactional elements arising during task completion. However, with more proficient learners, unknown linguistic elements can be deliberately built into the task to provide sufficient occasions for beneficial focus on form. Nevertheless, there should be only occasional opportunities for focus on form so that the flow of interaction is maximized. Furthermore, linguistic problems arising during oral-visual interaction that do not interfere with the flow of interaction should be dealt with when the task is completed.

6.4 Learner fit

The criterion of learner fit addresses task appropriateness from two perspectives: evidence that suggests that (1) "the targeted linguistic forms are at an appropriate level of difficulty of the learners" and (2) that "the task is appropriate to learners' individual characteristics" (Chapelle, 2001, p. 68). Data in Section 5.2.3 indicates that both the on-campus and distance participants perceived that all the tasks were set at an appropriate level of difficulty, despite the fact that their Chinese language proficiency varied. Analysis of such consensus further reveals that variations exist even within this general parameter of agreement.

6.4.1 Consensus and its variations

A comparison of the comments on the level of difficulty of tasks revealed an interesting consensus: although the participants' proficiency was different, they all believed, with a different understanding of the level of difficulty, that the task was set at the right linguistic level. It was also found from participant feedback that participants perceived differently what the right level of difficulty was. Their attitude towards the level of difficulty also differed. For example, Student 3 had the highest proficiency and believed that the task was quite easy, but she preferred this level because practising speaking, listening and responding was more important to her (see Section 5.2.3). Similarly, Student 2, who had the lowest proficiency, also believed that the task was at the right level for her but indicated it was not easy (see Section 5.2.3). Student 1's response was quite complicated in that he believed that the task was difficult, but at the same time requested it be harder so that he could learn more of the language (see Section 5.2.3). This indicates that there was still room for even more difficult tasks for this particular student. The same pattern also appeared in the responses from the distance participants, all of whom believed that the level of the tasks was within their grasp. From these responses, the right level of difficulty does not fall on a certain fixed point, but within a certain range. Within this range, each participant occupied a different place. This consensus indicates that learners have a wide scope of tolerance to the level of difficulty of a task.

6.4.2   Reasons for the consensus at the task design level

At the task design level, to ensure learner fit, the following characteristics of the participants from both the on-campus and distance groups were identified:

1.   Both groups of participants only possessed basic Chinese proficiency, which would limit the topics covered in the tasks.

2.   The distance participants had a lower level of proficiency in Chinese in respect to their listening, speaking and interactional skills.

Thus, in designing the tasks, special attention was paid to the learners' linguistic repertoire and abilities. In comparison with the on-campus students who had just finished their first year Chinese learning with 5 contact hours a week, the distance students with a similar length of studying the language had a lower Chinese proficiency, especially in terms of interactional skills, due to lack of exposure to spontaneous oral-visual interaction. This was confirmed in Stage One and Stage Two of the evaluation. In other words, the distance participants only had a basic level of proficiency with a limited number of structures and vocabulary at their disposal, in terms of their speaking skills. To ensure that the level of the tasks was within the capability of these distance students, textbooks for the first two study periods (CHN11 & CHN12) were used as a basis for the level of difficulty of the mega task as a whole and for some themes of the subtasks designed for this evaluation. Also taken into consideration in task design was the level of proficiency of the first year on-campus participants to ensure the topics in the tasks were within familiar territory.

Closely related to the language proficiency of the participants was the way the tasks were designed and conducted in the trials. The framework of the tasks was set at a certain level (for example, about applying for a job), but the level of language use was adjusted and controlled by the teacher during task performance in accordance with each participant's level of proficiency. Thus the tasks were designed to contain a certain degree of flexibility, providing opportunities for the development of different linguistic levels. This was achieved more at the task performance level.

6.4.3 Reasons for the consensus at the task performance level

In view of the differences in linguistic levels of different learners, within the same task frame, I deliberately guided the conversation to a slightly more sophisticated level with the on-campus students. For example, with the distance students, I would ask a simple question such as "do you have a brother?", while with the on-campus students, the same question would be extended to "could you please tell me if you have a brother?". This was to ensure a smooth performance of the tasks by both groups of students, and at the same time to provide sufficient and more complicated input for learners of higher proficiency. Here the advantage of the one-to-one nature of NetMeeting was clearly demonstrated because it allowed the instructor to adjust the conversation to a level suitable to an individual learner's linguistic ability, making the tutorial more effective than multiple-point conferencing. This experience indicates that one-to-one videoconferencing can be effective, especially when the learners' levels of proficiency vary or are not high enough to perform group collaborative tasks. (For detailed discussion on one-to-one interaction, see Section 6.3.1)

The above discussion reveals that at both the task designing and performing levels, the participants' linguistic capabilities and individual characteristics were taken into consideration, as suggested by Chapelle (2001).

6.4.4 Recommendations for learner fit

In view of the fact that most distance language learners only possess a basic level of speaking proficiency, at the task designing level, videoconferencing tasks should be planned and conducted in an oral context, starting at the very basic level, at least for the first few sessions. Room for adjustments and flexibility should be embedded in task design, and various levels of modification should be introduced at the task performance level. For example, useful phrases for maintaining the flow of oral-visual interaction should first be sent (e-mailed, or posted on the Web) to the learner, and occasions should be created for those phrases to be used in task completion. After a solid foundation is laid in interactional skills, more complicated tasks can be brought in for the subsequent videoconferencing sessions. More importantly, language professionals should consciously adjust the level of task difficulty according to each individual's needs and characteristics, and the one-to-one mode of the Internet-based videoconferencing tools allows for such personalized teaching and for such personal interaction.

6.5 Authenticity

The analysis of the authenticity of the tasks seeks evidence in regard to the connection between videoconferencing tasks and real world tasks. The findings in Section 5.2.4 correspond to Chapelle's (2001, p. 90) argument that "authenticity needs to be considered in a more-or-less fashion rather than as an all-or-nothing attribute of a task, and it needs to be considered relative to a context of interest rather than in absolute terms".

6.5.1 Progressive improvement on the authenticity of the tasks

Data contained in Section 5.2.4 further supports the contention of O'Conaill et al. (1993) and O'Dowd (2000) that videoconferencing is more suitable for planned tasks than for casual conversations and general discussions due to its practical limitations. Section 5.2.4 reveals that the first set of tasks was designed out of consideration for its usefulness and practicality in real life situations, with a job application as the main theme. On-campus participants evaluated this set as useful and related to their own life experiences. Based on the suggestion of the on-campus students that a variety of topics be included, a free chat section was then added to the original tasks in Set 2. The distance participants enjoyed the free chat but found it hard to switch roles from themselves to the roles in the role-play. O'Dowd (2000, p. 59) proposed that videoconferencing sessions "should start off with ice breaker activities such as short quizzes or vocabulary games where both groups get to interact with each other". The results from this research show that a free chat at the beginning of each task serves as an effective ice breaker activity, and the participants endorsed it. This finding corresponds with what Hampel & Hauck (2004, p. 78) discovered in their investigation. The warm-up activities in their audio conferencing "not only helped to get into a German-speaking frame of mind' but also are "essential to get people talking and to create a relaxed and open online atmosphere".

Set 3 was then introduced with more topics about oneself and one's family and daily life. At the same time, certain basic linguistic forms were highlighted in this set to raise the participants' awareness. Doughty (1991) argues that CALL materials with explicitly specified linguistic forms can offer better language potential than those without. This new set of tasks was greatly favoured by the distance participants and found to be more suitable to their level of proficiency. More natural language production was observed when the tasks related more to the participants' life experiences. At the same time, participants consciously employed the specified linguistic forms during task completion. Consequently a favourable environment for language acquisition was created. The above findings suggest that progressive improvement in the authenticity of tasks can be necessary and inevitable for the promotion of language acquisition. Language professionals should be alert to such necessity and adjust task authenticity accordingly. This is especially true as videoconferencing is still a new form of language learning and teaching.

6.5.2   Participants' perceptions of the authenticity of tasks

Both the on-campus and distance participants were positive about the authenticity of the three sets of tasks and their usefulness in improving their language proficiency. Although the major theme was a job application, in sets 1 and 2, the inclusive nature of the tasks provided participants with opportunities to engage in talking about their life experiences, prices, ordering drinks and food and explaining directions. Set 3 offered the participants even more opportunities to relay their life experience and less role-playing, making it more relevant to their everyday life. This finding supports Nunan's (1993) contention that task authenticity promotes meaningful interaction and encourages more personal involvement in the tasks.

In summary, none of the on-campus participants found role-playing difficult. Their ready acceptance of the role-playing tasks may come from their familiarity with this type of pedagogical exercise, thanks to their frequent engagement in such tasks in their face-to-face lectures and tutorials. In contrast, the distance participants generally found it difficult to assume a role in interaction, and constantly reverted to talking about themselves. A number of reasons contributed to this difficulty. First, they had been learning the language alone without interacting with others, and had never taken part in any role-playing tasks. Second, closely related to the first reason, is their lack of ready-to-use linguistic repertoire to interact naturally with other people. Third, also due to lack of exposure to interaction with others, they did not possess sufficient interactional skills to conduct a role-play with ease. Naturally, talking about themselves with less interaction with others seemed easier. Fourth, most distance language learners are adults who often may find role-plays awkward.

To summarize, the findings in regard to the authenticity of tasks confirm the general argument in the literature that task authenticity promotes more meaningful interaction in the target language, which in turn generates more comprehensible language production and provides the learner with more specific learning goals and more active personal involvement.

6.5.3   Recommendations for task authenticity

First, a combination of pedagogical and real-world tasks should be offered with an emphasis on the relevancy to the learner's life experiences. Pedagogical tasks, such as role-plays and games, can be gradually introduced when the learner's proficiency is improved and they become more comfortable with spontaneous oral-visual interaction. Furthermore, when designing role-plays, the characteristics of adult learners should be taken into consideration. Second, topics involving basic sentence structures and vocabulary are recommended for those distance learners who are using videoconferencing for the first time, as most of them would not have possessed sophisticated interactional skills and fluency for engaging in in-depth discussions on serious social issues. Third, recycling of language usages and sentence structures should be embedded in task design and is deemed important for distance language learners because of their limited exposure to the target language environment. Fourth, warm-up activities, such as a free chat in the target language, should be provided to facilitate a relaxed target language learning environment.

6.6 Positive impact

Chapelle (2001, p. 90) states that "[d]escriptions of CALL throughout the past 30 years abound with statements about the positive influence of CALL activities on language classrooms". This is because these CALL activities have enriched classroom teaching. However, the impact of videoconferencing on DLE is far more significant than just enriching the activities in distance language teaching. It, impacts on DLE in many revolutionary ways by providing DLE with what it has been crucially lacking: spontaneous oral-visual interaction. Participants' improvement in Chinese through the five hours of videoconferencing is a prime indicator of such a positive impact. As this impact has been discussed in sections 5.2.2 and 6.3.3, this section will concentrate on the analysis of the impact of the video, the impact on the sense of isolation, and the impact on participants' confidence building and enthusiasm in learning. Again, it can be argued that the positive impact of the five videoconferencing sessions was much more keenly felt by the distance group than by the on-campus group.

6.6.1 The impact of the video

Findings in Section 5.2.5 indicate a distinctive difference between the impact of the video on the on-campus and distance participants. On the whole, the on-campus participants were more critical of the video quality, and did not think video was absolutely necessary to language learning. For example, Student 2 believed that video was only important in the first few sessions and then became a distraction after the people involved in the videoconference had got to know each other. Most on-campus participants concentrated more on listening than looking at the video image on the computer screen. In fact, none of them looked at the video all the time. Two factors may contribute to their attitude towards the video. They had been attending my lectures on campus for a whole year and there was little further need to identify me during the two-way conversation. However, if it were a multi-way conferencing session, the need to identify the speaker would be greater. Besides, the on-campus participants could have used the quality of face-to-face lectures as a reference when judging the quality of the video. Thus the 'poor' video quality did not encourage them to consistently watch the video.

In contrast, despite the fact that the video quality was not as good as that in the Intranet condition, and even problematic at times, all of the distance participants believed that it was most important to have the video, and they all looked at the video constantly during the sessions. The importance of the video in providing paralinguistic cues and in establishing a personal link was emphasized repeatedly in the interviews. This positive perception of the video corresponds with what Ibañez & Duque (1999, p. 2) report about the LEVERAGE project. Their participants regard the video as "the most important tool" and "the best of the sessions".

Table 4.11 also shows that video was ranked only second to audio by the distance participants while most of the on-campus participants favoured the whiteboard more than the video. (see Section 4.2.4)

Such differences between the perceptions of the on-campus and distance participants can be analyzed from both linguistic and social perspectives. Linguistically, the on-campus participants had been accustomed to a much richer input of non-verbal and paralinguistic cues in face-to-face interaction, while the distance participants only had access to text-based interaction. A popular belief is that text-based interaction lacks the access to nonverbal and paralinguistic cues important in face-to-face interaction (for example, Sproull and Kiesler, 1986). Although this notion was challenged by others such as O'Malley et al. (1996), conversational and interactional cue limitations in text-based interaction have been generally recognized in the literature. For example, Walther et al. (1994, p. 465), while admitting the existence of cue limitations in CMC (text-based), claimed that it "is a question of rate, not capability". This is because "due to cue limitations of CMC [text-based], the medium cannot convey all the task-related as well as social information in as little time as multichannel face-to-face communication". In a videoconferencing environment, certain cue limitations are still present, such as body movement below the shoulders. However, body movement above the shoulders, facial expressions and certain hand gestures are all available in real-time. In other words, the limitation of paralinguistic cues is the limitation of the scope of the Web Camera itself, not of videoconferencing. It therefore can be concluded that videoconferencing can generate a learning environment and interaction much closer to that of face to face than can other media. Having been deprived of any visual interaction, the distance participants appreciated any opportunity to interact orally and visually with another human being in the target language, regardless of the not-so-perfect video quality.

From a social perspective, the on-campus participants had enjoyed a closer learning community, which had been unavailable to the distance participants. Stacey (1999, p. 30) points out the importance of learning community by saying: "[l]earners at a distance can often lack the social student network of the on-campus student, which provides them with a comparative perspective of their progress with the course". This also explains why the distance participants valued the personal link established through the video between themselves and the teacher. The importance of this visual link was frequently mentioned in the interviews. The following excerpt from the post-trial survey indicates that Participant A felt strongly about being able to see her tutor:

> [...] I also really liked putting a face to my tutor's name, which I have not been able to do in
> any other open learning units. (PTS -2.5)

The fact that we had never met before and that they had never been exposed to any oral-visual interaction in the language may have played a significant part in their extremely positive perception of the impact of the video on their learning experience. The linguistic and social benefits of the video were neatly summed up by Participant E in her following remarks:

> The very best thing was having the chance to engage in spontaneous conversation, and to
> develop a personal relationship with my tutor. I also really enjoyed seeing my Chinese progress,
> and think that regular conversation like this would be an invaluable addition to study. (PTS-2.5)

In summary, video was perceived to be especially important for distance students who worked in isolation. It was observed that the Open Learning students were genuinely delighted to see me, especially on the first occasion, and they watched the video much more constantly than the on-campus students.

The enthusiasm and improvement in the language proficiency of the distance participants echo Riddle's (1990) contention that face-to-face meeting helps to establish a rapport that can lead to better interaction. This is especially true of the distance language learning environment, where face-to-face contact is limited or non-existent. The establishment of a personal link between the teacher and the learner plays a fundamental role in fostering the participants' positive perception of videoconferencing. The provision of video had helped to reduce the linguistic and social insecurity and anxiety felt by most distance language learners and promote motivation for learning.

6.6.2   The impact on the sense of isolation

Feelings of isolation have been documented extensively in DE literature and are regarded as one of the reasons for the high average rate of dropout (e.g. Bernard & Amundsen, 1989), and low quality of learning attainment (e.g. Abrami & Bures, 1996). Isolation is inherent in DE because of physical distance (Bullen, 1998; Bernard et al., 2000). The impact of isolation was also clearly evident in the learning of the distance participants in this study. For this reason, the distance participants received videoconferencing with more enthusiasm than did the on-campus participants. Their appreciation of the personal links generated by videoconferencing was one of the most noticeable differences between the on-campus and the distance group. Because of the physical distance separating the distance participants from each other and from their education provider, no learner community had been formed to support a social network, which had been a crucial part of the learning experience for the on-campus learners. As a result, such isolation often brings frustration, especially when learners encounter problems and difficulties in their learning. Isolation was more keenly felt by distance language learners than by learners of other disciplines because they were learning a language for communication but often found that they had no one to communicate with. Videoconferencing certainly helped to reduce the sense of isolation in their learning and to "humanize" the distance-learning experience by providing a platform for communication and interaction in the target language. Participant D's remark is typical and to the point:

> I really liked being able to converse face to face. With no other Chinese speakers to converse with, this was of immense benefit. I was able to ask questions and receive immediate answers, was able to practise speaking and gain confidence, and was able to 'humanise' what had previously been an isolated academic experience. (PTS-2.5)

It was the strong need to communicate with others in the target language and to establish a personal link with the teacher that gave rise to the enthusiasm and acceptance of videoconferencing and, as a result, they became more tolerant of the present service standard of the technology.

6.6.3 The impact on confidence building

Similar to the findings in regard to the impact of the video and the reduction of isolation, data in Section 5.2.5 suggests that confidence building was never an issue with the on-campus group, probably because they enjoyed plenty of opportunities to speak Chinese with other people in face-to-face interaction. However, it was just such interaction that the distance language learners were lacking. As a result, at the start of the trial, the distance participants were very nervous when speaking the language and being spoken to in the language. Again a sharp contrast emerged between the on-campus and distance participants. The on-campus participants were much more relaxed and carried the conversations with more ease. In contrast, panic, apprehension and frustration could easily be observed among the distance participants, especially in the first two sessions. Such nervousness even existed before the trial started, as Participant A described:

I am excited about it, but a little nervous too, I have never really used my Chinese like this. I have no problem writing (especially with my dictionary!), but my mind just goes blank when I am put on the spot and even in exams! I have difficulty remembering the words...

However, data from both the post-session interviews and post-trial written survey (see Section 5.2.5) indicates that the distance participants felt more confident as the sessions progressed. This confidence came from knowing that they could speak the language with more ease and less nervousness, and that their spoken Chinese was improving with each videoconferencing session. Despite the fact that they encountered more technical problems than the on-campus participants did, they were not discouraged. On the contrary, they appeared to be more tolerant of technical difficulties. This attitude was clearly reflected in the following remark from Participant A:

But compared to the hundreds of positives I experienced with netmeeting [NetMeeting], this [video delay] is really just a very minor inconvenience, and will only get better as technology improves – which is very rapid these days! To put it this way, if it was not for having the opportunity of these netmeeting [NetMeeting] sessions, I would be 500% worse at speaking and understanding Chinese than I am now! So in the big scheme of things, these minor delays were really not an issue.

In fact, the increased confidence in speaking and learning the target language was strongly emphasized by all the distance participants. It can be said that videoconferencing task performance and completion were a process of confidence building for the distance participants. The importance of this process cannot be overlooked, as lack of confidence was one of the reasons for the low retention rate in distance education (see Bullen, 1998). In other words, confidence building is crucial to distance learning success. Without videoconferencing, their nervousness and lack of confidence in learning and using the target language would not be overcome and would affect their language acquisition and its actual use in real life.

6.6.4   The impact on participants' enthusiasm in videoconferencing supported DLE

The distance learners' enthusiasm for the provision of oral-visual interaction supported by videoconferencing was one of the most obvious and valuable experiences emerging from this trial. Such enthusiasm forms a distinctive contrast to that of the on-campus students who did not exhibit much keenness for such interaction, mainly because they had never been deprived of face-to-face interaction. All distance participants recommended the inclusion of videoconferencing in their language learning for linguistic and other benefits (e.g. confidence building and the establishment of a learning community). This strong need for spontaneous interaction in DLE further establishes the significance and urgency of this research. It is hoped that findings from this research will speed up the process of incorporating videoconferencing in DLE.

In conclusion, the positive impacts generated by videoconferencing are significant and manifold, especially for the distance participants. **Videoconferencing provides them with what they need most in their learning: synchronous oral-visual interaction in the target language**. Such interaction is not an added advantage; it is a crucial component that has been missing in their learning. Although this research focuses its discussion on the above areas of positive impact, the impact of videoconferencing on DLE may be much more far reaching, and needs ongoing assessments by distance language professionals.

6.6.5   Recommendation for increasing positive impact

Drawing on the above discussion, the following recommendations for generating a positive impact on learners' learning experiences are suggested.

Due to isolation from others, most learners are too nervous to speak the target language. Thus, in task design and performance, more attention should be paid to strategies to increase the learner's confidence. At the beginner's level, learners should be encouraged to use the target language whenever possible, for example, to clarify meaning and request information in the target language. For more advanced learners, it may be desirable to provide opportunities for learners to lead the conversation.

Furthermore, videoconferencing should be incorporated into distance language programs as an ongoing measure to establish regular personal contact between the learner and the teacher, and among the learners themselves. Thus a learning community with peer support can be created and the sense of isolation can be effectively reduced.

6.7 Summary

Following Chapters 4 and 5, which contain the results from stages one and two of the evaluation of NetMeeting, this chapter has conducted an in-depth analysis of these findings in regard to the technological capabilities and pedagogical values of oral-visual interaction via videoconferencing. In accordance with the criteria underpinning the selection of videoconferencing tools and task appropriateness, and drawing on the theories and practices in L2 literature, this chapter has examined the practicality of NetMeeting, the language potential of the videoconferencing tasks designed for this study, the fit between the learner and the level of difficulty of these tasks, the authenticity and the positive impact of the tasks on the learner. This examination has led to the conclusion that desktop videoconferencing is a mature and powerful medium that can successfully support (at least, one-to-one) oral-visual interaction in meaning-based tasks, despite the existence of latency and limitations in Internet bandwidth. Overall, these findings contribute to our understanding of the capabilities of the present generation videoconferencing tools and of the scope and depth of oral-visual interaction supported by videoconferencing. Even though the participants' levels of Chinese proficiency were low and varied, the positive impact of such interaction on the participants' language acquisition has been ascertained. Furthermore confidence building emerged strongly. Both groups of participants felt that the advantages of the videoconferencing outweighed the limitations in the present generation of Internet technology, and that the videoconferences had been a very worthwhile and rewarding experience. All the distance participants proposed the incorporation of videoconferencing into their Chinese learning program.

Especially significant is the validity of the criteria for evaluating the appropriateness of videoconferencing-supported tasks, and the recommendations in relation to each of these criteria. These criteria were first proposed in Section 3.4.2 in reference to Chapelle's criteria for evaluating the appropriateness of CALL tasks, and then further verified and enriched in the two-stage evaluation of NetMeeting. They proved to be comprehensive, but not exhaustive, as videoconferencing is still new to language professionals. Future research and practice will no doubt benefit from these criteria and recommendations. Most significantly, these criteria have helped to evaluate data in relation to the second subsidiary research question: *what are the benefits and limitations of videoconferencing-supported oral and visual interaction in the process of L2 acquisition?* On the basis of data on this second subsidiary question, recommendations have been made on each of the criteria.

Thus far, this research has successfully answered the central research question from both a theoretical and empirical perspective:

In what ways is real-time oral-visual interaction, enabled by videoconferencing, able to facilitate L2 acquisition at a distance?

This study now proceeds to the concluding chapter, Chapter 7, with conclusions and implications for future research.

Chapter Seven

Conclusion

7.1 Introduction

This study has set out to find a solution for a practical need which is evident with all language learning at a distance: the need for provision of oral-visual interaction. It argues that oral-visual interaction is an indispensable component when communicative language learning is the goal. Unfortunately, such interaction has been sadly lacking in most distance language programs. In finding a solution to this core problem facing DLE, this study has examined the technological and pedagogical values of oral-visual interaction via Internet-based desktop videoconferencing. In this examination, meaning-based communicative tasks with occasions of focus on form were designed and tested in order to investigate the benefits and limitations of videoconferencing-supported interaction required for distance language learning. Rich data was collected from this empirical study that shed light on many issues concerning DLE, issues such as our understanding of the needs of the distance language learners, the depth and scope of videoconferencing-based interaction and the potential of such technology-mediated interaction for a new generation of distance language education. In so doing, this data provides definitive answers to the central research question, that is, **in what ways is real-time oral-visual interaction via videoconferencing able to facilitate L2 acquisition at a distance?**

This chapter draws conclusions on the major contributions of this study to the fields of distance language education and the study of CMC. These contributions include:

- ♦ the identification of the most urgent needs facing distance language learners;
- ♦ the redefinition of distance education;
- ♦ the proposal of a theory on an emerging fourth generation DLE;
- ♦ the creation of a new taxonomy of interaction in the context of CMC;
- ♦ the development of criteria for evaluating the technological capabilities of videoconferencing tools;
- ♦ the development of criteria for evaluating the appropriateness of meaning-based videoconferencing tasks;
- ♦ the evaluation of findings of the *technological* capabilities of videoconferencing-supported oral-visual interaction for L2 acquisition at a distance; and

♦ the evaluation of findings of the *pedagogical* values of videoconferencing-supported oral-visual interaction for L2 acquisition at a distance.

Following this summary, implications for future research are discussed, thus answering the third subsidiary research question: W*hat are the implications and potential of oral-visual interaction via videoconferencing for L2 acquisition in distance mode*? Some final remarks point to the significance of this research for distance language education.

7.2   Contributions of this research

As pointed out in Section 3.5, the contribution of this research must be qualified by the small case study sample and limited to students with elementary Chinese proficiency. The sample would seem to limit the generalizations available from the research finding. However, as Yin (1990, p. 21) points out, "case studies, like experiments, are generalizable to theoretical propositions and not to populations or universes". The contributions and implications of this study are therefore discussed in the context of established theories in L2 acquisition and evaluation criteria, and in reference to other empirical studies on the use of CMC in distance education. Although the sample is limited, it provides rich and in-depth data, which would be impossible to gather in a larger and more varied sample. With the above qualifications, the research findings may extend beyond the case study sample.

The contributions of this study are not discussed in order of importance. Instead, this discussion follows the progressive process of this study, in order to demonstrate its importance and originality step by step, leading to the most significant contribution of this study, which is discussed in Section 7.2.8.

7.2.1   The identification of the most urgent needs facing distance language learners

This research has been informed not only by the literature on distance language learning and the use of CMC in language teaching and learning, but also by the practical problem facing distance language learning imposed by distance itself. My observations of the distance language students at Griffith University and the surveys in the preliminary studies of this research confirmed the severity of the problem of lack of exposure to oral-visual interaction in distance language learning (see sections 1.4 & 3.1). The serious consequence of this problem later became more concrete in Stage Two of the evaluation of the NetMeeting supported oral-visual interaction, in which the distance participants were found to have a very limited level of listening, speaking and interactional skills (see sections 5.2.2 & 6.3.2). This in itself demonstrates the gravity of this problem. At the same time, it provided a basis from which to search for a solution.

7.2.2 The creation of a new taxonomy of interaction in the context of CMC

In the investigation of the technologies to support oral-visual interaction, CMC emerged as a core solution to the provision of oral-visual interaction in DLE. The literature review in this study examined CMC supported interaction, in terms of its evolving nature, its scope and depth. This scrutiny addressed some of the confusions over the definitions of CMC. It then redefined CMC in order to reflect developments in this fast-changing field. The new definition of CMC developed in this study identifies CMC as communications between human beings via a computer network. Consequently the content and scope of CMC was extended in this redefinition to include the use of audio and videoconferencing tools. In line with this new definition, this study proposes a new taxonomy of interaction in the context of CMC in terms of its potential for language learning and learner goals, that is, written interaction (e.g. supported by e-mail and online chat), oral interaction (e.g. supported by audio conferencing) and oral-visual interaction (e.g. supported by videoconferencing). This new taxonomy classifies more accurately the technologies and capabilities of each type of CMC-based interaction. This research further points out that each of the three types of interaction caters for different language learning goals, which, at the same time, can be complementary. Consequently future research should address them individually and in combination in order to maximize their potential. It is believed that this new taxonomy will shed light on future application and research of CMC in L2 learning in distance mode, and will allow future research to focus on the appropriate and specific type(s) of interaction in their attempt to provide an optimal environment for distance language learning. (see Section 2.3.2; Wang, 2004a)

7.2.3 The redefinition of Distance Education (DE)

The identification of the distance learners' need for oral-visual interaction led this study to an examination of DLE history. This research revealed an inadequacy in the previous definitions of Distance Education (DE) by various scholars (e.g. Keegan, 1983, 1996), and a need to enrich the definition. This research thus enhanced the definition of DE by identifying characteristics of DE that were not included in the previous definitions developed by various scholars, such as learner characteristics and the issue of social distance. Furthermore, this redefinition also embraces the developments of DE at the beginning of the 21st century, such as the impact of real-time Internet technology (see Section 2.4.1). On the basis of this redefinition, this research proposed a new theory on the emergence of a fourth generation DLE. (see below)

7.2.4   The proposal of a theory on an emerging fourth generation DLE

My attempt to find a solution to the problem of lack of interaction in distance education also guided this research to an extensive review of what had been achieved in the provision of interaction in DLE since its inception. Moreover, the use of advanced computer technology, in particular, synchronous and real-time Internet technology, warrants a constant reappraisal of the distance teaching and learning paradigm, especially in the case of language learning. This reappraisal is required largely because language learning relies even more heavily on the use of technology than do most other areas of distance education. Technology, computer technology in particular, has major repercussions for the area of language learning because of the communicative nature of such learning. Drawing on the reappraisal of the characteristics and achievements of the first three generations, this research put forward a theory of the emergence of a fourth generation distance language education, challenging the commonly held three generation theory.

The traits of this fourth generation are largely determined by the use of cutting edge technologies, especially Internet-based real-time technology, in the provision of oral-visual interaction in DLE, and can be summarized as follows:

- ♦ greater choice of mode of subject matter delivery;
- ♦ wider physical coverage – reaching more learners;
- ♦ more authentic language learning environments; and, most importantly;
- ♦ the provision of synchronous and real-time multi-way interaction, for the first time in DLE history.

The creation of this new generation advances and challenges the three-generation theory commonly held by the existing literature. This new division redefines the dividing line for the third and fourth generations, and categorizes more precisely the roles played by different computer technologies in distance education for language learning. Furthermore, by way of depicting the present situation and the capabilities of today's educational technologies, this research suggests a re-conceptualization of DE. The advancement in network technology and its extensive use in education blur the distinction between distance-learning and campus-based education. It is hoped that this division will help the distance language educator and learner to better understand the capabilities and potential of DLE in its fourth phase and what technologies can be utilized to further improve the distance mode of language learning. (see Section 2.4.6)

7.2.5 The development of criteria for evaluating the technological capabilities of videoconferencing tools

After the theoretical context of this research was firmly established, the study proceeded to its empirical dimension, by examining the capabilities of a particular CMC technology – videoconferencing. However, as videoconferencing is still an emerging medium, criteria for selecting and evaluating its capabilities have not been substantially established in the literature. In view of this lacuna and informed by the limited existing literature on, and my empirical knowledge of, videoconferencing tools, this research developed five criteria for evaluating the technological capabilities of videoconferencing tools: *user friendliness, video and audio quality, other features of pedagogical value, reliability* and *cost*. The five criteria were then applied in the two-stage evaluation of NetMeeting and improved as the evaluation proceeded. They proved to be comprehensive. The development of these criteria bridges a gap in the research of videoconferencing, thus enriching our knowledge and understanding of the educational potential of this new medium. More importantly, future research can employ these criteria as both theoretical and empirical guidelines in selecting the appropriate videoconferencing tools. (see Section 3.4.1)

7.2.6 The development of criteria for evaluating the appropriateness of meaning-based videoconferencing tasks

Following the evaluation of the *technological* capabilities of videoconferencing-support oral-visual interaction using the above criteria, a task-based approach was adopted for evaluating the *pedagogical* potential of such interaction. Drawing on research in CALL task design, especially guidelines developed by Skehan (1998) and Chapelle (2001), this research proposed a set of criteria for evaluating the appropriateness of videoconferencing-supported tasks. These criteria are: (a) practicality, (b) language learning potential, (c) learner fit, (d) authenticity and (e) positive impact (see Section 3.4.2). Their validity was tested in the two-stage evaluation of NetMeeting, and they were found to be beneficial, providing the evaluation with depth and scope. In many ways, these criteria fill a void in videoconferencing task design and evaluation.

7.2.7 The evaluation of findings and resulting recommendations regarding the technological capabilities of oral-visual interaction via videoconferencing

Another major contribution of this research is the findings from the two-stage evaluation in regard to the technological capabilities of NetMeeting, providing original data to the criterion of practicality. The evaluation conducted in four different network environments yielded a wealth of data, which not only strongly supports the use of Internet-based desktop videoconferencing in DLE for the provision of oral-visual interaction, but also advances our understanding of the potential of this medium.

The ease of installation and use makes NetMeeting a user-friendly videoconferencing tool, a merit that was unanimously agreed upon by both the on-campus and distance participants.

A major contribution of this study is the confirmation of the state-of-the-art audio and video quality in supporting one-to-one real-time interaction. Without reliable sound and video quality, videoconferencing would be impossible. Particularly significant is the high performance standard of NetMeeting in the LAN-Internet-LAN environment, which indicates that with improved Internet bandwidth, quality one-to-one videoconferences at a distance will be easily attainable. At the same time, this study acknowledges the constraints of the Internet bandwidth, latency and the computing power of the individual PC on the quality of a videoconference.

Another major finding is that, in contrast to most commercially available videoconferencing tools, NetMeeting offers features of great pedagogical value such as the whiteboard, Document Sharing and File Transfer. The evaluation of these features confirmed their technical maturity and reliability in supporting a multimodal online learning environment.

This research also confirmed the reliability of NetMeeting as a language learning tool. NetMeeting itself proved to be very reliable, despite the fact that the Internet could pose potential problems due to limited bandwidth and latency.

Last but not least, NetMeeting is an economically viable tool for learners. The fact that NetMeeting can be freely downloaded from the Internet and that there is no maintenance cost involved effectively reduces the cost to both educational institutions and the learner, making it a more economically viable and sustainable option. Based on the above findings, comprehensive recommendations for employing videoconferencing tools in DLE have been suggested in reference to each of the criteria. (see Chapter 4 and Section 6.2)

It has been argued throughout this research that distance language professionals should not just wait for the improvement of technology, despite the inevitable Internet development and the realization of broadband. Instead, in order to make distance language more interactive and effective, distance language professionals should work within the constraints of the existing technologies and maximize the advantages that they offer. Although there is a wealth of research on the use of computer technology in distance education, a mode of instruction seemingly welcomed by most distance educators, the use of Internet-based desktop videoconferencing tools has not been widely accepted in language teaching at a distance. This research points out that, while the technology is in place, changes at the institutional, conceptual and practical levels are now needed to keep up with technological advancement.

In summary, the empirical study of this research has extended our knowledge of the technological capabilities of videoconferencing tools and broadened our horizons by opening up new possibilities for providing oral-visual interaction in distance language learning. The significance of the empirical studies of this research lies in its confirmation that 4th generation technology is ready and capable, and will improve with the advancement of Internet technology in the near future. How to take advantage of this effective technology will be largely determined by the needs of teaching and learning. This was precisely what the next step of this research achieved – the investigation into the pedagogical values of videoconferencing-supported interaction in addressing the practical needs of the distance language learner.

7.2.8 The evaluation of findings and resulting recommendations regarding the pedagogical values of oral-visual interaction via videoconferencing

The contributions discussed above finally lead to the most significant contribution of this study: the evaluation of findings and resulting recommendations regarding the *pedagogical* values of oral-visual interaction via videoconferencing. Instead of investigating only the technological level of videoconferencing-support interaction, as most existing studies do (see Salaberry, 2000, p. 29), this research has furthered our understanding of videoconferencing-based interaction by examining its pedagogical values in task completion. To achieve this, meaning-based interactive tasks were designed and performed in a videoconferencing environment. Criteria proposed by this research for evaluating the appropriateness of meaning-based tasks supported by videoconferencing were applied in the evaluation. The appropriateness of videoconferencing tasks was judged in terms of their *language learning potential, learner fit, authenticity* and *positive impact.*

As the most important criterion of the five criteria for evaluating videoconferencing tasks, *language learning potential* was teased out and investigated in great detail, in terms of the provision of occasional focus on form and participants' perceived improvement in Chinese. Opportunities of interactional modification, an important contributor to focus on form, were tallied and analyzed using the Varonis and Gass's (1985) model. This in-depth analysis revealed the scope and depth of negotiation of meaning in videoconferencing-supported interaction. The support afforded by NetMeeting (e.g. the video, the whiteboard, etc) also proved essential for oral-visual interaction. The combination of video, audio, the Whiteboard, File Transfer and Document Sharing helps to create an authentic language learning environment, in which the participants could rely on these NetMeeting features to interact with the teacher. In addition, in such a multimodal environment, all senses were mobilized and their potential was maximized. As a result of such interaction, the participants' Chinese proficiency was improved, qualified by both the researcher's observation and the participants' self-perception.

The one-to-one nature of NetMeeting on the one hand enables the teaching to cater for individual needs of the learner. On the other, it promotes intensive interaction in, and production of, the target language. Personalized feedback from the teacher became immediately available to the individual learner. In a way it reproduced L1 (First Language) learning experience where one-to-one interaction is the basis for language learning. At the same time, the disadvantages of one-to-one interaction, such as lack of collaborative learning and inefficiency in terms of time and resource management, have also been acknowledged in this research. A combination of one-to-one and multi-way interaction is most desirable in distance language learning, and this study has directed our attention to the potential of multi-way interaction supported by desktop videoconferencing, and prepared us both theoretically and empirically for the research and employment of this advanced form of videoconferencing. (see Section 6.3.3)

The findings in regard to *learner fit* contribute to our understanding of the learner's receptiveness of task difficulties. In order to achieve a fit between learner's level of language proficiency and the level of task difficulty, tasks should be designed in such a way that their level of difficulty can be adjusted in accordance with an individual learner's proficiency and needs at the task performance level. Again the one-to-one interaction supported by videoconferencing is invaluable for addressing an individual distance learner's needs and characteristics during task performance. (see Section 6.4)

The inquiry into the *authenticity of the tasks* (that is, task relevancy to the real world) designed for this evaluation leads to the conclusion that constant improvement of task authenticity during task performance is necessary in order to promote more authentic target language production and interaction. Data shows that the more the tasks are closely related to the learner's life experience, the easier it is for the learner to engage in interaction in the target language. (see Section 6.5)

The positive impact of videoconferencing-supported tasks proved to be manifold and significant. Four features emerged as the most significant impact of videoconferencing: the positive impact of the video, confidence building, the reduction of the sense of isolation and increased enthusiasm in learning the language. These findings contribute to our understanding of the impact of oral-visual interaction supported by videoconferencing. The addition of such interaction further enriches the content and scope of distance language learning, changing it from text-based to orally and visually interactive for the first time in its history. The video in videoconferencing exposes the learner to the non-verbal aspects of the spoken language which would normally be lost in written and oral only interaction, but are nevertheless essential to L2 acquisition. In this virtual learning environment, deep level learning occurred in which students acquire knowledge on how to learn and use the target language in real life. The significance of oral-visual interaction goes far beyond linguistic benefits. From a social perspective, videoconferencing provides the distance learner with a sense of connectedness, as one participant pointed out, videoconferencing "humanized" their learning experience (PTS-2.5). Through videoconferencing, a learning community can be formed for distance learners who have otherwise been working in isolation. Closely related to the reduction of isolation is the issue of confidence building with the use of videoconferencing. Participants repeatedly emphasized that they felt more confident in speaking and learning Chinese as the videoconferencing sessions advanced. Consequently, they were extremely enthusiastic about this form of learning and adamant about the incorporation of videoconferencing in their learning. Distance no longer separates the learner and the education provider in the same way as it did before. (see Section 6.6)

Thus, data in relation to the five criteria (practicality, language learning potential, learner fit, authenticity and positive impact) has so far answered the central research question from various angles: **in what ways is real-time oral-visual interaction, enabled by videoconferencing, able to facilitate L2 acquisition at a distance**?

This research further contributes to distance language education by providing recommendations for each of the criteria. These recommendations were drawn from the evaluation findings and offer beneficial and comprehensive guidelines for future research.

To summarize, this research has contributed to distance language education both in theory and practice by shedding light on issues not considered by previous research. The results from this evaluation suggest that task-based interactive language learning at a distance can be adequately supported by videoconferencing, with the important finding that Internet-based desktop videoconferencing tools may emerge as a viable tool for generating oral-visual interaction in distance language learning. This is because it fulfils the two major rationales of distance language education – access and cost savings. The capabilities of videoconferencing in fostering spontaneous oral-visual interaction align it more closely with modern conceptions of language teaching emphasizing communicative task-based learning models.

7.3 *Implications for future research*

Dede (1996, p. 34) points out that "[t]he most significant influence on the evolution of distance education will not be the technical development of more powerful devices...but rather the professional development of wise designers, educators and learners". In this context, the implications for future research will be addressed under three broad headings: designers, educators and learners.

7.3.1 Implications for course designers of a distance language learning program

There are a number of implications from this research for the course design of a distance language learning program with interaction as its indispensable component. Ways of incorporating videoconferencing in distance language learning are suggested below.

Firstly, activities using videoconferencing should be incorporated into the course as part of the assessable items. This is to avoid the pitfall of learners' treating it as peripheral. For example, assessable speaking tasks can be designed in such a way that they require the employment of a videoconferencing tool to cooperate and communicate among learners. Advanced learners can be encouraged to use videoconferencing to complete such tasks as role-plays among themselves or with a native speaker on a regular basis. At the same time, the video can help the distance learners build a learning community, an essential social environment for successful language learning.

Videoconferencing tools can also be used to provide regular speaking tutorials similar to the sessions in the evaluation conducted in this research. This is especially viable when the enrolment number is low, as in the case of the advanced level of the Open Learning Chinese Program at Griffith University. Tasks with clearly established and achievable goals for each videoconferencing session should be set beforehand and carried out in these tutorials. Learners should be encouraged to take advantages of videoconferencing features such as the video, audio, the whiteboard, File Transfer and Document Sharing. The video can be used to demonstrate conversational prompters (e.g. a book, a photo etc.) to promote target language production. The whiteboard is especially valuable in showing character writing, grammar explanations, and negotiation for meaning. Learners can transfer large sized document to the other party through File Transfer, and share documents on their desktop with the other party through Document Sharing. All these features are beneficial for effective interaction in the target language.

Moreover, one-to-one videoconferencing can add a new dimension to language testing in that, for the first time in the history of distance language learning, speaking tests can be conducted in real-time. More authentic and cheat-proof than the telephone, videoconferencing supports interaction between the student and instructor in much the same way as in face-to-face interaction. However, the possible inconsistent audio and video quality should be taken into consideration when grading students' performance.

Videoconferencing can also be employed for individual consultation. The Open Learning Chinese program at Griffith University is an example, as videoconferencing can replace or partly replace the telephone consultation service, which at the moment is the only venue for lecturer-student oral communication. Videoconferencing-based consultation can be a more academically and economically viable option compared with telephone consultation. Instead of picking up a phone, the students can invite their teacher online to answer their questions more effectively with built-in conferencing functions such as the Whiteboard, Document Sharing and File Transfer.

However, videoconferencing is unlikely to provide the full range of learning for distance language education. For this reason, a combination of technologies is needed in the fourth generation of DLE, as Kaye (1989) points out:

> These technologies [CMC and other on-line services] should not be considered as a substitute for existing media and methods which have already proved their worth for distance education. CMC will not in every case replace teachers, texts, telephone tuition, or residential seminars – for the majority of learners it will complement these earlier technologies, and in so doing vastly enrich the distance education experience. And for particular groups – the housebound, the handicapped… – CMC may well become the major lifeline to interactive learning opportunities. (p. 9)

Due to the emergence of a great variety of CMC tools, such as e-mail, audio conferencing, and videoconferencing, the choice of medium or media poses some degree of difficulty. Based on the experience of this research, a bottom-up approach is suggested, that is, in selecting the appropriate CMC for distance language learning, the examination of the technological capabilities of a particular CMC tool should proceed after the learner's needs and learning objectives have been determined. The tasks meeting the learning objectives may then be designed in accordance with the learner's needs, proficiency and the practicality of the technology. The use of other CMC tools to supplement the one chosen can enhance the effectiveness of the teaching and learning process. For example, in my research e-mail was used occasionally to send lecture notes and so on for the purpose of supporting task completion during or after videoconferencing sessions, and e-mail proved to be very effective. The web can also be utilized to offer online technical and academic support for videoconferencing activities.

A number of suggestions for meaning-based videoconferencing task design have been discussed in Chapter 6, in terms of language learning potential, learner fit, authenticity, and positive impact. During the evaluation of videoconferencing-supported tasks, it became evident that occasional focus on form promotes acquisition, while too frequent focus on form is detrimental to the flow of interaction. Thus to maintain a beneficial frequency of focus on form at the task design and performance levels remains an ongoing challenge to language professionals. A fit between task difficulty level and the level of learner's proficiency requires the embedding of room and flexibility for adjustments in task design. This is to ensure the introduction of levels of modification at the task performance level, in accordance with individual needs and proficiency. Another balance that needs to be struck is the one between the pedagogical and real-life tasks. Pedagogical tasks are often set with specific learning objectives, while tasks that use real-life experience help the learner with their communicative competence and promote motivation for learning the target language. Thus both types of task benefit language production and reproduction, and together they can generate improved learning outcomes. In order to promote learners' confidence and enthusiasm, and to reduce the sense of isolation, the use of video and video clips could be explored to take full advantage of their potential. For example, for beginners, task design can include a variety of conversational prompters, such as a book or a piece of clothing, that can be viewed through the video function of a videoconferencing tool to further promote language production. For more advanced learners, role-plays and discussion on certain topics using video clips of a movie can be an excellent catalyst for language production.

7.3.2 Implication for educators

As videoconferencing is still new to distance language learning, there are a number of issues facing distance language educators. This new teaching paradigm requires them to be prepared technologically, pedagogically and psychologically.

This research indicates that most videoconferencing tools are very user friendly. One does not have to be a computer expert to be able to use them. However, the more a language professional knows about computers and the Internet, the more confident he/she will be. As language professionals are the first contact point when the learner encounters a technical problem, the technologically competent teacher has more opportunity to offer better support to the learner. Furthermore, ongoing technical training for teachers needs to be made available by distance education institutions. At the same time, language professionals should become more alert to technological changes and keep themselves up-to-date with these changes. In other words, training for technological readiness should be an ongoing effort from the distance language professionals and institutions.

At the same time, distance language professionals need to train for pedagogical readiness. As videoconferencing facilitates a new context for oral-visual interaction, effectively managing this multimodal learning environment will pose new challenges to distance language professionals.

Different from a face-to-face lecture, the one-to-one nature of desktop videoconferencing enables the teacher to provide more intensive and individualized teaching through the use of video, audio, text chat, etc. The intensive nature of such teaching requires more activities to be designed into the tasks in order to take full advantage of online time. Providing personalized assistance to the learner also calls for careful planning, awareness and sensitivity of an individual learner's needs. For example, with students of higher proficiency, the teacher can offer help discreetly. Conversely, the teacher can guide the task performance more explicitly when the learner has a lower level of proficiency.

In view of the instability of the Internet, distance language teachers need to develop a back-up plan, to be used when the videoconferencing sessions fail to proceed due to technical difficulties, such as a failed connection due to temporary Internet disruption or congestion. For example, e-mail can be used to forward lecture notes, or to rearrange a time for the abandoned tutorial.

Last but not least, distance language professionals need to be ready psychologically. Interaction in a videoconferencing environment is similar to that of face-to-face but differs from it in important ways. For example, the combination of video, audio, text and other links enriches the learning environment, but at the same time can place considerable pressure and strain on the teacher as well as the learner. In such a multimodal environment, how to cope with the intensive demands of the technology and the learner is a new challenge to teachers, who have to constantly adjust themselves psychologically to this new teaching environment. Furthermore, due to a variety of reasons, especially the instability of the Internet services, videoconferencing sessions can fail. Distance language professionals have to be prepared for failures of this kind and encourage themselves and the learner to persevere. The psychology of interaction in the videoconferencing environment deserves more attention and research from language professionals as this new teaching and learning medium becomes widely used.

7.3.3   Implication for learners

The fact that only five out of the 11 students enrolled in the Open Learning program participated in the trial may suggest that not all learners are ready for videoconferences in terms of their computer skills and psychological preparedness. After all it is easier to remain in familiar comfort zones than venturing into unchartered territory. It was also discovered in the evaluation of NetMeeting that some learners possessed only very basic computer knowledge and easily became panicky when encountering a technological problem. This led to some apprehension of videoconferencing among the participants.

Most distance language learners also lacked confidence in their listening and speaking competence in the target language. Wegerif (1998, p. 38) noted a "threshold experience" among online students. Those who have crossed the threshold participate actively, but those who fail to make it to the threshold usually become onlookers of the learning community. These learner characteristics should be taken into consideration when using videoconferencing. It is suggested that one or two induction sessions be conducted before the substantial use of videoconferencing commences in order to provide learners with the opportunity to familiarize themselves with the technology and ready themselves psychologically for videoconferencing-supported learning.

Ultimately the success of Internet-based distance language learning relies on the attitudes and the concerted work of course designers, educators and learners. In her discussion of the future of distance language learning, White (2003, p.321) also contends that "it is the participants [the learners, the teachers and support staff] themselves, and the attention that is paid to the participants within each context of delivery, that will determine the future of language learning in distance education, far more than any single innovation".

7.4 Final remarks

To my knowledge, there has been little empirical research in the literature which evaluates the use of NetMeeting in a distance language learning context. This study therefore fills a long existing gap in DLE by addressing a real need in distance learning and offering a model for integrating videoconferencing into distance language learning, one which serves not as an extension or add-on component of the existing program, but as a vital solution to what has been practically lacking. For the first time in the history of distance language education, the whole distance-learning process can be transformed from asynchronous and non-real-time to orally and visually synchronous and real-time. Although the physical distance between the learner and the education provider is still there, its effect can be minimized. It is not an exaggeration to conclude that Internet-based real-time technology is changing distance education qualitatively as well as quantitatively, advancing it into a fourth generation with oral-visual interaction as its defining feature. A whole new dimension has been opened to the field of DLE with the use of videoconferencing. Now deep learning and communicative competence can be expected from distance language education, and this research represents only the beginning of the important effort to make distance language learning a more worthwhile endeavour.

The issue of obsolescence of technology was recognized early in this research (see Section 3.6). However, the scope of this book only allows the examination of the capabilities of one Internet-based desktop videoconferencing tool: NetMeeting. This was selected not only for its state-of-the art quality and capability, but also because it represents the future of the technology of its kind. I acknowledge the possibility that by the completion of this research, more advanced videoconferencing tools may be emerging to replace NetMeeting. In fact Microsoft has now integrated MSN with NetMeeting, in an attempt to simplify connection procedures. However, the basic characteristics and capabilities of videoconferencing tools discussed here are still applicable. More importantly, videoconferencing-supported task design distilled from this research and participants' positive perceptions of videoconferencing will not fade into oblivion in the near future. On the contrary, these findings are gaining in importance as research in the use of desktop videoconference in learning has started to grow in recent years. Although the technology is changing rapidly, the larger pedagogical issues contained in this book are beyond obsolescence. In addition, these findings are applicable to any language learning at a distance and the approach of this research can be generalized and applied to other teaching and research. This research urges distance language professionals to be open to the use of whatever technology available to maximize the level and quality of oral-visual interaction, and in so doing, to create a more effective and efficient learning environment for distance language learners.

The results of this research promise more than just a model for integrating videoconferencing tools into distance language learning, or even, for that matter, the option of making distance language learning more effective and attractive. The results help us visualize a globalized future of distance language learning and suggest a reconceptualization of distance education as a whole. When the distance factor in distance education is minimized or even neutralized by technology, the distinction between distance and campus-based education is also blurred. The "guided didactic conversation" put forward by Holmberg (1986) will soon be as interactive as that of face-to-face interaction. This further enhances our confidence in this expanding mode of learning. The results of this research demonstrate that the technology to support synchronous distance language learning is in place, and it is improving rapidly.

Finally, Gravener (1998, p.108) points out that "the real barriers to excellent Web-based education are not technological, but psycho-social, economic, and political". The challenge now is for designers, educators and learners to overcome these barriers to exploit the potential that videoconferencing offers.

Appendix A – Survey of difficulties in learning Chinese

28 July 2000

Dear

I invite you to participate in a short survey to identify the major problems you might have experienced in learning Chinese by distance mode and to improve the course by finding ways to solve or ease problems.

I, therefore, invite you to answer the attached questions and return the response sheets to me together with your next assignment, as soon as possible, but not later than **8 September 2000.**

I will send you the results for confirmation and I am also happy to discuss the results with you either over the telephone or through email.

To make it easier for me to follow up the survey, I have included your student number on your response sheets. However, these responses will be analyzed with no student numbers and I assure you that your responses will be treated confidentially. I also will use these results anonymously in my research on language learning by distance mode. Your responses are important to the course and your achievements as a student. Thank you for your help.

Yours faithfully

Yuping Wang

Modern Chinese (Open Learning CHN12 & 22)

Course Evaluation

Student No. _____

Please give a detailed response to the following 3 questions. Please PRINT.

Why did you enrol in this Chinese course in distance mode?

What are your main problems with this course? Please comment on the four skills.

Speaking

Listening

Reading

Writing

What improvements would you suggest?

Thank you again for your time and efforts.

Please send all response sheets in with your next assignment.

Appendix B – CNET user evaluation results

Microsoft NetMeeting 3.01

89% positive   11% negative   (1,698 votes)

Average User Rating	1	2	3	4	5
Features				•	
Ease of use				•	
Stability				•	
Speed				•	

CUseeMe 5.0

59% positive   41% negative   (37 votes)

Average User Rating	1	2	3	4	5
Features				•	
Ease of use				•	
Stability			•		
Speed			•		

ICUII 4.9

79% positive   21% negative   (533 votes)

Average User Rating	1	2	3	4	5
Features				•	
Ease of use				•	
Stability			•		
Speed			•		

Video VoxPhone Gold 2.0

88% positive   12% negative   (34 votes)

Average User Rating	1	2	3	4	5
Features				•	
Ease of use				•	
Stability				•	
Speed					•

For detailed user comments, see the following sites:

http://download.cnet.com/downloads/1,10150,0-10001-103-0-1-7,00.html?tag=srch&qt=NetMeeting&cn=&ca=10001 (Accessed on 28 November 2001)

http://download.cnet.com/downloads/0-3364651-100-5976507.html?tag=st.dl.10001-103-1.lst-7-6.5976507. (Accessed on 28 November 2001)

http://download.cnet.com/downloads/0-3364651-100-7978697.html?tag=st.dl.10001-103-1.lst-7-1.7978697. (Accessed on 28 November 2001)

http://download.cnet.com/downloads/0-3364652-100-4538974.html?tag=st.dl.10001-103-1.lst-7-1.4538974. (Accessed on 28 November 2001)

Appendix C – Student Handbook for on-campus participants

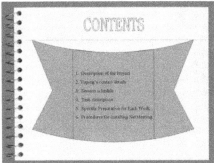

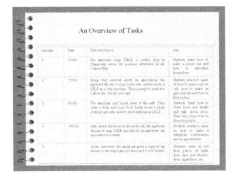

Session TWO

Mega task: Job Application

Subtask 2

Session Three

Mega task: Job Application

Subtask 3

Notes

Session Four

Mega task: Job Application

Subtask 4

Notes

Session Five

Mega task: Job Application

Subtask 5

Procedures for Installing NetMeeting

To install Internet Explorer

Procedures for Installing NetMeeting

To install NetMeeting 3.01

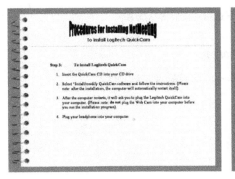

Procedures for Installing NetMeeting
To install Logitech QuickCam

Step 3:   To install Logitech QuickCam

1. Insert the QuickCam CD into your CD drive

2. Select "Install/modify QuickCam software and follow the instructions. (Please note: after the installation, the computer will automatically restart itself)

3. After the computer restarts, it will ask you to plug the Logitech QuickCam into your computer. (Please note: do not plug the Web Cam into your computer before you run the installation program)

4. Plug your headphone into your computer

Procedures for Installing NetMeeting
To open a hotmail account

Step 4:   To open a hotmail account

Note: if you don't have a Hotmail or MSN account, you need one to participate in NetMeeting.

1. Run NetMeeting
2. go to CALL and select Directory
3. click on "Click here to sign up for a Hotmail Account" and follow the instructions.

Please note don't forget to record your Hotmail address and password on a piece of paper because you need to use them every time you log on to NetMeeting.

Procedures for Installing NetMeeting
To install MSN Messenger

Step 5:   To install MSN Messenger

Note: if you have already installed MSN Messenger, go to Step 6

1. Open Internet Explorer
2. go to http://listen.download.com/
3. in the "Search" section, type in "MSN"
4. click on "MSN Messenger 6.6" and save it onto desktop.
5. When downloading is completed, go to desktop and double click on the "messenger.exe" icon.
6. Complete the installation, following the instructions.

Procedures for Installing NetMeeting
To log on to NetMeeting

Step 6:   To log on to NetMeeting

1. go to MSN (After MSN is installed, an icon will appear at the right hand corner of your computer, and click on the MSN icon.

2. click on "Click here to sign in"

3. type in your hotmail account password as prompted.

4. In the MSN Messenger Box, click "Add contact" and follow the instructions to add my email address (yeman02@hotmail.com)

5. In the MSN Messenger Box, put your name in Typing and right click to find "Start NetMeeting". Click on "Start NetMeeting" and Typing will receive your invitation. Now you are NetMeeting with Typing.

in emergency:

Ring Yaping on 937 57537 or

Email Yaping at X.Wang@botany.ga.edu.au

Appendix D – Post-trial survey

Summary of results from Stage two evaluation

N = 4 Participant C did not complete the Post Trial Survey due to her withdrawal.

Part One – Background Information

1. How long have you been learning Chinese?   **PTS – 1.1**

2. Apart from the Open Learning Chinese program you are now enrolled in, at what other places
    have you studied Chinese? Please indicate the appropriate bracket (s) with an X. You may
    select more than one.   **PTS – 1.2**
    - (a) None   ( )
    - (b) An institution in China   ( )
    - (c) An institution in Australia   ( )
    - (d) An institution in Taiwan   ( )
    - (e) Other (please specify) _____   ( )

3. How did you practice your speaking skills before this trial? Please indicate the appropriate
    bracket (s) with an X. You may select more than one.   **PTS – 1.3**
    - (a) Never practiced   ( )
    - (b) With Chinese friends   ( )
    - (c) With my neighbours   ( )
    - (d) With tapes   ( )
    - (e) With my colleagues   ( )
    - (f) With people in my family   ( )
    - (g) Other (please specify) _____   ( )

Summary of results of Part One

Participants	Q1: Length of learning Chinese	Q2: other places of study	Ways of practicing speaking Chinese before this trial
Participant A	10 months	none	Never practised
Participant B	Started in the 1970s and continued intermittently	Taiwan and Germany	With tapes, Rosetta Stone (an online course)
*Participant C	10 months	none	With tapes
Participant D	10 months	none	With tapes and Chinese speakers
Participant E	2 years	Anther institution in Australia	With tapes and colleagues

Part Two – Evaluation of NetMeeting

1. Please rank the following features of NetMeeting according to their usefulness in learning Chinese. Number 1 represents most useful and Number 5 least useful. Please put a number in each bracket. **PTS – 2.1**
    - (a) Video (the image) ( )
    - (b) Audio (the sound) ( )
    - (c) File Transfer ( )
    - (d) Sharing (sharing document on your desktop ( )
    - (e) Whiteboard ( )
    - (f) My Video (the self image window) ( )

	No. 1	No. 2	No. 3	No. 4	No. 5	No. 6
audio	4					
video		3	1			
File Transfer		1		1	2	
Sharing				2		
Whiteboard	1		3			
My Video					2	2

Note: Participant E put number 1 for both audio and the Whiteboard. Sharing was not rated by Participant D and E.

2. Below is a list of possible strengths of NetMeeting for language learning. Please put an X in the appropriate bracket (s) when NetMeeting helped you. You may select more than one: **PTS – 2.2**

Strengths	*Results*
(a) Building my confidence in speaking Chinese	(4)
(b) Reducing my anxiety in learning Chinese	(2)
(c) Reducing isolation in learning in distance mode	(3)
(d) Increasing my motivation in learning the language	(3)
(e) Seeing the person I am talking to	(3)
(f) Allowing instant feedback from the teacher	(4)
(g) Allowing mistakes to be corrected on the spot	(4)
(h) Providing me the opportunity to interact spontaneously with someone	(4)
(i) Negotiating for meaning using Chinese	(3)
(j) Allowing me to ask for more information using Chinese	(4)
(k) Allowing me to clarify meaning using Chinese	(4)
(l) Inferring meaning according to the context	(3)
(m) Improving my listening skill	(4)
(n) Other (please specify) <u>having fun</u>	

253

3. Below is a list of possible weakness of NetMeeting for language learning. Please put an X in
    the appropriate bracket (s). You may select more than one.   **PTS – 2.3**
    (a)   It's too difficult to use   (0)
    (b)   It's too difficult to set up   (1)
    (c)   It's one-to-one mode only   (1)
    (d)   The quality of the video is not good enough for language learning   (1)
    (e)   The quality of the audio is not good enough for language learning   (0)
    (f)   It lacks support for group discussion   (0)
    (g)   The Internet transmission was not reliable   (3)
    (h)   NetMeeting was not reliable   (1)
    (i)   You have to do it at certain times because of Internet congestion   (3)
    (j)   Other (please specify) _____   (0)

4. How reliable was NetMeeting? Please indicate on the diagram below with an X.
    (Please Note: reliable here refers whether or how often NetMeeting crashed)   **PTS – 2.4**

Very reliable								Not reliable	
1	2	3	4	5	6	7	8	9	10
	(2)	(1)						(1)	

Please explain why

- ♦ I have marked 2, basically very reliable, as even though the system froze a couple of times,
  it was quickly remedied by either inviting the person to netmeet again, or a quick restart of
  the computer. As I say, it only happened a few times, but was easily fixed. **(Participant A)**

- ♦ The problems I experienced were not due to the Netmeeting program itself, but more to the
  connection between my school and Griffith University. Once we had established successful
  contact the meetings were very smooth. **(Participant E)**

- ♦ Seemed quite reliable in terms of program stability, I can only remember having to re-boot
  it once or twice during the sessions**. (Participant B)**

- ♦ My net meeting [NetMeeting] trial had a lot of problems. Beyond the hardware problems,
  there was difficulty with the Internet connection and its speed, the netmeeting application.
  We tried to achieve success many times, and only had one successful attempt.
  (Participant D)

5. Please write down what you liked when using NetMeeting for learning Chinese
    and why.   **PTS – 2.5**

- ♦ It was just so nice as a distant student learning a difficult language to have face to face
  tutor contact. Distance students normally are studying via distance ed because they are

busy – so it was a bonus to be able to practice speaking Chinese with my tutor in my own home! Before the sessions, I used to freeze when I tried to string a sentence together spontaneously! Netmeeting has enabled me to overcome that initial fear of being asked a question in Chinese, to only feel embarrassed that I cannot think of a response, even though I have learned the words! I am not quite fluent yet (ha ha!), but I definitely have the confidence now to take on further challenges in Chinese conversation! I also really liked putting a face to my tutor's name, which I have not been able to do in any other open learning units. **(Participant A)**

♦ I liked the one on one nature of the medium which provided for very intensive lessons. Plus the features of Netmeeting that allowed for instant feedback (e.g. whiteboard), and introduction of other materials e.g.: documents (sharing) and video [sending a video clip] (although it did not work in my case) relevant to the context of the face to face dialogue. **(Participant B)**

♦ The very best thing was having the chance to engage in spontaneous conversation, and to develop a personal relationship with my tutor. I also enjoyed seeing my Chinese progress, and think that regular conversation like this would be an invaluable addition to study. **(Participant E)**

♦ I really liked being able to converse face to face. With no other Chinese speakers to converse with, this was of immense benefit. I was able to ask questions and receive immediate answers, was able to practice speaking and gain confidence, and was able to 'humanise' what had previously been an isolated academic experience. **(Participant D)**

6. Please write down what you did not like when using NetMeeting for learning Chinese and why. **PTS – 2.6**

♦ The first 20 seconds or so, the video and sound sticks, freezes and delays, but it seemed to go alright after that. Occasionally during the session the video and sound would freeze again. This, when it happened, made listening a little difficult, and the delays meant not being able to equate the sound with facial expressions etc. But compared to the hundreds of positives I experienced with netmeeting, this is really just a very minor inconvenience, and will only get better as technology improves – which is very rapid these days! To put it this way, if it was not for having the opportunity of these netmeeting sessions, I would be 500 per cent worse at speaking and understanding Chinese than I am now! So in the big scheme of things, these minor delays were really not an issue. **(Participant A)**

♦ It was very difficult to attain success. A lot of the time, we did not know what was going wrong, so perhaps more technical support would be of benefit. It was quite a difficult exercise. Other than that, I found the whiteboard difficult to use in that the Chinese characters were difficult to decipher. I don't think my character recognition was helped by netmeet [NetMeeting]. **(Participant D)**

♦ Although not related to the program per se, the difficulties encountered with unreliable Internet transmission was a real nuisance, particularly when then sound broke up or was not transmitted at all. These problems do not seem to be insurmountable with e.g. faster Internet connections on both ends and judicious timing of link-up. (**Participant B**)

♦ I often found the technological aspects of the communication very frustrating, experiencing a wide range of set-up and communication problems. (**Participant E**)

7. Through the five NetMeeting sessions, what aspects of Chinese language learning did you feel improved? Please put an X in the appropriate bracket (s) below that best describe your own experience. You may select more than one. **PTS – 2.7**

    (a) My fluency (3)
    (b) My pronunciation (3)
    (c) My listening ability (4)
    (d) My vocabulary (3)
    (e) My grammar and structures (3)
    (f) My reading (0)
    (g) My writing (0)
    (h) My speaking ability (4)
    (i) My conversational tactics (e.g., asking in Chinese for repetition and clarification of meaning, inferring meaning from the context, etc.) (4)
    (j) Spontaneous replies (3)
    (k) Other (please specify) _____ (0)

8. How important do you believe is the video in NetMeeting to the improvement of listening and speaking skills? Please indicate on the diagram below. **PTS – 2.8**

Important								Not important	
1	2	3	4	5	6	7	8	9	10
(1)	(1)	(1)	(1)						

Please explain why

♦ The video is very important, because it is more personal to speak to each other face to face than on the phone. Silence is not a problem while you think of a response, because your tutor can see that you are thinking (very hard!). You can see facial expressions which is very important to try and guess what on earth your tutor just said when you can't understand any of the words! And again it is nice to have that face to face contact, and put a face to the name, both for student and teacher. The video can be a little scary at first, especially if you have not used netmeeting before in other situations. But like any new technology, it is also exciting, and any nerves of using the video quickly disappear! (**Participant A**)

- The importance of the video image lies in the fact that one gets the dialogue with the appropriate body language and facial expression, which do not only aid in understanding meaning but are part of the message itself. More specifically it seems to me that to achieve accurate pronunciation the opportunity of seeing the actual sound being formed by a native speaker is very helpful. It also would allow the teacher to do on the spot correction of mistakes through sound and visual demonstration. **(Participant B)**

- The video quality I experienced was never good enough to allow me to see my tutor's lips clearly, but I still got a lot from my sessions. I would love to experience the difference a good picture could make. [Because she used a laptop, the video quality was affected by the limited power of her computer.] **(Participant E)**

- I think it is important, because it is helpful to 'see' your teacher. To have a telephone conference would not be as good. Seeing your teacher is more personal, and it makes you more comfortable, which assists with learning. Of course video is not as important as audio, but it is still significant. **(Participant D)**

9. If you were given a choice between one-to-one and many-to-many interaction (i.e. a group discussion) supported by a videoconferencing tool, which one would you choose? Please explain why **PTS – 2.9**

- I think for beginners, one to one maybe better, to give them the confidence and practice. Then maybe for advanced students with a wider vocab, a group chat session would be better. I found that when I did not understand something, my tutor had to keep asking me again and again until I worked out the meaning. This is the best way to help a beginner like myself get used to hearing and understanding, but I think other students would get a little bored of waiting! Group discussion would be great for more experienced students, but I have never been involved in one, so I do not know how the technology would cope, i.e. delays etc. **(Participant A)**

- In an ideal world I would like to experience both, but if asked to choose, I would definitely choose the one-to-one option because it provides more efficient communication in the short time available. However, many-to-many would probably allow more variety of communication. **(Participant E)**

- I would choose one-to-one, because I feel a videoconference [with more than one person] would be very difficult to learn and contribute to. I have been part of a video conference before, and I did not find it to be beneficial. I would love to take part in a group that was face-to-face, but with netmeet [NetMeeting], I would prefer to speak with just one other person. **(Participant D)**

- [one-to-one interaction is] particularly useful, because it allows for an intensity of interaction which one rarely gets in the regular classroom setting. **(Participant B)**

10. Are there any other feature(s) do you think important for language learning? (other features include File Transfer, the Whiteboard, Sharing Document, My Video and audio.) **PTS – 2.10**

- ◆ Yeah the whiteboard helped heaps. When I could not understand a word my tutor could write it on the board. (Well at first the character, which I was none the wiser with!), but writing the pinyin was good, as sometimes I thought I was hearing a totally different sound. The more this happened though, the more I got used to the way my tutor pronounced the words. (the correct way as opposed to my incorrect way!). We used the sharing files feature was to talk about family photos. But this feature could be used for endless conversation possibilities. **(Participant A)**

- ◆ We used all those features at time and they were largely useful of specific purposes e.g. video in conjunction with audio gives the opportunity to see body language and facial expressions which contribute to the communication process. **(Participant B)**

- ◆ The whiteboard proved useful for instant demonstration of written language w.o. [without] Having to go to cumbersome keyboard input methods [the use of the mouse to write characters]. **(Participant D)**

- ◆ Perhaps more phone support at times could be helpful in order to motivate and reduce isolation. **(Participant E)**

11. How important do you believe is the oral-visual interaction provided by NetMeeting to your learning of Chinese? Please indicate on the diagram below with an X. **PTS – 2.11**

Important								Not important	
1	2	3	4	5	6	7	8	9	10
(1)	(3)								

Please explain why

- ◆ I think I have covered this response in my comments above. **(Participant A)**

- ◆ Important in providing visual cues to involved in the communication process useful also for demonstrating and correcting sound formation in establishing correct Pronunciation. **(Participant B)**

- ◆ If you cannot speak with and see anyone while you are learning a language, it is very difficult to improve and to become fluent. It is integral that a student be able to practice what they are learning. **(Participant D)**

- ◆ It creates more of a classroom feeling which is a useful adjunct to all of the individual study that must be done by a distance education student". **(Participant E)**

12. How easy was it to use NetMeeting? Please indicate on the diagram below with an X. **PTS – 2.12**

Very easy								Very difficult	
1	2	3	4	5	6	7	8	9	10
(1)		(1)	(1)	(1)					

Please explain why

♦ Netmeeting was very easy to use, as the program is user friendly, and simple to follow. **(Participant A)**

♦ Because of technical difficulties I did not find the Netmeeting program easy to use – that is I experienced difficulties making connection, but this was a problem with firewalls. Once these technical difficulties were fixed, the actual Netmeeting program is very user friendly, and easy to operate. My low rating is due to the initial connection difficulties. **(Participant E)**

♦ There were many problems in my trial. NetMeeting seemed to have a lot of unexplainable technical problems that we were largely unable to rectify. **(Participant D)**

♦ The visual layout of the program window and the conveniently arranged buttons for the ancillary features (whiteboard, file share etc) were not too numerous and complex. Plus in case of difficulties the person experienced with the program was able to give immediate face to face help. The big bugbear was the reliability of the connection. **(Participant B)**

13. Do you think that NetMeeting should be incorporated into the Open Learning Chinese Program after the trial? Why? **PTS – 2.13**

♦ Yes I do think that netmeeting should be incorporated into the OLA Chinese Program, because of all the reasons above! The trial has been a great opportunity for me to improve my Chinese, and therefore using netmeeting as a set part of the course would obviously be nothing but advantageous for students and their results, and most importantly their enthusiasm and motivation by having fun learning Chinese! **(Participant A)**

♦ Yes, I do. Although my trial had a lot of technical problems, I can certainly see the immense benefit in having NetMeeting in the Open Learning Chinese Program. Without it, Chinese is extremely difficult to learn without any other support. I think Netmeeting is almost a necessity. **(Participant D)**

♦ Provided the technical problems related to unreliable and slow connection can be at least minimized, I would strongly support the incorporation of NetMeeting into the Chinese program. All the features of the program provide useful aids for the language learner, e.g.: sharing, video, whiteboard. Initially one might consider using NetMeeting as the preferred form of liaising with the tutor during the regular time slot provided for the purpose. **(Participant B)**

♦ I rarely found the quality of the picture really sharp, so it didn't really assist my learning to see my tutor. However I absolutely loved having the opportunity to converse with someone in Chinese. Apart from being exciting, it motivated me to continue studying, and gave me some much needed contact with someone. Therefore I think some kind of video conferencing should be used. The very best thing would be for some opportunity to speak with small groups including other students on some occasions, and the opportunity to speak only with the tutor on other occasions. I think I learned a lot in a short time while talking with my tutor, and would like to see continued opportunity to develop spontaneous conversation skills in this way. **(Participant E)**

14. Other comments **PTS – 2.14**

♦ Thank you for the opportunity, I have appreciated it very much! **(Participant A)**

♦ The trial really showed me that it is possible to learn a language through distance education. Although it is still difficult, and there are a range of technical problems, it is a great idea, and I would recommend it as a significant educative tool. **(Participant D)**

♦ In my view, it is difficult to learn Chinese by distance education unless there is a component of conversation included. Netmeeting could be an effective way to build some regular conversation practice into Chinese studies. **(Participant E)**

♦ **No comment from Participant B**

This is the end of the questionnaire.

Thank you very much for helping me with this project.

Appendix E – Excerpts of Stage One interviews

Data in relation to the sound quality of NetMeeting

Interviews with Student 1 reveals that the fading in and out of the sound affected his understanding:

Session Four

Student 1:	The sound quality? Still comes in and out.
R:	Not stable?
Student 1:	Hm
R:	Did that affect your understanding?
Student 1:	Sometimes.
R:	But most of the times, it was OK?
Student 1:	Most of the times it's OK.

The Sound quality was confirmed to be good enough for teaching purposes. For example, at the end of *Session One*, Student 2 reported:

Student 2:	The sound quality was good…
R:	…But do you think the sound quality is good enough for teaching purposes?
Student 2:	Yeah. Yeah.

Session Two

Student 1:	The picture was a bit more steady. Sometimes maybe once or twice it actually blacked out.
R:	Really? That didn't happen to me. But from my side, when you move, the picture became blurred, I can't see your eyes and mouse. Did you have that?
Student 1:	No.
R:	It's just that I disappeared and came back again?
Student 1:	Yeah.

Data in relation to the other features of NetMeeting

Session Five

R:	Oh. Did you think NetMeeting was helpful with your performance of the tasks?
Student 1:	Yeah, it was good.
R:	Can you explain a bit more? I mean about the NetMeeting.

Student 1:	Because of the tools it has. They can help you convey your message across. Because it has a lot of tools, the whiteboard, the camera, the, what do you call it?
R:	File transfer?
Student 1:	File transfer.

Session Five

Student 2:	Umm I think I enjoyed all of them, I think a variety was very good.
[....]	
R:	...Comparing video with the whiteboard, which one is more important to you?
Student 2:	I'm not sure, I think it probably depends on what the topic of the conversation is. If it's easy conversation probably the video, but if it's difficult and you need clarification on opinion, probably the visual; the whiteboard.
R:	And also Sharing and the Whiteboard, which one do you think is more useful?
Student 2:	I'd say both are useful but more so the whiteboard. Umm because, I also have other Chinese programs open, so I could copy your character into my thing to get the Pinyin [romanization].

Appendix F – Excerpts of Stage Two interviews

Data in relation to the sound quality of NetMeeting

When asked about the sound quality in *Session One* at the post-session interview, Participant A reported,

Participant A:	Sometimes it's really good, and sometimes it broke, broke into little, eee, hard to understand little fragments, kind of thing. And then, then the video would go very very slow and stop, and it would take, you know 10 to 20 seconds... , but (.) you know, disregarding, you know, the quality. It's hard, like the technology is new and]
R:	hm]
Participant A:	It's hard to explain. It was, it was. How do I put it without making it sound very bad. Like the quality wasn't fantastic, but again, hadn't it for the net conferences, I wouldn't have that kind of communication, I wouldn't have net conferences.
[...]	
Participant A:	The fact that the quality is not perfect, is, is probably not that important.
R:	OK, Alright. Maybe we can get used to it. [(hahh), I don't know.
Participant A:	[yeah yeah] and you know, I mean, technology will probably get better as well.
R:	Mmhmm yeah OK. Oh, and I've got a few rating here, very good, good, OK, poor, very poor. The sound quality of the video... NetMeeting? So which one do you say...
Participant A:	I'd say OK.
R:	Next question: was it good enough for learning Chinese?
Participant A:	Mm (7)
R:	Yes or no (hahh)
Participant A:	Mm that's a difficult... I'd say yes.
R:	Mm, why?
Participant A:	I'd say yes. Mm, it was very, like even in everyday conversation, if you were talking to me, you know on the phone, I would find it very difficult to understand and pick up the syllables that you speak. And so, the sound quality I think is good enough to learn Chinese. Yes.

Session Three

Participant A:	For the majority of the session, I'd say, I'd say very good.
R:	OK. Compared with the last session... Do you say it's better, the same... ?
Participant A:	I think it's the same.
Participant A:	It's probably, but I didn't have any problems.

Session Five

Participant A:	Good. Just at the very start, I think I can see a pattern now. When we start NetMeeting, for the first, say 20 seconds or so, the sound is very bad. Then, then it gets better. Then it's fine.
R:	OK, OK.
Participant A:	And I notice that. You know because we had to log on again.
R:	Yeah?
Participant A:	We logged on again for the second time. Again for the first 20 seconds, the sound was really bad. Then it was, then it was fine.
R:	Yeah, yeah. I found the same thing too. Mm, compared with the last session, was it better, same or worse?
Participant A:	It was the same.
R:	The same. OK. So was it still good enough for learning Chinese?
Participant A:	Yeah!

Participant C commented on the sound quality at the end of **Session Two**:

Participant C:	Well, (hahh). At times actually your, your picture was, sort of frozen went quite, um that was before it. I think that was part of the connection issue. But when it was running alright, it was fine. The picture was clear and the voice was very clear.
R:	When you could hear it, it was very clear. But sometimes it lost.
Participant C:	Yeah. That was actually worse as it got to later in the morning.
R:	Compared with the previous session, was the sound better, worse or the same?
Participant C:	Probably a little worse as it progressed today, I think. But that delay was quite noticeable at times.
R:	Was it good enough for learning Chinese?
Participant C:	Ah, yes! I could start to pick up, just even using those phrases, like 'I can't hear' or 'say it again', was useful.

Participant D also confirmed the good quality of the sound at the end of **Session Five**:

Participant D:	I thought it was, I thought it was quite good. Um there were times when it crackled a little and maybe I missed a couple of things, but no, it was quite good.
R:	Oh, that's good. Um.
Participant D:	A slight delay.
R:	A slight delay, was it?
Participant D:	Yeah.
R:	OK, OK. On my side, it was quite good. Just one time, I think we lost a sentence.
Participant D:	Yeah, there was that one time.

R:	How many times did that happen on your end?
Participant D:	There was only that one time that was bad, but sometimes it, it just flicked a bit maybe in and out. Just a couple of times, like not it wasn't bad, it was just a slight, a slight distraction.
R:	So early in the morning is good, isn't it?
Participant D:	I think, yeah I think so. Anyway I think I just get too slow, my connection gets too slow.
R:	So the quality of the sound, was it good enough for learning Chinese?
Participant D:	Um, yes, yeah, I think it was. Maybe, maybe pronunciation might be a little difficult at times, but no, I thought it was good.

Session One

Participant E:	Not, not quite good enough to always get meaning over. […] you know at crucial times, I would get a crackling sort of interference which was just enough to stop me from hearing (.) a sentence to string a sentence together.
R:	OK, OK. It does interfere with your understanding?
Participant E:	Yeah, it does.
R:	So how do you rate the sound, very good, good, OK, poor or very poor?
Participant E:	Oh, that's hard. Say good. I wouldn't say very good because to be very good, I think I have to get some meaning from it relatively easily, you know I had to ask you to repeat yourself quite a number of times not because I wasn't understanding the words but because I couldn't hear them properly and connect into a meaning.

The sound quality of **Session Three** was considered to be the best of all.

R:	So what did you think of the sound quality today?
Participant E:	Much better than we had.
R:	Yes, it was much better than last time, than the previous two times.
Participant E:	Yes, it was.
R:	Was it good enough for learning Chinese?
Participant E:	I think so.

Data in relation to the video quality of NetMeeting

In modem-Internet-modem environment

The following excerpt was taken from the interview with Participant A immediately after **Session One**. When asked about the quality of the video, Participant A answered:

Participant A:	Again, OK. Sometimes there were delays, and the video stopped and it would take a little while to catch up. But I don't think too many problems.

R:	Mm, Mm, OK. Was it good enough for learning Chinese?
Participant A:	Eh yes!

At the end of *Session Two*, Participant C commented on the quality of the video:

Participant C:	Most of the time, it's very good. Yeah.
R:	OK. Was it blurred, continuous, stilled or delayed?
Participant C:	Yeah, it was a bit delayed.
R:	But it was not blurred?
Participant C:	No, no, it's, at one stage, that was when I was actually closed the computer down and, re, rebooted everything, it got very distorted. I think that was my computer, I probably clicked something I shouldn't do or something, but the rest of the time, a good clear picture that was moving mostly.
[...]	
R:	The video quality: was it better, worse or the same?
Participant C:	I think it was probably very similar.
R:	Very similar.
Participant C:	Yeah, very similar. The picture was quite clear and I could see you quite well.
R:	So the picture, was it good enough for learning Chinese?
Participant C:	Ah, yes. Yes.

In LAN-Internet-modem environment

At the end of *Session Three*, Participant A described the sound quality on her side.

Participant A:	Mm, fine. I know my picture [video image] was pretty dark, wasn't it? But that's something to do with the lighting in my office. We'll get a brighter light in there.
R:	Maybe...
Participant A:	But yours [my video image on her side] is fine.
R:	So, was it continuous or, or very still? What kind of picture on your side?
Participant A:	It was probably better than previous sessions. It, it was, it delayed a few times but not much. Quite continuous.
R:	But, quite continuous all the time, or most of the time.
Participant A:	Most of the time, yeah.
R:	OK, yeah. Mm, so was it good enough for learning Chinese?
Participant A:	Yes, yes.

The interview with Participant A at the end *of Session Four* reveals delays in transmission of video and sound.

R:	What did you think of the video quality?
Participant A:	Em, good. Again just a few little delays.
R:	Yeah. Compared with the previous sessions, it's getting better or, the same or worse?
Participant A:	Tonight it seemed a little bit worse.
R:	Oh, even the video?
Participant A:	Yeah. Because it's the, it's the delay of the video that actually makes the sound a little bit distorted. Do you know what I mean? Those delays make the sound bad and, do you know what I mean?
R:	Yeah. Yeah.
Participant A:	When, when the delays are occurring, it affects the video and the sound.
R:	Yeah, yeah. I see what you mean. Congestion in the network, I think. Yeah, on my side, it's clear and the video is good too because I use the local network. So it's a wider band, it's a broader band. But on your side, you're still using the Internet. So
Participant A:	So it's a shame you can't see it, isn't it, from my [side]...
R:	Yeah. It's true.
Participant A:	It would be hard for me. If I could see it if yours were a lot better, I could say probably say yeah mine is not very good. Hahh. Yeah, it's clear enough for me to see it and the delay is there. I can deal with the delays.

Participant C also confirmed the capability of the video in supporting distance language learning.

Session Three

R:	[the video] very clear. Good. Back to the video quality, do you think it was good enough for learning Chinese?
Participant C:	Yeah.
R:	Good.
Participant C:	I could see, you know, the movements of your lips and so on when I needed to.
R:	Oh good. That's good. So it's very continuous and clear?
Participant C:	Yeah!

LAN – Internet –LAN environment

Session One

Participant E:	Very good. Although I suppose I had one, I had expected it to maybe seeing mouth movement, making sounds. You can't do that. It's not that sophisticated. So you still mainly reply on the auditory, the sound quality to hear rather than what you can see to learn from. But it's nice to see who you are speaking to.

Participants' perceived improvement

Participant B was affirmative of his progress at the completion of *Session Five*:

R:	Through the five sessions, do you think your speaking skills have been improved?
Participant B:	Yes, definitely.
R:	Why did you say so?
Participant B:	Well, I feel just to, you know, just to be able to actually use Chinese in a one to one situation. I just got the feeling that I, well, I'm becoming also more aware of the mistakes I was making, more than anything else. Sometimes as I'm speaking, I am making mistakes. But I think that's a, that's good process as well.
R:	It's just a process of getting used to speaking Chinese, is it? In what way, more specifically that you think your speaking has been improved?
Participant B:	The main thing is just confidence to know you actually can do it.

Appendix G – Student Handbook for distance participants

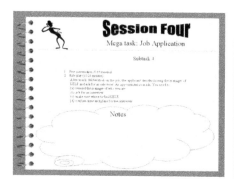

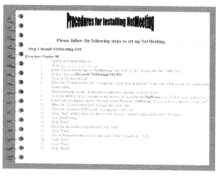

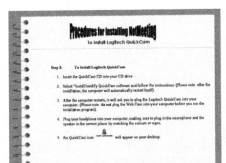

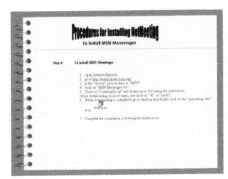

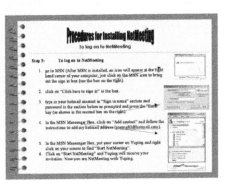

Appendix H – Pre-trial survey

Date

Dear

I am writing to you to ask your help with a problem facing many Open Learning students. My research indicates that the biggest problem facing students in the Open Learning Chinese program is the lack of opportunity for speaking practice. To help to ease this problem, we have decided to pilot test an Internet videoconferencing tool called NetMeeting. Our initial evaluation reveals that NetMeeting can support both video and audio conferencing on a one-to-one basis. This means through NetMeeting, the students and teacher can both hear and see each other, much like a face-to-face conversation.

The trial of NetMeeting is scheduled in Study Period 1, between April and May 2002. Five lessons will be planned for each participant according to his or her level of proficiency in Chinese and each lesson will last about 30 minutes. Through NetMeeting students can role-play with the teacher using Chinese and/or do pronunciation and tone practice. I invite you to participate in the trial and benefit from direct contact with your teacher. Everything will be provided to help you participate in the trial successfully.

I invite you to answer the attached questions and return the response sheet to me by email as soon as possible, but not later than 28 March 2002. This survey will take about 5 minutes of your time.

I assure you that your responses will be treated confidentially. I also will use these results anonymously in my research on language learning by distance mode. Your responses are important to the course and your achievements as a student. Thank you for your help.

Best wishes

Yours sincerely

Yuping Wang
Lecturer, Chinese Language

Open Learning Chinese CHN 21

Note: please indicate with an X

Part One: Trial of NetMeeting

1. Do you intend to participate in the trial?

    Yes ☐   No ☐

2. If **yes**, why _____

3. If **no**, why _____

Part Two: Availability of resources

1. What kind of computer do you have? Please indicate as many as possible.

    Pentium 1 ☐   Pentium 2 ☐   Pentium 3 ☐
    Other (please specify) _____

2. What window system do you have?

    Windows 95 ☐   Windows 98 ☐   Windows 2000 ☐
    Other (please specify) _____

3. What videoconferencing tools have you used before?

    None   ☐

    NetMeeting   ☐

    Iphone   ☐

    VoxPhone   ☐

    CUseeMe   ☐

    ICUII   ☐
    Other (please specify) _____

4. Have you used MSN before?

Yes ☐   No ☐

5. What Internet browser do you use?

Internet Explorer 4.0   ☐

Internet Explorer 5.0   ☐

Internet Explorer 6.0   ☐

Other version of Internet Explorer _____

Netscape   ☐

This is the end of the survey.

Thank you very much for your help.

Appendix I – Post-installation survey results in Stage Two

Videoconferencing for Providing Oral-visual Interaction in Chinese

Student evaluation

NetMeeting: Set up

1. How easy or difficult was it to set up NetMeeting? Please put an X in the appropriate bracket.

very easy ( )   easy ( )   OK ( )   difficult ( )   very difficult ( )

I-Q1

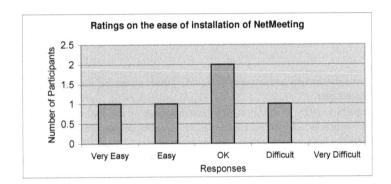

2. Were the instructions (in the Student Handbook) for installing NetMeeting easy or difficult to follow? Please put an X in the appropriate bracket.

very easy ( )   easy ( )   OK ( )   difficult ( )   very difficult ( )

I-Q2

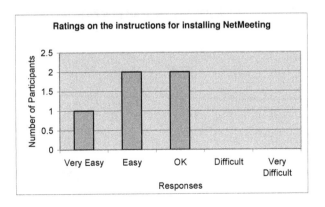

3. How long did it take you to set up everything?

I-Q3

Participant A	Participant B	Participant C	Participant D	Participant E
1 hour	1 and half hours	1 hour	20 minutes	A few weeks *

Comments:

1. Not long at all to set it all up, maybe an hour or so (because of downloading times also) but I played for a few hours with the video software afterwards!
2. A few weeks because a faulty netcam [Web Camera] needed to be returned. Sorting out the initial problem took a few visits to computer technicians. Once I received new equipment the installation was straight forward.

4. Other comments

I-Q4

1. Using the hotmail messenger system [MSN] made organizing a netmeeting much easier.
2. A problem might be to identify the right audio jack for the headset and knowing how to set the microphone as the recording device. This would probably not pose a problem if you are computer savvy. I got around the problem by using my son's expertise. The installation of the program is pretty straight forward.
3. Initial difficulties with technology are easing with more use.
4. The instructions were clear and concise with the steps clearly outlined. Maybe some tips on how to set up lighting and background for the camera shot could be given. Or perhaps this does not matter? Otherwise the setup has been a simple and enjoyable process.

Thank you very much for your help.

Appendix J – Video transcripts of NetMeeting sessions (Stage One)

Focus on form in oral-visual interaction

In *Session Three*, Stage One, when I, the teacher, who played the role of the friend of Student 2 in the role-play scene at a coffee shop, apologized for being late (*wo lai wan le*), the participant could not understand *lai wai*, because she had not learned this phrase before. She was trying to understand 'lai wan' by negotiating with the teacher:

R:	Dui buqi, wo lai wan le (Sorry I was late).
Student 2:	[looking puzzle and did not say anything]
R:	Wo lai wan le. Ni zhidao ma? 'lai wan' (I was late. Do you know 'to be late'?)
Student 2:	Zhidao. (I know) [sounding not very sure]
R:	Dui buqi, wo lai wan le (Sorry I was late).
Student 2:	Ni jintian wanshang zuo shenme (What are you going to do tonight)?

At this point, I realized that the student must have mixed up *wanshang* with *lai wan*, so I wrote the characters for '*lai wan*' on the whiteboard. This time the student seemed to understand. I wanted to confirm the participant's understanding of '*lai wan*':

R:	Ruguo wo shuo, 'dui buqi, wo lai wan le', ni yinggai shuo shenme (If I say, 'Sorry I was late", what should you say?)
Student 2:	Wo yinggai shuo, 'wo ye lai wan le' (I should say, 'I was also late').
R:	[laughed] zhen de ma (Is that true?)
Student 2:	[laughed and nodded]
R:	Ruguo wo shuo, 'dui buqi, wo lai wan le', ni yinggai shuo 'mei guanxi' (If I say, 'Sorry I was late", you should say 'It doesn't matter'.)
Student 2:	[laughed] Mei guanxi (It doesn't matter.)

Appendix K – The teacher's diary

Name	Participant A
Sex	Female
Occupation	Housewife
Nationality	Australian
Language level	Learned Chinese for 6 months
Been to China?	No
Place of Residence	Brighton, Queensland

Session One – Participant A

Date	8 May 2002
Time and duration	From 5:00pm to 6:00pm
Connection	*Problem:* At first the student could not contact me through the IP address that I gave her. She then called my mobile and I got her IP address and initiated another call. This time we got through successfully.
	Solution: It was found out that when using a modem, the IP address changes each time you log on. So it may be a good idea for us MSN. Procedures for setting up MSN were emailed to the first two students as a back up scheme.
Video/audio quality	The student seemed to be delighted to see me for the first time. The sound and video quality was not as good as in a LAN environment as expected. The main problem was it was not stable. When it was clear, it was acceptable. But when it was not clear, conversation would have to stop. Patches of sound and video were lost on several occasions resulting in half of the sentences been lost. Repetition was needed. Patches of data were congested sometimes resulting in still pictures. It might be a busy time at 5:00pm on Wednesday?
Other features of NetMeeting	The whiteboard was used frequently to show characters and pronunciations.
Technical problems	No
Linguistic problems/grammar/ pronunciation/usages	Linguistic problems
	Linguistic insecurity
	The student was very nervous when she spoke. She could hardly understand me at first. But as the session unfolded, she seemed to get better and her listening was better too. I think this nervousness is mainly caused by the lack of speaking practice in her learning, as she also mentioned in her email before the first session. As a result, she used English when she could not understand me.
	Lack of basic linguistic repertoire for conversation tactics such as clarification requests, repetition requests and confirmation checks. She did not understand "hao bu hao"? or dong le ma? At the beginning, no interaction could be achieved in Chinese.
	Solution: I will email them a list of classroom languages for them to learn and use in the session.

Low listening capacity: I have noted a serious mismatch between what they have learnt with books and tapes and what is needed in everyday conversation. For example, a simple sentence such as ni xihuan xue zhongwen ma? Was lost to the student. She did not get the meaning of xihuan. But when I wrote them on the board, she recognized the characters and knew the meaning. This means they could not understand the words they have learned because they have never or seldom heard about them being spoken. This is a problem typical of non Romanized languages such as Chinese. This also indicates the importance of oral-visual interaction in distance language education.

It was also observed that when the student read from what she prepared the sentences were quite complicated and long and correct. However when speaking, she could not form a complete sentence. The same applied to her listening. She knew what she was saying but when I repeated what she just said, she could not understand the same sentence. Lack of speaking and listening practice clearly contributes to this low level of listening and speaking ability.

Interactional skills	Lack of conversational skills such as inferences. When the student could not understand a word in a sentence, she gave up easily by saying in English that she did not understand. However, I encouraged her to use "bu dong" instead of "I didn't understand". She got used to that quickly and kept saying, bu dong, bu dong.
Listening skills	Very poor listening capacity.
Affective factors	Confidence building – the student seemed to become more confident as the session went on. This is also reflected in the interview.
Task completion	The role play was more or less one way because the student could not understand me in Chinese. The student was prepared and read out the sentences she prepared. When I gave an answer or asked a question, she sometimes ignored them because she could not understand. The task was completed in a sense we asked and answered more questions with the help of English, but spontaneous interaction in Chinese was not achieved. (10% success rate?), because often there was not acknowledgement of receipt of information and comprehension of the questions being asked.
General impression	The student was nervous at first and became more confident later on. She was very positive about this type of teaching.

Session Two – Participant A

Date	15 May 2002
Time and duration	5:00pm to 6:00pm
Connection	No problem. We used MSN and she initiated the call.
Video/audio quality	Both audio and video qualities were better than last time, probably because this session was done at home. I was told by Michael, our LAL technician that because dial up at the Uni has to go though the local telephone network and the switchboard reducing the quality of connection where at home the telephone line goes straight to the server. The sound was clear and continuous and there was little freezing of the movie.
Other features of NetMeeting	The whiteboard was used frequently to show characters and pronunciations and also a location of the café was drawn by the student on the whiteboard.

Technical problems	No
Linguistic problems/grammar/ pronunciation/usages	The student was getting better with her sentence construction although mistakes such as misplace of the time and places in the sentence.
	Her pronunciation was good. She spoke more Chinese this time than last time.
Interactional skills	She used the phrases I emailed her whenever the need arose. E.g. she used Chinese to make clarification, repetition requests. She could give more correct spontaneous response. We actually interacted in Chinese much more than last time.
Listening skills	Noticeable improvement in listening. At the beginning of the session, when we chatted in Chinese, I asked the same questions that I asked last time and she could understand them almost instantly and replied with the correct grammar.
	As she suggested in her earlier email that we should use the free chat time to talk about what they were learning in the present unit. So I used the vocabulary and structures in Uni 12 but she could not understand me. Even if she had used the phrases such as SBS and News, she still could not understand them when I used them. This is probably because she has never heard them being spoken. It was noticed that the words we used in the previous session were quickly understood by the students.
Affective factors	The first thing the student said in the interview was that she was not so nervous and more relaxed. This was also observed during the session. She looked more relaxed and could understand and produce more.
General impression	She got more used to NetMeeting and the sound and video quality was better when doing it at home.

Session Three – Participant A

Date	19 June 2002
Time and duration	5:15pm to 6:40pm
Topic	Task 1, set 2: talking about oneself.
Connection	I could not hear or see her at first and she said that she could see me but could not hear me. As she clicked on NetMeeting, a message popped up saying an illegal operation was performed and NetMeeting shut itself down. I asked the student to restart the computer but we still could not hear or see each other at first. I suspected that it may be caused by our inviting each other at the same time and that confused NetMeeting. I asked her to wait for me to invite her, and this time it worked.
Video/audio quality	This is the first time I used the LAN to do videoconferencing. It was found the quality of the audio and video were much better than using the Internet on my side. The student thought it was a bit better or the same. In other words, on her side the improvement was not so obvious. I could hear her clearly and the there was also most no delay.
Other features of NetMeeting	The whiteboard was used frequently to show characters and pronunciations. The student initiated the use of whiteboard.
Technical problems	No other technical problems apart from the beginning.

Linguistic problems/grammar/ pronunciation/usages	Subtask 1 of the second set of the task was used today. The structure of "shi... de" was dealt with. The pronunciation of qing wen (4) not qing (2) was emphasized. Student prefers to talk about herself.
Interactional skills	The student used Chinese to check understanding and asking for clarification of meaning: qing ni zai shuo yi bian or xx yong zhongwen zenme shuo.
Listening skills	The student felt a big improvement and I noticed the same progress too.
Affective factors	She was very happy and more confident.
Task completion	Successful. She was well prepared. In her email she wanted to do tasks 1, 2, and 3 together but she only prepared for task 1. She found the task was easier and enjoyed it.
General impression	The lesson itself lasted about one hour and she spoke a lot and asked me a lot of questions. She is a conscientious student and was very keen to improve her speaking.

Session Four – Participant A

Date	26 June 2002
Time and duration	5:15pm to 6:15pm
Connection	Instant. It was found that the students often forgot to click on video in Tools.
Topic	Task 3, set 2: talking about family
Video/audio quality	The sound was very clear and not much delay on my side and the video was clear and continuous, much better than the session on the same day with Pauline at 3:00pm. Probably because Participant A is in Queensland while Pauline in Victoria. The picture of the student was a bit dark due to insufficient light in her room but better than last time.
Other features of NetMeeting	The whiteboard was used frequently to show characters and pronunciations.
	Sharing was used to share my family photo and lecture notes on age and was found to be very clear and of high quality.
	The student also used the video to show me her family photos and a dog. The quality of the picture was not very good again partially due to the light in her room and partially due to the small size of the pictures but they were clear enough to enable conversations around them. The student also used My Video to adjust the photo and made it more focused.
Technical problems	No
Linguistic problems/grammar/ pronunciation/usages	We dealt with how to talk about age. We also dealt with the sound 'j'. The student seemed to be able to pick up the difference between the correct and the wrong pronunciation. Her pronunciation is improving too. Sentence structures such as
	Subj. + place or time + verb were practiced and emphasized where the time and place should be.
Interactional skills	She used a lot of the phrase on the list I emailed her.
Listening skills	Much better. We actually had a longer conversation in Chinese. She could understood me quite well although sometimes she took time to think in her mind first before she spoke.

Affective factors	More relaxed and confident.
Task completion	Successful
General impression	Every time I noticed a big improvement in her listening and speaking and she was very quick to pick up thing I explained and used. For example, I introduced "zhen de ma?" she started to use it every time the situation aroused. We had a good time together.

Session Five – Participant A

Date	3 July 2002
Time and duration	5:15pm to 6:30pm
Topic	3, set 2
Connection	Good
Video/audio quality	On my side the video was better than last time and the audio was as clear as last time. But the students felt both the video and the audio quality was still the same. Clear enough for language learning.
Other features of NetMeeting	The whiteboard was used frequently to show characters and pronunciations.
Technical problems	For the last few minutes, when I clicked on the whiteboard, it caused a crash of NetMeeting. When we tried to restart NetMeeting, it didn't work. We tried twice and the same problem persisted. The same whiteboard came up again as an automatically saved file. We could not see or hear each other anymore. So the meeting was ended. Fortunately the lesson was nearly finished.
Linguistic problems/grammar/ pronunciation/usages	A big improvement of pronunciation and fluency. She was quick to understand the grammar and used "le" conscientiously. The structure "shi...de" was explained and used.
Interactional skills	When she tended to be lazy and asking questions in English, I would raise my eye brow and did not say anything. She then realized that she has to speak Chinese.
Listening skills	Much improved
Affective factors	More confident each time
Task completion	Nearly successful
General impression	She enjoyed it very much and was very positive.

Name	**Participant B**
Sex	Male
Occupation	Bookkeeper
Nationality	Australian/German
Language level	Learned Chinese for 1 year
Been to China?	Live in Taiwan for one year and China for 4 weeks. At present, he does not have Chinese friends to speak Chinese to.
Place of residence	Adelaide, South Australia

Session One – Participant B

Date	11 May 2002 (Saturday)
Time and duration	6:50pm to 7:20pm
Connection	Very good. We used MSN to call each other and no congestion was experienced during connection.
Video/audio quality	Audio was much better than the session with Participant A. It was quite clear and continuous although there was a bit delay in sound transmission from one end to the other. This sometimes caused overlapping/false starts in turn taking. The better audio and video quality probably was due to the time of the videoconferencing – Saturday evening, there might be less Internet traffic. It may be also because my home computer is better than the office one as this session was done at home.
Other features of NetMeeting	The whiteboard was used only once to show the characters of zhichi (support). The student's proficiency in listening and speaking was very good.
Technical problems	No problems experienced in this session, but student mentioned in the interview that he had a bit of a problem in setting up NetMeeting but got help from his son, because he did not know a lot about computers.
Linguistic problems/grammar/ pronunciation/usages	Apart from a few grammatical mistakes, for example, use of Ma as a question word when there is a question word in the sentence (e.g. Wo yao gongzuo duoshao ge xiaoshi ma?), he was a fluent speaker.
Interactional skills	Turn taking and clarification of meaning was all done naturally, although there were few occasions for the use of such skills. Everything went smoothly.
Listening skills	Very good
Affective factors	He mentioned in the interview that he needed to get used to this type of teaching. He is very positive about it and wondered if we could continue to use it after the trial.
Task completion	Successfully done. He prepared well.
General impression	The task seemed to be quite easy for him although he thought it was the right level. More occasions of use of interactional skills need to build in with his task, for example, use of new vocabulary for clarification of meaning or negotiation of meaning. Use of paralinguistic cues etc.

Session Two – Participant B

Date	15 May 2002
Time and duration	8:25pm to 9:20pm (Brisbane time)
Connection	We could not hear or see each other at first. I asked him to initiate the call, but same problem happened. He used IP to call me but could not get through. I invited him again and this time it was on.
Video/audio quality	The sound quality was very bad. Often half of the sentences were lost and the sound seemed to get stuck a few times resulting lose of words or intelligible sounds. However, when the sound did come through, it was quite clear although sometimes it became very loud and faint alternatively.
Other features of NetMeeting	The whiteboard was used frequently to show characters and pronunciations and the student drew on the board to show location of the café.
Technical problems	A part from Internet congestions and no sound and video at the beginning, no other technical problem was experienced.
Linguistic problems/grammar/ pronunciation/usages	Although the sound was not good, we managed to have a free chat and complete the task. No major problems there apart from a few words he did not know.
Interactional skills	He has good interactional skills and used the sentences on the list I emailed him. He used filled pauses and interjection naturally.
Listening skills	His listening was exceptionally good considering the poor sound quality. He had to guess a lot.
Affective factors	Despite the problem with the sound, he was still confident and relaxed.
Task completion	Finished quite successfully.
General impression	The importance of the timing of the session became quite clear. 8:00pm–9:00pm is probably the busiest time in the evening when everyone has finished dinner and is on the net, in addition to the fact that he was in Adelaide, thousands of miles away from Brisbane.
Student's suggestions	1. Do pronunciation drills with closer image of the teacher and students.
	2. Use of body language by sitting back a bit from the camera.
	3. Feedback at the end of the session on the mistakes that the student made then email them.

Session Three – Participant B

Date	18 May 2002
Time and duration	10:30pm to midnight
Connection	*Problem 1:* I tried several times but could not get on the University server at first. The call was through but a message popped up saying that the connection time was out because the remote computer was not responding. More detailed explanation was that there may be a problem with the server. Ensure to check with 55555. It is probably necessary to have a backup server?
	Problem 2: We could not start NetMeeting. After the initial invitation and acceptance, the ringing tone did not come through to the people who initiated the call, resulting no connection between the two. The call was finally

established after the student restarted his computer. Why?

Problem 3: The student tried to use the "my view" function, but every time he clicked on it, the NetMeeting was gone. This seemed to happen when I tried to use the whiteboard at the same time.

Video/audio quality	The audio quality was great, even better than the first time. The video image on my side froze all the time, but my video was very continuous and clear. On the student side, he could not use My Video function because it caused the NetMeeting window to shutdown twice. However, my image was very clear and continuous.
Other features of NetMeeting	The whiteboard was used frequently to show characters and pronunciations. Sharing was used to share the Menu on my desktop, but it took about 1 minute to load on to the screen on the student site. I also tried to share a photo on my desktop but the student did not get the photo, only the frame of the file. Ask Sun why this happened. Was it because the capacity of his computer was not big enough?
Technical problems	No other problem apart from the above.
Linguistic problems/grammar/ pronunciation/usages	As student suggested, I gave instant feedback to a few mistakes he made. We had a longer conversation today.
Interactional skills	His interactional skills are very good.
Listening skills	Good listening
Affective factors	He was very understanding and tolerant about these technical difficulties and seemed determine to continue with this trial. He was kept waiting for more than an hour because of the difficulty in logging into the network. This did not seem to have affected his interest in the technology.
Task completion	Successful
General impression	The sound was much better and made the whole session enjoyable. We laughed and talked for about an hour although the conversation was interrupted twice because of the shutting down of NetMeeting.

Session Four – Participant B

Date	22 May 2002
Time and duration	7:30pm to 8:30pm
Connection	NetMeeting could not start although we were shown to be in a call. No sound or video came up. We tried a few times but failed. I had to ask the student to restart his computer and then the connection was successful.
Video/audio quality	As the session started early in the morning, both the video and audio were much better (before 8:00) than last session although the last session was also quite good. After 8:00 there were a few occasions that the sound was lost and the background noise present. I had "my video" on and it didn't affect the student image.
Other features of NetMeeting	The whiteboard was not used because as soon as I tried to write on the whiteboard, it caused NetMeeting to crash. We had to restart NetMeeting. File transfer was used to send a video clip but the transmission was very slow. It was still being sent when we finished our task. I had to send it by email after class.

	Because we could not use the whiteboard I was asked to show him the new characters using my hand to draw in front of the camera. This is a very good way to use the camera.
Technical problems	Why the whiteboard caused a crash?
Linguistic problems/grammar/ pronunciation/usages	It was a very basic conversation and the student finished the task with ease.
Interactional skills	I tried to explain liuyan in Chinese and the student understood it as to leave a message. He has a very good communicative ability, good at inferring and kept the conversation flow.
Listening skills	Very good
Affective factors	Confident, positive even about the technical problems
Task completion	Successful
General impression	No major problem. A very good session with good video and audio quality.

Session Five – Participant B

Date	25 May 2002 (Saturday)
Time and duration	9:30am to 11:00am
Connection	The connection was instant, but I could see him but could not hear him. His son helped him to turn on the microphone. Then I could hear him but later he could not hear me. They did something then he could hear me. When asked what happened, he said he did not know. After than everything went smoothly.
Video/audio quality	We had the best video and audio quality of all the sessions so far. This was confirmed by the student too. The video image was very stable and continuous. The sound was clear and continuous too. The video was used to show a business card as a prompter for communication.
Other features of NetMeeting	The whiteboard was used frequently to show characters and pronunciations. The participant used File transfer to send me his "resume". The transfer was instant.
Technical problems	This time, the whiteboard did not cause the crash of NetMeeting. The reason for the crashes was still not certain. It might be caused by the capacity of computer or a bug in NetMeeting.
Linguistic problems/grammar/ pronunciation/usages	After the trial we talked about a few grammatical problems: The use of Nong cuo le. The structure of "shi…de" The use of guo and le
Interactional skills	Although he was good at inferring the meaning from the context, he also wanted to know the English equivalent of the Chinese phrases. I tried to explain the meaning of certain words in Chinese and he could understand me perfectly.
Listening skills	Very good
Affective factors	He said the main thing about this trial was to build up his confidence in speaking the language.
Task completion	Successful

General impression   An excellent session. In the interview, he mentioned that he found it hard to switch roles from himself to someone else. He would like to talk about something freely not in a controlled situation. He felt he was limited to the situation and could not speak more. He also mentioned that there should be more explanations on grammar. A good point. Probably I should give students a list of topics to talk about instead of talking about applying for a job for the entire five sessions. Possible topics are:

1. shopping
2. eating in a restaurant
3. weather
4. family
5. your likes and dislikes
6. talking about your past experience

Name	**Participant C**
Sex	Female
Occupation	Teacher
Nationality	Australian
Language level	Basic
Been to China?	Yes
Place of Residence	Victoria

Session One – Participant C

Date	26 May 2002
Time and duration	10:00 to 11:30
Connection	At first the student did not sign into MSN but tried to call me through NetMeeting. I could not get in contact with her because I did not have her mobile phone number. But later she told me that she could not get mobile phone connections at home. She finally figured out that she should use the MSN and then NetMeeting was started. She could hear or see me but I could only see hear. We restarted NetMeeting and this time everything worked fine. According to her, she had plugged the microphone and speakers at the wrong place.
Video/audio quality	The video on my side was clear with a bit delay. On her side she said it was very good, clear and continuous. The sound quality on my side was good but getting worse because more and more people were getting on the Net. But the sound on her said was very good according to her. Considering the fact that this was the first time she used NetMeeting, it must be very clear and continuous for her to say so. She mentioned there were a few occasions when the sound got stuck but these did not worry her. Sometimes I was not sure if she were saying something because I could see her lips moving but cannot hear the sound. I checked with her a few times and it turned out that she was repeating the sentences she heard silently to herself.
Other features of NetMeeting	The whiteboard was used frequently to show characters and pronunciations. No crash of NetMeeting happened due to the use of whiteboard. The student was delighted to see the whiteboard.
Technical problems	No
Linguistic problems/grammar/ pronunciation/usages	Student's level of proficiency was very low. Her listening was similar to Participant A's but her grammar and vocabulary were worse in that she could not make up a correct sentence even after she had prepared them. Because of her poor pronunciation, she could not understand me even if she has just used the same words herself. She did not have the basic conversational language to conduct a simple dialogue. The words for making a phone call or numbers have been learned long time ago but could not be remembered for the conversation. She even did not know how to reply to thank you. As she had never used what she had learned before, it took a long time for her to get them back and use them. Her basic grammatical structures are also a mess.
	A pronunciation drill needs to be worked out for such level students especially on zhi chi shi zi ci si ji qi xi.

Interactional skills	Not good at inferring although tried hard. She did not know how to use Chinese to clarify meaning or negotiate for meaning.
Listening skills	Very poor and slow to response. It seems she had to write the sound down to be able to understand it. She could not make spontaneous dialogues.
Affective factors	Was very nervous at the beginning but getting more confident.
Task completion	Partially successful because she prepared a few sentences to ask me and we managed to start and end the telephone conversation properly, although the conversation was interrupted frequently to deal with unknown words and pronunciation.
General impression	She needs a lot of personalized help in pronunciation and grammar. We need to work from the basic level in listening and speaking.

Session Two – Participant C

Date	1 June 2002
Time and duration	Scheduled for 9:00 but started at 10:00 and finished at 11:00
Connection	I could not see or hear her for the first hour. She rebooted her computer several times. She forgot to send her video to me so I could not see her. She did not put the microphone to her mouth so I cannot hear her. I tried to communicate with her through MSN chat but she did not know how to use it at first. But she could hear or see me clearly. She tried to use the whiteboard to talk to me and we managed to write to each other just one sentence and she was gone again. She told me after the trial that her computer had gone frozen several times so she had to restart it. Finally she figured out how to send a video with my instruction and put her microphone to her mouth. Her computer skills are very poor.

Thoughts: when the students' basic computer skills are poor, it may take a long time to set up NetMeeting because the student may forget to turn on the video or did not know who to use the chat to contact me. Furthermore, there was no one there to help her. |
Video/audio quality	Both the audio and video was more or less the same as last time. It was better at the beginning but getting was as the session progressed. It might be caused by the congestion in the Network as more and more people are getting on the Net. Sometimes the sound was clear sometimes the sentences were lost. It was better than the second session with Joachim.
Other features of NetMeeting	The whiteboard was used frequently to show characters and pronunciations.
Technical problems	Internet congestion and student's inability to set up NetMeeting at first.
Linguistic problems/grammar/ pronunciation/usages	She used the second set of tasks and we talked about family members. She prepared a little and was not so nervous. She concentrated more on listening and her listening was getting much better. She could pick up a lot of things I said and used the phrases I emailed her frequently.
Interactional skills	Tried to infer meanings and use Chinese to clarify meaning and affirming understanding and incomprehension.
Listening skills	Getting better and more confident. Learned to listen the whole sentence and get the gist of it. Tried to avoid getting stuck with an unknown word.
Affective factors	Getting more confident and less nervous and afraid of speaking or hearing the

	language.
Task completion	Mostly successful. We talked about how to ask about family members and their ages.
General impression	The connection was not good and the student performed better linguistically.
Further action	Email student to congratulate her on her improvement.

Session Three – Participant C

Date	26 June 2002
Time and duration	3:00pm to 4:10pm
Topic	Task 3 of set 3: talking about what happened yesterday.
Connection	No problem. The connection was quick with no hassles at all
Video/audio quality	Both video and audio quality was much better than the previous two sessions on Saturdays because we used LAN. The video was continuous and quite clear and sound was clear too but with some feedback from my speaker because I had to turn the volume up for recording. This was not a problem before but the sound was quite low today.
Other features of NetMeeting	The whiteboard was used frequently to show characters and pronunciations. The Sharing function was used to share a photo I took with Webcam and the student reported that the quality was superb and the function was useful.
Technical problems	No
Linguistic problems/grammar/ pronunciation/usages	The student still had difficulty understanding longer sentences. It seemed she had never had the chance to speak or listen to Chinese. She mentioned that she could only pick up words and tried to guess the meaning, inferring meaning from the context as I told her. While it was an improvement, but her improvement was not obvious as Participant A's. She still doesn't have enough language repertoire to communicate in Chinese. Also her pronunciation was so bad that I could not understand her most of the time. I feel that some listening strategies need to be introduced to the students.
Interactional skills	Very basic. She even had to refer to the list of frequently used words to say 'dong le'.
Listening skills	Very poor
Affective factors	She became more interested in the project and more confident and relaxed because we were connected to each other almost immediately and the sound and video quality was better. She was quite happy and impressed today.
Task completion	We talked about past tense, the use of le and mei. The task was completed.
General impression	The student was getting more confident with NetMeeting. Improvement in both listening and speaking can be seen but not was not as big as I expected. Everything went smoothly. Although the session was done during the day, 3:00pm–4:00pm, the quality of video and audio on both sides were better when using the LAN than we did it on Saturdays when using the Internet. This means bandwidth is still a problem with the Internet.

Participant C withdrew from the trial for personal reasons.

Name	**Participant D**
Sex	Male
Occupation	Student
Nationality	Australian
Language level	Basic Better than Participant A and C
Been to China?	No
Place of Residence	Gold Coast

Session One – Participant D

Date	30 May 2002
Time and duration	7:00am to 7:30am
Connection	Connection was instant.
Video/audio quality	Video was great, very clear and continuous.
	Audio was problematic – he could hear me clearly but I could not hear him. We checked the plugging in, the volume control and the set up in NetMeeting. The student got his housemate to check for him and said probably his sound card was faulty.
Task completion	Unsuccessful. I spoke some Chinese and he text chatted with me for a few minutes.

Session Two – Participant D

Date	4 July 2002
Time and duration	7:30 to 8:30
Connection	The connection was instant.
Video/audio quality	Video was clearer than before but I still could not hear him. He still used his computer because he did not have a chance to pick up the one I lent him. He could hear me but the sound was broken up a bit.
Other features of NetMeeting	The whiteboard was used to show characters and file transfer was used to transfer a video clip but it would take 84 minutes. So it was cancelled. I also tried to transfer a Word file but he could receive it but could not find it where it had gone. I still think his computer doesn't have enough memory.
Technical problems	He kept on dropping off from MSN and this had never happened before. However we could still see each other and he could still hear me. This means the NetMeeting was still on while MSN was gone.
Task completion	Unsuccessful.

Session Three – Participant D

Date	28 October 2002
Time and duration	9:30 to 10:00 (Brisbane time)
Connection	Connection was very slow. It seems that the Internet was very congested. He dropped out of MSN several times.
Video/audio quality	The video was clear but became still after one minute or so. He could hear me but only broken sentences and then the video and sound got stuck. I could see him clearly but the image became still soon but I could not hear him at all. We tested the microphone and speaker on NetMeeting, his microphone did not light up when he spoke. This can mean that he plugged into a wrong socket or his microphone was faulty??? We will try again this Wednesday at 6:30 Brisbane time and 7:30 Sydney time.
Task completion	Unsuccessful

Session Four – Participant D

Date	28 November 2002
Time and duration	8:00 Queensland (QLD) time, 9:00 New South Wales (NSW) time
Connection	Very slow. Took about 1 minute for the other party to respond. He was thrown off MSN several times. Why? This has never happened to other students. Ask Sun??
	Two problems were solved after the session:
	1. It was found out that my microphone was not plugged in. I don't know why it was unplugged.
	2. The firewall was found to be back on because the University recently did a security check and tightened the security. The technician lifted it again for me.
	The student told me that he was using the computer we provided and found the new headphone works with the new computer but not working with his old computer. Neither headphone works with his old computer. This suggested that the sound card of his old computer may be faulty.
Video/audio quality	I could not see or hear him at all. He could see me once when he invited me first. But if I invited him, neither of us could see or hear anything. The image became frozen after one minute. So the Internet was very congested at that time.
Task completion	Unsuccessful. Will try tomorrow at 6:00am Queensland (QLD) time.

Session Five – Participant D

Date	29 November 2002 (first successful session)
Time and duration	6:00am to 7:00am excluding interview
Connection	Instant without any problem. We were delighted to see each other.
Video/audio quality	Both video and audio were very good quality. Clear and continuous. I only observed at one time that the student's image became still and he did not get my sentences. It seemed one packet was lost. But the student reported to have noticed about 2 lost packets. The video and audio were very stable too.
Other features of NetMeeting	The whiteboard was used frequently to show characters and pronunciations. But the student commented that it was hard to read the characters on the board because even with print, he did not recognize a lot of characters. But he did find it a useful tool.
Technical problems	No problem
Linguistic problems/grammar/pronunciation/usages	As he has not used Chinese for a long time, his Chinese is a bit rusty but he has good grammar and pronunciation and intonation and was very quick to pick up or recall things. The conversation was generally flowed. English was used when there were problems. On the whole, the task was completed successfully.
Interactional skills	He has basic interactional skills and was quick to learn. I have emailed him the frequently used phrases for him to use in class.
Listening skills	Very good considering he has not practiced much.
Affective factors	Very positive about this type of teaching
Task completion	Successful
General impression	He can benefit a lot from these NetMeeting sessions. He enjoyed talking about basic things.
	The only problem for me is that I have to get up at 5:00am, not really convenient.

Session Six – Participant D

Date	2 December 2002
Time and duration	6:00am to 6:40am
Connection	I initiated an invitation but there was no response for a while. I asked him to invite me and it took a long time for him to respond. It seemed even the messages could not get through at times. A message said that my invitation could not be delivered. We finally got connected and both the sound and video quality was great but the connection only lasted about 5 minutes and then everything became still. The student signed out MSN but could not sign in again for some reason. Every time he tried there was a message saying that he was behind a firewall. I asked him to try to connect through IP address, but a message saying on his side that there was no response from me. On my side nothing happened. So we had to give up this time. I sent an email to Professors Sun, Giscard and Haifeng.
Task completion	Unsuccessful

Name	**Participant E**
Sex	Female
Occupation	Teacher
Nationality	Australian
Language level	Good
Been to China?	Yes
Place of residence	Victoria

Session One – Participant E

Date	24 July 2002 (Wednesday)
Time and duration	4:30pm to 6:00pm
Connection	It took a long time to connect. First of all, she could not sign into MSN. A message came up asking her id?? I asked her to apply a new account and sign in with a new password. She finally got into MSN and tried to call me through NetMeeting but failed. She rang me and I told her that I would invite her through MSN. At first, I could not see her and asked her to send the video. Then I could see her and hear her clearly, the best quality I had never had before. She was using Netplace as the Internet Service Provider and may have a wider bandwidth. Unfortunately she cannot hear or see me. Her school technician said it may be due to a firewall in Netplace because they have bypassed the school firewall.
	She will install Internet at her place and we will try again.
Video/audio quality	Excellent video and audio on my side. This means if the bandwidth is big enough, very good video and audio quality can be achieved, for example, using LAN at both sides or cable.
Task completion	Unsuccessful

Session Two – Participant E

Date	26 July 2002 (Friday)
Time and duration	4:00
Connection	I was waiting for the student to be on MSN but could not see her. She rang me and said she was on. I looked at MSN but could not find her. As I clicked on her name, MSN asked me to sign in again and I did. This time, I could see her. Very strange. This has never happened before. Then the connection was instant. She seemed to be able to figure out how to accept my invitation. She confirmed this step over the phone.
Video/audio quality	Video is good but the sound was too broken to be intelligible on both sides. It seemed that there was a huge congestion in the Internet. We gave up and decided to try on Saturday morning when there is less Internet traffic.
Task completion	Unsuccessful

Session Three – Participant E

Date	27 July 2002
Time and duration	8:00am to 8:30am
Connection	No trouble with inviting and accepting calls as the student is now familiar with the process.
Video/audio quality	Video was OK on my side but student mentioned occasional fuzzy pictures on her side. The sound on my side was very broken, no complete sentences could be received. There were huge delays. But the student could sometimes hear a sentence very clearly but sometimes lost a few words.
Technical problems	The bad sound quality and delays were probably due to the Network congestion but it was hard to explain that there is heavy traffic early Saturday morning, especially on my side, the sound quality was not much better than yesterday at 4:00.
	I suspect her Internet was not quick enough.
	She was also using a laptop. Does that mean that her laptop was not powerful enough? The student was still determined to preserver with the trial. She said she was delightedly at the prospect of being able to speak to someone in Chinese.
	Talk with Professor Sun
	1. The ISP (Internet Service Provider) may have a long delay and limited bandwidth which they don't often tell their customers.
	2. Laptop has limited capacities because a lot of things are compressed.
	3. Within 100 msec delay is often unnoticed in conversation but usually a modem has a 150–200 msec delay and a LAN has 40 msec delay.
	4. Firewall is often set by the institution, not ISP. Ask the student to check with her technician again to ensure the firewall was lifted.
Task completion	Unsuccessful.
	1. She will ask her Internet provider to see the capacity of the Internet.
	2. Change to a desktop computer. And try again this morning.

Session Four – Participant E

Date	31 July 2002
Time and duration	4:15pm to 4:40pm
Connection	Quick connection but I still cannot hear or see her. We can establish calls if I invited her but if she invited me, we could not establish calls. A message appeared on my side saying the person is unable to accept NetMeeting calls. It still seemed to be a block here although their technician was sure that they have bypassed the school firewalls and checked that their Internet Provider-Netspace does not have a block. We also checked that her video works too because she could see herself in 'My View'.
Video/audio quality	Excellent sound and video quality on my side.
Task completion	Unsuccessful

Session Five – Participant E

Date	7 August 2002
Time and duration	4:00 to 6:00
Connection	We gave up trying at her school. This session was carried out at GSAT, the science/technology facility at Deakin Uni. At first, we could not see or hear each other at all, although our names appeared in the NetMeeting box. Then the technician updated the video drive and the new version of NetMeeting, then we could see and hear each other. The student will find out what the technician actually did to enable the videoconferencing.
Video/audio quality	The video quality was OK, with occasional fizzy pictures. The sound was a bit faint at the first on my side and became louder after the volume on my machine was pushed up. No feedback was detected with the speakers on. Why? The student did not think the sound was great but she could understand me easily.
Other features of NetMeeting	The whiteboard was used frequently to show characters and pronunciations
Technical problems	No apart from the first problem in connection.
Linguistic problems/grammar/ pronunciation/usages	She has a good proficiency, second to Joachim and very good pronunciation and tones. She mentioned that her biggest problem was spontaneity. Her grammar and structures were good but lack of vocabulary to express her ideas.
Interactional skills	Better interactional skills then others except Joachim.
Listening skills	Very good listening skills although I had to repeat the sentences sometimes.
Affective factors	She was frustrated with the problem with connection.
Task completion	Successful
General impression	She was a good learner and determined to do this project. This was the first time that we were able to converse through NetMeeting and she was not so positive about the sound quality and thinks it was better to use the telephone. She still liked the video and watch it all the time but could not see clearly my mouth movements.

Session Six – Participant E

Date	9 August 2002
Time and duration	3:00pm to 4:00pm
Connection	We tried her from her school first but same problem appeared. She could not receive my video and audio. She then went to GSAT and we got connected straight away.
Video/audio quality	According to her, the video on her side was not good at all. The picture was pixelled and she could not see me clearly. Such quality stayed all the time during the session. I wonder if it was her laptop capacity that causing the bad quality of picture. I have asked her to use a normal computer at GSAT. Her sound was worse than the last session. She looked frustrated sometimes because of the background noise in the network. On my side the picture and sound was quite good, continuous and clear most of the time with occasional

	noise and a little bit of delay. Need to find out what kind of network she used, dial up through a modem or LAN?
Other features of NetMeeting	The whiteboard was used frequently to show characters and pronunciations. File transfer was used to transfer a video clip of my family. The transfer was successful and very quick.
Technical problems	
Linguistic problems/grammar/pronunciation/usages	She did not seem to be prepared. She used Nianji (age) wrongly was corrected. Did not see any improvement in her language and pronunciation probably due to the poor video and audio quality on her side. The lecture note on age was sent to her after the session via email.
Interactional skills	She referred to the list I email her on useful phrases.
Listening skills	Good
Affective factors	Disappointed at the poor video and audio quality today. Her confidence level was down a bit.
Task completion	Successful
General impression	She felt frustrated with the sound and video quality although most of the time she could understand me perfectly. She mentioned that she often missed out the important words due to the bad sound quality.

Session Seven – Participant E

Date	14 August 2002
Time and duration	4:00pm to 5:20pm
Connection	She connected to me from GSAT and the connection was instant.
Video/audio quality	The sound quality was much better today than the previous two sessions and she was very pleased about it. The video was slightly better than before but still blurred on her side. Both the video and audio quality on my side was better today too. Probably there was less congestion in the network because it is the exhibition holiday in Brisbane.
Other features of NetMeeting	The whiteboard was used frequently to show characters and pronunciations.
Technical problems	None
Linguistic problems/grammar/pronunciation/usages	She did not seem to be prepared. We talked about a range of things today although we were supposed to concentrate on what happened yesterday. I corrected her use of le and mei in a couple of places and she seemed to understand their usage but not used to them. We talked about food and exercises. She has a large vocabulary and used some big words like air pollution and to prevent heart attack. I was really impressed by her language ability. She doesn't seem to go through the process of translating from English into Chinese and her response was almost spontaneous although a bit slow sometimes. She used the list I gave her to clarify meanings.
Interactional skills	She referred to the list I email her on useful phrases.
Listening skills	Good – better than before
Affective factors	More confident
Task completion	Successful

General impression	She was really happy about today's lesson and said she felt rewarding. She is more positive and relaxed today.

Session Eight – Participant E

Date	16 August 2002
Time and duration	1:40pm to 3:30pm
Connection	She connected to me from GSAT and the connection was instant.
Video/audio quality	The sound quality was not as good as last time today. She mentioned crackling noise interferes her listening. Sometimes I have to repeat a few times before she could work out the meaning. I think it was a combination of both the sound and her Chinese listening. The video was slightly better than before. Both the video and audio quality on my side stayed the same today too. I still think that her laptop contributes to the poor quality on her side.
Other features of NetMeeting	The whiteboard was used briefly to show characters and pronunciations.
Technical problems	The connection dropped once when the student tried to enlarge her video.
	I tried to use the whiteboard and the sharing function but the whiteboard worked once and then both the sharing and the whiteboard indicated not in a call. So I did not use sharing but used MSN to send the menu to her. That was successful.
Linguistic problems/grammar/ pronunciation/usages	She was prepared. We talked about a range of things today around tasks 4 and 5. Her proficiency and spontaneity has improved from my observation.
Interactional skills	Quite spontaneous
Listening skills	Good – better than before.
Affective factors	Felt more used to NetMeeting.
Task completion	Successful
General impression	She was quite happy about today's session.

Appendix L – Transcription notation

The transcription symbols employed in this book are commonly used for conversation analysis and were developed by Gail Jefferson (see Atkinson and Heritage, 1984: ix-xvi)

(.)	A dot in brackets indicates A short pause in talk of less than 0.2 of a second.
(3 secs)	The time in bracket indicates the length of pause.
Over [lap	Square brackets between adjacent lines of concurrent talk
[overlap	indicate the start of overlapping speeches.
[…]	Indicates omission of speeches in the extract.
Goo:d	Colons indicate the speaker has stretched the preceding sound to give an emphasis.
↑	Indicates rising intonation.
(( ))	Sentences in a double bracket indicate a non-verbal activity. For example ((looking puzzled))

Appendix M – Post-session survey – summary of results (Stage One)

	Session 1	Session 2	Session 3	Session 4	Session 5
Question 1 Usefulness of **"Whiteboard"**	Very useful Very useful Useful	Very useful Very useful Very useful	N/A	N/A	N/A
Question 1 Usefulness of **"Sharing" function**	N/A	N/A	Very useful Very useful Very useful	Useful Very useful	
Question 1 Usefulness of **"File Transfer"**	N/A	N/A	N/A	Very useful	Very useful
Question 2 Usefulness of **task** for improving fluency	Very useful Useful Useful	Very useful Very useful Very useful	Very useful Very useful Useful	Very useful Very useful	Very useful Very useful
Question 3 Usefulness of **NetMeeting** for improving fluency	Very useful Useful Useful	Very useful Useful OK	Very useful Very useful OK	Very useful Very useful	Very useful Very useful
Question 4 Aspects improved	Grammar Speaking Listening Spontaneous responses Pronunciation Tones	Grammar Vocabulary Speaking Listening Fluency Spontaneous responses Pronunciation Tones	Grammar Vocabulary Listening Speaking Spontaneous responses Tones Pronunciation	Grammar Vocabulary Speaking Listening Spontaneous responses Pronunciation Tones	Vocabulary Grammar Speaking Listening Fluency Spontaneous responses
Question 5 Other comments	♦ Because delayed response, you must concentrate on listening.	♦ Reception was much clearer than last time. Conversation flowed much better. Whiteboard was very useful for directions. ♦ More comfortable with this day.	♦ Background knowledge + preparedness is important. ♦ Perhaps discuss a few more topics – like cover a range of little situations to expand conversation and to keep it flowing.	♦ Need to see the dialogue written when looking at "new words" on the whiteboard. ♦ Non verbal communication is good when you get used to the feature.	♦ Still have trouble with having consinent structures.

Bibliography

Abrami, P. C., & Bures, E. M. (1996). Computer-supported collaborative learning and distance education. *The American Journal of Distance Education, 10*(2), 4-36.

Adair-Hauck, B., Willingham-McLain, L., & Yongs, B. E. (2000). Evaluating the integrations of technology and second language learning. *CALICO Journal, 17*(2), 269-306.

Ahmad, K., Cornett, G., Rogers, M., & Sussex, R. (1985). *Compute, language learning and language teaching.* Cambridge: Cambridge University Press.

Aist, G. (1999). Speech recognition in Computer-Assisted Language Learning. In K. Cameron (Ed.), *CALL: Media, design and application* (pp. 165-182). Lisse: Swets & Zeitlinger.

Altrichter, H., Evans, T., & Morgan, A. (1991). *Windows: Research and evaluation on a distance education course.* Geelong, Vic.: Deakin University.

Anderson, R. C., & Pearson, P. D. (1988). A schema-theoretic view of the basic processes in reading comprehension. In P. Carrell, J. Devine & D. Eskey (Eds.), *Interactive approaches to second language reading* (pp. 37-55). Cambridge: Cambridge University Press.

Annand, D. (1999). The problem of computer conferencing for distance-based universities. *Open Learning, 14*(3), 47-52.

Appel, C., & Gilabert, R. (2002). Motivation and task performance in a task-based web-based tandem project. *ReCALL, 14*(1), 16-31.

Arnold, R. (1999). Will distance disappear in distance studies? Preliminary considerations on the didactic relevance of proximity and distance. *Journal of Distance Education, 14*(2), 1-9.

Atkins, M., J. (1993). Theories of learning and multimedia applications: an overview. *Research Papers in Education, 8*, 251-271.

Atkinson, J. M., & Heritage, J. (1984). *Structures of social action: Studies in conversation analysis.* Cambridge: Cambridge University Press.

Auld, L., & Pantelidis, V. S. (1999). *The virtual reality and education laboratory at East Carolina University.* Retrieved 8 August 2001, from http://www.thejournal.com/magazine/vault/A2371.cfm.

Baath, J. A. (1980). *Postal two-way communication in correspondence education.* Lund: Gleenup.

Baath, J. A. (1985). A note on the origin of distance education. *ICDE Bulletin*(7), 61-62.

Baker, B., Frisbie, A., & Patrick, K. (1989). Broadening the definition of distance education in the light of the new telecommunications technologies. *The American Journal of Distance Education, 3*(1), 20-29.

Balet, S. (1985). Testing some current assumptions. *ELT Journal, 39*(3), 178-182.

Barnes, A., & Reid, A. (1993). Quality and computers in teaching and learning. In T. Nunan (Ed.), *Distance education futures* (pp. 503-516). Underdale: University of South Australia.

Barnes, S. (2000). What does electronic conferencing afford distance education? *Distance Education, 21*(2), 236-244.

Barnes, S. B. (1999). Electronic conferencing to support post-graduate students working at a distance. *Interact, 19*(October), 18-19.

Barson, J., Frommer, J., & Schwarrtz, M. (1993). Foreign language learning using e-mail in a task oriented perspective: interuniversity experiments in communication and collaboration. *Journal of Science Education and Technology, 2*(4), 565-584.

Barty, K. (1998). Interactive television: How interactive is it? *Babel, 33*(1), 28-30.

Bates, A. (1982). Trends in the use of audio-visual media. In John S. Daniel, Martha A. Stroud & J. R. Thompson. (Eds.), *Learning at a distance. A world perspective.* (pp. 8-15). Edmonton: Athabasca University, International Council for Correspondence Education.

Bates, A. W. (1988). Technology for distance education: a 10-year prospective. *Open Learning, 3*(3), 3-11.

Bates, A. W. (1991). The third generation distance education: the challenge of new technology. *Research in Distance Education, 3*(2), 10-15.

Bates, A. W. (1995). *Technology, open learning and distance education.* London: Routledge.

Bates, A. W. (1997). The impact of technological changes on open and distance learning. *Distance Education, 18*(1), 93-109.

Bates, T. (1984). Putting it together, now and the future. In A. W. Bates (Ed.), *The role of technology in distance education* (pp. 223-231). London & Sydney: Croom Helm.

Bates, T. (1993). Theory and practice in the use of technology in distance education. In D. Keegan (Ed.), *Theoretical principles of distance education* (pp. 213-233). London: Routledge.

Batt, D. (2003). *The Communicative Orientation of Virtual Language Teaching in Upper Primary and Lower Secondary Telematics in Western Australia.* Unpublished PhD, Queensland University of Technology, Brisbane.

Battenberg, R. W. (1971). *Epistolodidaktika.* Boston.

Beauvois, M. H. (1995). E-Talk: attitudes and motivation in computer-assisted classroom discussion. *Computers and the Humanities, 28*, 177-190.

Beller, M., & Or, E. (1998). The crossroads between lifelong learning and information technology: A challenge facing leading universities. *The Journal of Computer-Mediated Communication, 4*(2). http://www.ascusc.org/jcmc/vol4/issue2/beller.html

Benbunan-Fich, R., & Hiltz, S. R. (1999). Educational applications of CMCS: Solving case studies through asynchronous learning networks. *The Journal of computer-Mediated Communication, 4*(3). http://www.ascusc.org/jcmc/vol4/issue3/benbunan-fich.html

Berge, Z. (1998). Guiding principles in Web-based instructional design. *Education Media International, 71*(8), 323-326.

Berge, Z., & Collins, M. (1995). *Computer mediated communication and the online classroom in distance learning.* Cresskill, NJ: Hampton Press.

Bernard, R. M., & Amundsen, C. L. (1989). Antecedents to dropout in distance education: Does one model fit all. *Journal of Distance Education, 4*(2), 25-47.

Bernard, R. M., Rojo de Rubalcava, B., & St-Pierre, D. (2000). Collaborative online distance learning: Issues for future practice and research. *Distance Education, 21*(2), 260-271.

Bloomfield, D. (2000). Voices on the Web: Student teachers negotiating identity. *Asia-Pacific Journal of Teacher Education, 28*(3), 199-212.

Borady-Ortmann, C. (2002). Teachers' perceptions of a professional development distance learning course: A qualitative case study. *Journal of Research on Technology in Education, 35*(1), 107-116.

Born, F. (1999). *Technophile.* Retrieved 20 December 2000, from http://greco.dit.upm.es/~leverage/levenews/techno5.htm

Boyd, G. (1993). A theory of distance education for the cyberspace era. In D. Keegan (Ed.), *Theoretical principles of distance education.* (pp. 234-253). London & New York: Routledge.

Boyle, E., Anderson, A., & Newlands, A. (1994). The effects of visibility on dialogue and performance in a cooperative problem-solving task. *Language and Speech, 37*(1), 1-20.

Boyle, R. (1995). Language teaching at a distance: from the first generation model to the third. *System, 23*(3), 283-294.

Brandon, D. P., & Hollingshead, A. B. (1999). Collaborative learning and computer-supported groups. *Communication Education, 48*(2), 109-126.

Breen, M. (1987). Learner contributions to task design. In C. Candlin & D. Murphy (Eds.), *Language learning tasks* (pp. 23-46). Englewood Cliffs NJ: Prentice-Hall.

Brody, C. M. (1995). Collaborative or cooperative learning? Complimentary [sic] practices for instructional reform. *Journal of Staff, Program, & Organizational Development, 12*, 133-143.

Brown, J. D. (1989). Language program evaluation: A synthesis of existing possibilities. In R. K. Johnson (Ed.), *The second language curriculum* (pp. 222-241). Cambridge: Cambridge University Press.

Brown, J. D. (1995). Language program evaluation: Decision, problems and solution. *Annual Review of Applied Linguistics, 15*, 227-248.

Brown, K. (1996). The role of internal and external factors in the discontinuation of off-campus students. *Distance Education, 17*(1), 44-71.

Bruce, V. (1996). The role of the face in communication: implications for video-phone design. *Interacting with Computers, 8*(2), 166-176.

Bruffee, K. A. (1993). *Collaborative learning: Higher education, interdependence, and the authority of knowledge.* Baltimore, MD: John Hopkins Press Ltd.

Brundage, D. H., & Mackeracher, D. (1980). *Adult learning principles and their application to program planning.* Ontario: Ontarion Institute of Studies in Education.

Buckett, J., & Stringer, G. (1997a). *ReLaTe: A case study in language teaching using the MBone.* Retrieved 28 November 2001, from http://www.ex.ac.uk/pallas/relate/papers/ukerna97.html

Buckett, J., & Stringer, G. (1997b). *ReLaTe (Remote Language Teaching): progress, problems and potential.* Paper presented at the CALL'97, Exeter.

Buckett, J., & Stringer, G. (1999). *Internet Videoconferencing's 3Ms: Multiway, Multimedia, Multicast.* Retrieved 28 November 2001, from http://www.ex.ac.uk/pallas/relate/papers/peg99/stringer.htm

Buckett, J., Stringer, G., & Datta, N. K. J. (1999). Life after ReLaTe: Internet videoconferencing's growing pains. In K. Cameron (Ed.), *CALL and the learning community* (pp. 31-38). Exeter: Elm Bank Publications.

Bullen, M. (1998). Participation and critical thinking in online university distance education. *Journal of Distance Education, 13*(2), 1-32.

Burge, E. (1994). Learning in computer conferenced contexts: The learner's perspective. *Journal of Distance Education, 9*(1), 19-43.

Burke, C., Lundin, R. & Daunt, C. (1997). Pushing the boundaries of interaction in videoconferencing: A dialogical approach. *Distance Education, 18*(2), 349-360.

Bygate, M. (2001). Effects of task repetition on the structure and control of oral language. In M. Bygate, P. Skehan & M. Swain (Eds.), *Researching pedagogic tasks: Second language learning, teaching and testing* (pp. 23-48). Harlow, England: Pearson Education Limited.

Bygate, M., Skehan, P., & Swain, M. (2001). *Researching pedagogic tasks: Second language learning, teaching and testing.* Harlow, England: Pearson Education Limited.

Campion, M., & Kelly, M. (1988). Integration of external studies and campus-based education in Australian higher education: the myth and the promise. *Distance Education, 9*(2), 171-201.

Canale, M., & Swain, M. (1980). Theoretical bases of communicative approaches to second language teaching and testing. *Applied Linguistics, 1*(1), 1-47.

Candlin, C. (1987). Towards task-based language learning. In C. Candlin & D. Murphy (Eds.), *Language learning tasks* (pp. 5-22). Englewood Cliffs, N.J.: Prentice-Hall International.

Carey, J. (1980). *Paralanguage in computer mediated communication.* Paper presented at the Eighteenth Annual Meeting of the Association for Computational Linguistics and Parasession on Topics in Interactive Discourse: Proceedings of the conference.

Carr, W., & Kemmis, S. (1986). *Becoming critical: Education, knowledge and action research.* Basingstoke, Hants: Falmer Press.

Carrell, P. (1983). Background knowledge in second language comprehension. *Language Learning and Communication, 2*, 25-34.

Chacon, F. (1992). A taxonomy of computer media in distance education. *Open Learning, 7*, 12-27.

Chapelle, C. A. (1997). Call in the year 2000: Still in search of research paradigms? *Language Learning & Technology, 1*(1), 19-43.

Chapelle, C. A. (1998). Multimedia CALL: Lessons to be learned from research on instructed SLA. *Language Learning & Technology, 2*(1), 22-34.

Chapelle, C. A. (2000). Is networked-based learning CALL? In M. Warschauer & R. Kern (Eds.), *Network-based language teaching: Concepts and practice* (pp. 204-228). Cambridge: Cambridge University Press.

Chapelle, C. A. (2001). *Computer applications in second language acquisition: Foundations for teaching, testing and research.* Cambridge: Cambridge University Press.

Chen, Y., & Willits, F. K. (1999). Dimensions of educational transactions in a videoconferencing learning environment. *The American Journal of Distance Education, 13*(1), 45-59.

Chou, C. C. (2001). Formative evaluation of synchronous CMC systems for a learner-centered online course. *Journal of Interactive Learning Research*(Summer-Fall), 173-187.

Chun, D. (1994). Using computer networks to facilitate the acquisition of interactive competence. *System, 22*(1), 17-31.

Chun, D. M., & Plass, J. L. (2000). Networked multimedia environments for second language acquisition. In M. Warschauer & R. Kern (Eds.), *Network-based language teaching: Concepts and practice* (pp. 151-170). Cambridge, England: Cambridge University Press.

Clark, R. (1985). Evidence of confounding in computer-based instruction studies: Analyzing the meta-analyses. *Educational Communication and Technology Journal, 33*, 249-262.

Clifford, R. (1998). Mirror, mirror, on the wall: Reflections on computer assisted language learning. *CALICO Journal, 16*(1), 1-10.

Cohen, K. (1982). Speaker Interaction: video teleconferences versus fact-to-face meetings. *Proc. Teleconferencing and Electronic Communications*, 189-199.

Collins, M., & Berge, Z. (1994). *Guiding design principles for interactive teleconferencing.* Paper presented at the Pathways to Change: New Directions for Distance Education and Training Conference, University of Maine at Augusta.

Collins, M., & Berge, Z. (1996). *Facilitating interaction in computer mediated on-line courses.* Retrieved 8 December 2001, from http://star.ucc.nau.edu/~mauri/moderate/flcc.html

Collis, B. (1996). *Telelearning in a digital world: The future of distance learning.* London: International Computer Press.

Collis, B. (1997). Pedagogical re-engineering: A pedagogical approach to course enrichment and redesign with the WWW. *Educational Technology Review, 8*, 11-15.

Collis, B. (1998). WWW-based environments for collaborative group work. *Education and Information Technologies, 3*, 231-245.

Cook, M., & Lalljee, M. (1972). Verbal substitutes for visual signals in interaction. *Semiotica, 3*, 212-221.

Cook, V. (2001). *Second language learning and language teaching* (3rd edn). London: Arnold.

Crowder, E. M. (1996). Gestures at work in sense-making science talk. *The Journal of Learning Sciences, 5*(3), 173-208.

Cunningham, S., Tapsall, S., Ryan, Y., Stedman, L., Bagdon, K.& Flew, T. (1998). *New media and borderless education: A review of the convergence between global media networks and higher education provision*: Commonwealth of Australia.

Curzon, A. J. (1997). Correspondence education in England and in the Netherlands. *Comparative Education, 13*(3), 249-261.

Cuskelly, E., & S., G. (1994). Perspectives on computer mediated communication. In T. Evans & D. Murphy (Eds.), *Research in distance education.* (pp. 115-126). Geelong: Deakin University Press.

Dallos, R. (1984). Tutors and media. In A. W. Bates (Ed.), *The role of technology in distance education* (pp. 185-193). London & Sydney: Croom Helm.

Daniel, J. S. (1997). *The Open University in a new era: Reviewing the vision, renewing the mission, refreshing the Image.* Milton Keynes: OU, Internal Paper.

Darrouzet, C., & Lynn, C. (1999). *Presentation at the creating a new architecture for learning and development capacity-building workshops.* Paper presented at the Creating a New Architecture for Learning and Development Capacity-Building Workshops, Tokyo.

Daugherty, M., & Funke, B. L. (1998). University faculty and student perception of Web-based instruction. *Journal of Distance Education, 13*(1), 21-39.

Davis, N. F. (1978). The use of the telephone in distance teaching. *English Language Teaching Journal, 32,* 287-291.

Dede, C. (1996). The evolution of distance education: emerging technologies and distributed learning. *The American Journal of Distance Education, 10*(2), 4-36.

Devitt, S. (1997). Interacting with authentic texts: Multilayered process. *Modern Language Journal, 81*(4), 457-469.

Dias, J. (1998). The teacher as chameleon: Computer-mediated communication & role transformation. In P. Lewis (Ed.), *Teachers, learners, and computers: Exploring relationships in CALL* (pp. 17-26). Tokyo: JALT.

Dinsdale, W. A. (1953). Inception and development of postal tuition. *The Statist,* 572-575.

Doughty, C. (1991). Theoretical motivations for IVD software research and development. In M. D. Bush, A. Slaton, M. Verano & M. E. Slayden (Eds.), *Interactive videodisc: The "Why" and the "How"* (pp. 1-15) *(CALICO monograph series)* (Vol. 2).

Doughty, C. (1991). Second language instruction does make a difference: evidence from an empirical study of SL relativization. *Studies in Second Language Acquisition, 13,* 431-469.

Doughty, C. (2001). Cognitive underpinnings of focus on form. In P. Robinson (Ed.), *Qualitative research, theory, method and practice* (pp. 206-257). Cambridge: Cambridge University Press.

Doughty, C., & Long, M. H. (2003). Optimal Psycholinguistic environments for distance foreign language learning. *Language Learning & Technology, 7*(3), 50-80.

Doughty, C., & Williams, J. (1998a). *Focus on form in classroom second language acquisition.* Cambridge: Cambridge University Press.

Doughty, C., & Williams, J. (1998b). Issues and terminology. In C. Doughty & J. Williams (Eds.), *Focus on form in classroom second language acquisition* (pp. 1-11). Cambridge: Cambridge University Press.

Doughty, C., & Williams, J. (1998c). Pedagogical choices in focus on form. In C. Doughty & J. Williams (Eds.), *Focus on form in classroom second language acquisition* (pp. 197-261). Cambridge: Cambridge University Press.

Duffy, T. M., Dueber, B., & Hawley, C. L. (1998). Critical thinking in a distributed environment: A pedagogical base for the design of conferencing systems. In C. J. Bonk & K. S. King (Eds.), *Electronic collaborators: Learner-centred technologies for literacy, apprenticeship and discourse* (pp. 51-78). Hillsdale, N.J.: Lawrence Erlbaum Associates.

Duschatel, P. (1997). A Web-based model for university instruction. *Journal of Educational Technology Systems, 25*(3), 221-228.

Egbert, J., Chao, C. C., & Hanson-Smith, E. (1999). Computer-enhanced language learning environment: An Overview. In J. Egbert & E. Hanson-Smith (Eds.), *Computer-enhanced language learning* (pp. 1-13). Alexandria, VA: TESOL Publications.

Ellis, R. (1986). *Understanding second language acquisition.* Oxford: Oxford University Press.

Ellis, R. (1990). *Instructed second language acquisition.* Oxford: Blackwell.

Ellis, R. (1994). *The study of second language acquisition.* Oxford: Oxford University Press.

Evans, T., & Nation, D. (1993). Distance education, educational technology and open learning: converging futures and closer integration with conventional education. In T. Nunan (Ed.), *Distance education futures* (pp. 16-35). Underdale: University of South Australia.

Feeberg, A. (1989). The written world: on the theory and practice of computer conferencing. In R. Mason & A. Kaye (Eds.), *Mindweave: Communication, computers and distance education* (pp. 22-39). Oxford: Perganmon Press.

Felix, U. (1999). Web-based Language Learning: A window to the authentic world. In R. Debski & M. Levy (Eds.), *WORDCALL: Global perspective on computer-assisted language learning* (pp. 85-98). Lisse: Swets & Zeilinger.

Felix, U. (2002). The web as a vehicle for constructivist approaches in language learning. *ReCALL, 14*(1), 2-15.

Fernández-García, M., & Martínez-Arbelaiz, A. (2002). Negotiation of meaning in nonnative speaker-nonnative speaker synchronous discussions. *CALICO Journal, 19*(2), 279-294.

Flagg, B. N. (1990). *Formative evaluation for educational technologies.* Hillsdale, New Jersey: Lawrence Erlbaum Associates Publishers.

Follows, S. B. (1999). *Virtual learning environments.* Retrieved 11 November 2001, from http://www.thejournal.com/magazine/vault/A23742.cfm

Foot, C. (1994). Approaches to multimedia audio in language learning. *ReCALL, 6*(2), 9-13.

Fristsch, H. (1991). Drop in and drop out: The need of definition. In B. Holmberg & G. E. Ortner (Eds.), *Research into Distance Education* (pp. 184-191). Frankfurt am Main: Peter Lang.

Ganderton, R. (1998). New strategies for a new medium? Observing L2 reading on the World Wide Web. *On-CALL, 12*(2), 2-9.

Ganderton, R. (1999). Interactivity in L2 Web-based reading. In R. Debski & M. Levy (Eds.), *WORDCALL: Global perspective on computer-assisted language learning* (pp. 49-66). Lisse, The Netherlands: Swets & Zeitlinger.

Garrison, D. R. (1985). Three generations of technological innovations in distance education. *Distance Education, 6*, 235-241.

Garrison, D. R. (1993). A cognitive constructivist view of distance education: An analysis of teaching-learning assumptions. *Distance Education, 14*(2), 199-211.

Garrison, D. R. (1997). Computer conferencing: the post-industrial age of distance education. *Open Learning, 12*(2), 3-11.

Garrison, D. R. (1999). Will distance disappear in distance studies? A reaction. *Journal of Distance Education, 14*(2), 10-13.

Garrison, D. R., & Shale, D. (1987). Mapping the boundaries of distance education: problems in defining the field. *The American Journal of Distance Education, 1*(1), 4-13.

Gass, S. M. (2003). Input and interaction. In C. J. Doughty & M. H. Long (Eds.), *The handbook of second language acquisition* (pp. 224-255). Malden, MA: Blackwell Publishing Ltd.

Gass, S. M., & Varonis, E. M. (1994). Input, Interaction, and second language production. *Studies in Second Language Acquisition, 16*, 283-302.

Godwin-Jones, R. (1998). *Language interactive: Language teaching and the Web.* Retrieved 16 March 1999, from http://www.fln.vcu.edu/cgi/1.html

Goldman-Segall, R. (1991). A multimedia research tool for ethnographic investigation. In I. Harel & S. Papert (Eds.), *Constructionism* (pp. 467-496). Norwood, New Jersey: Ablex Publishers.

Goodfellow, R. (1999). Evaluating performance, approach and outcome. In K. Cameron (Ed.), *CALL: Media, design and application* (pp. 109-140). Lisse: Swets & Zeitlinger.

Goodfellow, R., Manning, P., & Lamy, M. (1999). Building an online open and distance language learning environment. In R. Debski & M. Levy (Eds.), *WORDCALL: Global perspective on computer-assisted language learning* (pp. 267-286). Lisse: Swets & Zeitlinger.

Goodman, K. (1976). Reading: a psycholinguistic guessing game. In H. Singer & R. R (Eds.), *Theoretical models and process of reading* (2nd edn, pp. 495-505). Newark, Del.: International Reading Association.

Grabe, W. (1988). Reassessing the term "interactive". In P. Carrell, J. Devine & D. Eskey (Eds.), *Interactive approaches to second language reading* (pp. 56-70). Cambridge: Cambridge University Press.

Grabe, W. (1991). Current developments in second language reading research. *TESOL Quarterly, 25*(3), 376-407.

Gravener, P. (1998). Education on the Web: a rejoinder. *Computers and the Humanities*(September), 107-108.

Green, J. N. (1999). *Interactive videoconferencing improves performance of limited English proficient students.* Retrieved 6 June 2000, from http://www.thejournal.com/magazine/vault/A2038.cfm.

Grice, H. P. (1975). Logic and conversation. In P. Cole & J. Morgan (Eds.), *Syntax and semantics 3: Speech acts* (pp. 41-58). New York: Academic Press.

Haastrup, K. (1987). Using think aloud and retrospection to uncover learner's lexical inferencing procedures. In C. Faerch & G. Kasper (Eds.), *Introspection in second language research.* Clevedon Avon, England: Multilingual Matters.

Hall, J. W. (1998). Leadership in accreditation and networked learning. *The American Journal of Distance Education, 12*(2), 5-15.

Hall, K. J. (1995). "Aw, man, Where you goin?": Classroom interaction and the development of L2 Interactional competence. *Issues in Applied Linguistics, 5*, 37-62.

Halliday, M. A. K. (1973). *Explorations in the functions of language.* London: Edward Arnold.

Halliday, M. A. K. (1978). *Language as a social semiotic.* London: Edward Arnold.

Hamburger, H., Schoelles, M., & Reeder, F. (1999). More intelligent CALL. In K. Cameron (Ed.), *CALL: Media, design and applications* (pp. 183-202). Lisse: Swets & Zeitlinger.

Hampel, R. (2003). Theoretical perspectives and new practices in audio-graphic conferencing for language learning. *ReCALL, 15*(1), 21-36.

Hampel, R., & Baber, E. (2003). Using Internet-based audio-graphic and video conferencing for language learning. In U. Felix (Ed.), *Language learning on-line: Towards best practice* (pp. 171-191). Lisse, The Netherlands: Swets & Zeitlinger.

Hampel, R., & Hauck, M. (2004). Towards an effective use of audio conferencing in distance language courses. *Language Learning & Technology, 8*(1), 66-82.

Hampel, R., & Stickler, U. (2005). New skills for new classrooms: Training tutors to teach languages online. *Computer Assisted Language Learning, 18*(4), 311-326.

Harasim, L. (1989). On-line education: A new domain. In R. Mason & A. Kaye (Eds.), *Mindweave: Communication, computers and distance education* (pp. 50-62). Oxford: Perganmon Press.

Harasim, L. (1990). *Online education: Perspectives on a new environment.* New York: Praeger.

Harasim, L., Hiltz, S.R., Teles, L. & Turoff, M. (1995). *Learning networks: A field guide to teaching and learning online.* Cambridge: the MIT Press.

Harrington, M., & Levy, M. (2001). CALL begins with a "C": interaction in computer-mediated language learning. *System, 29*, 15-26.

Hauck, M., & Haezewindt, B. (1999). Adding a new perspective to distance (language) learning and teaching - the tutor's perspective. *ReCALL, 11*(2), 46-54.

Hearnshaw, D. (2000). Effective desktop videoconferencing with minimal network demands. *British Journal of Educational Technology, 31*(3), 221-228.

Heath, C. (1997). The analysis of activities in face to face interaction using video. In D. Silvermann (Ed.), *Qualitative research: Theory, method and practice* (pp. 183-200). London: SAGE Publications.

Hegelheimer, V., & Chapelle, C. A. (2000). Methodological issues in research on learner-computer interactions in CALL. *Language Learning & Technology, 4*(1), 41-59.

Henri, F. R., C. (1996). Collaborative distance education and computer conferencing. In T. Liao (Ed.), *Advanced educational technology: Research issues and future potential* (pp. 45-76). Berlin: Springer-Verlag.

Heritage, J. (1997). Conversation analysis in institutional talk: Analyzing data. In D. Silvermann (Ed.), *Qualitative research* (pp. 161-181). London: Sage.

Herring, S. (1996). Introduction. In S. Herring (Ed.), *Computer-mediated communication: Linguistic, social and cross-Cultural perspectives* (pp. 1-10). Amsterdam/Philadelphia: John Benjamins Publishing Company.

Hewer S., Kötter, M., Rodine, C. R., & Shield, L. (1999). *The Right Tools for the Job: criteria for the choice of tools in the design of a virtual, interactive environment for distance language learners and their tutors.* Paper presented at the CAL 99, London.

Higgins, J. (1998). *Language, learners and computers: Human intelligence and artificial unintelligence.* Singapore: Longman.

Hiltz, S. R. (1994). *The virtual classroom: Learning without limits via computer networks.* Norwood, New Jersey: Ablex Publishing Corporation.

Hiltz, S. R., & Wellman, B. (1997). Asynchronous learning network as a virtual classroom. *Communications of the ACM, 40,* 44-49.

Holland, V. M., Kaplan, D. J., & Sams, M. R. (Eds.). (1995). *Intelligent language tutors: Theory shaping technology.* Mahwah, New Jersey: Lawrence Erlbaum.

Holmberg, B. (1977). *Distance education: A survey and bibliography.* London: Kogan Page.

Holmberg, B. (1986). *Growth and structure of distance education.* London: Croom Helm.

Holmberg, B. (1989). The concept, basic character and development potentials of distance education. *Distance Education, 10,* 127-134.

Holmberg, B. (1995). The evolution of the character and practice of distance education. *Open Learning, 10*(2), 47-53.

Holstein, J. A., & Gubrium, J. F. (1997). Active interview. In D. Silvermann (Ed.), *Qualitative research, Theory, method and practice* (pp. 113-129). London: SAGE Publications.

Howell, F. (1996). Student needs and expectations. In M. Farquhar & P. McKay (Eds.), *China connection: Australian business needs and university language education* (pp. 125-142). Canberra: NLLIA.

Hutchby, I. (2001). *Conversation and technology: from the telephone to the Internet.* Malden, MA: Blackwell Publishers Inc.

Hutchby, I., & Wooffitt, R. (1998). *Conversation analysis: Principles, practices and applications.* Cambridge: Polity Press.

Hutchinson, T., & Waters, A. (1987). *English for specific purposes.* Cambridge: Cambridge University Press.

Ibañez, A., & Duque, M. (1999). *Pedagogical issues.* Retrieved 20 December 2000, from http://greco.dit.upm.es/~leverage/levenews/pedagog5.htm

Jafari, A. (1997). *Issues in distance education.* Retrieved 12 October 1999, from http://www.thejournal.com/past/OCT/1097exclu3.html.

James, R. (1996). CALL and the speaking skill. *System, 24*(1), 15-21.

Jonassen, D., Prevish, T. Cjrostu, D. & Stavrulaki, E. (1999). Learning to solve problems on the web: Aggregate planning in a business management course. *Distance Education, 20*(1), 49 - 65.

Jones, A., Scanlon, E., & Blake, C. (2000). Conferencing in communities of learners: Examples from social history and science communication. *Educational Technology & Society, 3*(3), 215-226.

Jones, C., & Fortescue, S. (1987). *Using computers in the language classroom*. London: Longman.

Kaplan, N. (1995). *E-literacies*. Retrieved 6 June 1999, from http://raven.ubalt.edu/staff/kaplan/lit/E-literacies_612.html

Kaye, A. (1989). Computer-mediated communication and distance education. In R. Mason & A. Kaye (Eds.), *Mindweave: Communication, computers and distance education* (pp. 3-21). Oxford: Perganmon Press.

Kearsley, G. (1998). Educational technology: A critique. *Educational Technology, 4*, 47-51.

Keegan, D. (1983). On defining distance education. In D. Sewart, D. Keegan & B. Holmberg (Eds.), *Distance Education: International Perspectives* (pp. 6-18). London: Croom Helm.

Keegan, D. (1991). The study of distance education: terminology, definition and the field of study. In B. Holmberg & G. E. Ortner (Eds.), *Research into distance education/Fernlehre und Fernlehrforschung* (pp. 36-45). Frankfurt am Main: Peter Lang.

Keegan, D. (1996). *The foundations of distance education* (3rd edn). London: Croom Helm.

Kenning, M. M., & Kenning, M. J. (1990). *Computer and language learning: Current theory and practice*. Chichester, UK: Ellis Horwood.

Kern, R. (1996). Computer-mediated communication: Using e-mail exchanges to explore personal histories in two cultures. In M. Warschauer (Ed.), *Telecollaboration in foreign language learning* (pp. 105-119). Honolulu, HI: University of Hawaii, Second Language Teaching & Curriculum Centre.

Khan, B. H. (1997). Web-based instruction (WBI): What is it and why is it? In B. H. Khan (Ed.), *Web-based instruction* (pp. 5-19). Englewood Cliffs, NJ: Educational Technology Publications.

Kinginger, C. (1998). Videoconferencing as access to spoken French. *The Modern Language Journal, 82*(iv), 502-213.

Kitade, K. (2000). L2 learners' discourse and SLA theories in CMC: Collaborative interaction in Internet chat. *Computer Assisted Language Learning, 13*(2), 143-166.

Kitao, K., & Kitao, K. (1999). Using on-line chat in language teaching. In K. Cameron (Ed.), *CALL & the learning community* (pp. 251-260). Exeter: Elm Bank Publications.

Kleinke, C. L. (1986). Gaze and eye contact: a research review. *Psycho. Bull, 100*, 78-100.

Knowles, M. (1980). *The modern practice of adult education*. Chicago: Follett Publishing Company.

Kolb, D. (1984). *Experiential learning: Experience as the source of learning and development*. New Jersey: Prentice-Hall, Englewood Cliffs.

Kötter, M. (2001). Developing distance language learners' interactive competence - Can synchronous audio do the trick? *International Journal of Educational Telecommunications, 7*(4), 327 - 353.

Kötter, M. (2003). Negotiation of meaning and codeswitching in online tandems. *Language Learning and Technology, 7*(2), 145-172.

Kötter, M., Shield, L., & Anne, S. (1999). Real-time audio and email for fluency: promoting distance language learners' aural and oral skills via the Internet. *ReCALL, 11*(2), 55-60.

Kramsch, C. J. (1986). From language proficiency to interactional competence. *Modern Language Journal, 10*(3), 366-372.

Krashen, S. (1988). *The input hypothesis: Issues and implications*. London: Longman.

Kress, G., & van Leeuwen, T. (2001). *Multimodal discourse: The modes and media of contemporary communication*. London: Arnold.

Künzel, S. (1995). Processors processing: Learning theory and CALL. *CALICO Journal, 12*, 106-113.

Kubala, T. (1998). *Addressing student needs: Teaching on the Internet*. Retrieved 12 December 1999, from http://www.thejournal.com/98/mar/398feat4.html.

Lake, D. (1999). Reducing isolation for distance students: An on-line initiative. *Open Learning, 14*(3), 14-23.

Lamy, M., & Goodfellow, R. (1999). "Reflective conversation" in the virtual language classroom. *Language Learning & Technology, 2*(2), 43-61.

Lantolf, J. P. (1994). Sociocultural theory and second language learning: Introduction to the special issue. *Modern Language Journal, 78*(4), 418-420.

LaQuey, T. (1993). *The Internet companion: A beginner's guide to global networking*. Reading, MA:: Addison-Wesley.

Larsen-Freeman, D., & Long, M. H. (1991). *An introduction to second language acquisition research*. London: Longman.

Lecourt, D. (1999). The ideological consequences of technology and education: The case for critical pedagogy. In M. Selinger & J. Pearson (Eds.), *Telematics in education: Trends and issues* (pp. 51-75). Amsterdam: Pergamon.

Lee, L. (1998). Going beyond classroom learning: Acquiring cultural knowledge via on-line Newspapers and Intercultural Exchanges via on-line chatrooms. *CALICO Journal, 16*(2), 101-120.

Lee, L. (2004). Learner's perspectives on networked collaborative interaction with native speakers of Spanish in the US. *Language Learning & Technology, 8*(1), 83-100.

Lee, L. (2007). Fostering second language oral communication through constructivist interaction in desktop videoconferencing. *Foreign Language Annals, 40*(4), 635-650.

Leow, R. P. (1993). To simplify or not to simplify: A look at intake. *Studies in Second Language Acquisition, 15*, 333-355.

Levy, M. (1997). *Computer assisted language learning: Context and conceptualization*. New York: Oxford University Press.

Levy, M. (1997). Theory-driven CALL and the development process. *Computer Assisted Language Learning, 10*, 41-56.

Levy, M. (1998). Two conceptions of learning and their implications for CALL at the tertiary level. *ReCALL, 10*(1), 86-94.

Levy, M. (1999). Theory and design in a multimedia CALL project in Cross-Cultural Pragmatics. *Computer Assisted Language Learning, 12*(1), 29-57.

Levy, M. (2000). Scope, goals and methods in CALL research: Questions of coherence and autonomy. *ReCALL, 12*(2), 170-195.

Levy, M. (2004, in press). Effective of CALL technologies: Finding the right balance. In R. Donaldson & M. Haggstrom (Eds.), *Changing Language Education Through CALL*. Lisse, The Netherlands: Swets & Zeitlinger.

Levy, M., & Kennedy, C. (2004). A task-cycling pedagogy using stimulated reflection and audio-conferencing in foreign language learning. *Language Learning & Technology, 8*(2), 50-69.

Liddell, P. (1994). Learners and second language acquisition: A union blessed by CALL? *Computer Assisted Language Learning, 7*, 163-173.

Lightbown, P., & Spada, N. (1993). *How languages are learned*. Oxford: Oxford University Press.

Littlewood, W. (1981). *Communicative Language Teaching: An Introduction*. Cambridge: Cambridge University Press.

Ljoså, E. (1993). Understanding distance education. In D. Keegan (Ed.), *Theoretical principles of distance education* (pp. 175-188). London: Routledge.

Long, M. H. (1981). Input, Interaction, and second language acquisition. In H. Winitz (Ed.), *Native Language and Foreign Language Acquisition: Annals of the New York Academy of Sciences* (Vol. 379, pp. 259-278).

Long, M. H. (1983a). Does second language acquisition make a difference? A review of research. *TESOL Quarterly, 17*(3), 359-382.

Long, M. H. (1983b). Native speaker/non-native-speaker conversation and the negotiation of comprehensible input. *Applied Linguistics, 4*(2), 126-141.

Long, M. H. (1988a). *Focus on form: A design feature in language teaching methodology.* European-North-American Symposium on Needed Research in Foreign Language Education, Bellagio, Italy: Rockefeller Centre.

Long, M. H. (1988b). Instructed interlanguage development. In L. Beebe (Ed.), *Issues in second language acquisition: Multiple perspectives* (pp. 115-141). New York: Newbury House.

Long, M. H. (1991). Focus on form: A design feature in language teaching methodology. In K. d. Bot, R. Ginsberg & C. Kramsch (Eds.), *Foreign Language Research in Cross-Cultural Perspective* (pp. 39-52). Amsterdam: John Benjamins.

Long, M. H. (1996). The role of the linguistic environment in second language acquisition. In W. C. Ritchie & T. K. Bhatia (Eds.), *Handbook of research on language acquisition. Vol. 2: Second language acquisition* (pp. 413-468). New York: Academic Press.

Long, M. H. and Crookes, G. (1992). Three approaches to task based syllabus design. *TESOL Quarterly, 26*(1): 27-56.

Long, M. H., & Crookes, G. (1993). The authors respond. *TESOL Quarterly, 27*(4), 729-733.

Long, M. H., & Robinson, P. (1998). Focus on form: theory, research and practice. In C. Doughty & J. Williams (Eds.), *Focus on form in classroom second language acquisition* (pp. 15-41). Cambridge: Cambridge University Press.

Lyman-Hager, M. A. (1995). Multimedia and distance education in a foreign language programme. *Open Learning, 10*(1), 51-55.

Mackenzie, O., Christensen, E., & Rigby, P. (1968). *Correspondence institution in the United States.* New York: McGraw-Hill.

Mak, L. (1996). *Language learning of a new kind.* Retrieved 8 October 1999, from http://www.hku.hk/ssrc/newLearn.html

Marsh, D., Arnold, I., Ellis, N., Halliwell, J., Hodgins, C., & Malcom, S. (1997). Project MERLIN: A learning environment of the future. *ReCALL, 9*(1), 52-54.

Mason, R. (1989). An evaluation of CoSy on an Open University course. In R. M. A. Kaye (Ed.), *Mindweave: Communication, computers and distance education* (pp. 115-145). Oxford: Perganmon Press.

Mason, R. (1994). *Using communications media in ppen and flexible learning.* London: Kogan Page.

Mason, R., & Kaye, A. R. (1990). Towards a new paradigm for distance education. In L. M. Harasim (Ed.), *Online education: Perspectives on a new environment* (pp. 279-288). New York: Praeger.

Mathews, D. (1999). *The origins of distance education and its use in the United States.* Retrieved 11 December 2000, from http://www.thejournal.com/magazine/vault/A2222.cfm

McAndrew, P., Foubister, S. P., & Mayes, T. (1996). Videoconferencing in a language learning application. *Interacting with Computers, 8*(2), 207-217.

McCarthy, B. (2002). Resisting obsolescence in CALL. *CALL-EJ Online, 3*(2), 1-13.

McCarthy, M. (1991). *Discourse analysis for language teachers.* Cambridge: Cambridge University Press.

McCarthy, M., & Carter, R. (1994). *Language as discourse: Perspectives for language teaching.* London: Longman.

McConnell, D. (1994). *Implementing computer supported cooperative learning.* London: Kogan Page.

McGinnis, S. (1997). Tonal spelling versus diacritics for teaching pronunciation of Mandarin Chinese. *The Modern Language Journal, 81*(ii), 228-236.

McKay, P. (1994). *Communicative Orientation and Language Outcomes in Australian Junior Secondary Foreign Language Classes.* Unpublished PhD, University of Queensland, Brisbane.

McKay, P. (1996). Setting the scene: Language policy and language teaching. In M. Farquhar & P. McKay (Eds.), *China connections: Australian business needs and university language education* (pp. 9-37). Australia: The National Language and Literacy Institute of Australia.

McLoughlin, C., & Oliver, R. (1995). Analysing Interactions in technology supported learning environments. In R. Oliver & M. Wild (Eds.), *Learning without Limits* (pp. 49-62). Perth: Australian Computers in Education Conference.

McMeniman, M. (1992). Once more up the methodology road: A critical view of the communicative approach. *Asian Studies Review, 15*(3), 2-16.

Meredith, R. (1983). Materials and equipment: The new generation. *The Modern Language Journal, 67*, 424-430.

Miller, J., & Glassner, B. (1997). The 'inside' and the 'outside': finding realities in interviews. In D. Silvermann (Ed.), *Qualitative research, theory, method and practice* (pp. 99-112). London: SAGE Publications.

Mills, D. G. (1999). Interactive Web-based language learning: The state of the art. In R. Debski & M. Levy (Eds.), *WORLDCALL: Global perspectives on computer-assisted language learning.* (pp. 117-132). Lisse: Swets & Zeitlinger.

Mitchell, R., & Myles, F. (1998). *Second Language Learning Theories.* London: Arnold.

Mohan, B. (1992). Models of the role of the computer in second language development. In M. C. Pennington & V. Stevens (Eds.), *Computers in applied linguistics* (pp. 110-126). Avon: Multilingual Matters.

Moore, M. G. (1972). Learner autonomy: The second dimension of independent learning. *Convergence*(Fall), 76-88.

Moore, M. G. (1973). Toward a theory of independent learning and teaching. *Journal of Higher Education, 44*, 666-679.

Moore, M. G. (1989). Editorial: Three types of interaction. *The American Journal of Distance Education, 3*(2), 1-6.

Moore, M. G. (1990). Background and overview of contemporary American distance education. In M. G. Moore (Ed.), *Contemporary issues in American distance education* (pp. xii-xxvi). New York: Pergamon.

Moore, M. G. (1993). Theory of transactional distance. In D. Keegan (Ed.), *Theoretical principles of distance education* (pp. 22-38). London; New York: Routledge.

Moore, M. G., & Kearsley, G. (1996). *Distance education: A systems view.* Belmont, CA: Wadeworth.

Motteram, G. (2001). The role of synchronous communication in fully distance education. *Australian Journal of Educational Technology, 17*(2), 131-149.

Murray, G. L. (1999). Exploring learners' CALL experiences: A reflection on method. *Computer Assisted Language Learning, 12*(3), 179-195.

Murray, J., Morgenstern, D., & Furstenberg, G. (1989). The Athena language project: Design issues for the next generation of computer-based language-tools. In W. F. Smith (Ed.), *Modern technology in foreign language education: Applications and projects* (pp. 97-118). Lincolnwood, IL: National Textbook Company.

Naidu, S. (1997). Collaborative reflective practice: An instructional design architecture for the Internet. *Distance Education, 18*(2), 257-283.

Negretti, R. (1999). Web-based activities and SLA: A conversation analysis research approach. *Language Learning & Technology, 3*(1), 75-87.

Neu, J. (1990). Assessing the role of nonverbal communication in the acquisition of communicative competence in L2. In R. C. Scarcella, E. S. Anderson & S. D. Krashen (Eds.), *Developing communicative competence in a second language* (pp. 121-138). New York: Newbury House Publishers.

Nipper, S. (1989). The third generation distance learning and computer conferencing. In R. Mason & A. Kaye (Eds.), *Mindweave: Communication, computers and distance education* (pp. 63-73). Oxford: Perganmon Press.

Noffinger, J. S. (1926). *Correspondence schools. lyceums, chatauguas.* New York: Macmillan.

Nunan, D. (1988). *The Learner-centred curriculum.* Cambridge: Cambridge University Press.

Nunan, D. (1989). *Designing tasks for the communicative classroom.* Cambridge: Cambridge University Press.

Nunan, D. (1991). Communicative tasks and the language curriculum. *TESOL Quarterly, 25*(2), 279-295.

Nunan, D. (1993). *Teachers interactive decision-making.* Sydney, NSW: National Centre for English Language Teaching and Research, Macquarie University.

O'Conaill, B., Whittaker, S., & Wilbur, S. (1993). Conversation over video conferences: an evaluation of the spoken aspects of video-mediated communication. *Human-Computer Interaction, 8*(4), 389-428.

O'Dowd, R. (2000). Intercultural learning via videoconferencing: a pilot exchange project. *ReCALL, 12*(1), 49 - 62.

Ohta, A. S. (1995). Applying sociocultural theory to an analysis of learner discourse: Learner-learner collaborative interaction in the zone of proximal development. *Issues in Applied Linguistics, 6*, 93-121.

Oliver, R. (1999). Exploring strategies for online teaching and learning. *Distance Education, 20*(2), 240-249.

Oliver, R., & Omari, A. (1999). Using online technologies to support problem based learning: Learners' perspectives and perceptions. *Australian Journal of Educational Technology*, 58-79.

O'Malley, C., Langton, S., Anderson, A., Doherty-Sneddon, G., & Bruce, V. (1996). Comparison of face-to-face and video-mediated interaction. *Interacting with Computers, 8*(2), 177-192.

Orton, J. (2001). Building "Bridges": Design issues for a Web-based Chinese course. In U. Felix (Ed.), *Beyond Babel - Language learning online.* Melbourne: Language Australia Ltd.

Oxford, R. L. (1995). *Patterns of cultural identity.* Boston: Heinle.

Oxford, R. L. (1997). Cooperative learning, collaborative learning, and interaction: Three communicative strands in the language classroom. *The Modern Language Journal, 81*(iv), 443-456.

Paiva, V. (1999). CALL and online journals. In R. Debski & M. Levy (Eds.), *WORDCALL: Global perspective on computer-assisted language learning* (pp. 247-265). Lisse: Swets & Zeilinger.

Palloff, R. M., & Pratt, K. (1999). *Building learning communities in cyberspace: Effective strategies for the online classroom.* San Francisco: Jossey Bass.

Papalia, A. (1987). Interaction of reader and text. In W. M. Rivers (Ed.), *Interactive language teaching* (pp. 70-82). Cambridge: Cambridge University Press.

Paramskas, D. M. (1999). The shape of computer-mediated communication. In K. Cameron (Ed.), *CALL: Media, design and application* (pp. 13-34). Lisse: Swets & Zeitlinger.

Pastor, E., Fernández, D., & Robles, T. (1998). *My teacher is on the network (Experiences using multimedia communication technologies in distance learning).* Retrieved 20 December 2000, from http://greco.dit.upm.es/~leverage/conf1/pastor.htm

Pawan, F., Paulus, T. M., Yalcin, S., & Chang, C. (2003). Online learning: Patterns of engagement and interaction among in-service teachers. *Language Learning &Technology, 7*(3), 119-140.

Pearson, J. (1999). Electronic conferencing in initial teacher education: Is a virtual faculty of education possible? *Computers and Education, 32*, 221-238.

Pellettieri, J. (2000). Negotiation in cyberspace: The role of chatting in the development of grammatical competence. In M. Warschauer & R. Kern (Eds.), *Network-based language teaching: Concepts and practice* (pp. 59-86). Cambridge, England: Cambridge University Press.

Pelton, J. (1991). Technology and education: Friend or foe? *Research in Distance Education, 3*(2), 2-9.

Pennington, M. C. (1989). *Teaching languages with computers*. La Jolla, CA: Athelstan Publications.

Pennington, M. C. (1989). Application of computers in the development of speaking and listening proficiency. In M. C. Pennington (Ed.), *Teaching languages with computers* (pp. 99-123). La Jolla, CA: Athelstan Publications.

Pennington, M. C. (1999). The missing link in computer-assisted writing. In K. Cameron (Ed.), *CALL: Media, design and application* (pp. 271-294). Lisse: Swets & Zeitlinger.

Peters, O. (1989). The iceberg has not melted: further reflections on the concept of industrialization and distance teaching. *Open Learning, 6*, 3-8.

Peters, O. (1991). Towards a better understanding of distance education: analyzing designations and catchwords. In B. Holmberg & G. Ortner (Eds.), *Research into distance education* (pp. 51-60). Frankfurt: Lang.

Peters, O. (1994). Distance education in a post industrial society (1993). In D. Keegan (Ed.), *Otto Peters on Distance Education: the Industrialization of Teaching and Learning* (pp. 220-240). London: Routledge.

Peterson, M. (1997). Language teaching and networking. *System, 25*(1), 29-37.

Phillips, J. K. (1998). Media for message: Technology's role in the standards. *CALICO Journal, 16*(1), 25-36.

Pica, T. (1994). Research on negotiation: what does it reveal about second language learning conditions, processes, and outcomes? *Language Learning, 44*(3), 491 - 527.

Pica, T., Kanagy, R., & Falodun, J. (1993). Choosing and using communication tasks for second language instruction. In G. Cookes & S. M. Gass (Eds.), *Tasks and language learning: Integrating theory & practice* (pp. 9-34). Clevedon, England: Multilingual Matters.

Piper, A. (1986). Conversation and the computer: A study of the conversational spin-off generated among learners of English as a foreign language working in groups. *System, 14*(2), 187-198.

Platt, J. (1992). "Case study" in American methodological thought. *Current Sociology, 40*, 17-48.

Pomerantz, A., & Fehr, B. J. (1997). Conversation analysis: An approach to the study of social action and sense-making practices. In T. Van Dijk (Ed.), *Discourse as a social interaction* (pp. 1-37). Thousand Oaks, CA: Sage.

Poon, S. (1993). Internet Relay Chat (IRC) - A real-time multi-user computer collaborative learning medium. In T. Nunan (Ed.), *Distance education futures* (pp. 63-72): University of South Australia.

Porter, L. R. (1997). *Creating the virtual classroom: Distance learning with the Internet.* New York: John Weley & Sons, Inc.

Portway, P., & Lane, C. (1994). *Guide to teleconferencing and distance learning.* San Ramon Calif.: Applied Business Communications.

Prabhu, N. S. (1987). *Second language pedagogy.* Oxford: Oxford University Press.

Price, K. (1987). The use of technology: Varying the medium in language teaching. In W. M. Rivers (Ed.), *Interactive language teaching* (pp. 155-169). New York: Cambridge University Press.

Prokop, M. (1996). *Using the Web for language exercises and readings of authentic texts.* Retrieved 12 November 1999, from http://www.ualberta.ca/~german/present.htm

Psathas, G. (1995). *Conversation analysis - The study of talk-in-interaction.* Thousand Oaks, CA: Sage.

Quarterman, J. S. (1993). *The global matrix of minds.* Cambridge, MA: the MIT Press.

Reeder, F., Hamburger, H., & Schoelles, M. (1999). Real talk: Authentic dialogue practice. In R. Debski & M. Levy (Eds.), *WORLDCALL: Global perspectives on computer-assisted language learning* (pp. 319 - 338). Lisse: Swets & Zeitlinger.

Reeves, T. (1986). Research and evaluation models for the study of interactive video. *Journal of Computer-Based Instruction, 13*, 102-106.

Richards, J., Platt, J., & Weber, H. (1985). *Longman dictionary of applied linguistics*. London: Longman Group Limited.

Richards, J. C., & Rogers, T. S. (1986). *Approaches and methods in language teaching*. Cambridge: Cambridge University Press.

Richmond, I. (1999). Is your CALL connected? Dedicated software vs Integrated CALL. In K. Cameron (Ed.), *CALL: Media, design and application* (pp. 295-314). Lisse: Swets & Zeitlinger.

Riddle, J. (1990). Measuring effective change: Students in a distance learning class. *Paper presented at the Annual Meeting of the Northern Rocky Mountain Educational Research Association, Greeley, CO (ERIC Document Reproduction No. ED 325 514.*

Rivers, W. M. (1987). Interaction as the key to teaching language for communication. In W. M. Rivers (Ed.), *Interactive language learning* (pp. 3-16). Cambridge: Cambridge University Press.

Robinson, B. (1984). Telephone teaching. In A. W. Bates (Ed.), *The role of technology in distance education* (pp. 121-137). London & Sydney: Croom Helm.

Roblyer, M. D. (1997). Videoconferencing. *Learning and Teaching with Technology, 24*(5), 58 - 61.

Roblyer, M. D., & Edwards, J. (2000). *Integrating educational technology into teaching* (2nd edn). Upper Saddle River, NJ: Prentice-Hall, Inc.

Rogers, C. (1961). *On becoming a person: A therapist's view of psychotherapy*. London: Constable.

Romiszowski, A. (1990). The Hypertext/hypermedia solution: But what exactly is the problem? In D. Jonassen & H. Mandle (Eds.), *Designing hypermedia for learning* (pp. 321-333). Berlin: Springer-Verlag.

Rosell-Aguilar, F. (2005). Task design for audiographic conferencing: Promoting beginner oral interaction in distance language learning. *Computer Assisted Language Learning, 18*(5), 417-442.

Rosell-Aguilar, F. (2006a). Online tutorial support in Open Distance Learning trough audio-graphic SCMC: tutor impressions. *JALT-CALL Journal, 2*(2), 37-52.

Rosell-Aguilar, F. (2006b). The face-to-face and the online learner: a comparative study of tutorial support for Open and Distance Language Learning and the learner experience with audio-graphic SCMC. In J. Liontas (Ed.), *The Reading Matrix 5th Anniversary Special Issue - CALL Technologies and the Digital Learner* (Vol. 6, pp. 248-268).

Rumble, G. (1988). *The Organization of academic work in distance teaching universities: Do we need new structures?* Hagen: FernUniversität.

Rumble, G., & Harry, K. (Eds.). (1982). *The distance teaching universities*. London: Croom Helm.

Rutter, D., & Stephenson, G. (1977). The role of visual communication in synchronizing conversation. *Euro. J. Social Psychol., 2*, 29-37.

Saba, F. (1999). Toward a systems theory of distance education. *The American Journal of Distance Education, 13*(2), 32-36.

Sacks, H., Schegloff, E., & Jefferson, G. (1974). A simple systematic for the organization of turn-taking for conversation. *Language, 53*, 361-382.

Salaberry, M. R. (2000). Pedagogical design of computer mediated communication tasks: Learning objectives and technological capabilities. *The Modern Language Journal, 84*(i), 28-37.

Salaberry, M. R. (2001). The use of technology for second language learning and teaching: A retrospective. *The Modern Language Journal, 85*(i), 39-56.

Salmon, G. (1999). Computer Mediated Conferencing in large scale management education. *Open Learning, 14*(2), 34-43.

Sampson, N. (2003). Meeting the needs of distance learners. *Language Learning & Technology, 7*(3), 103-118.

Santoro, G. (1995). What is computer mediated communication? In Z. Berge & M. Collins (Eds.), *Computer mediated communication and the online classroom in distance learning* (pp. 11-28). Cresskill, NJ: Hampton Press.

Satyanarayanna, M. (1996). keynote address to ACM Mobicom'96.

Schegloff, E. (1968). Sequencing in conversational openings. *The American Anthropologist, 70*(6), 1075-1095.

Schiffrin, D. (1994). *Approaches to discourse*. Cambridge, Mass.: Blackwell.

Schön, D. A. (1983). *The Reflective Practitioner: How Professionals Think in Action*. London: Temple smith.

Schuemer, R. (1991). Diagnosis and therapy: Theoretical and methodological aspects of drop-out research. In B. Holmberg & G. E. Ortner (Eds.), *Research into Distance Education* (pp. 194-195). Frankfurt am Main: Peter Lang.

Schweizer, K., Paechter, M., & Weidenmann, B. (2001). A field study on distance education: Experiences of a virtual tutor. *The Journal of Computer-Mediated Communication, 6*(2). Retrieved 30 December 2002, from http://www.ascusc.org/jcmc/vol6/issue2/schwerzer.html

Schwienhorst, K. (1997). Modes of interactivity: Internet resources for second language learning. In D. Kranz., L. Legenhausen & B. Luking (Eds.), *Multimedia - Internet - Lernsoftware: Fremdsprachenunterricht vor neuen herausforderungen* (pp. 103-110). Munster: Agenda Verlag.

Seliger, H. W., & Shohamy, E. (1989). *Second language research methods*. Oxford: Oxford University Press.

Sellen, A. (1995). Remote conversations: the effects of mediating talk with technology. *Human-Computer Interaction, 10*(4), 401-444.

Serwatka, J. A. (1999). *Internet distance learning: How do I put my course on the Web?* Retrieved 12 November 2000, from http://www.thejournal.com/magazine/vault/A2109.cfm

Sharan, S. (1994). *Handbook of cooperative learning methods*. Westport, CT: Greenwood Press.

Shield, L., Hauck, M., & Hewer, S. (2001). Talking to strangers - the role of the tutor in developing target language speaking skills at a distance. *Proceedings of UNTELE 2000, II*. Retrieved 7 July 2002, from http://fels-staff.open.ac.uk/lesley-shield/webbed/untele/shieldhauckhewer/talkingtostrangers.html

Shield, L., & Hewer, S. (1999). A synchronous learning environment to support distance language learners. In K. Cameron (Ed.), *CALL and the learning community* (pp. 379-390). Exeter: Elm Bank Publications.

Shield, L., & Weininger, M., J. (1999). Collaboration in a virtual world: Group work and the distance language learner. In R. Debski & M. Levy (Eds.), *WORDCALL: Global perspective on computer-assisted language learning* (pp. 99-116). Lisse: Swets & Zeitlinger.

Shield, L., Weininger, M. J., & Davies, L. B. (1999). A task-based approach to using MOO for collaborative language learning. In K. Cameron (Ed.), *CALL and the learning community*. Exeter: Elm Bank Publications.

Shield, L., Weininger, M. J., & Davies, L. B. (1999). *Mooing in L2: Constructivism and developing learner autonomy for technology-enhanced language learning*. Retrieved 19 August 2003, from http://jaltcall.org/cjo/10_99/mooin.htm

Shin, J., & Wastell, D. G. (2001). A user-centered methodological framework for the design of hypermedia-based CALL systems. *CALICO Journal, 18*(3), 517-537.

Short, J., Williams, E., & Christie, B. (1976). *The social psychology of telecommunication*. London: John Wiley.

Silvermann, D. (1993). *Interpreting qualitative data: Methods for analyzing talk, text and interaction.* London: Sage.

Sims, R. (1994). Seven levels of interactivity: Implications for the development of multimedia education and training. *Apitite,* 589-594.

Skehan, P. (1998). *A cognitive approach to language learning.* Oxford: Oxford University Press.

Skehan, P., & Foster, P. (2001). Cognition and tasks. In P. Robinson (Ed.), *Cognition and second language instruction* (pp. 183 - 205). Cambridge: Cambridge University Press.

Skinner, B., & Austin, R. (1999). Computer conferencing - does it motivate EFL students? *ELT Journal, 53*(4), 270-279.

Slatin, J. M. (1990). Reading hypertext: Order and coherence in a new medium. *College English, 52*(8), 870-883.

Slatin, J. M., & Sharir, Y. (1996). Multimedia in cyberspace: Teaching with virtual reality. *Syllabus, 10*(3), 16-20.

Slavin, R. E. (1988). *Student team learning: An overview and practical guide* (Second ed.). Washington, DC: National Education Association.

Smith, B. (2003). Computer mediated negotiated interaction: An expanded model. *The Modern Language Journal, 87*(1), 38-57.

Smith, F. (1982). *Understanding reading* (Third ed.). New York: Holt, Rinehart and Winston.

Smith, M., & Salam, U. (2000). *Web-based ESL courses: A search for industry standards.* Retrieved 9 September, 2001, from http://www.clec.ritsumei.ad.jp/english/callejonline//5-1/msith&salam.html.

Smith, P., & Kelly, M. (1987). *Distance education and the mainstream.* London: Croom Helm.

Smith, P. L., & Dillon, C. L. (1999). Comparing distance learning and classroom learning: Conceptual considerations. *The American Journal of Distance Education, 13*(2), 6-23.

Smith, P. L., & Dillon, C. L. (1999). Towards a systems theory of distance education: A reaction. *The American Journal of Distance Education, 13*(2), 32-36.

Snow, C. E. (1988). Conversations with children. In P. Fletcher & M. Garman (Eds.), *Language acquisition* (Vol. 2, pp. 69-89). Cambridge, UK: Cambridge University Press.

Sotillo, S. M. (2000). Discourse functions and syntactic complexity in synchronous and asynchronous communication. *Language Learning and Technology, 4*(1), 82-119.

Spears, R., & Lea, M. (1992). Social influence and the influence of the social in computer-mediated communication. In M. Lea (Ed.), *Context of computer-mediated communication* (pp. 30-65). New York: Harvester Wheatsheaf.

Spears, R., & Lea, M. (1994). Panacea or panopticon? The hidden power in computer-mediated communication. *Communication Research, 21,* 427-459.

Spitzer, D. R. (1998). Rediscovering the social context of distance learning. *Educational Technology, 38,* 52-56.

Spolsky, B. (1989). *Conditions for second language learning: Introduction to a general theory.* Oxford: Oxford University Press.

Sproull, L., & Kiesler, S. (1986). Reducing social context cues: Electronic mail in organizational communications. *Management Science, 32,* 1492-1512.

Stacey, E. (1997). *A virtual campus: The experiences of postgraduate students studying through electronic communication and resource access.* Retrieved 30 November 1999, from http://ultibase.rmit.edu.au/Articles/stace1.html

Stacey, E. (1999). Collaborative learning in an online environment. *Distance Education, 43*(2), 14-33.

Stake, R. E. (1983). The case study method in social inquiry. In G. F. Madaus, M. S. Scriven & D. L. Stufflebeam (Eds.), *Evaluation models* (pp. 279-286). Boston: Kluwer-Nijhoff.

Stenström, A. (1994). *An introduction to spoken interaction*. New York: Longman.

Stern, P. N. (1980). Grounded theory methodology: Its uses and process. *Image, 12*, 20-23.

Stevens, A. (1995). Issues in distance teaching in languages. *ReCALL, 7*(1), 12-19.

Stevens, A., & Hewer, S. (1998). From policy to practice and back. In *Proceedings of 1ˢᵗ LEVERAGE conference, 7-8 January 1998*. Cambridge.

Strambi, A., & Bouvet, E. (2003). Flexibility and interaction at a distance: A mixed-mode environment for language learning. *Language Learning & Technology, 7*(3), 81-102.

Strauss, A., & Corbin, J. (1998). *Basics of qualitative research: Techniques and procedures for developing grounded theory*. London: SAGE Publications.

Stringer, M., Shale, D., & Abrioux, D. (1982). Language learning at a distance: international comparisons. *Teaching at a Distance, 21*, 52-56.

Study Guide for Modern Standard Chinese: CHN11 &CHN12 (1992). Sydney &

Brisbane, Australia: School of Modern Languages, Macquarie University

Key Centre for Asian Languages and Studies, Griffith University.

Summerfield, Q. (1992). Lipreading and audio-visual speech perception. *Philosophical Trans. Royal Society of London, B335*, 71-78.

Sun, C., & Chen, D. (2002). Consistency maintenance in real-time collaborative graphics editing systems. *ACM Transactions on Computer-Human Interaction, 9*(1), 1-41.

Sussex, R. (1991). Current issues in distance language education and open learning: An overview and an Australian perspective. In G. L. Ervin (Ed.), *International perspectives on foreign language teaching* (pp. 177-193). Chicago: National Textbook Company.

Sussex, R. (1999). Introducing the Web: The language teacher, the maze, and the wise guide. *CALL-EJ Online, 1*(2). Retrieved: 23 July 2003, from http://www.clec.ritsumei.ac.jp/english/callejonline//4-2/sussex.html

Swain, M., & Lapkin, S. (1995). Problems in output and the cognitive processes they generate: A step towards second language learning. *Applied Linguistics, 16*, 371-391.

Swan, M. (1985a). A critical look at the communicative approach (1). *ELT Journal, 39*(1), 2-12.

Swan, M. (1985b). A critical look at the communicative approach (2). *ELT Journal, 39*(2), 76-87.

Swan, M. (1985c). Communicative competence: Some roles of comprehensible input and comprehensible output in its development. In S. M. Gass & C. Madden (Eds.), *Input in second language Acquisition* (pp. 235-253). Rowely, MA: Newbury House Publishers.

Tarone, E. (1982). Systematicity and attention in interlanguage. *Language Learning, 32*, 69-84.

Thomas, J. A. (1995). *Meaning in interaction: An introduction to pragmatics*. London: Longman.

Thompson, D. J. (1996a). Audioteleconferencing: myths and realities. *Open Learning, 11*(2), 20-27.

Thompson, G. (1996b). Some misconceptions about communicative language teaching. *ELT Journal, 50*(1), 9-15.

Thompson, M. M., & Chute, A. G. (1998). A vision for distance education: networked learning environments. *Open Learning, 13*(2), 4-11.

Trevino, K., Lengel, R., & Daft, R. (1987). Media symbolism, media richness, and media choice in organizations: A symbolic interactionist perspective. *Communication Research, 14*, 553-574.

Tsichritzis, D. (1999). Reengineering the university. *Communications of the ACM, 42*(6), 93-100.

Tudini, V. (2003). Using native speakers in chat. *Language Learning and Technology, 7*(3), 141-159.

Tudor, I. (1996). *Learner-centredness as language education*. Cambridge: Cambridge University Press.

Tuman, M. C. (1996). Literacy online. *Annual Review of Applied Linguistics, 16,* 26-45.

Turoff, M. (1972). 'Party-line' and 'Discussion' computerized conferencing systems. In S. Winkler (Ed.), *Computer Communication - Impacts and implications: Proceedings of the International Conference on Computer Communications* (pp. 161-170). Washington, DC: International Council for Computer Communication.

Underwood, J. (1984). *Linguistics, computers and the language teacher*. Rowley, MA: Newbury.

van Lier, L. (1996). *Interaction in the language curriculum: Awareness, autonomy & authenticity*. London: Longman.

Varonis, E. M., & Gass, S. M. (1985). Non-native/non-native conversation: A model for negotiation of meaning. *Applied Linguistics, 6*(1), 71-90.

Verduin, J. R. J., & Clark, T. A. (1991). *The foundations of effective practice*. San Francisco: Jossey-Bass Publishers.

Von Der Emde, S., Schneider, J., & Kotter, M. (2001). Technically speaking: Transforming language learning environment (MOOs). *The Modern Language Journal, 85*(ii), 210-225.

Vygotsky, L. S. (1978). *Mind in society: The development of higher psychological processes* (M. M. L.-M. Cole, A. R. Luria & J. J. Wertsch, Trans.). Cambridge, MA: Harvard University Press.

Walther, J. B. (1992). Interpersonal effects in computer-mediated interaction: A relational perspective. *Communication Research, 19,* 52-90.

Walther, J. B., Anderson, J., & Park, D. (1994). Interpersonal effects in computer-mediated interaction: A mateanalysis of social and antisocial communication. *Communication Research, 21,* 460-487.

Walther, J. B., & Burgoon, J. K. (1992). Relational communication in computer-mediated interaction. *Human Communication Research, 19,* 50-88.

Walther, J. B., & Tidwell, L. C. (1995). Nonverbal cues in computer-mediated communication, and the effect of chronemics on relational communication. *Journal of Organizational Computing, 5,* 355-378.

Wang, Y. (1999). Learning Chinese characters through multimedia. *Call-EJ Online, 1*(1). Retrieved 28 September 2001, from: www.lerc.ritsumei.ac.jp/callej/4-1/wang1.html

Wang, Y. (2004a). Distance language learning: Interactivity and fourth-generation Internet-based videoconferencing. *CALICO Journal, 21*(2), 373-395.

Wang, Y. (2004b). Internet-based desktop videoconferencing in supporting synchronous distance language learning. *Language Learning and Technology, 8* (3), 90-121.

Wang, Y. (2006). Negotiation of meaning in desktop videoconferencing-supported distance language learning. *ReCALL, 18*(1), 122-146.

Wang, Y. (2007). Task design in videoconferencing supported distance language learning. *CALICO Journal, 24*(3), 591-630.

Wang, Y., & Chen, N.-S. (2007). Online Synchronous Language Learning:

SLMS over the Internet. *Innovate, 3*(3).

Wang, Y., & Sun, C. (2000). Synchronous distance education: Enhancing speaking skills

via Internet-based real time technology. In X. Zhou, J. Fong, X. Jia, Y. Kambayashi, & Y. Zhang (Eds.), *Proceedings of the 1st International Conference on Web Information Systems Engineering* (pp. 168-172). Los Alamitos, CA: IEE Computer Society.

Wang, Y., & Sun, C. (2001). Internet-based real time language education: Towards a fourth generation distance education. *CALICO Journal, 18*(3), 539-561.

Warschauer, M. (1996). Comparing face-to-face and electronic communication in the second language classroom. *CALICO Journal, 13,* 7-26.

Warschauer, M. (1997). Computer-mediated collaborative learning: theory and practice. *The Modern Language Journal, 81*(iv), 470-481.

Warschauer, M. (1998). *Interaction, negotiation and computer mediated learning.* Retrieved 23 July 2000, from http://www.insa-lyon.fr/Departments/CDRL/interaction.html

Watson, A., & Sasse, M. A. (1996). Evaluating audio and video quality in low-cost multimedia conferencing systems. *Interacting with Computers, 8*(3), 255-275.

Watts, N. (1997). A learner-based design model for interactive multimedia language learning packages. *System, 25*(1), 1-8.

Webster, J., & Hackley, P. (1997). Teaching effectiveness in technology-mediated distance learning. *Academy of Management Journal, 40*, 12282-11309.

Wegerif, R. (1998). The social dimension of asynchronous learning networks. *Journal of Asynchronous Learning Networks, 2*(1), 34-49.

Wells, G. (1981). Language as interaction. In G. Wells (Ed.), *Learning through interaction: The study of language development* (pp. 22-72). Cambridge: Cambridge University Press.

White, C. (2003). *Language Learning in Distance Education.* Cambridge: Cambridge University Press.

White, M. A. (1982). Distance education in Australian higher education. *Distance Education, 3*(2), 255-278.

Wiesenberg, F. (1999). Teaching on-line: One instructor's evolong 'theory of practice'. *Adult Basic Education, 9*(3), 149-161.

Wild, A., & Quinn, C. (1997). Implications of educational theory for the design of instructional multimedia. *British Journal of Educational Technology, 29*, 73-82.

Wilkins, D. (1976). *National syllabuses.* Oxford: Oxford University Press.

Wilkinson, L. C. (1982). *Communicating in the Classroom.* New York: Academic Press.

Williams, S., & Sharma, P. (1988). Language acquisition by distance education: an Australian survey. *Distance Education, 9*(1), 127-146.

Windeatt, S. (1986). Observing CALL in action. In G. Leech & C. Candlin (Eds.), *Computers in English language teaching and research* (pp. 79-87). London: Longman.

Witmer, D. F. (1998). Introduction to computer-mediated communication: A master syllabus for teaching communication technology. *Communication Education, 47*, 162-173.

Wong, J., & Fauverge, A. (1999). LEVERAGE - Reciprocal peer tutoring over broadband networks. *ReCALL, 11*(1), 133-142.

Yin, R. K. (1989). *Case study research: Design and methods.* Newbury Park, CA: Sage.

Yin, R. K. (1993). *Applications of case study research.* Newbury Park, CA: Sage.

Yin, R. K. (1990). *Case study research: Design and methods* (second ed.). Newbury Park, CA: Sage.

Yule, G. (1996). *Pragmatics.* Oxford: Oxford University Press.

Zähner, C., Fauverge, A., & Wong, J. (2000). Task-based language learning via audiovisual networks. In M. Warschauer & R. Kern (Eds.), *Network-based language teaching: Concepts and practice* (pp. 186 - 203). Cambridge: Cambridge University Press.

Zuber-Skerritt, O. (1992). *Action research in higher education.* London: Kogan Page.

Zuber-Skerritt, O. (1992). *Professional development in higher education.* London: Kogan Page.

www.ingramcontent.com/pod-product-compliance
Lightning Source LLC
Chambersburg PA
CBHW071404050326
40689CB00010B/1752